樋口大輔

How much do we really know about our-
selves?
People around us... the town and the country we live in... We think we know, but in
fact, there's so much we don't know.
Ignorance is terrifying. Ignorance is sad.
Korea and Japan are near, and yet so far.
What's really frightening is the fact that we
are unaware of how much we don't know,
and that we don't even care about it.

    – Daisuke Higuchi

Daisuke Higuchi's manga career began in 1992 when the
artist was honored with third prize in the 43rd Osamu
Tezuka Award. In that same year, Higuchi debuted as
creator of a romantic action story titled *Itaru*. In 1998,
Weekly Shonen Jump began serializing *Whistle!*
Higuchi's realistic soccer manga became an instant hit
with readers and eventually inspired an anime series,
debuting on Japanese TV in May of 2002.

WHISTLE!
VOL. 18: CHANGE OVER

The SHONEN JUMP Manga Edition

STORY AND ART BY
DAISUKE HIGUCHI

English Adaptation/Drew Williams
Translation/Naomi Kokubo
Touch-up Art & Lettering/Jim Keefe
Cover Design/Sean Lee
Interior Design/Matt Hinrichs
Editor/Jonathan Tarbox

Editor in Chief, Books/Alvin Lu
Editor in Chief, Magazines/Marc Weidenbaum
VP of Publishing Licensing/Rika Inouye
VP of Sales/Gonzalo Ferreyra
Sr. VP of Marketing/Liza Coppola
Publisher/Hyoe Narita

Printed in the U.S.A.

Published by VIZ Media, LLC
P.O. Box 77010
San Francisco, CA 94107

SHONEN JUMP Manga Edition
10 9 8 7 6 5 4 3 2
First printing, January 2008
Second printing, March 2008

PARENTAL ADVISORY
WHISTLE! is rated A and
is suitable for readers of
all ages.
ratings.viz.com

THE WORLD'S
MOST POPULAR MANGA

www.shonenjump.com

www.viz.com

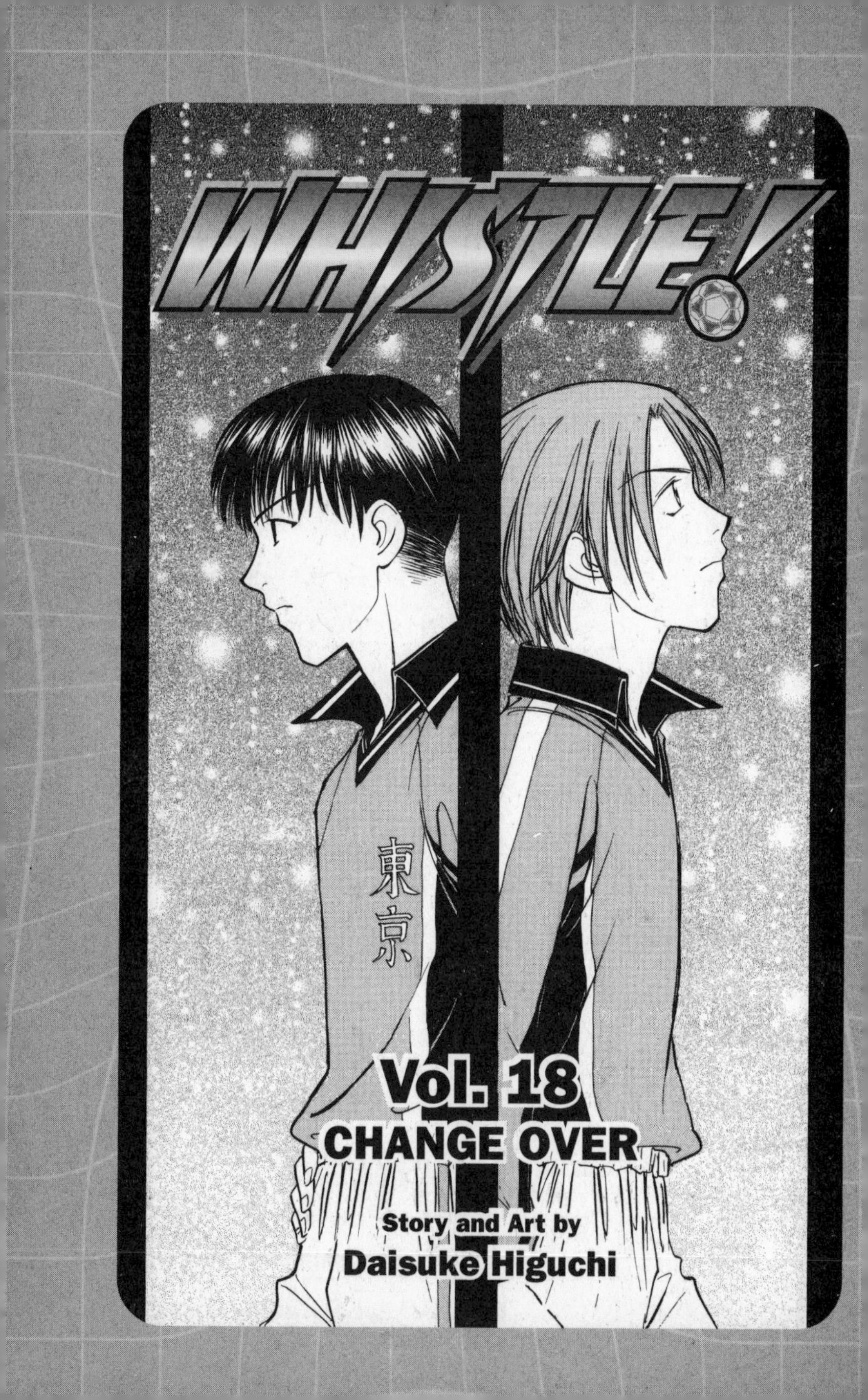
東京

WHISTLE!

Vol. 18
CHANGE OVER

Story and Art by
Daisuke Higuchi

SHŌ KAZAMATSURI

- JOSUI JUNIOR HIGH SOCCER TEAM FORWARD

AKIRA SAIONJI

SHIINA TSUBASA

TATSUYA MIZUNO

- JOSUI JUNIOR HIGH SOCCER TEAM MIDFIELDER

CHARACTERS

EISHI KAKU

ZŌSHIGAYAMINAMI JUNIOR HIGH

MIDDLE FIELDER

KENTARŌ KOZUTSU

YANAHARA JUNIOR HIGH

GOAL KEEPER

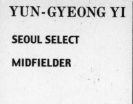

YUN-GYEONG YI

SEOUL SELECT

MIDFIELDER

STORY

TO REALIZE HIS DREAM, SHŌ KAZAMATSURI, A BENCHWARMER AT SOCCER POWERHOUSE MUSASHINOMORI, TRANSFERRED TO JOSUI JUNIOR HIGH SO HE COULD PLAY THE GAME HE LOVES.

DUE TO HIS REMARKABLE PERFORMANCE DURING A TOURNAMENT, SHŌ WAS INVITED TO TRY OUT FOR THE TOKYO SELECT TEAM. IN THE END, HE MADE THE TEAM--BARELY--AS A SUBSTITUTE.

AFTER COMPETING AGAINST TOP-NOTCH PLAYERS IN PRACTICE, SHŌ IMPROVED DRAMATICALLY. MEANWHILE, THE TOKYO SELECT TEAM TRAVELED TO SOUTH KOREA FOR THEIR FIRST FORMAL GAME.

EARLY IN THE MATCH, TOKYO SELECT IS OUT OF SORTS ON FOREIGN SOIL AND THREATENED BY THE POWER OF THE SEOUL SELECT TEAM...

WHISTLE!

**Vol. 18
CHANGE
OVER**

STAGE.153 Serious Game
7

STAGE.154 Snap Out of It!
27

STAGE.155 Play More
45

STAGE.156 The Control Tower Awakens
67

STAGE.157
Under the Snowy Skies of Seoul
86

STAGE.158 Testing the Trump Card
105

STAGE.159 Desperate Save
125

STAGE.160 Reliable Back
143

STAGE.161 Stare in Wonder
161

STAGE.162
Two Heroes (CHANGE OVER)
181

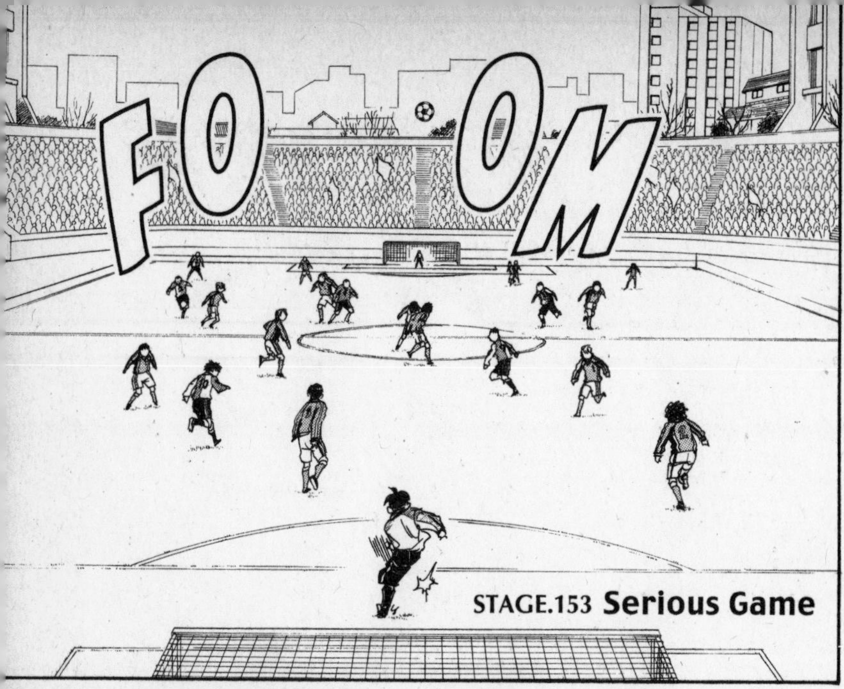
FO-OM

STAGE.153 Serious Game

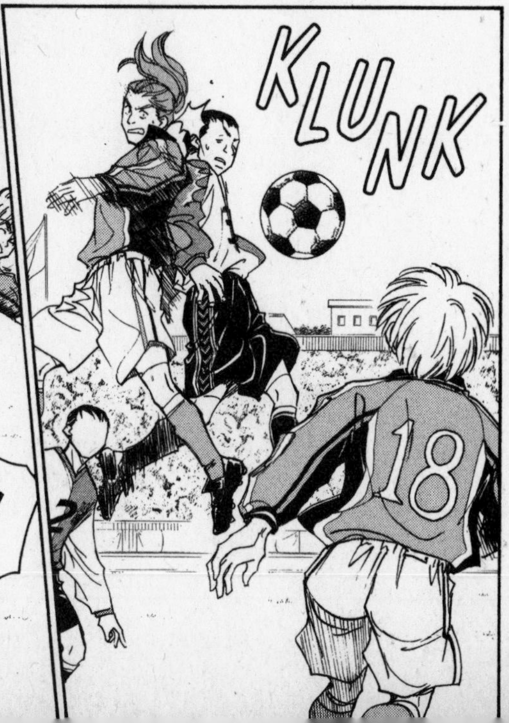
KLUNK

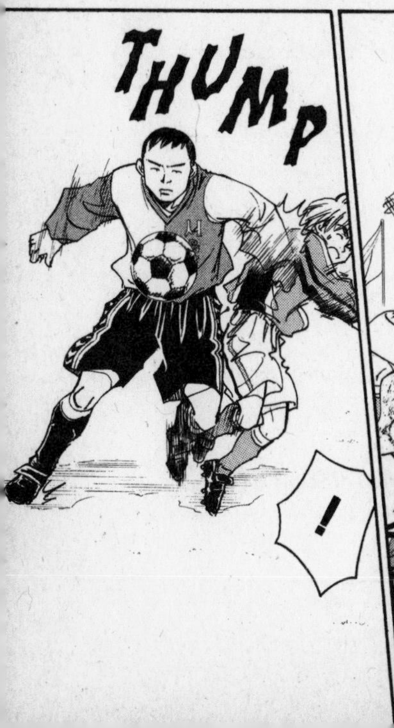
THUMP
!

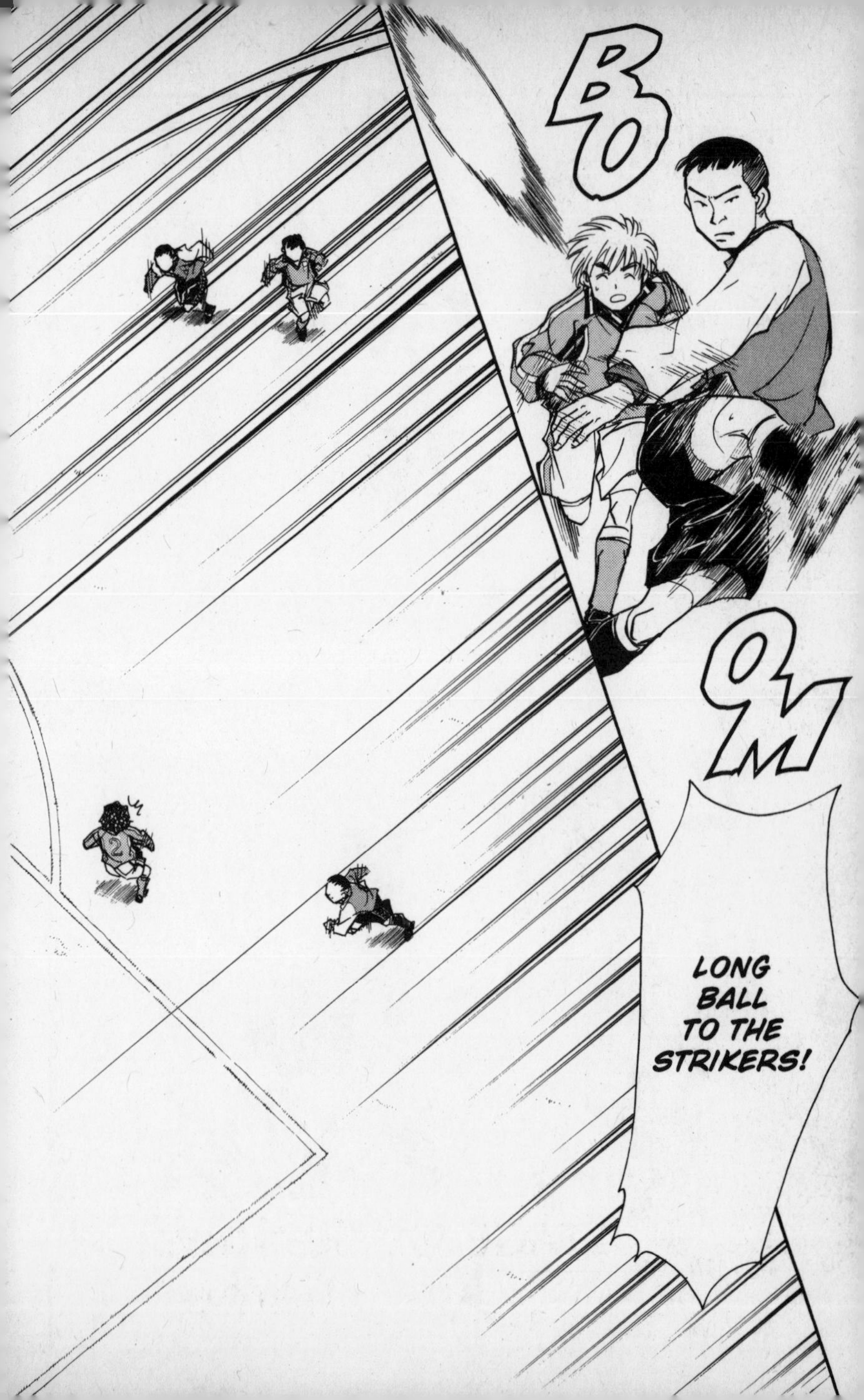
BOOM
LONG BALL TO THE STRIKERS!

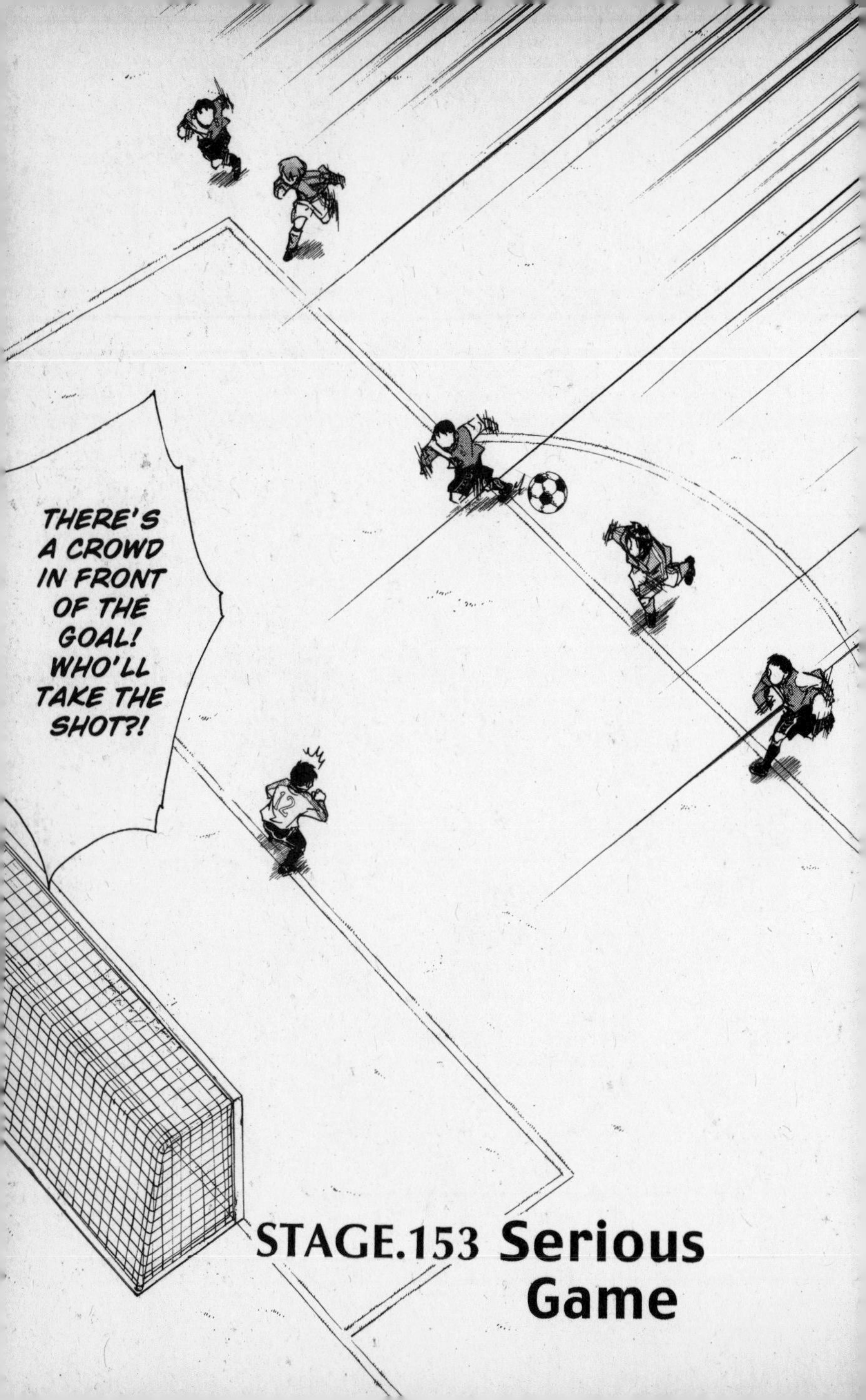
THERE'S A CROWD IN FRONT OF THE GOAL! WHO'LL TAKE THE SHOT?!
12

STAGE.153 Serious Game

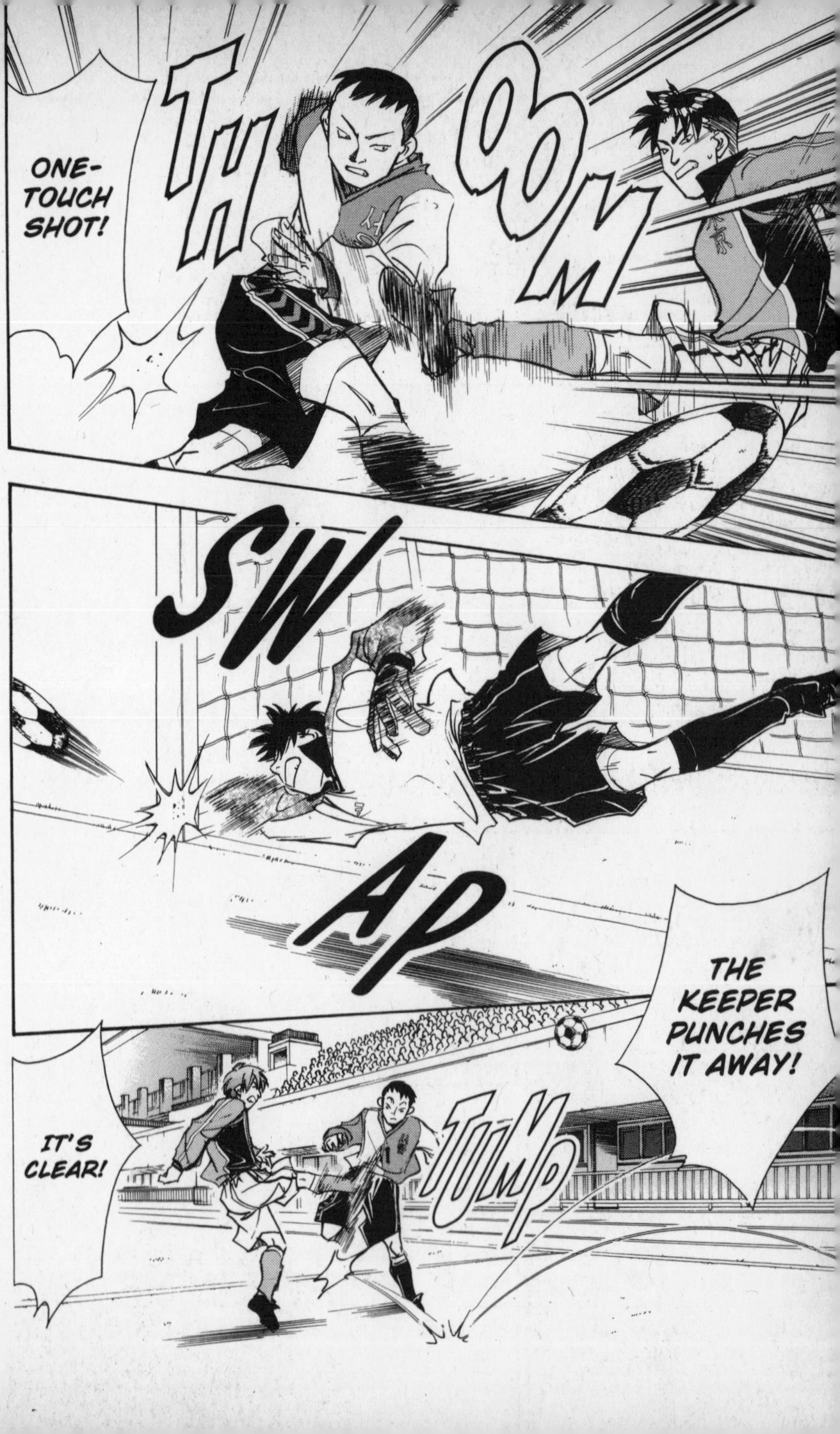
ONE-TOUCH SHOT!
THOOM
SWAP
THE KEEPER PUNCHES IT AWAY!
TUMP
IT'S CLEAR!

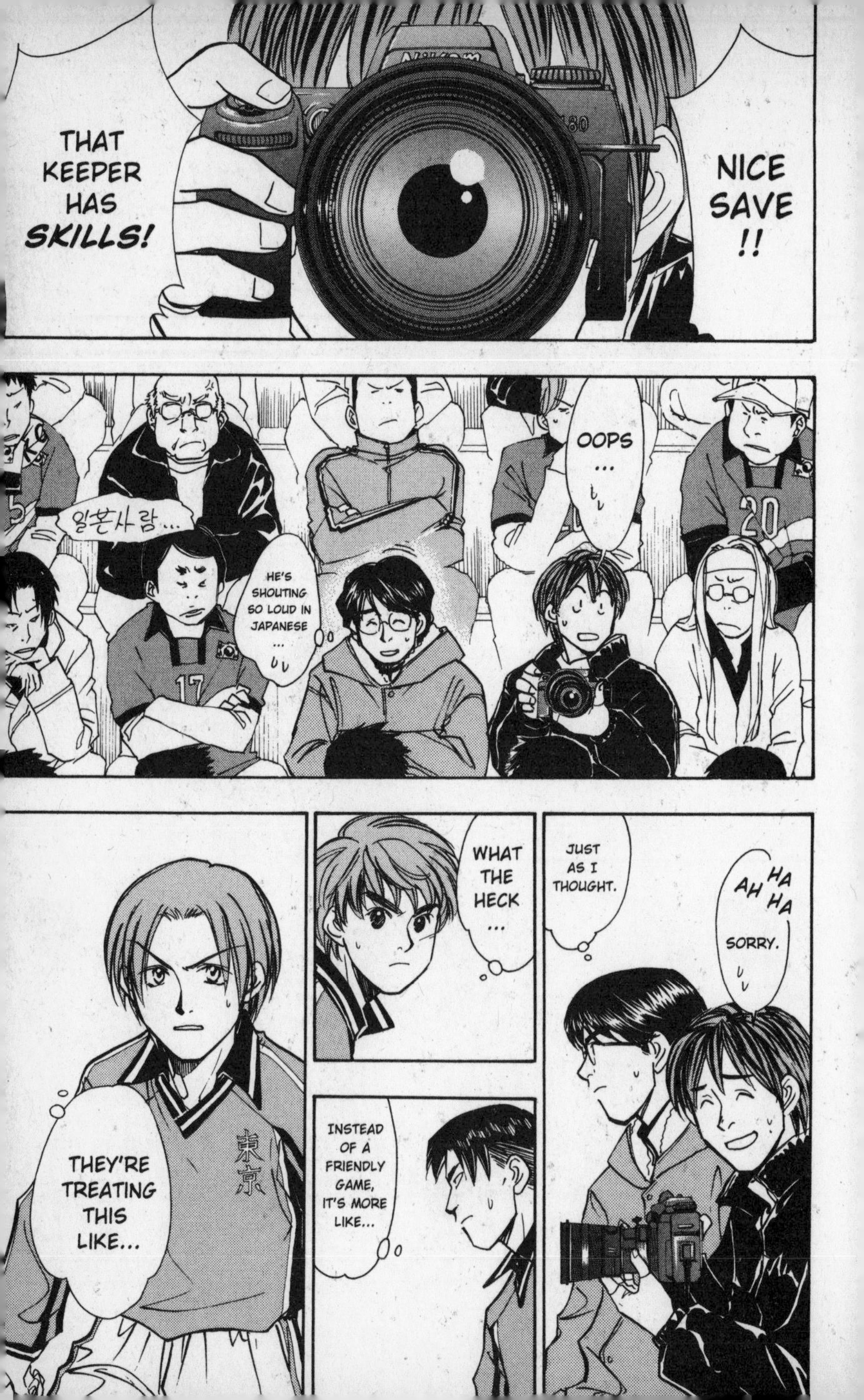
NICE SAVE !!
THAT KEEPER HAS SKILLS!
OOPS...
HE'S SHOUTING SO LOUD IN JAPANESE... ..
일본사람...
AH HA HA
SORRY. ..
JUST AS I THOUGHT.
WHAT THE HECK...
INSTEAD OF A FRIENDLY GAME, IT'S MORE LIKE...
THEY'RE TREATING THIS LIKE...

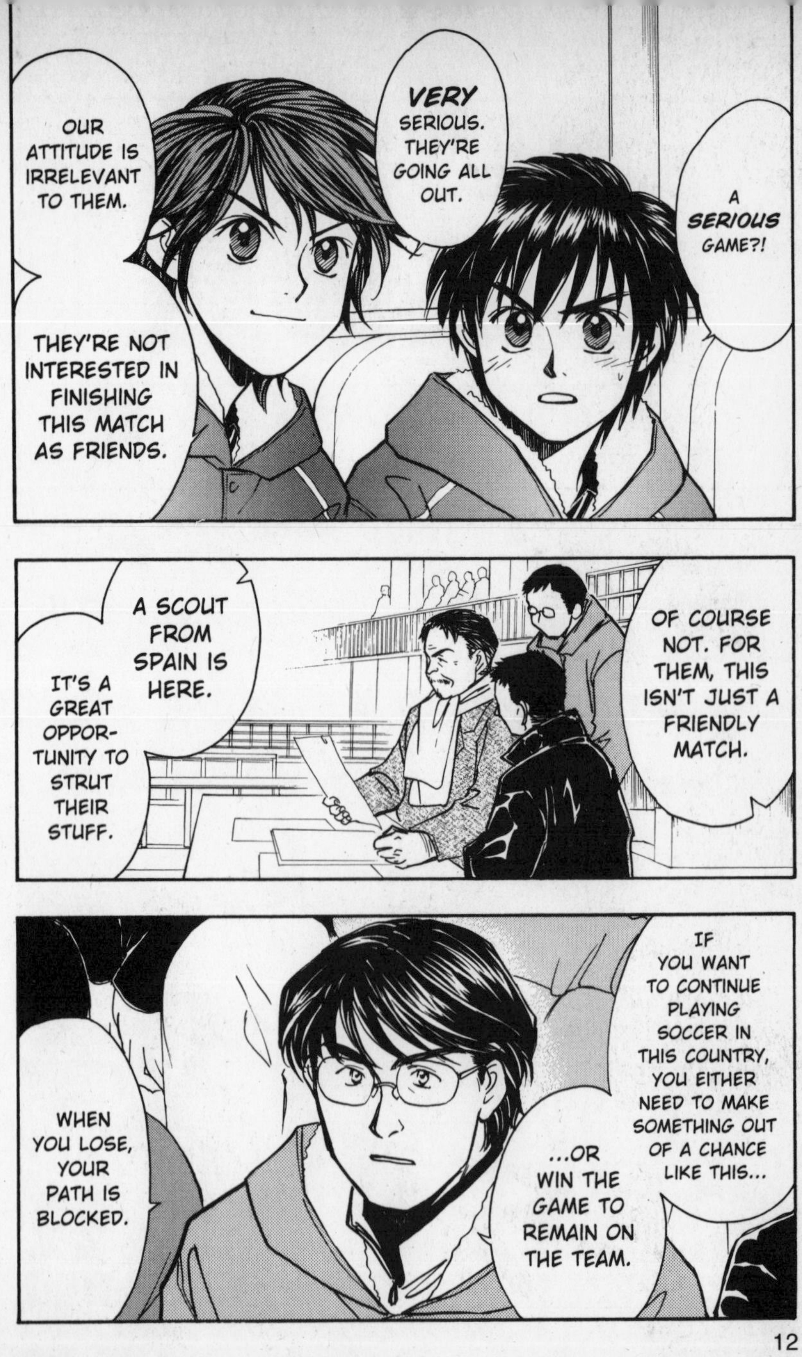
A SERIOUS GAME?!
VERY SERIOUS. THEY'RE GOING ALL OUT.
OUR ATTITUDE IS IRRELEVANT TO THEM.
THEY'RE NOT INTERESTED IN FINISHING THIS MATCH AS FRIENDS.
OF COURSE NOT. FOR THEM, THIS ISN'T JUST A FRIENDLY MATCH.
A SCOUT FROM SPAIN IS HERE.
IT'S A GREAT OPPORTUNITY TO STRUT THEIR STUFF.
IF YOU WANT TO CONTINUE PLAYING SOCCER IN THIS COUNTRY, YOU EITHER NEED TO MAKE SOMETHING OUT OF A CHANCE LIKE THIS...
...OR WIN THE GAME TO REMAIN ON THE TEAM.
WHEN YOU LOSE, YOUR PATH IS BLOCKED.

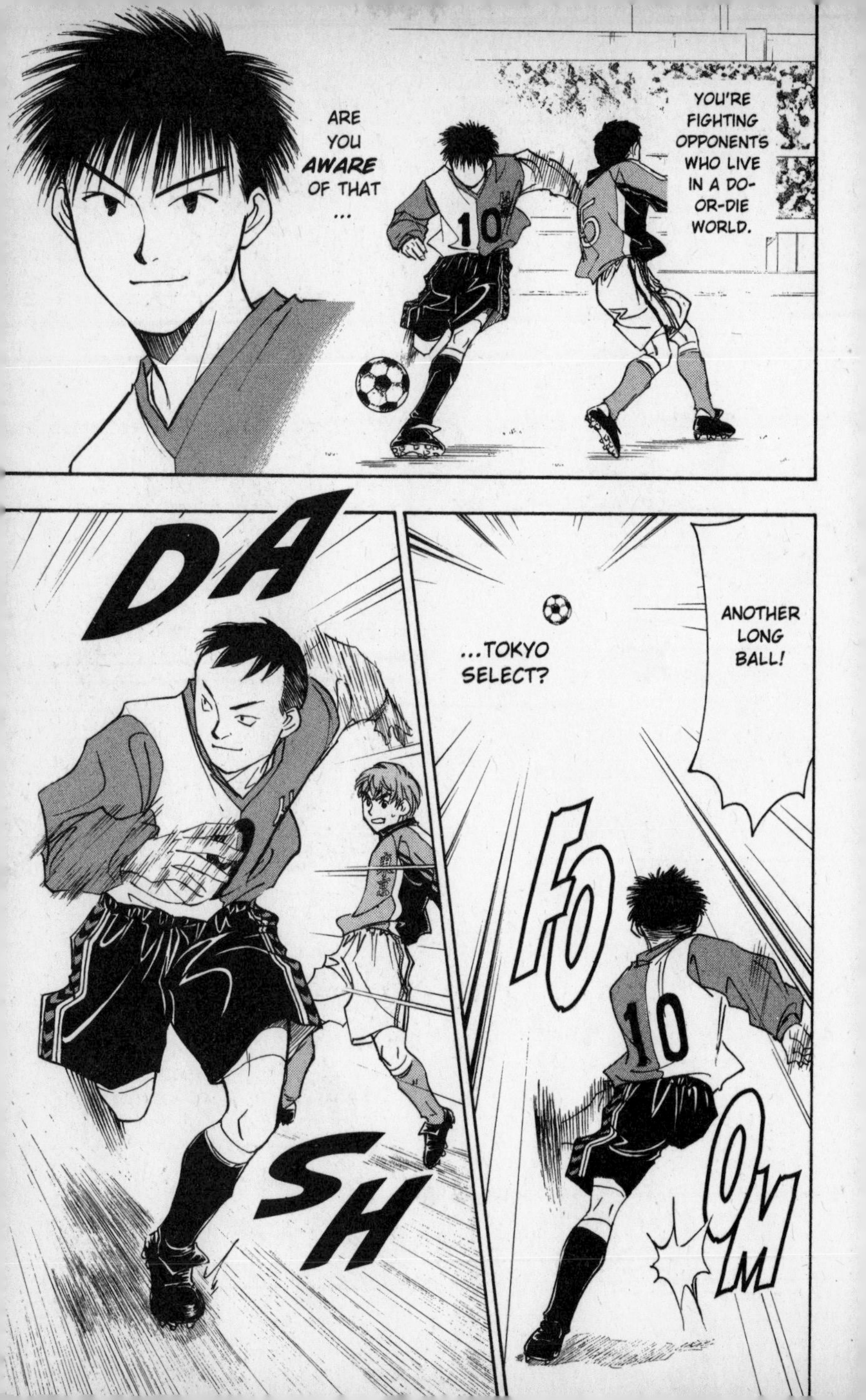
YOU'RE FIGHTING OPPONENTS WHO LIVE IN A DO-OR-DIE WORLD.
ARE YOU AWARE OF THAT ...
ANOTHER LONG BALL!
...TOKYO SELECT?
FOOM
DASH

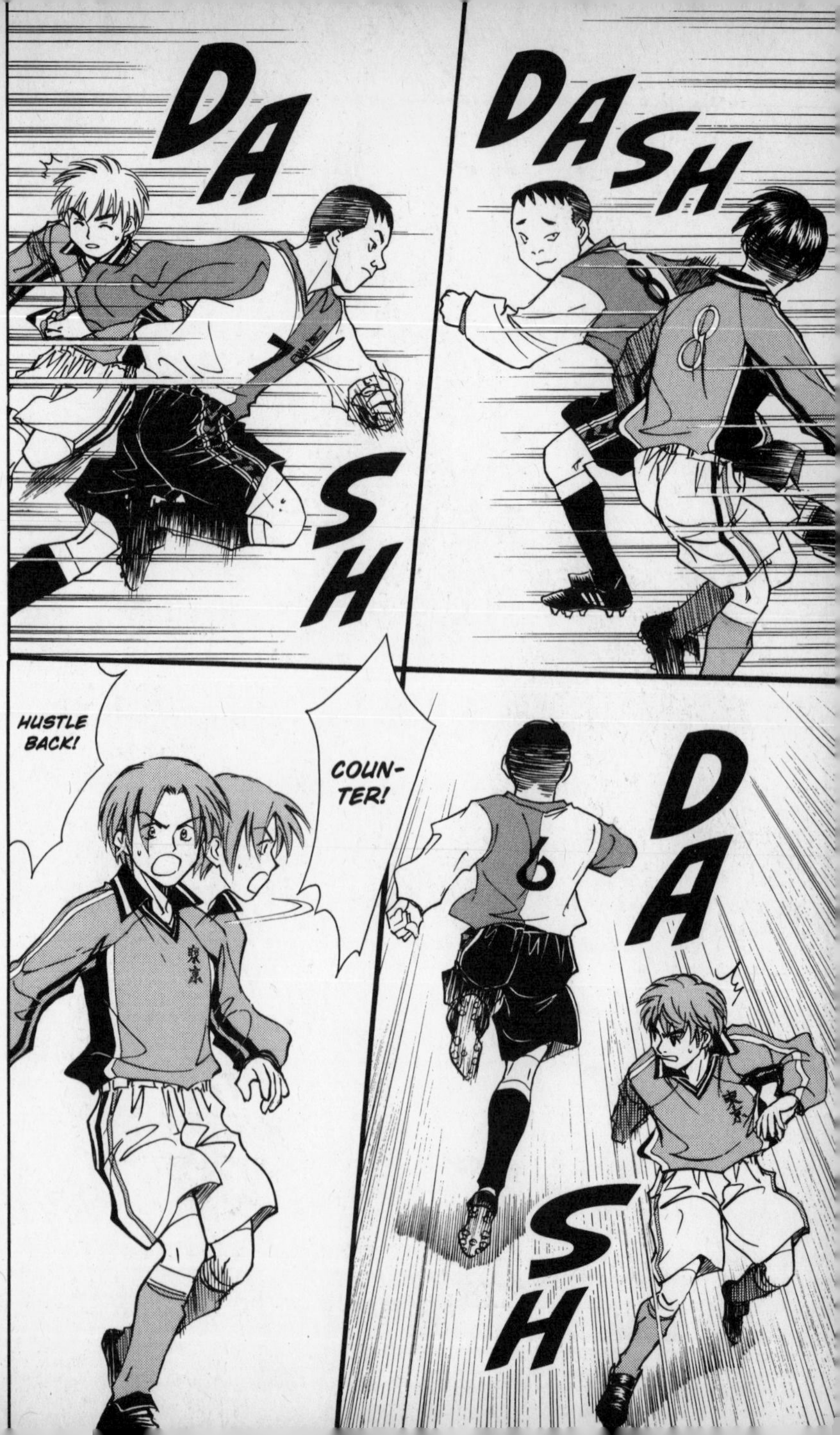
DASH
DASH
DASH
COUN-TER!
HUSTLE BACK!

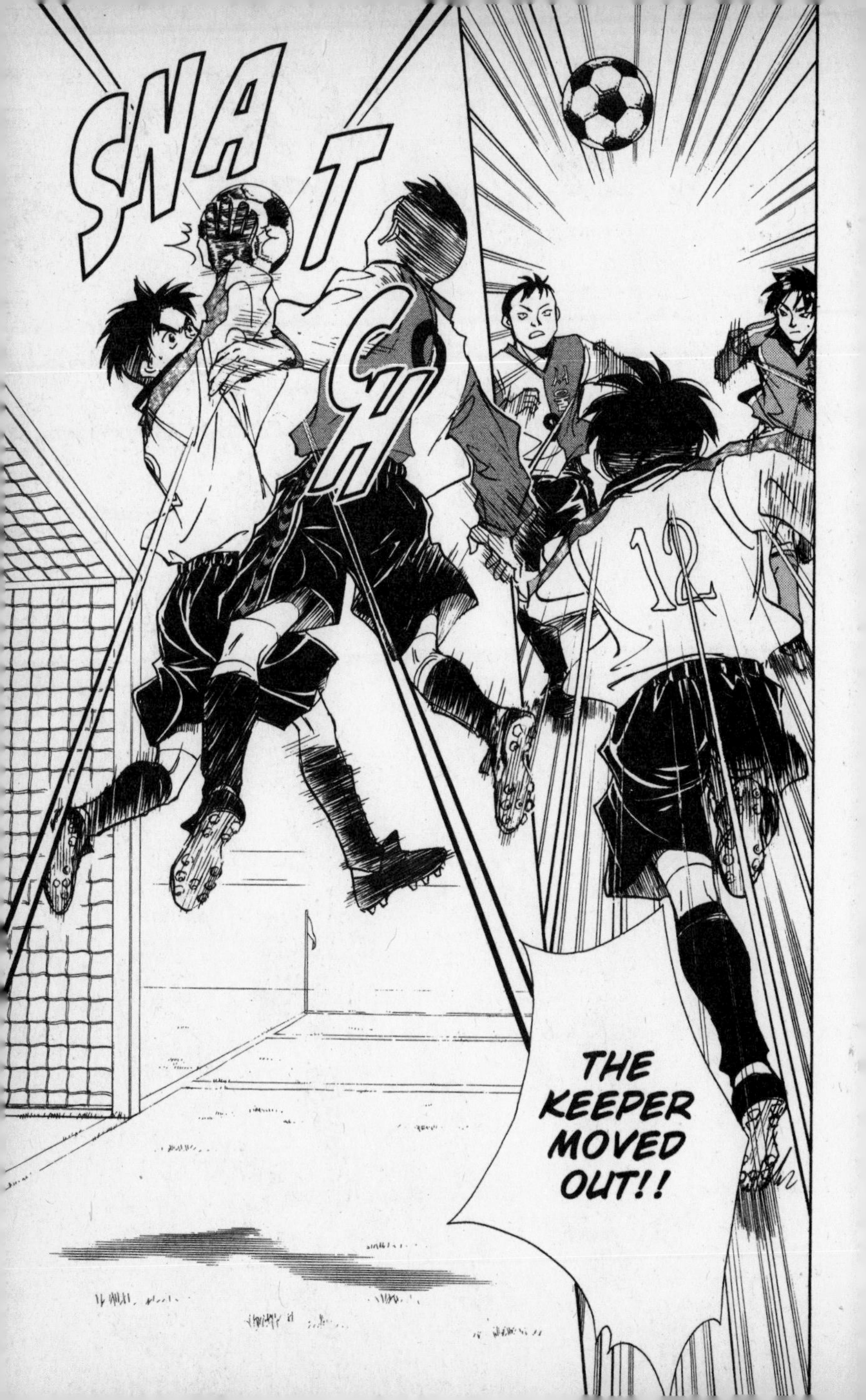
SNATCH
THE KEEPER MOVED OUT!!

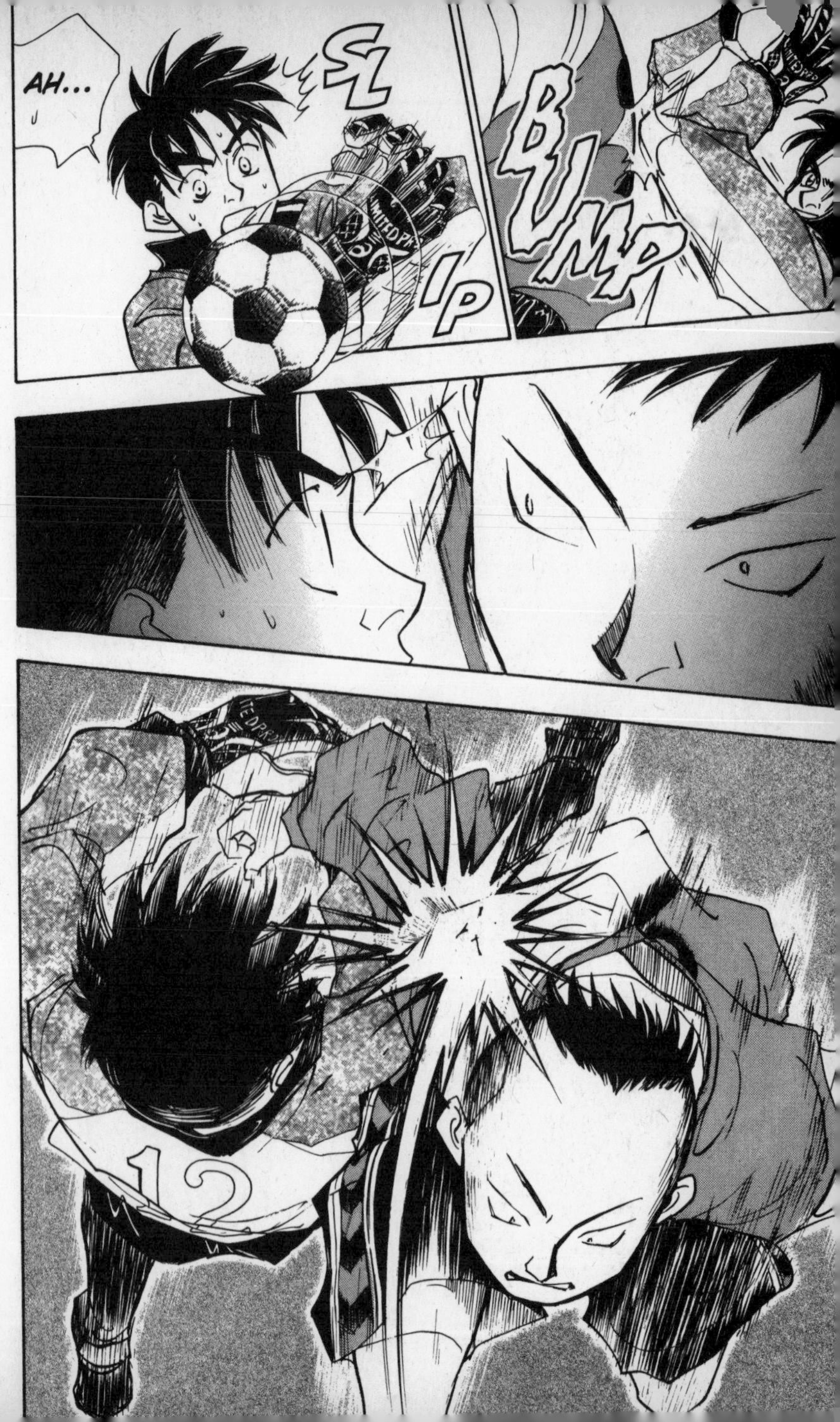
BUMP
AH...
SL
IP

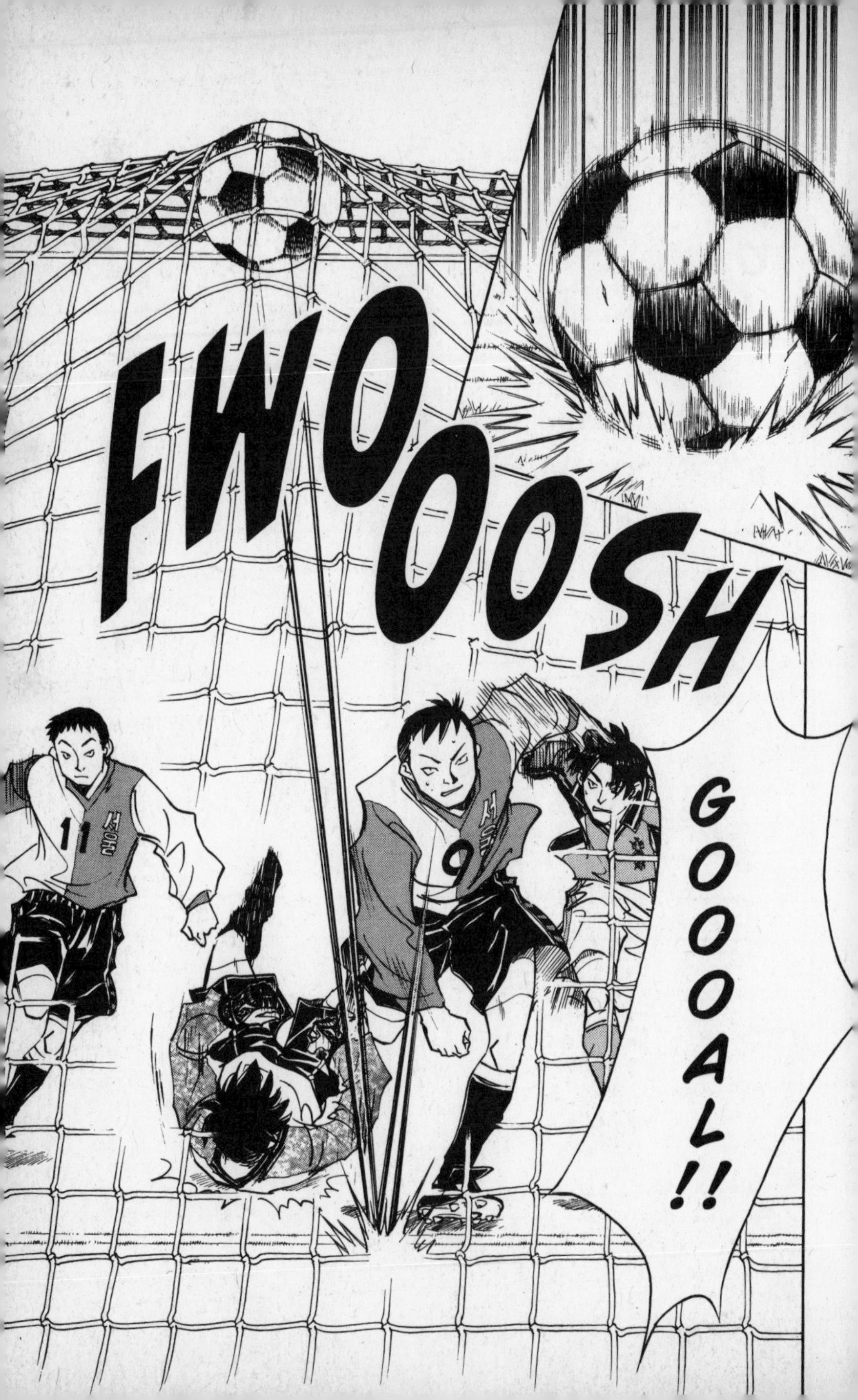
FWOOOSH
GOOOAL!!

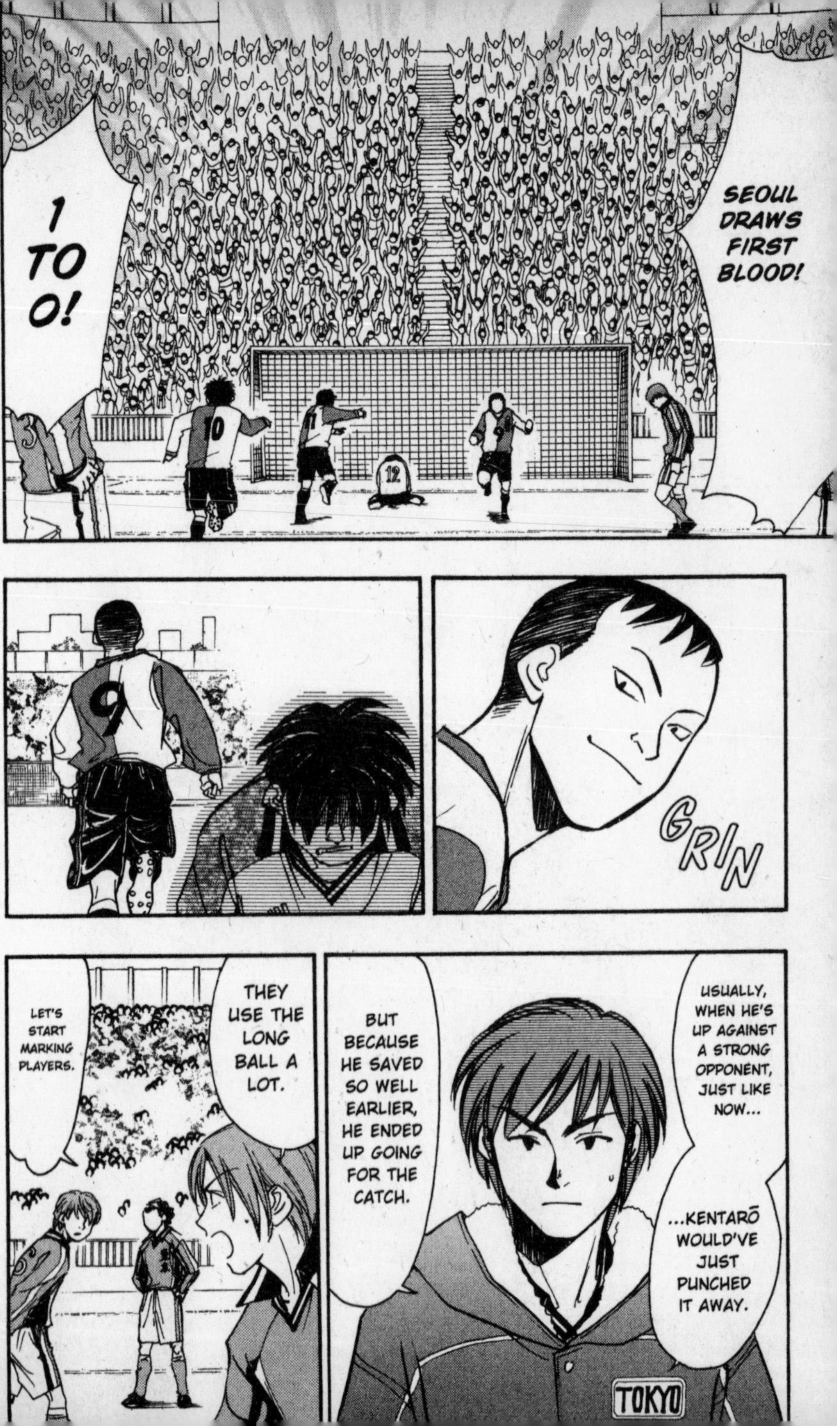
SEOUL DRAWS FIRST BLOOD!
1 TO 0!
GRIN
USUALLY, WHEN HE'S UP AGAINST A STRONG OPPONENT, JUST LIKE NOW...
...KENTARŌ WOULD'VE JUST PUNCHED IT AWAY.
BUT BECAUSE HE SAVED SO WELL EARLIER, HE ENDED UP GOING FOR THE CATCH.
TOKYO
THEY USE THE LONG BALL A LOT.
LET'S START MARKING PLAYERS.

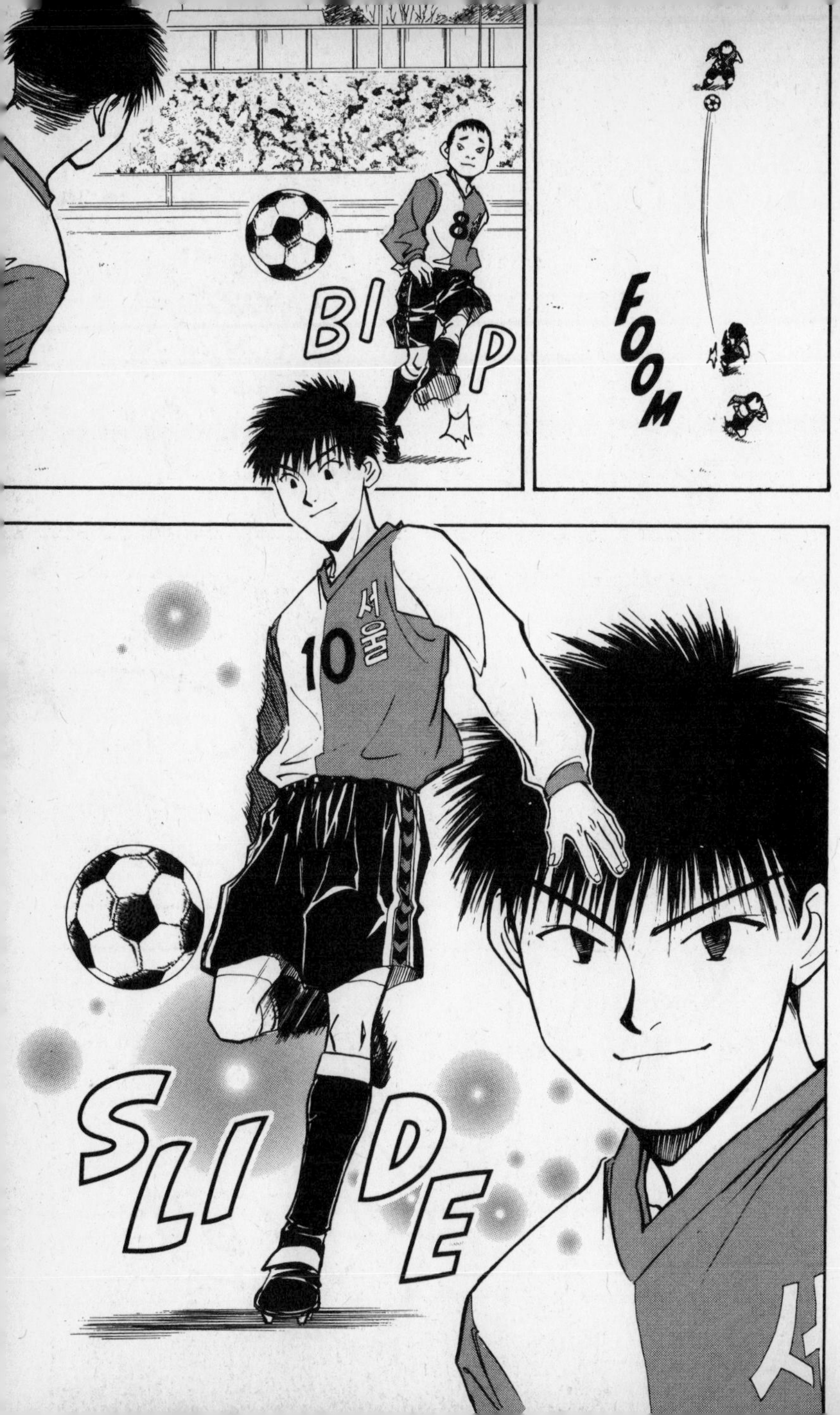
FOOM
BIP
서울
SLIDE

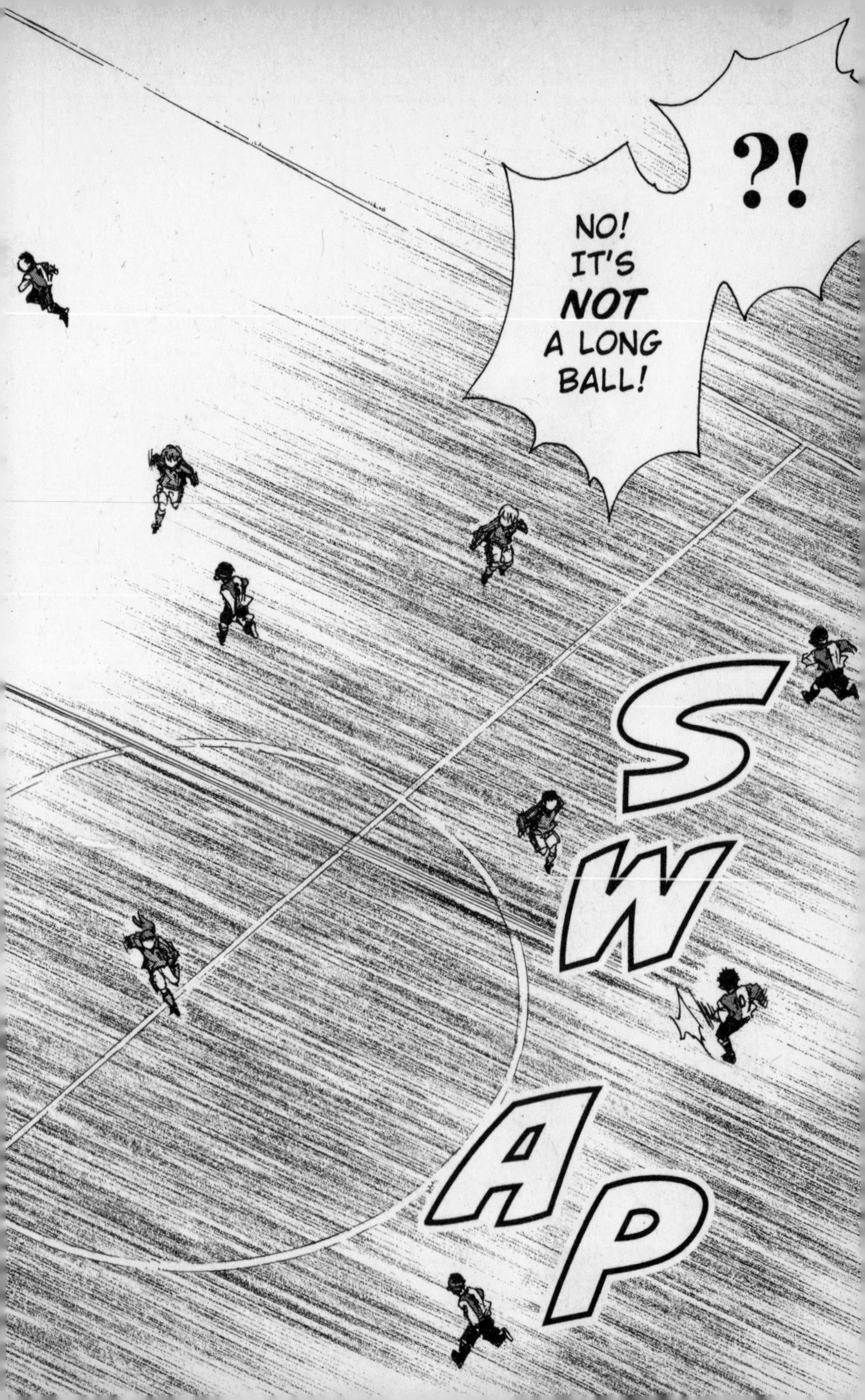
?!
NO! IT'S NOT A LONG BALL!
SWAP

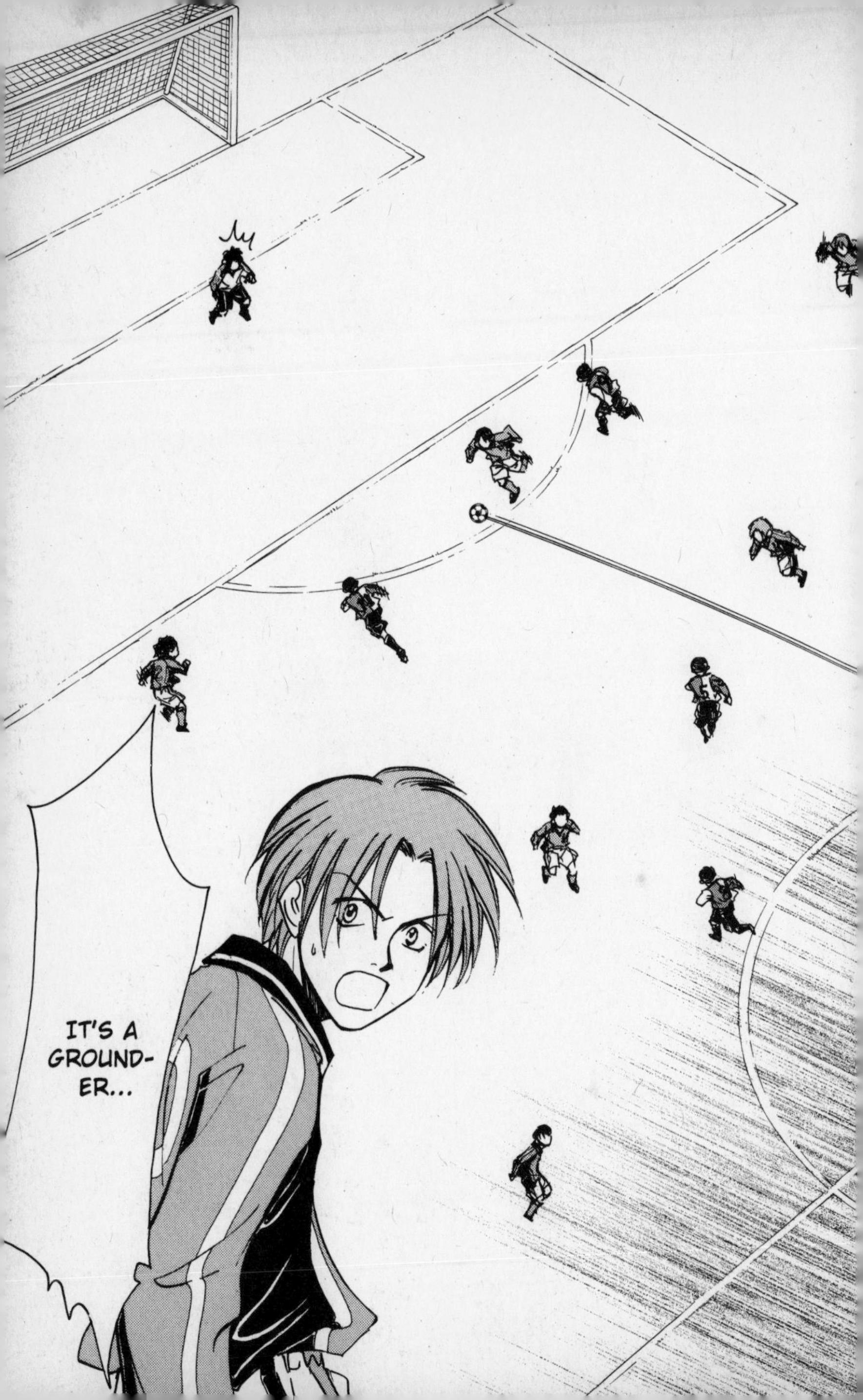
IT'S A GROUNDER...

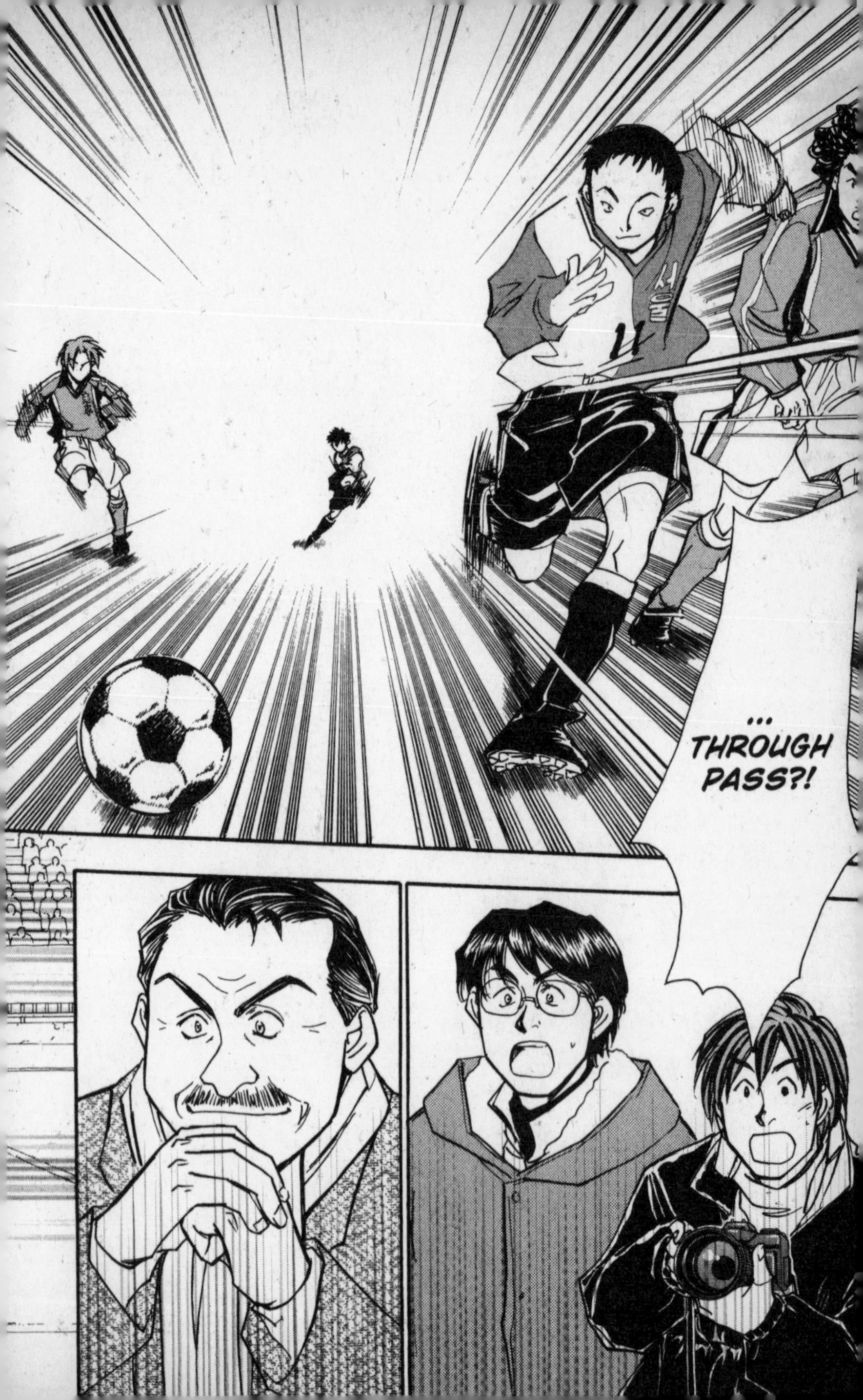
... THROUGH PASS?!

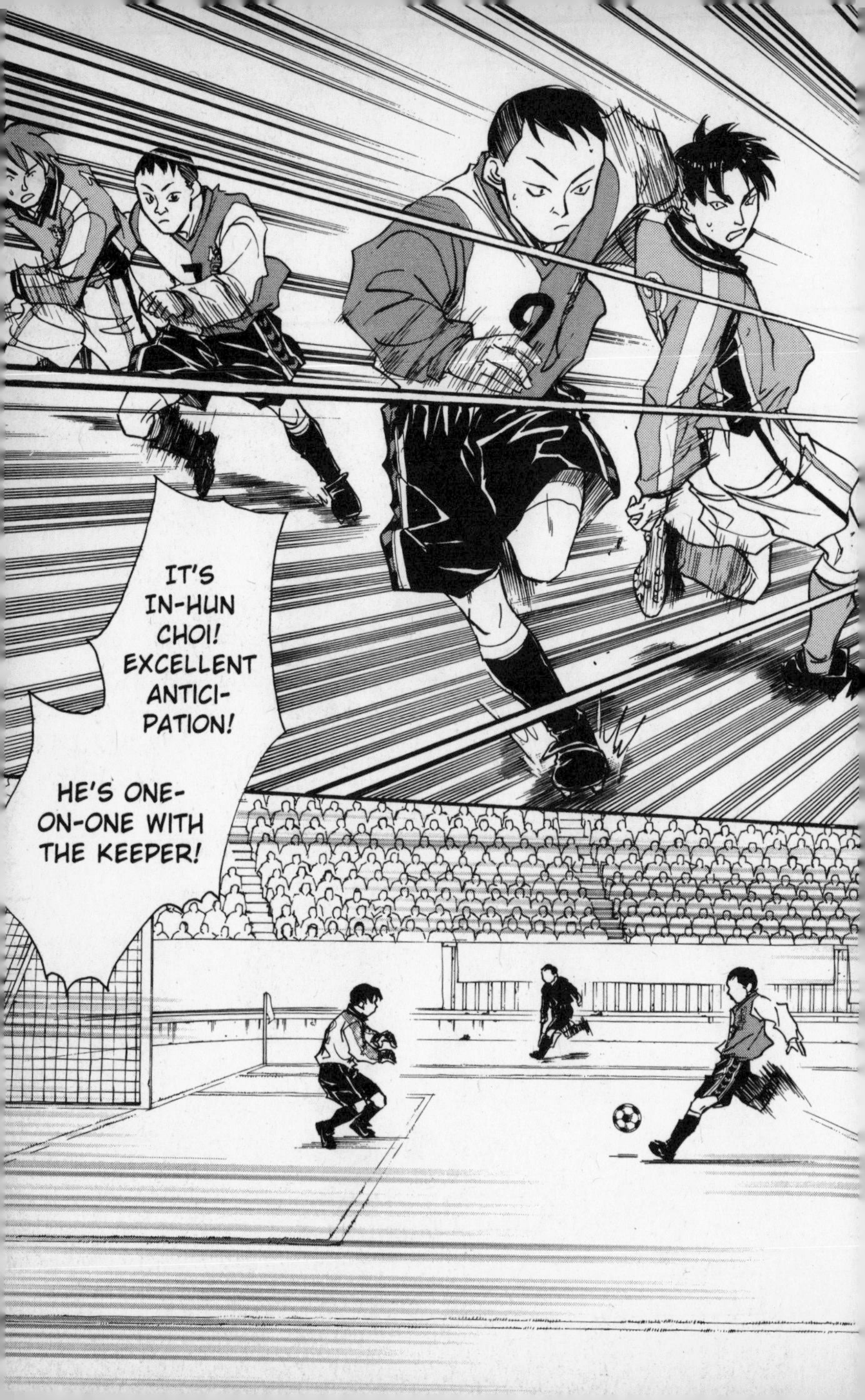
IT'S IN-HUN CHOI! EXCELLENT ANTICI-PATION!
HE'S ONE-ON-ONE WITH THE KEEPER!

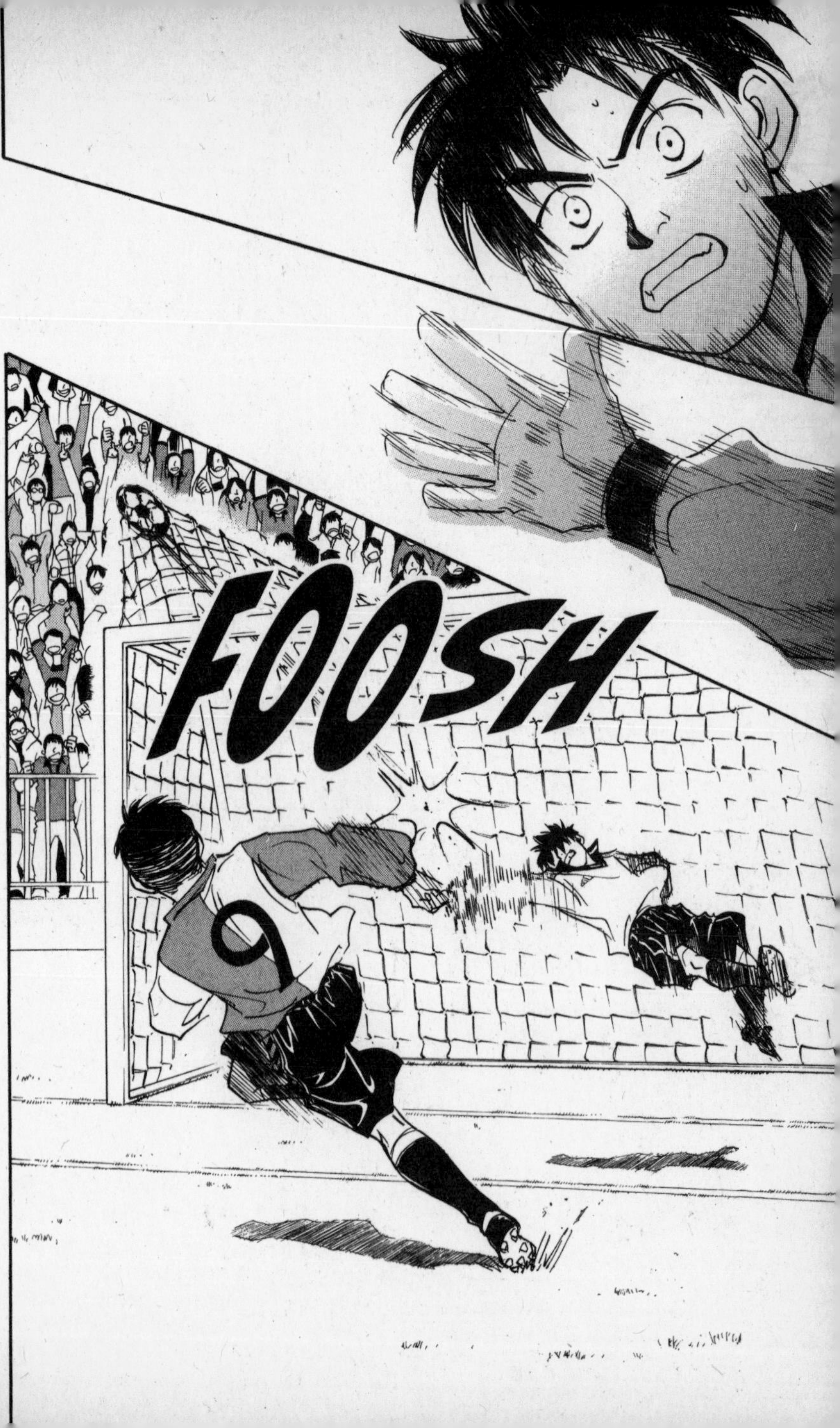
FOOSH

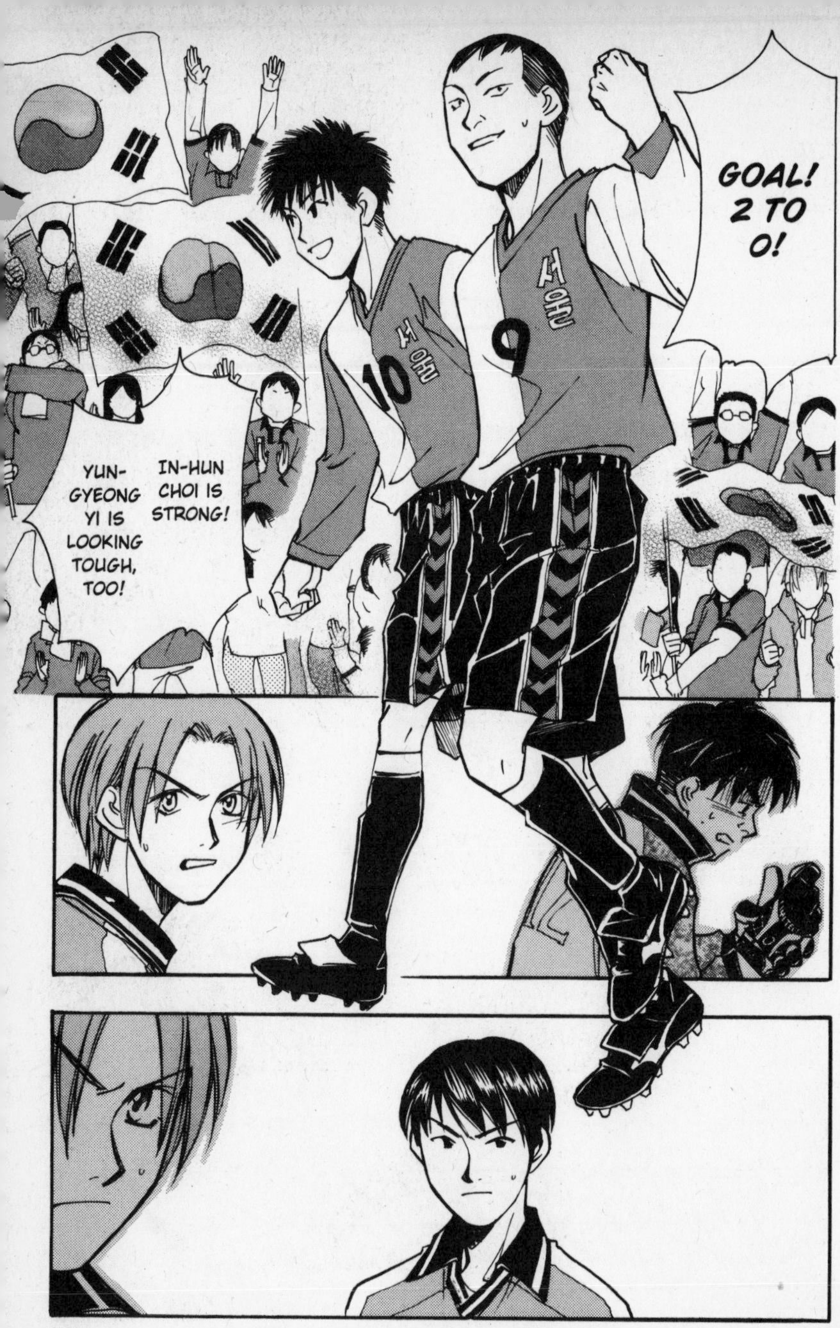
GOAL! 2 TO 0!
IN-HUN CHOI IS STRONG!
YUN-GYEONG YI IS LOOKING TOUGH, TOO!

WHISTLE!™

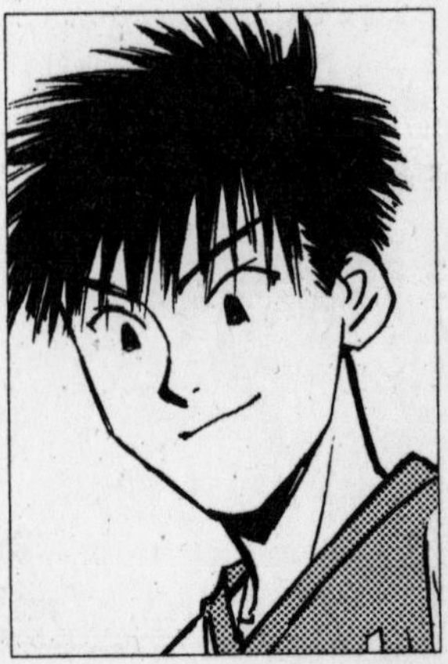

STAGE.154
Snap Out of It!

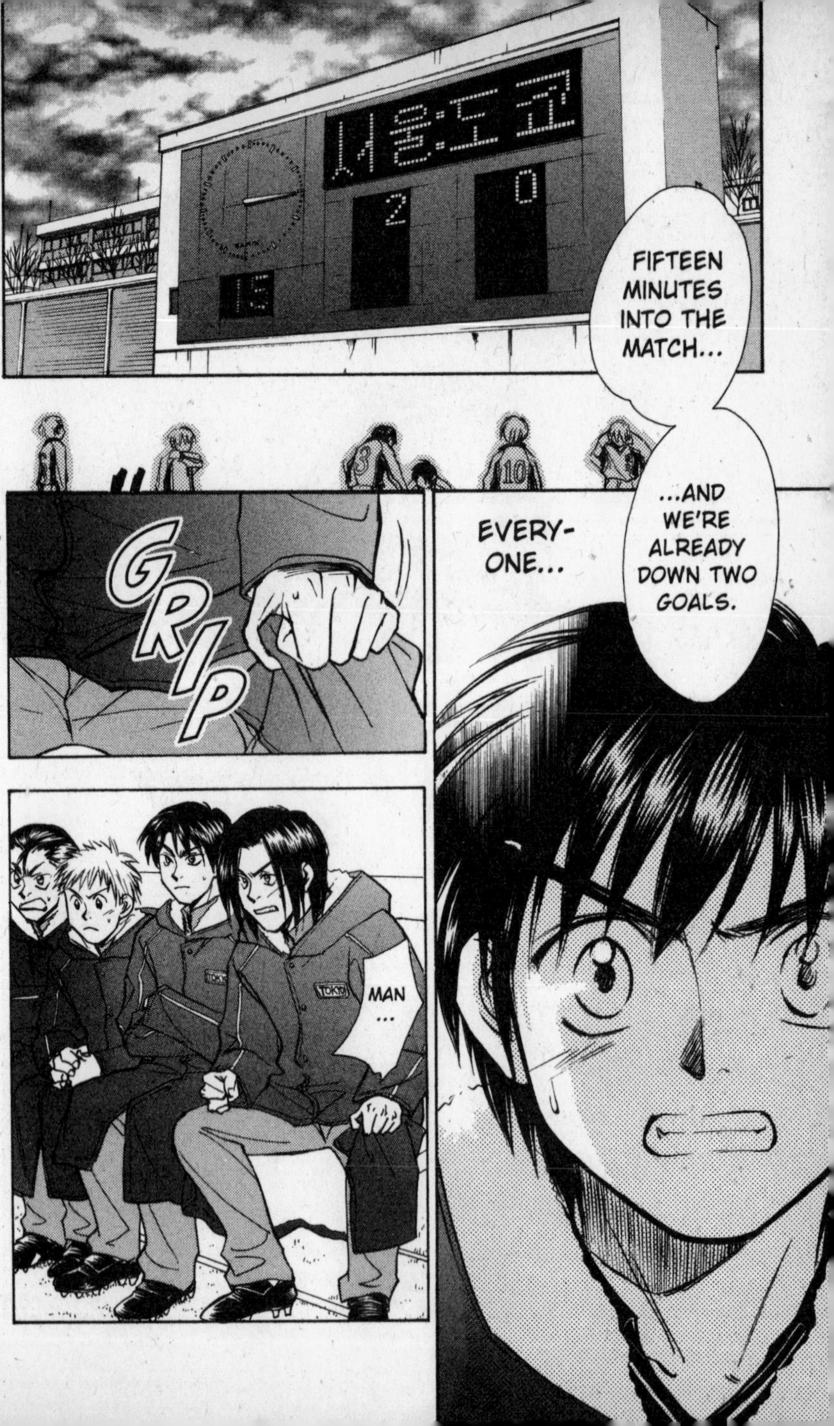
15
2
0
FIFTEEN MINUTES INTO THE MATCH...
...AND WE'RE ALREADY DOWN TWO GOALS.
EVERY-ONE...
GRIP
MAN...

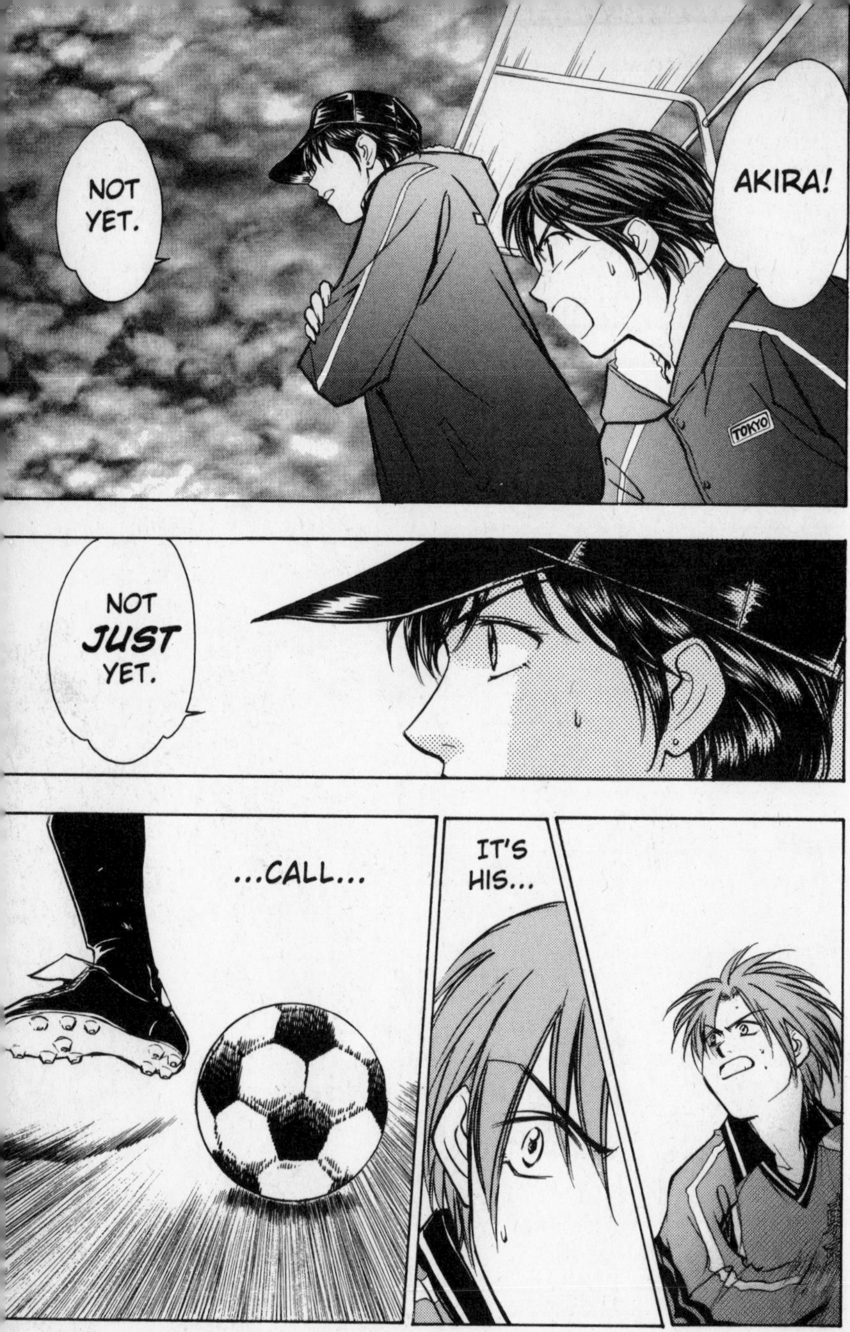
AKIRA!
NOT YET.
NOT **JUST** YET.
IT'S HIS...
...CALL...

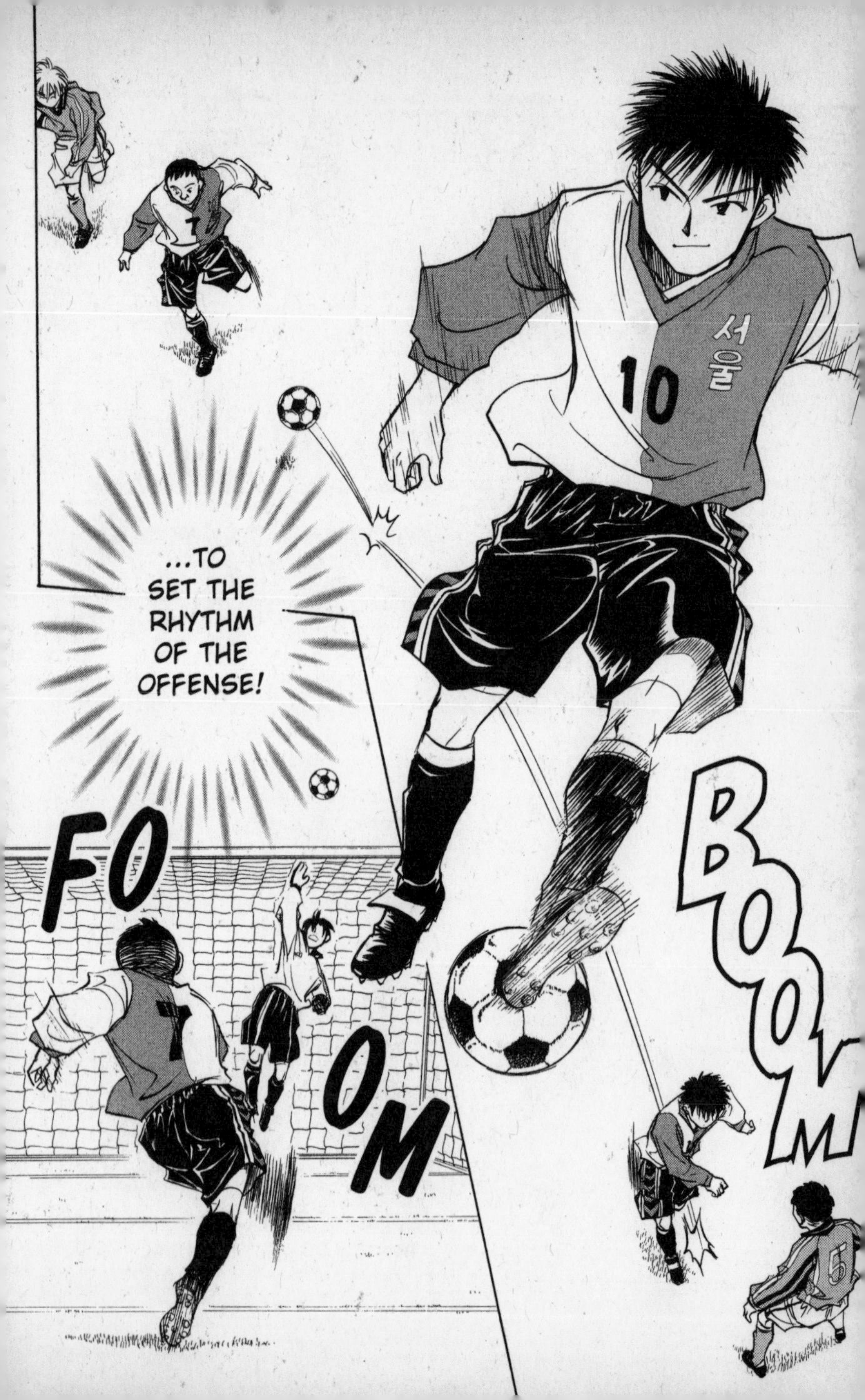
...TO SET THE RHYTHM OF THE OFFENSE!
BOOOM
FOOM

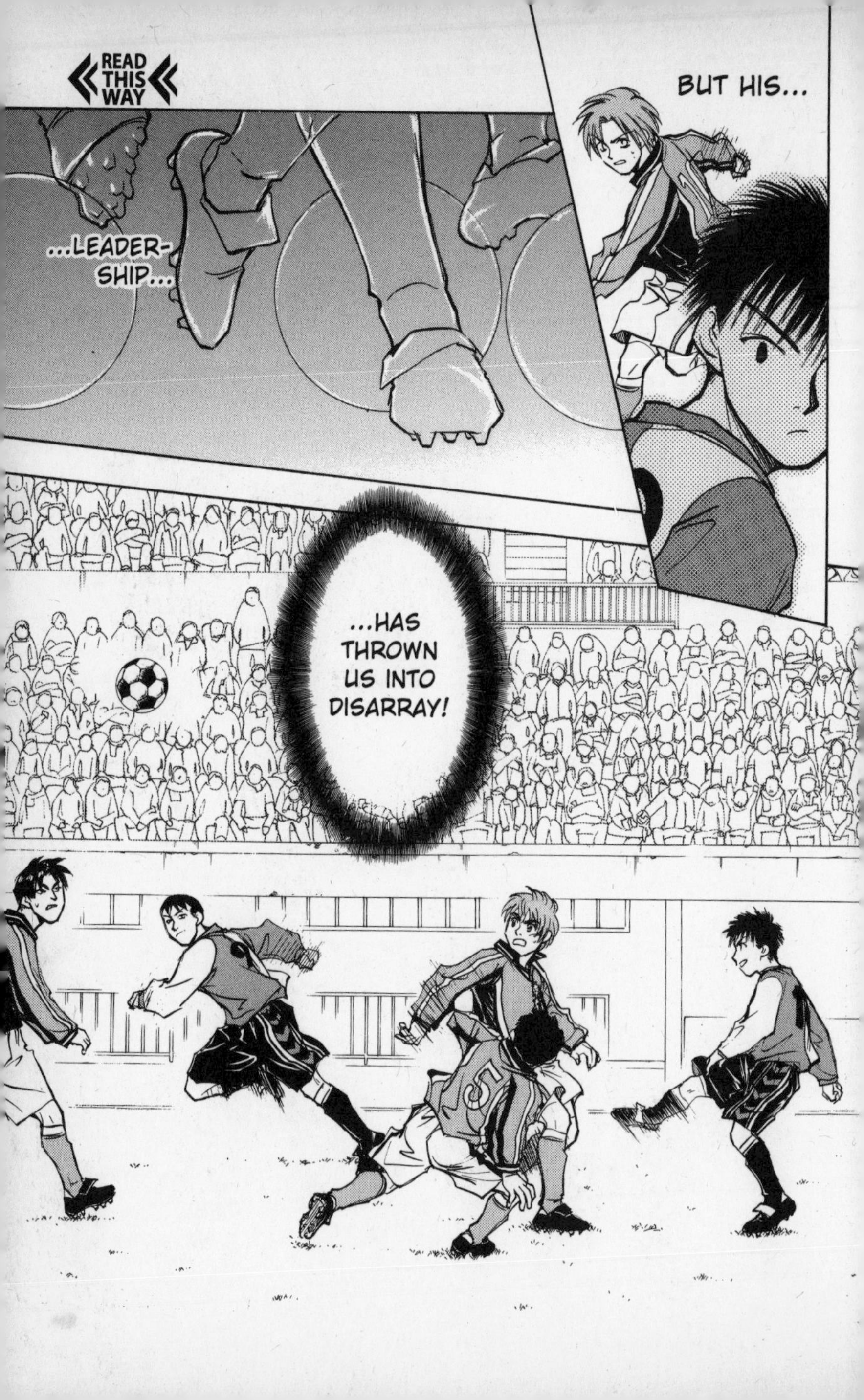
READ THIS WAY
BUT HIS...
...LEADER-SHIP...
...HAS THROWN US INTO DISARRAY!

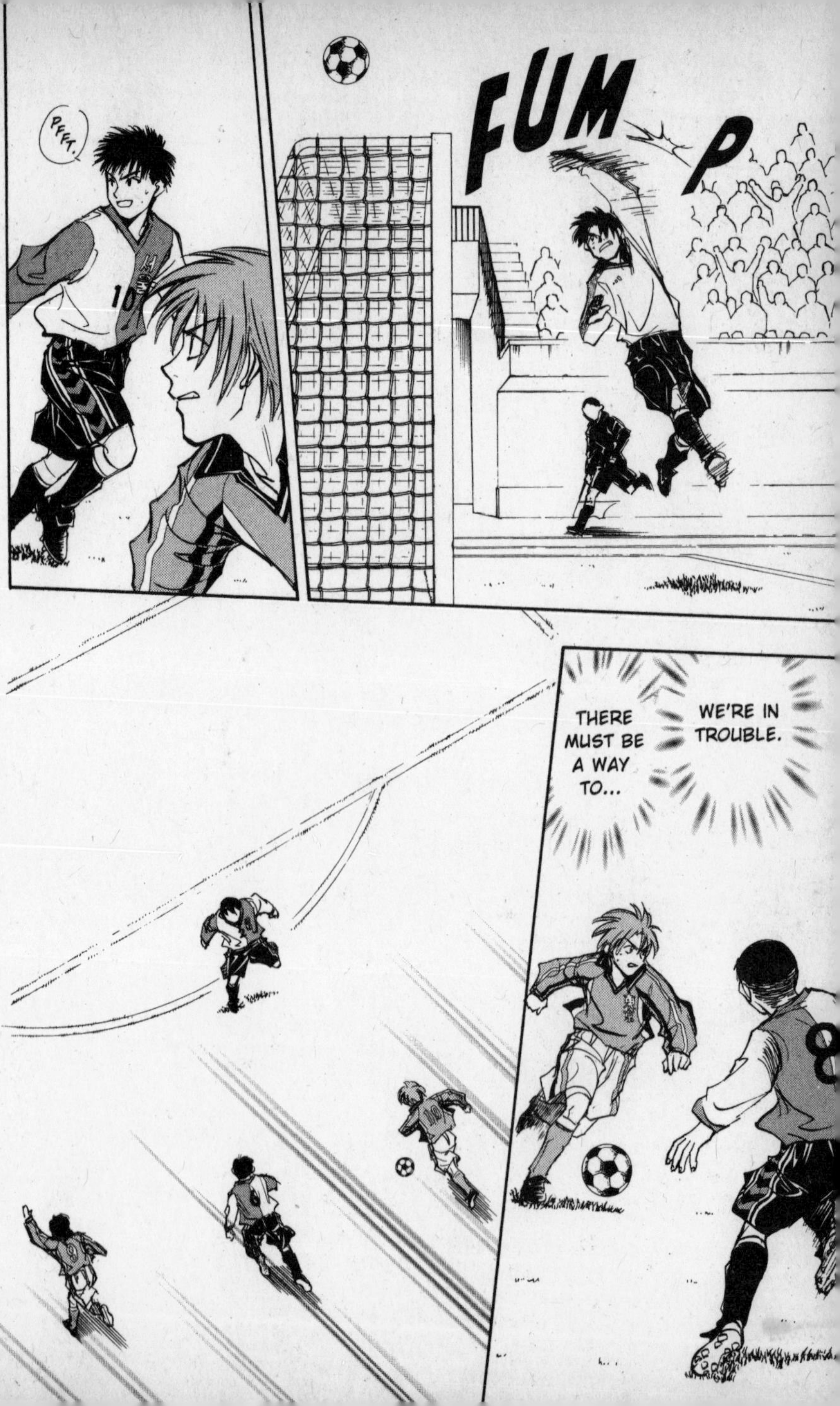
FUMP
PFFT.
WE'RE IN TROUBLE.
THERE MUST BE A WAY TO...

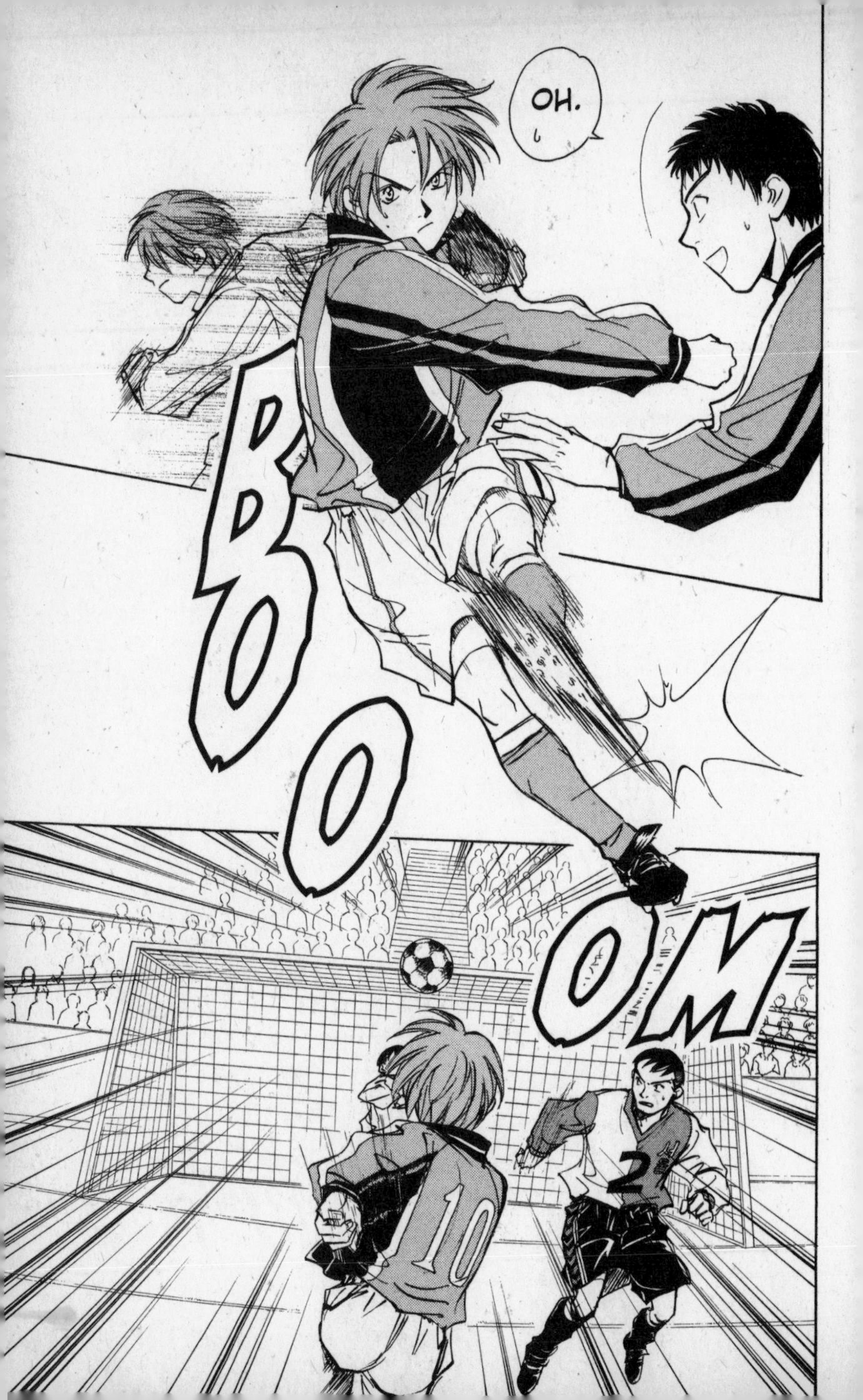
OH.
BOOOM

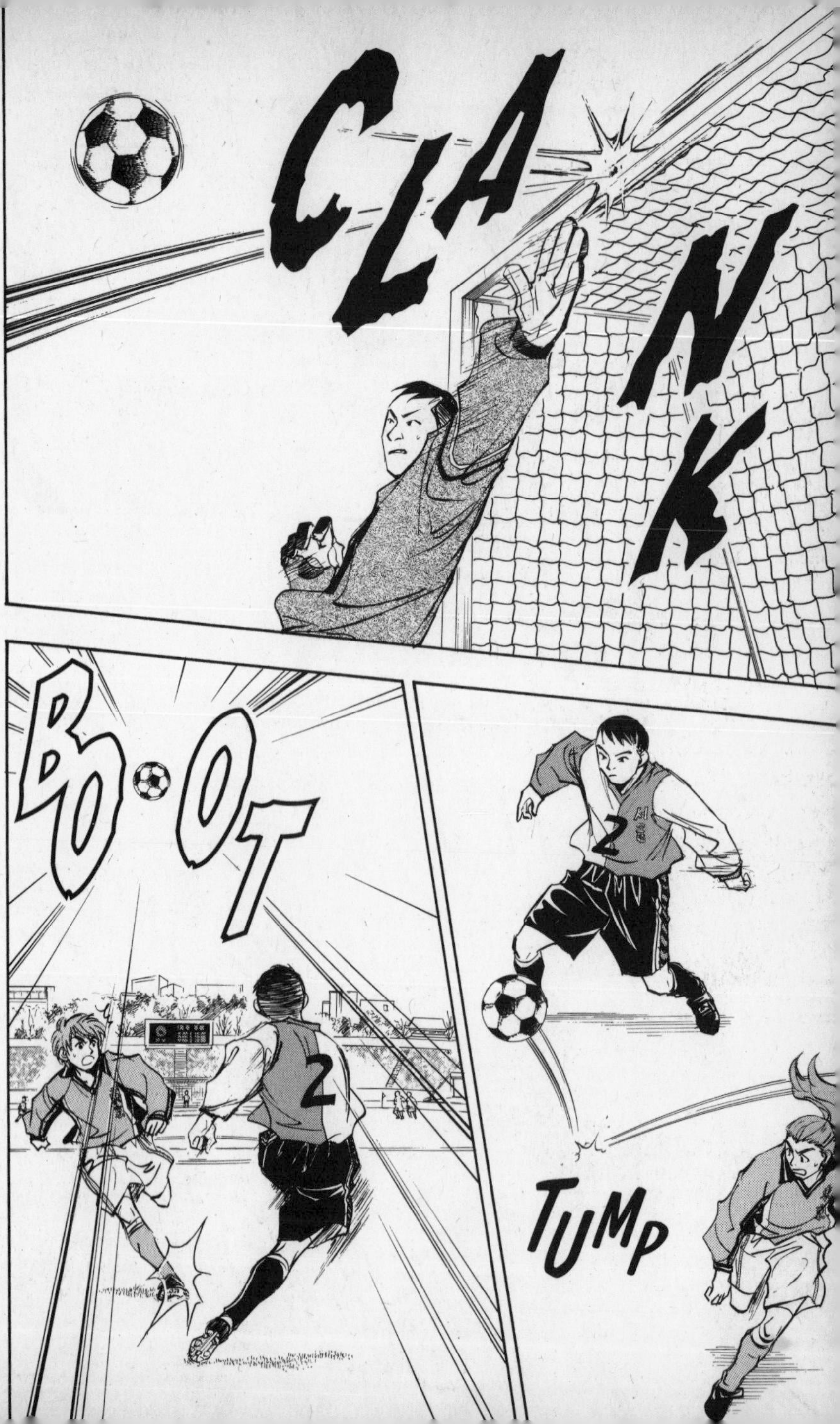
CLANK
TUMP
BOOT

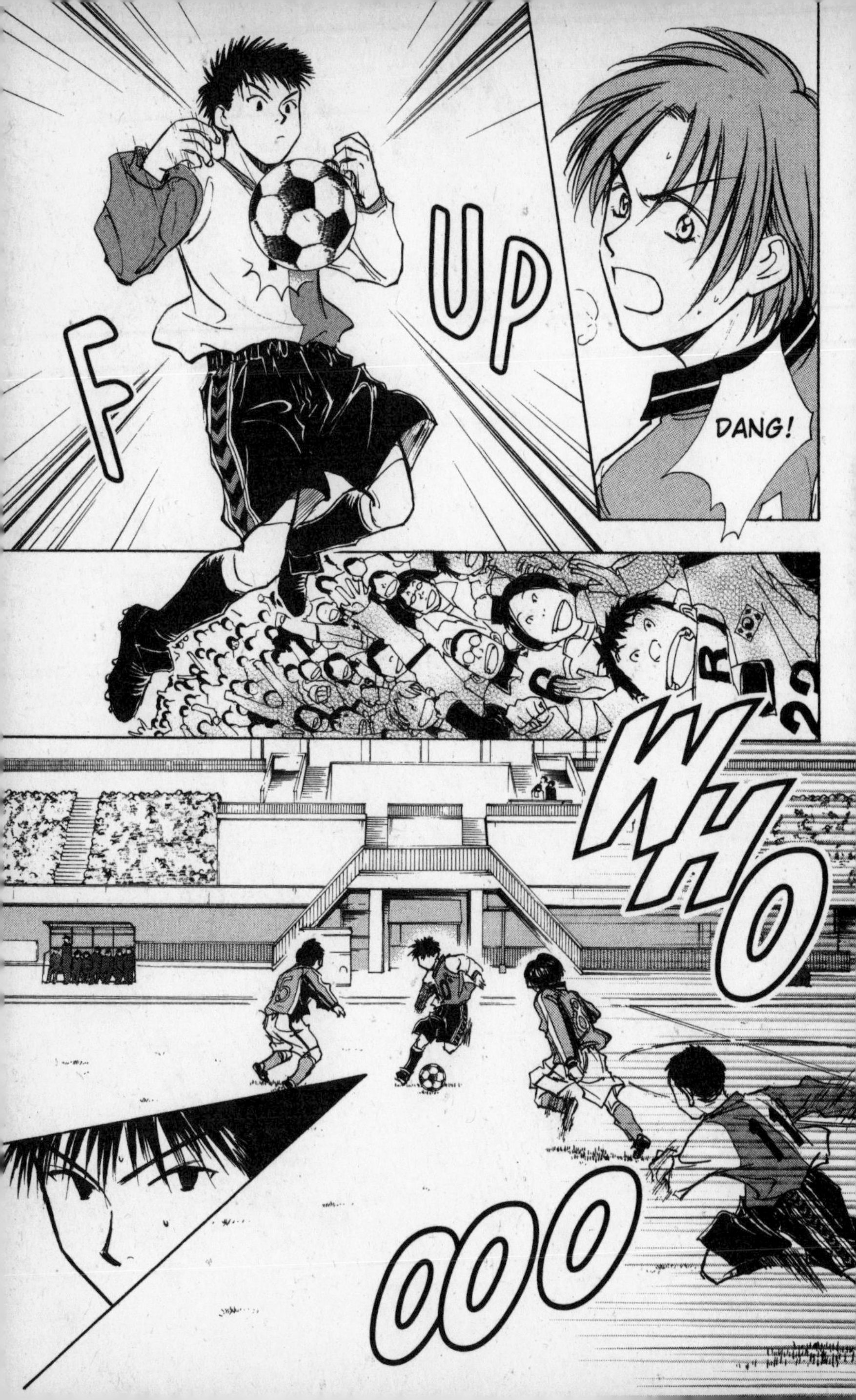
DANG!
FUP
WHOOOO

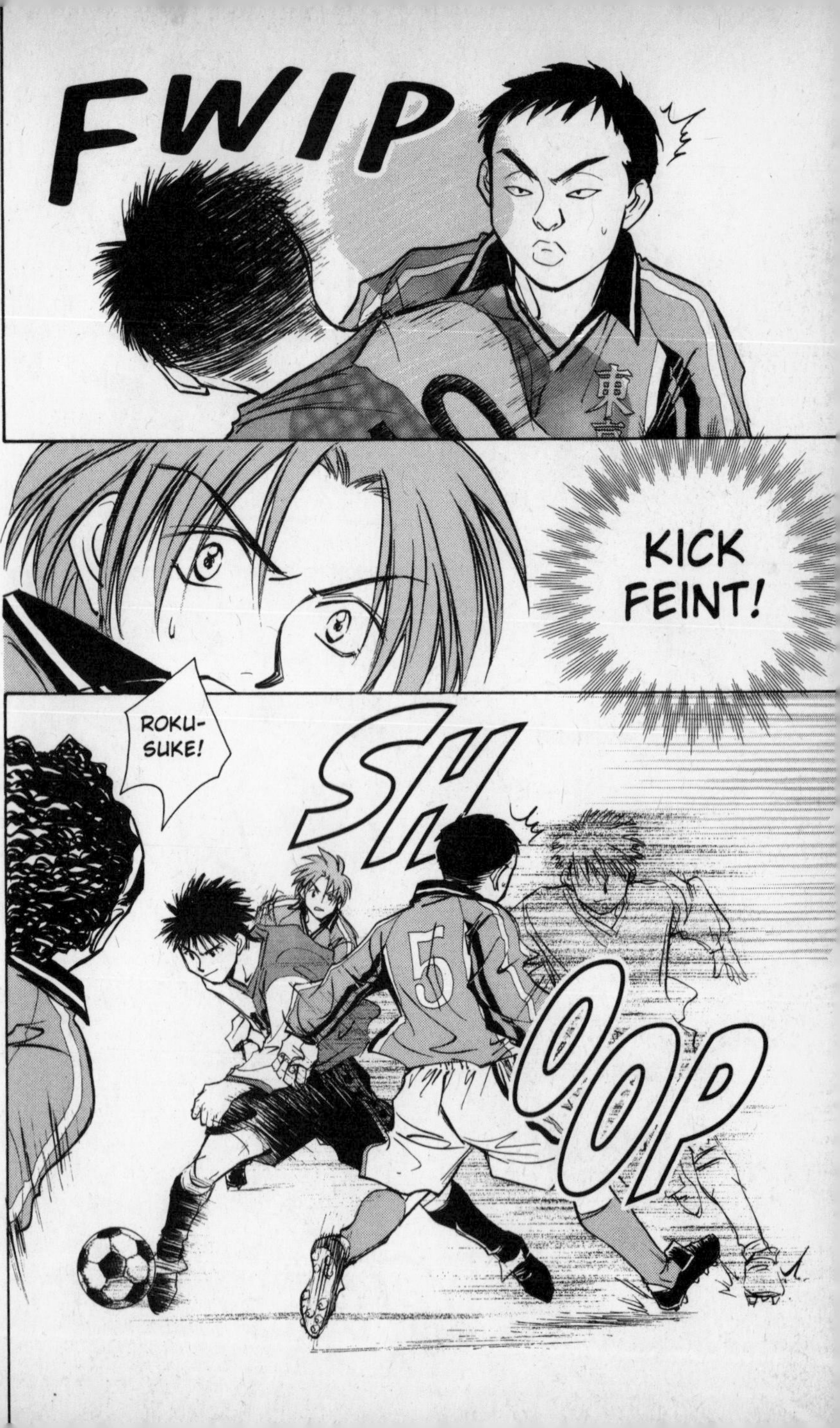
FWIP
KICK FEINT!
ROKU-SUKE!
SHOOP

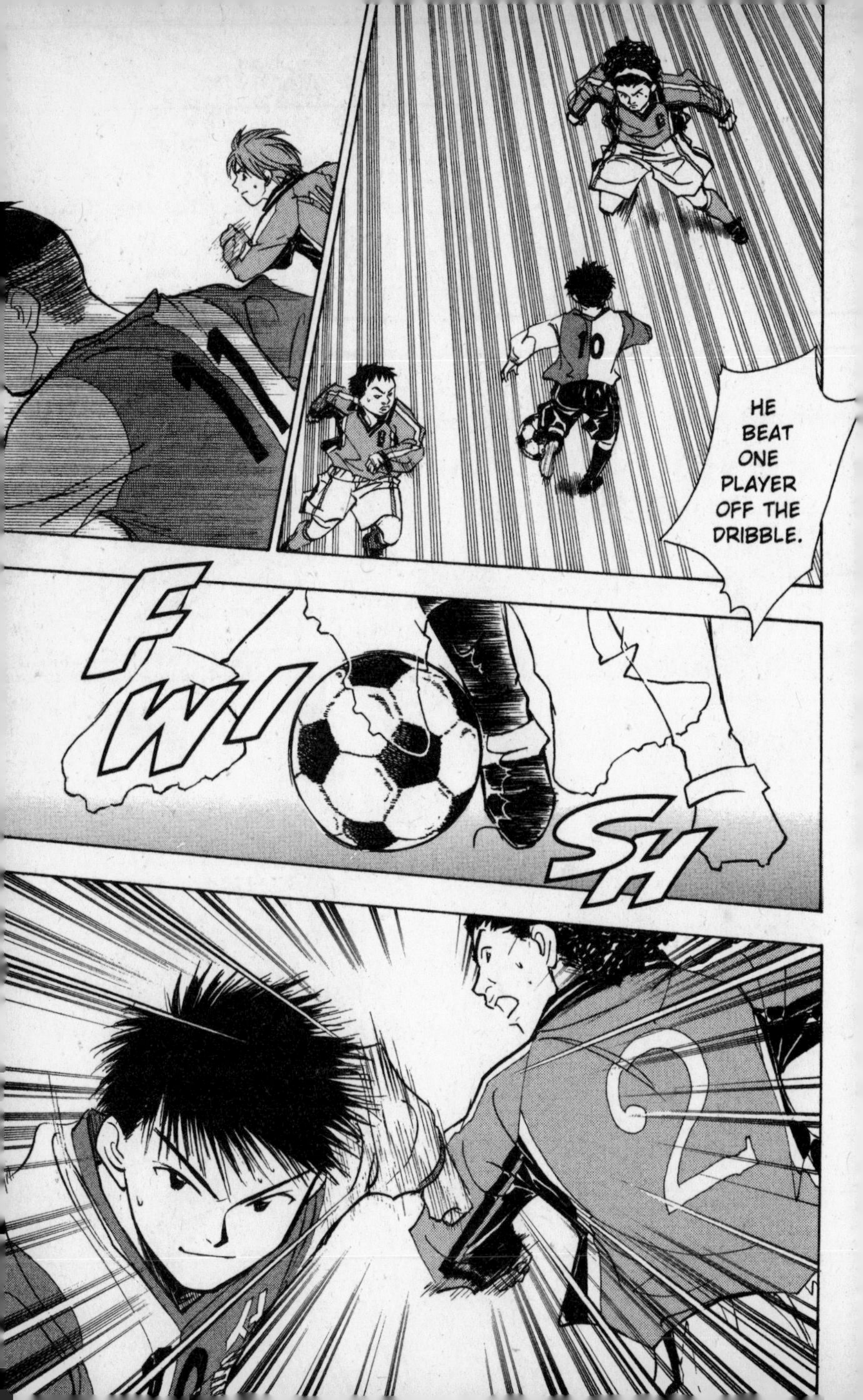
HE BEAT ONE PLAYER OFF THE DRIBBLE.
FWI
SH

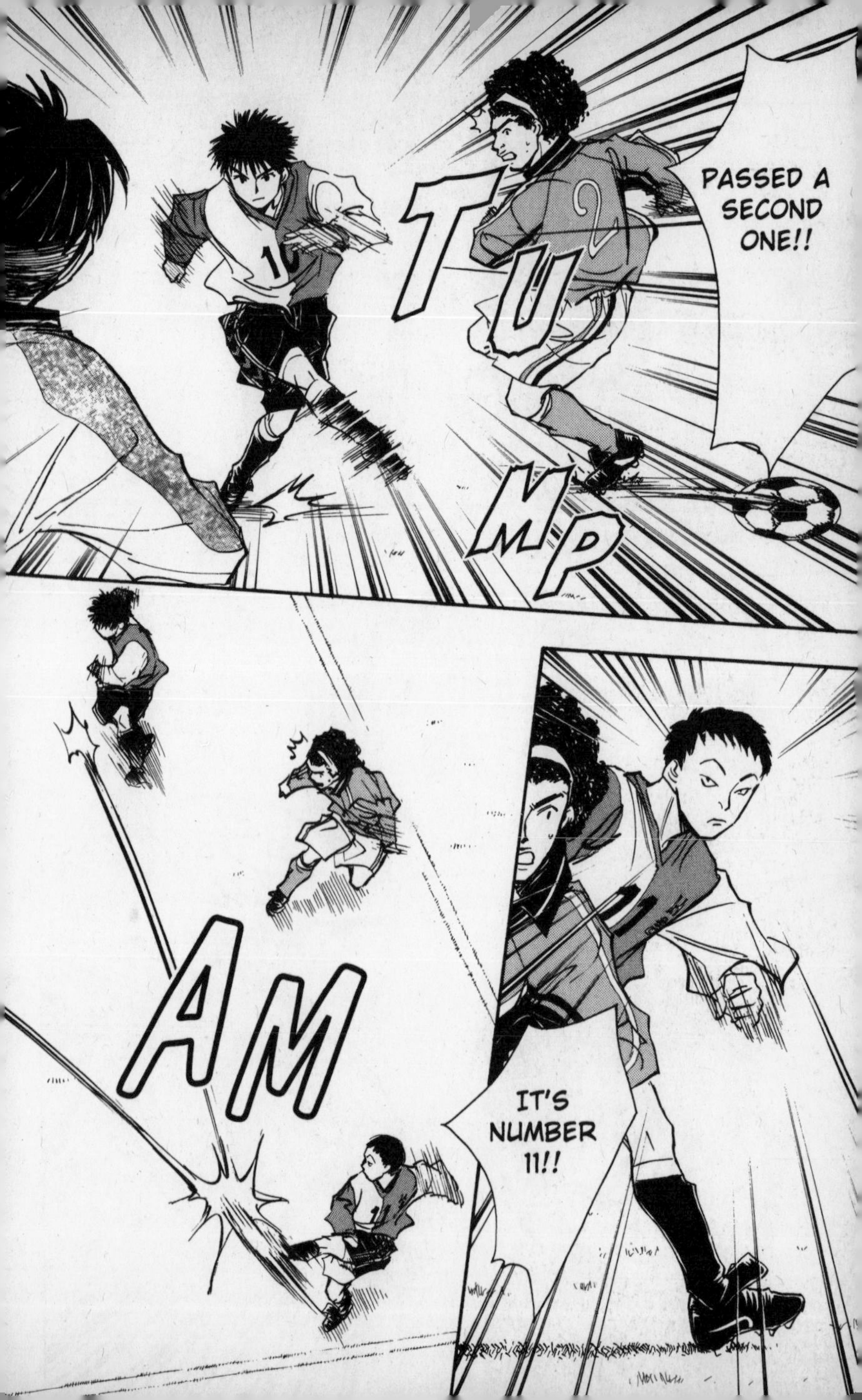
PASSED A SECOND ONE!!
TUMP
IT'S NUMBER 11!!
AM

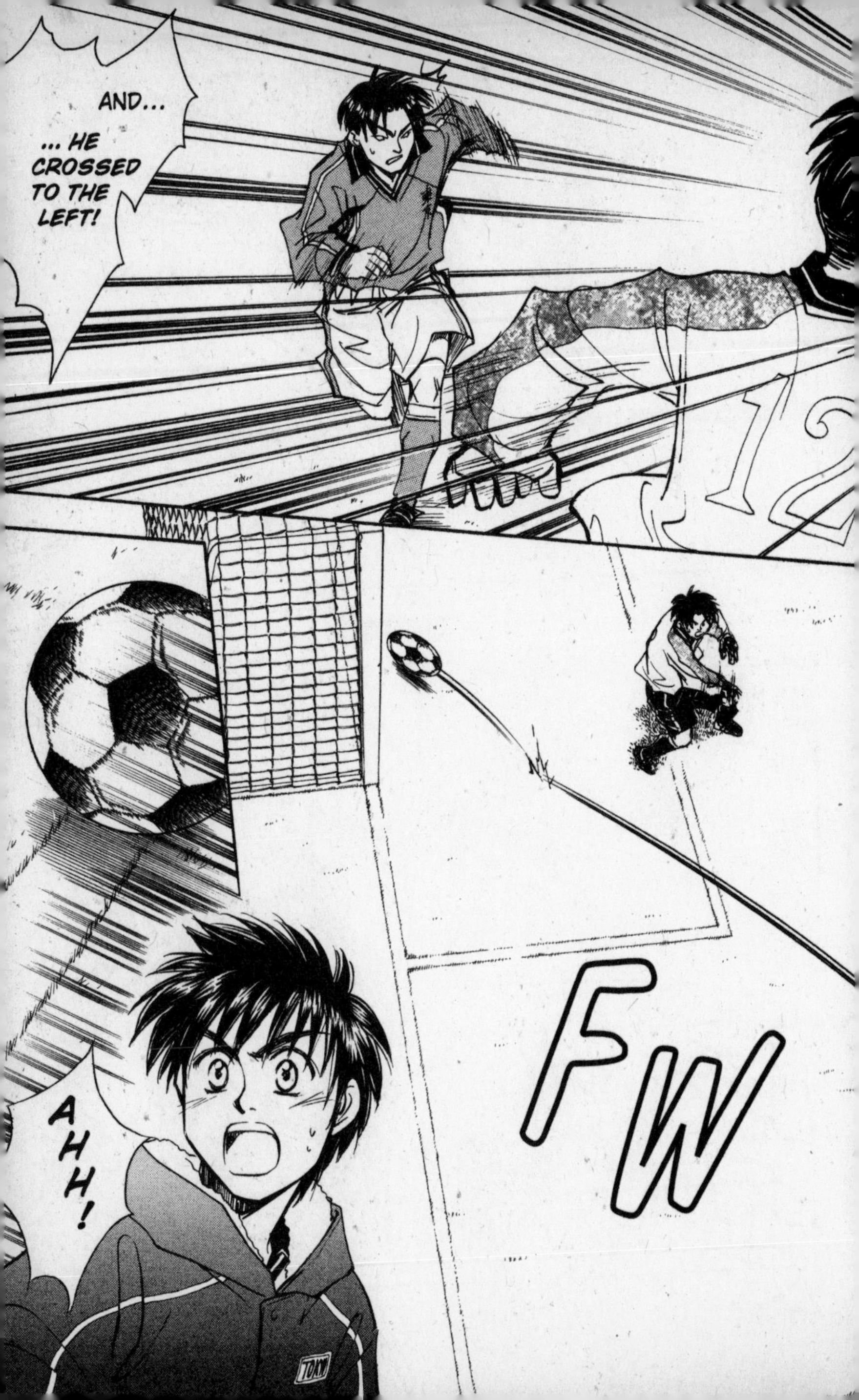
AND...
... HE CROSSED TO THE LEFT!
FW
AHH!

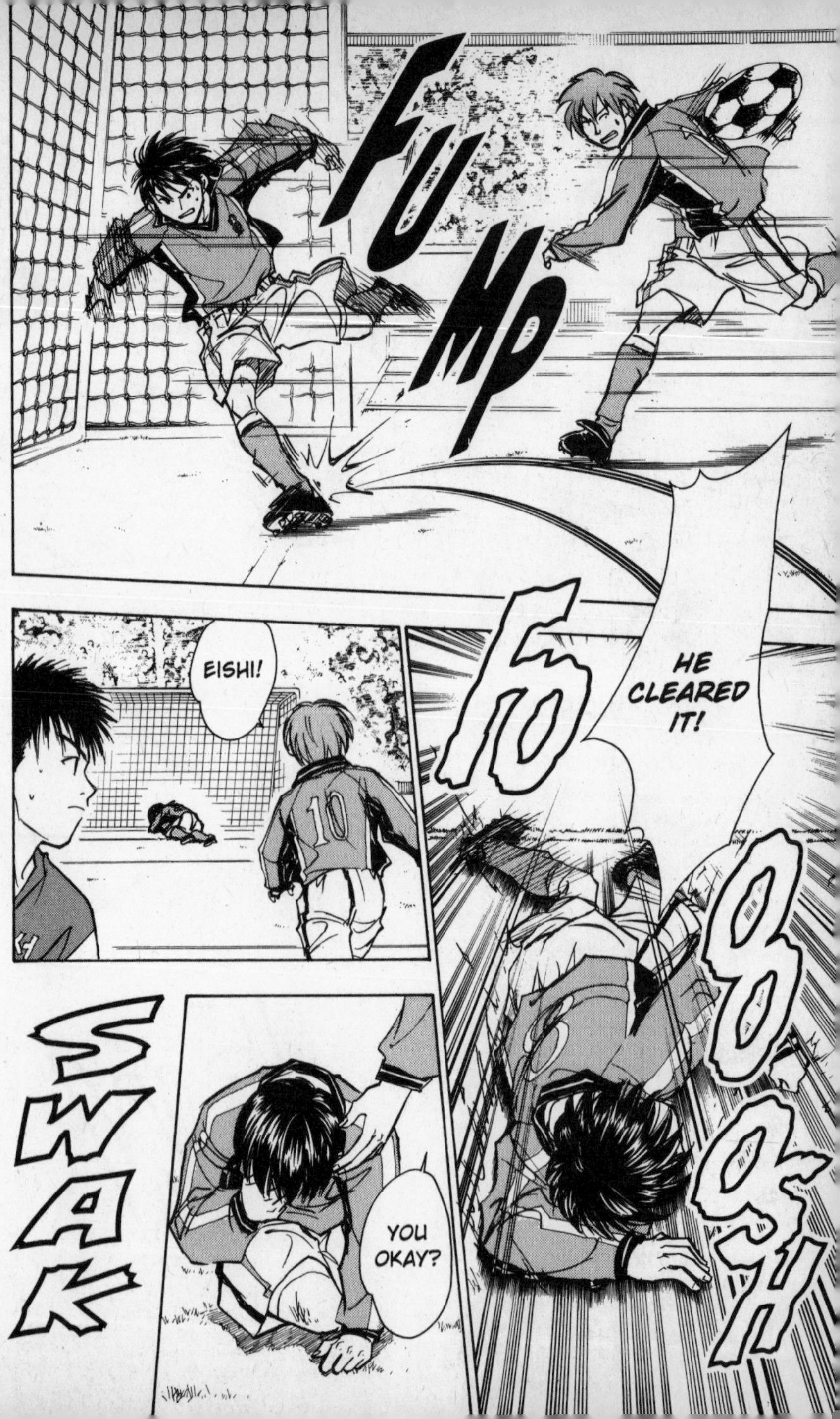
FUMP
HE CLEARED IT!
EISHI!
YOU OKAY?
SWAK

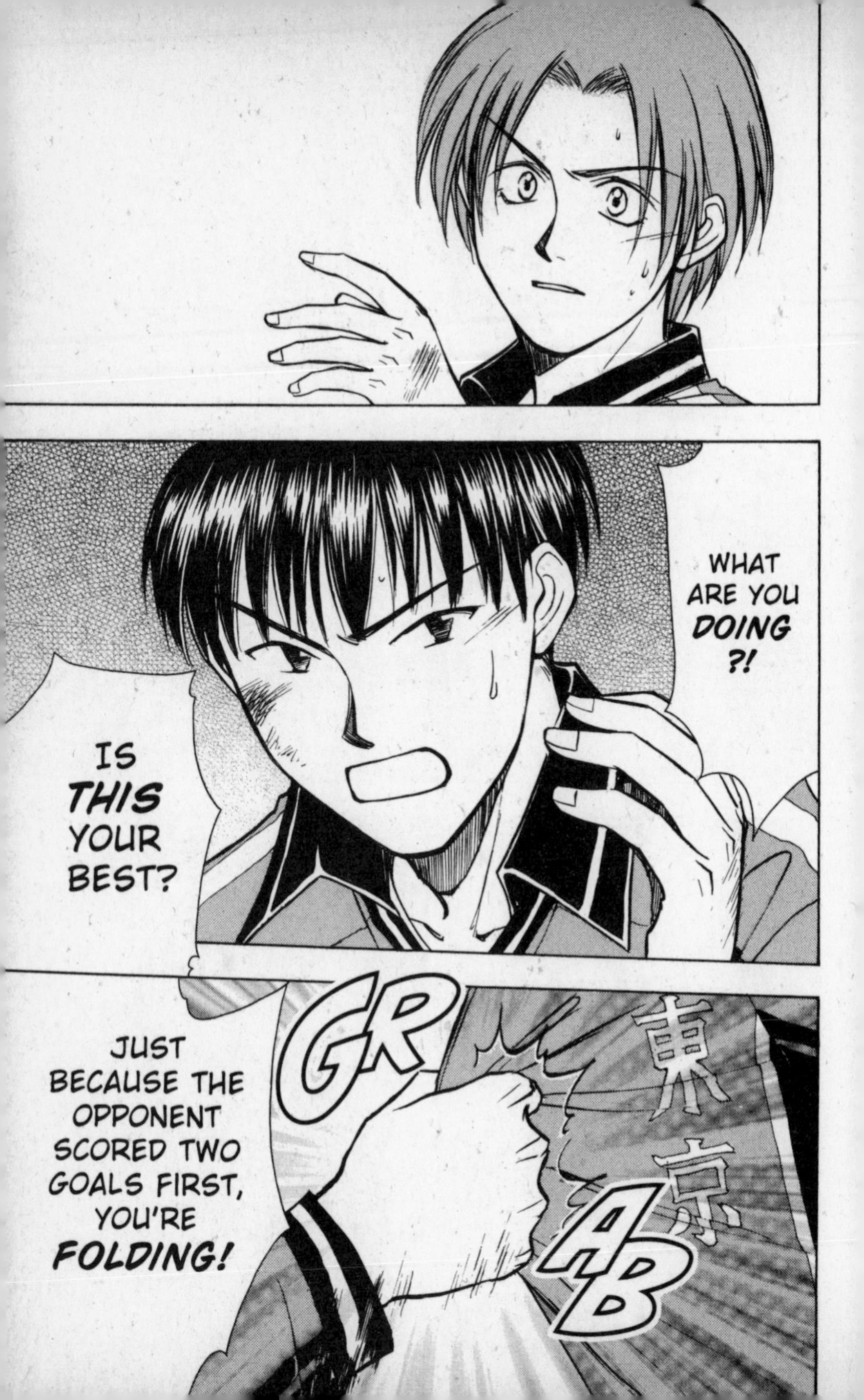
WHAT ARE YOU DOING ?!
IS THIS YOUR BEST?
GRAB
東京
JUST BECAUSE THE OPPONENT SCORED TWO GOALS FIRST, YOU'RE FOLDING!

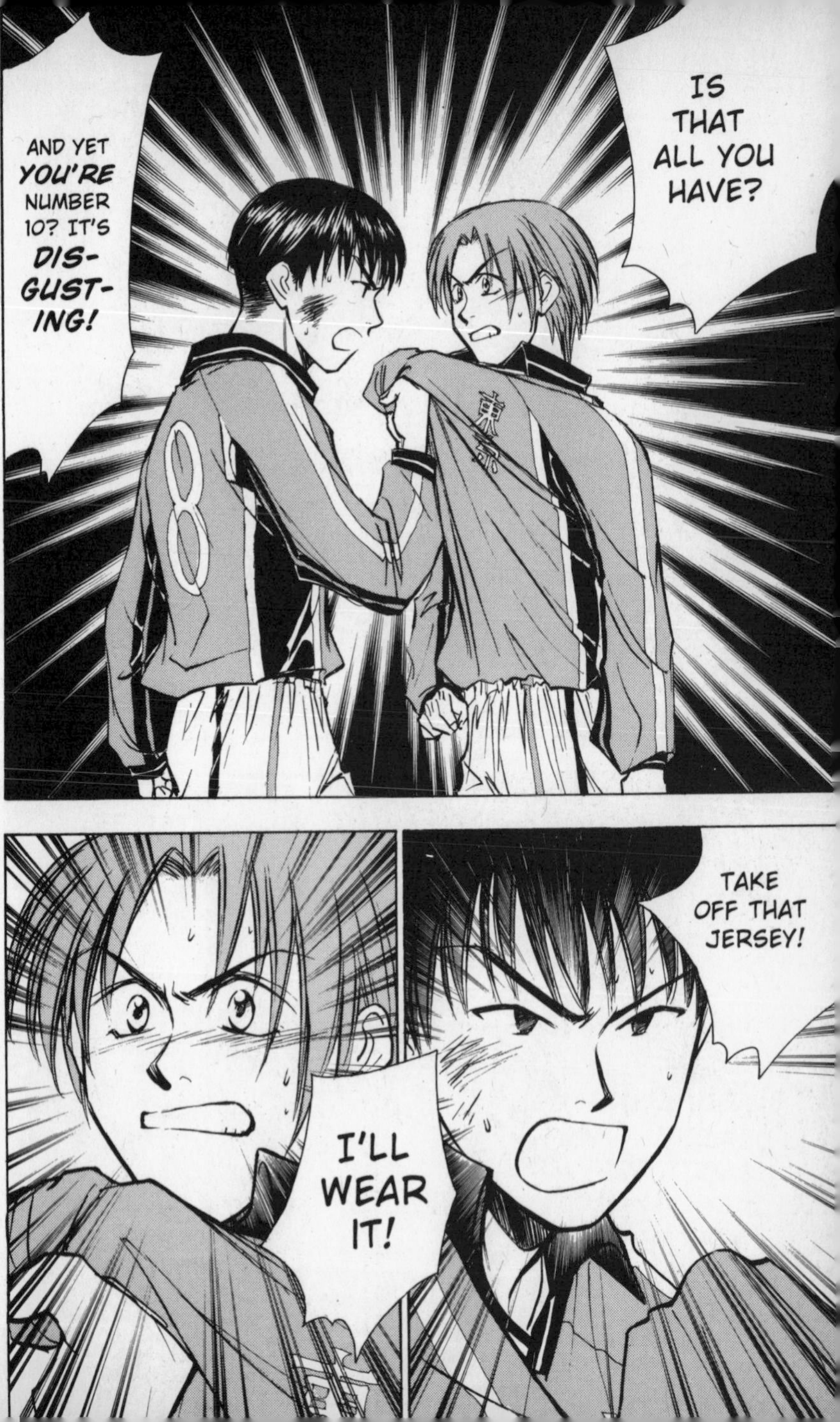
IS THAT ALL YOU HAVE?
AND YET *YOU'RE* NUMBER 10? IT'S *DIS-GUST-ING!*
TAKE OFF THAT JERSEY!
I'LL WEAR IT!

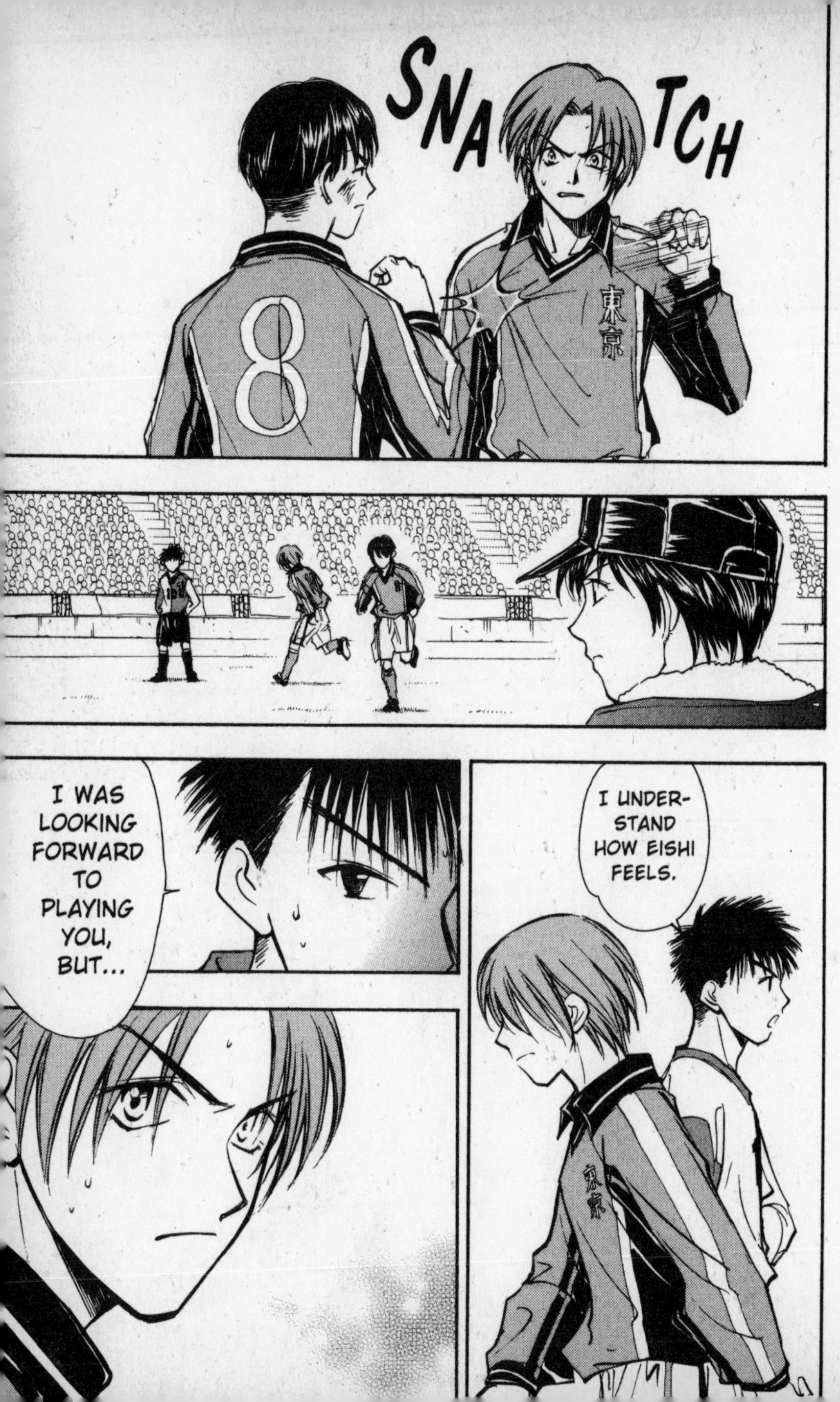
SNATCH
東京
I UNDER-STAND HOW EISHI FEELS.
I WAS LOOKING FORWARD TO PLAYING YOU, BUT...

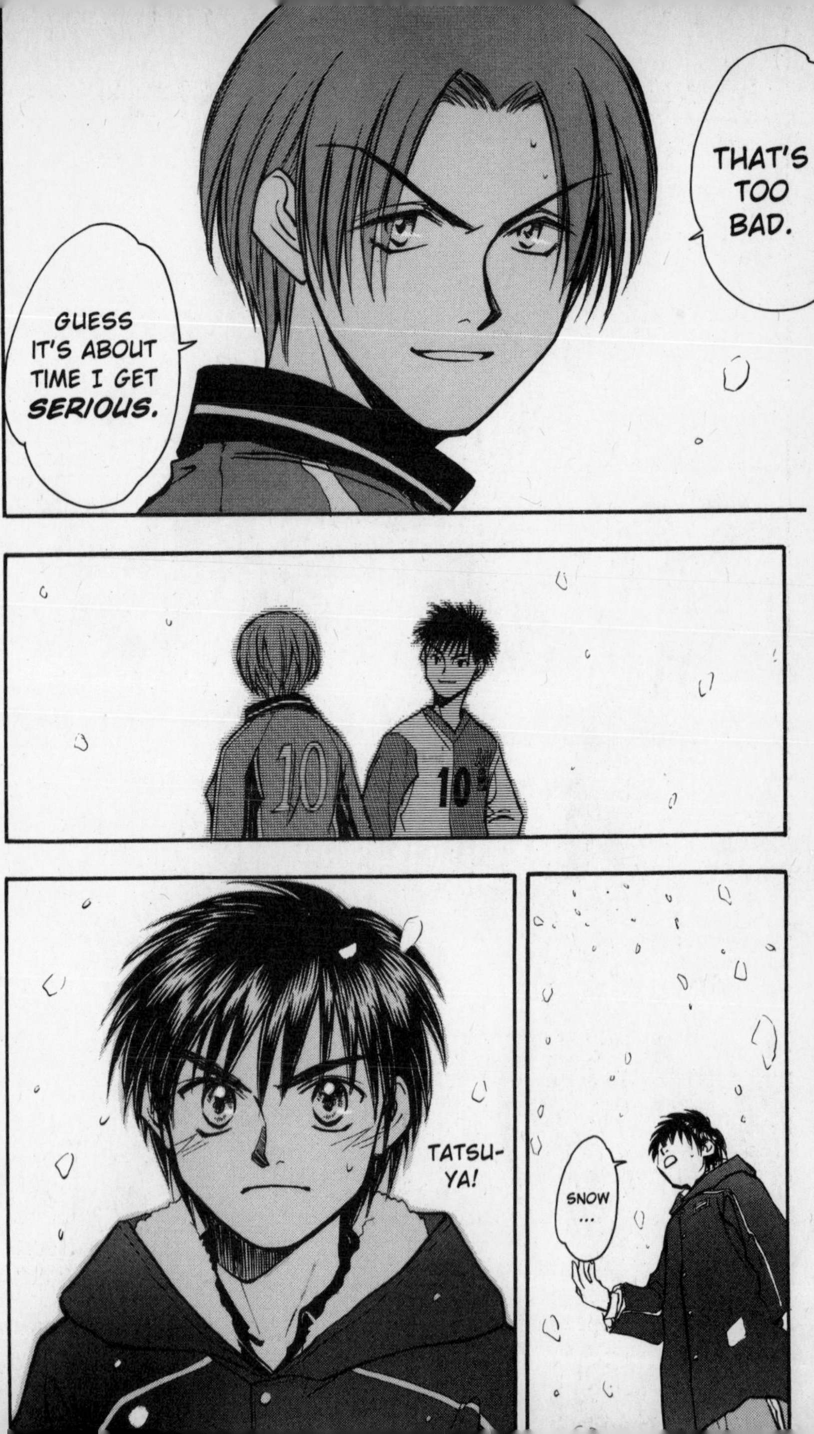
THAT'S TOO BAD.
GUESS IT'S ABOUT TIME I GET **SERIOUS.**
SNOW ...
TATSU-YA!

STAGE.155 Play More

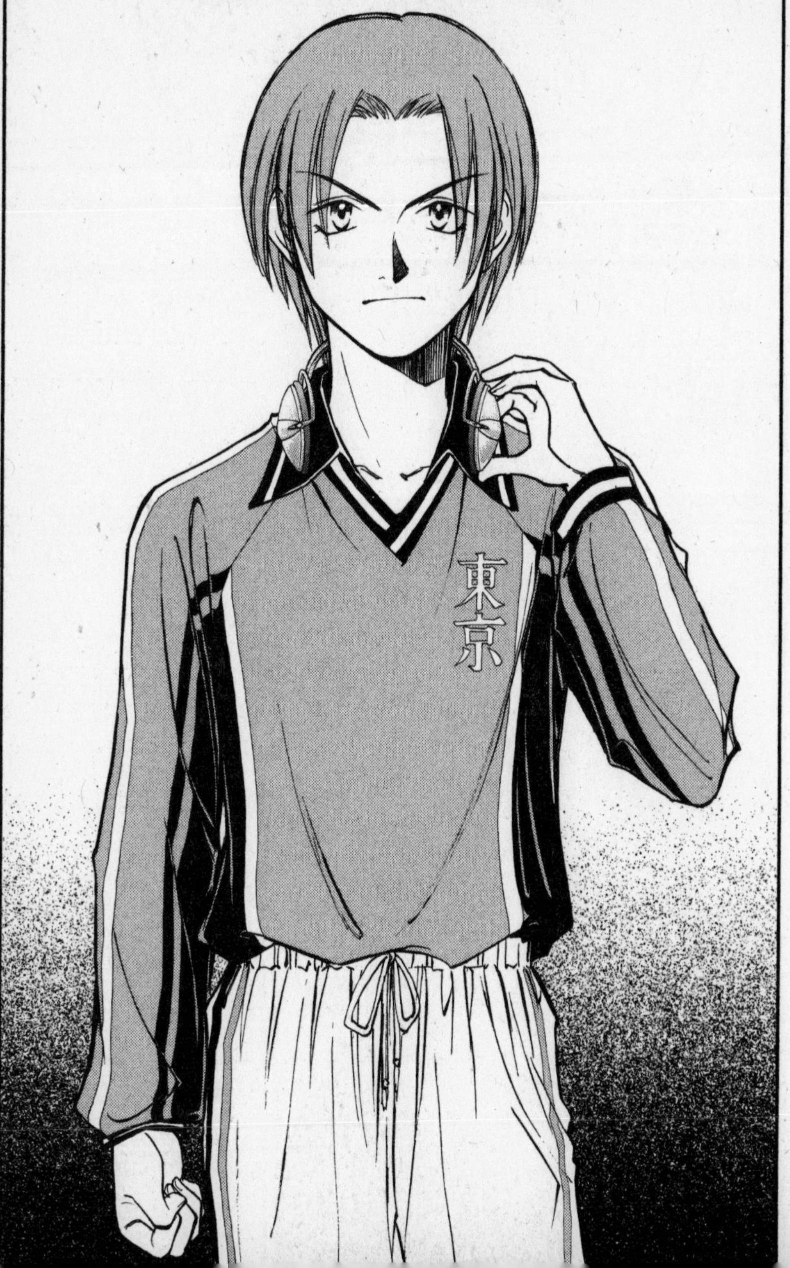
東京

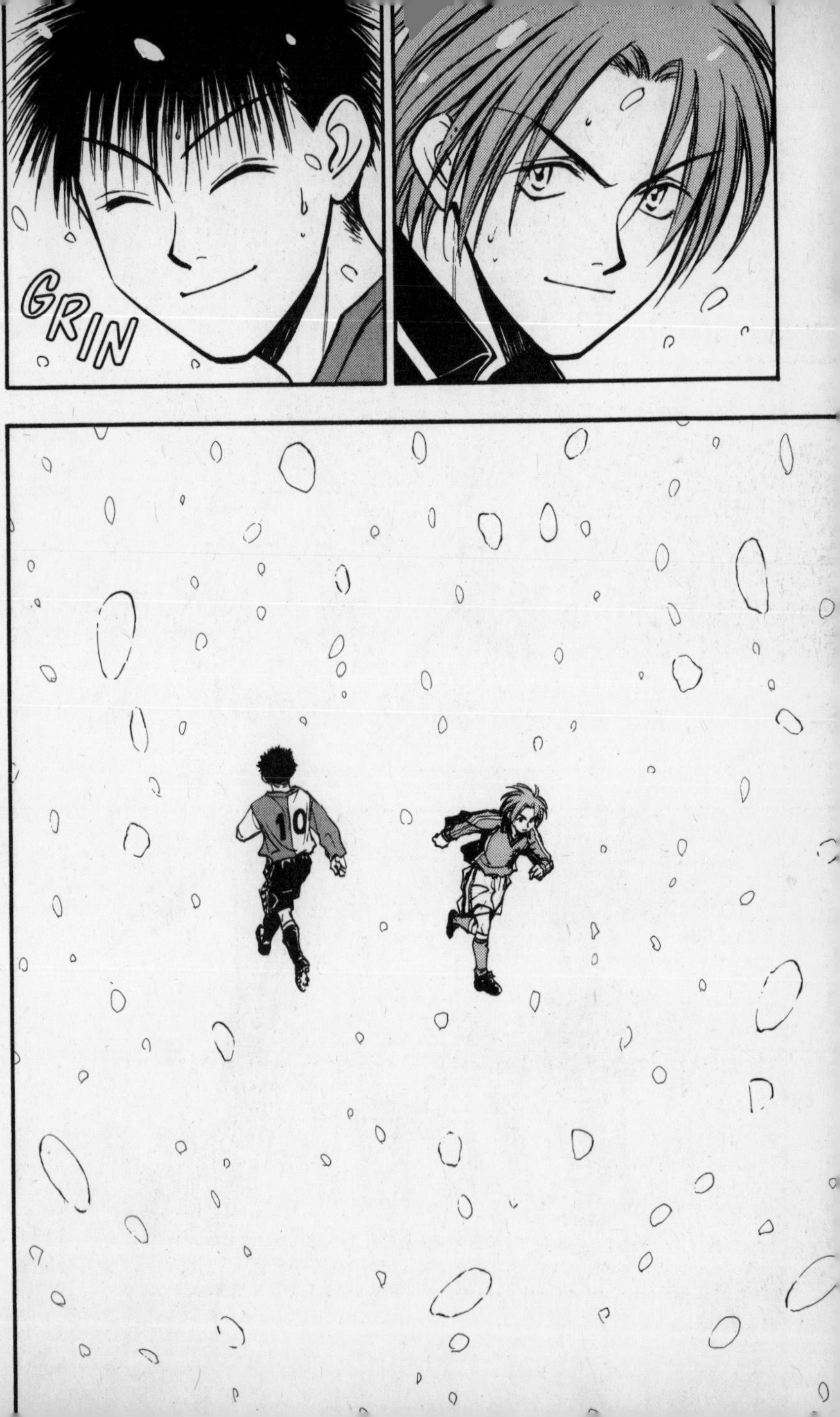
GRIN

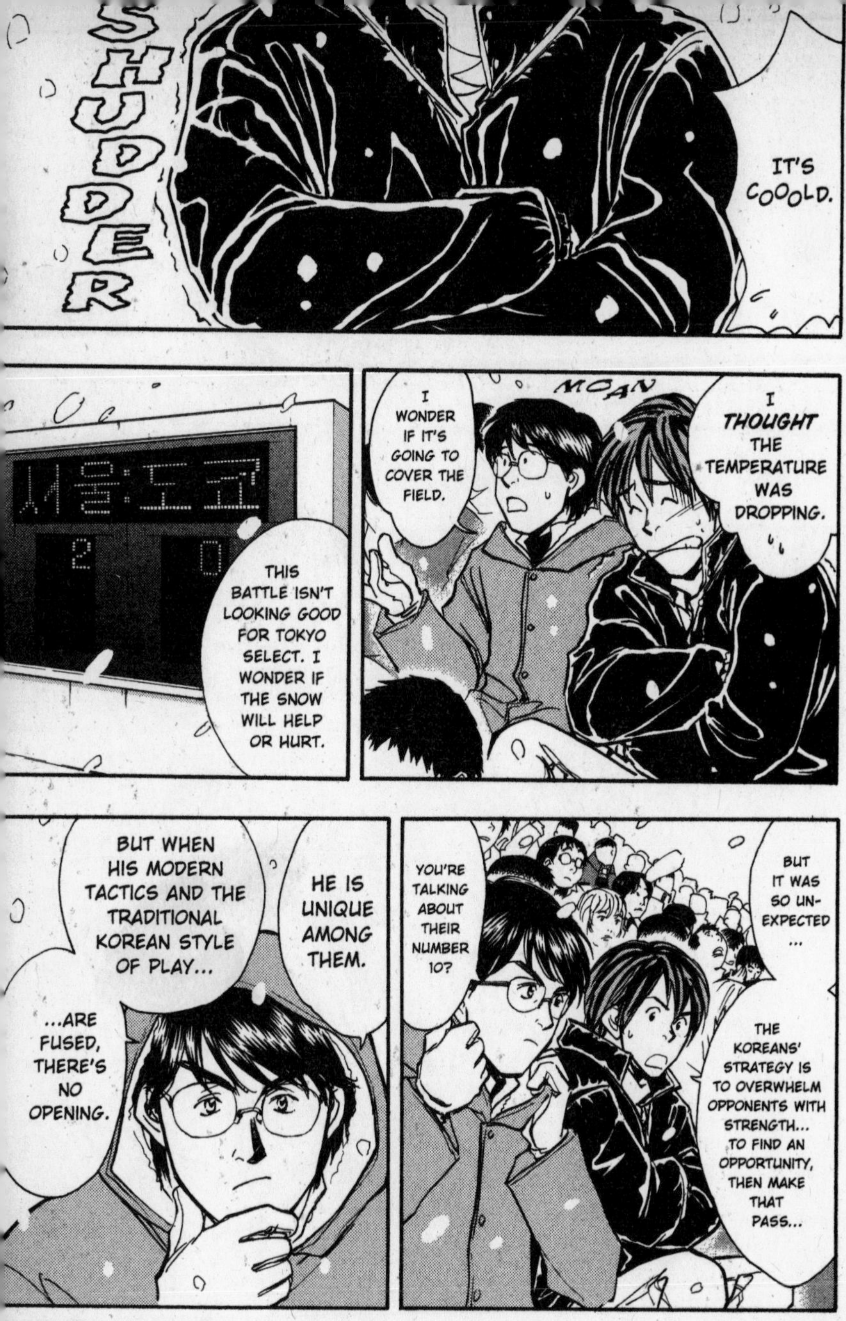
IT'S COOOLD.
SHUDDER
I THOUGHT THE TEMPERATURE WAS DROPPING.
MOAN
I WONDER IF IT'S GOING TO COVER THE FIELD.
서울:도쿄
2 0
THIS BATTLE ISN'T LOOKING GOOD FOR TOKYO SELECT. I WONDER IF THE SNOW WILL HELP OR HURT.
BUT IT WAS SO UN-EXPECTED...
THE KOREANS' STRATEGY IS TO OVERWHELM OPPONENTS WITH STRENGTH... TO FIND AN OPPORTUNITY, THEN MAKE THAT PASS...
YOU'RE TALKING ABOUT THEIR NUMBER 10?
HE IS UNIQUE AMONG THEM.
BUT WHEN HIS MODERN TACTICS AND THE TRADITIONAL KOREAN STYLE OF PLAY...
...ARE FUSED, THERE'S NO OPENING.

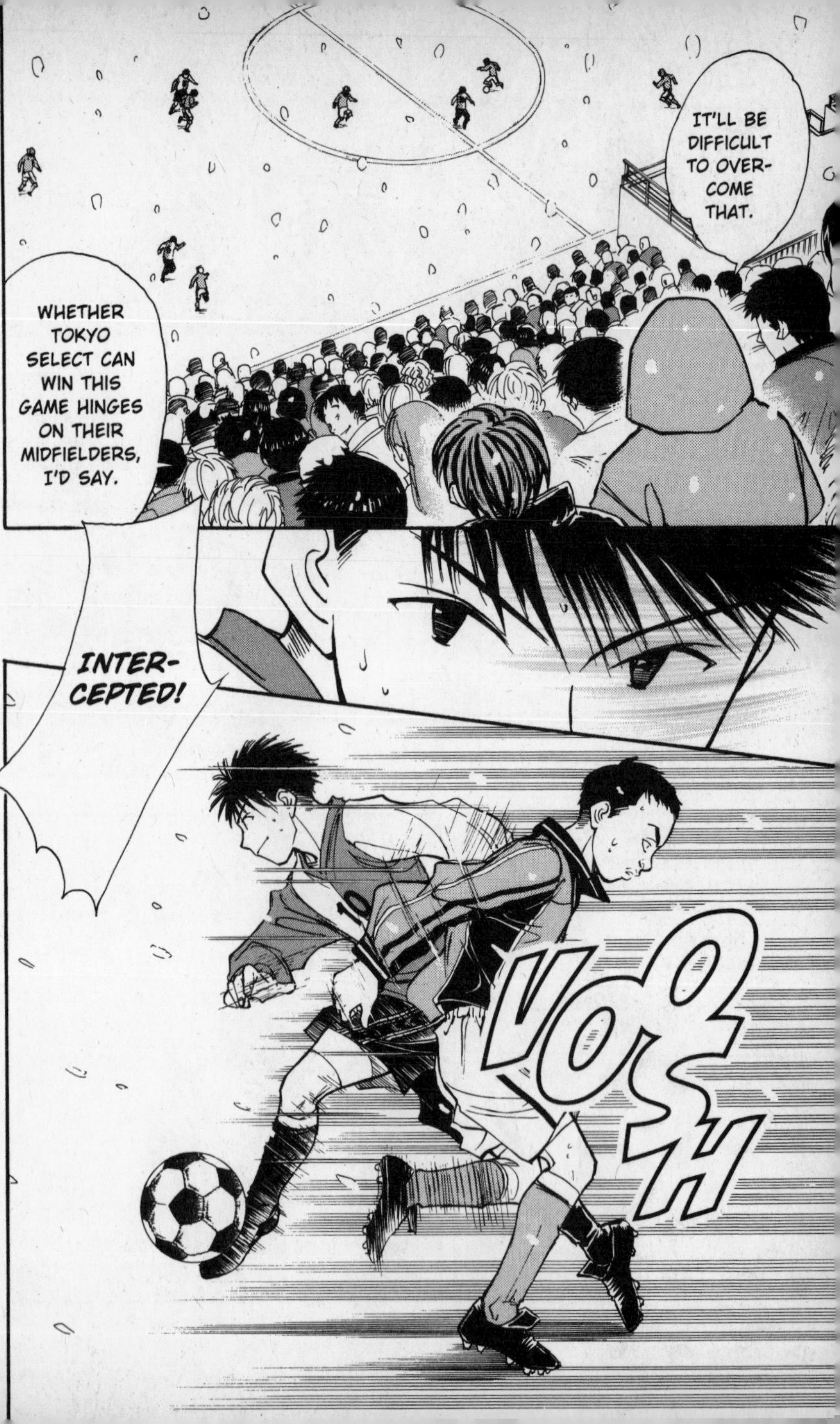
IT'LL BE DIFFICULT TO OVER-COME THAT.
WHETHER TOKYO SELECT CAN WIN THIS GAME HINGES ON THEIR MIDFIELDERS, I'D SAY.
INTER-CEPTED!
VOOSH

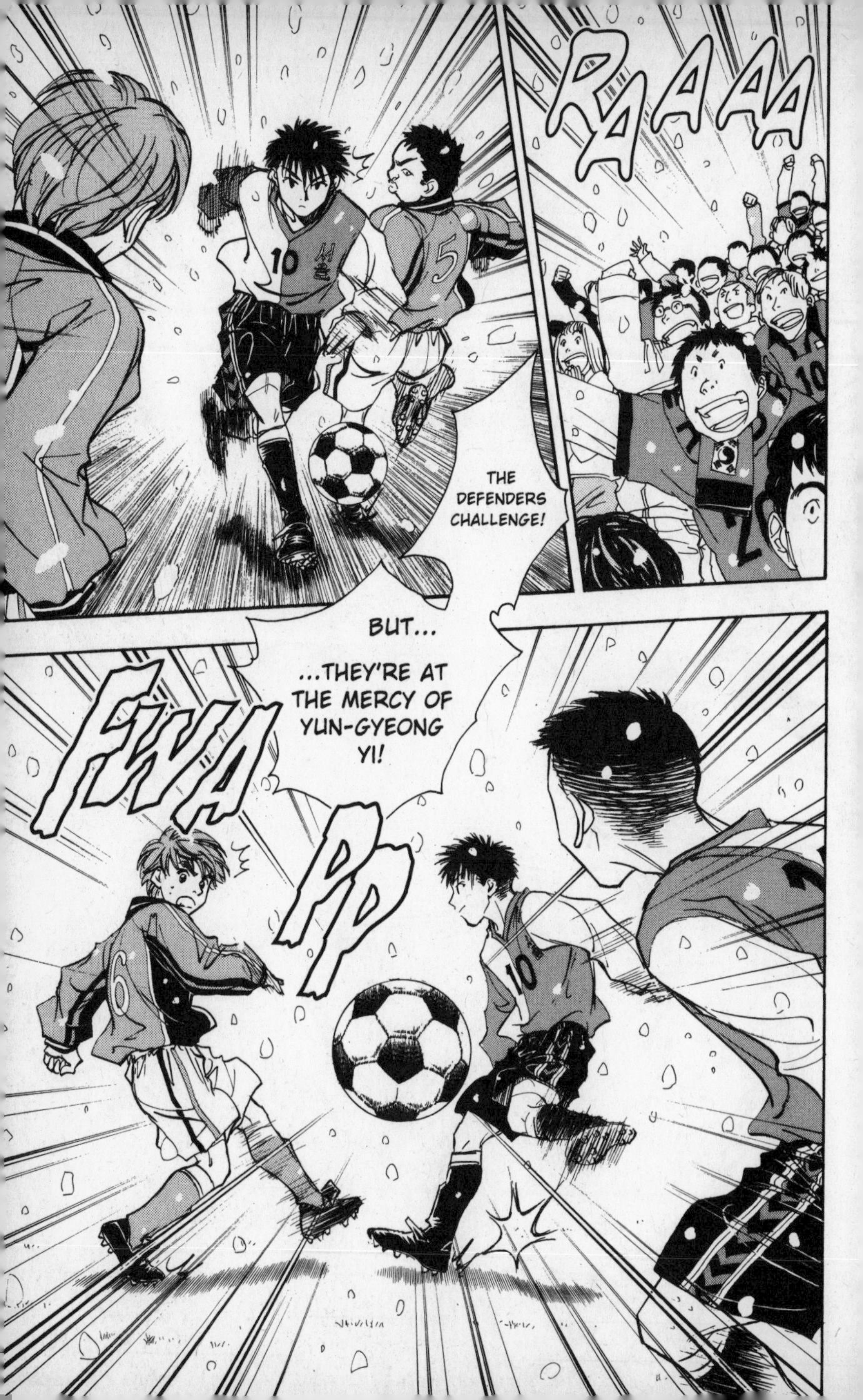
RAAAAA
THE DEFENDERS CHALLENGE!
BUT...
...THEY'RE AT THE MERCY OF YUN-GYEONG YI!
FWA
PP

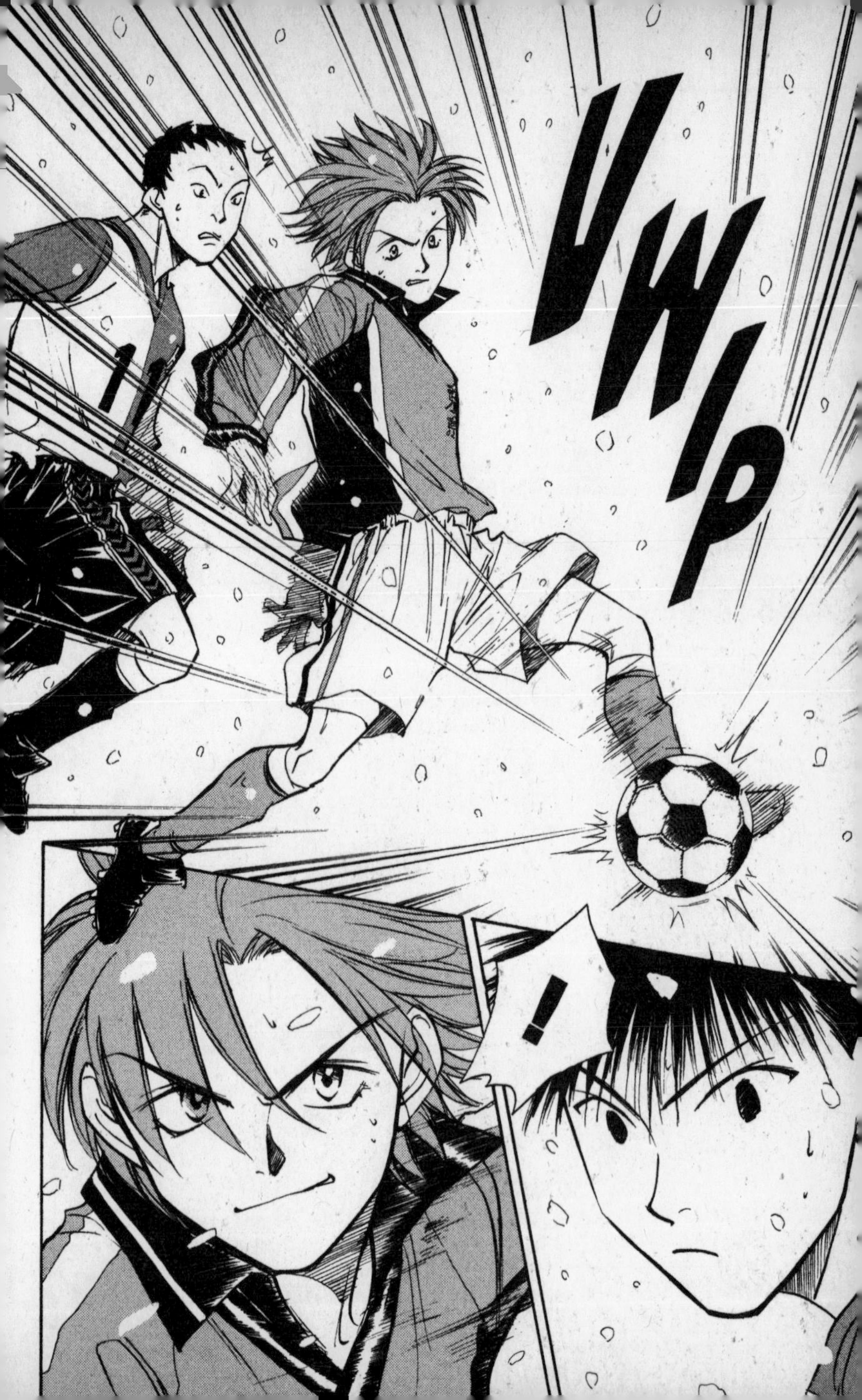
WHIP
!

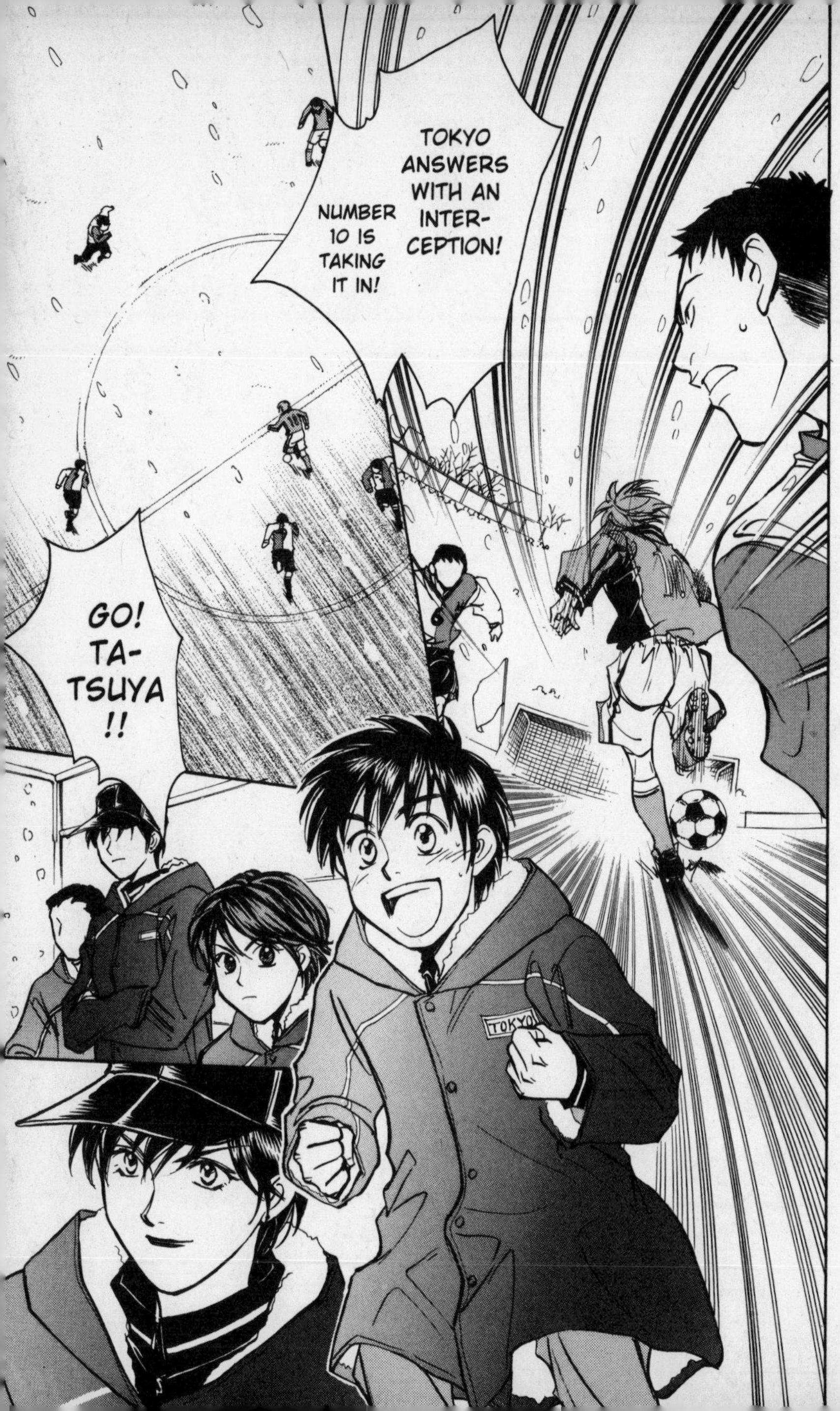
TOKYO ANSWERS WITH AN INTER-CEPTION!
NUMBER 10 IS TAKING IT IN!
GO! TA-TSUYA !!
TOKYO

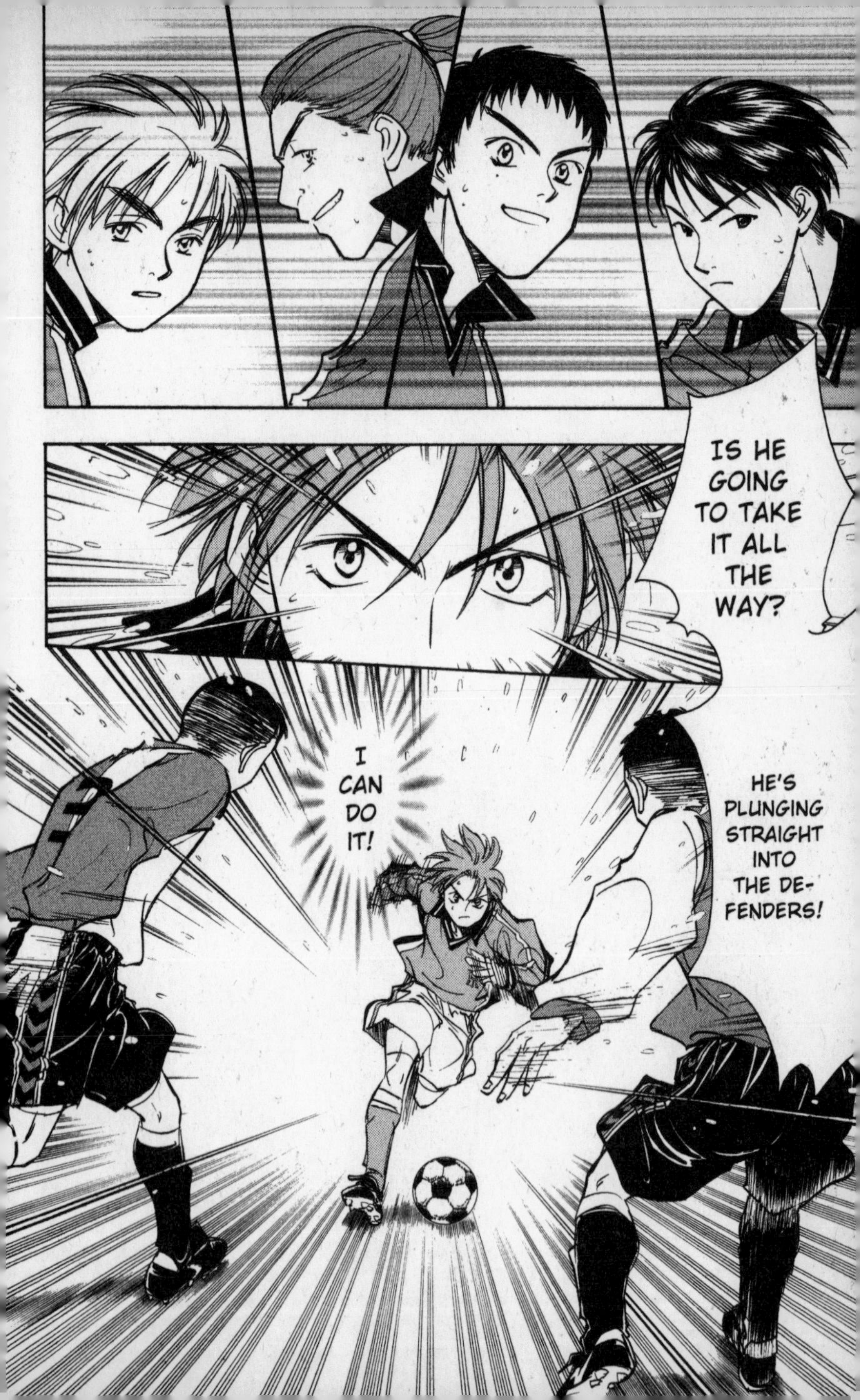
IS HE GOING TO TAKE IT ALL THE WAY?
HE'S PLUNGING STRAIGHT INTO THE DE-FENDERS!
I CAN DO IT!

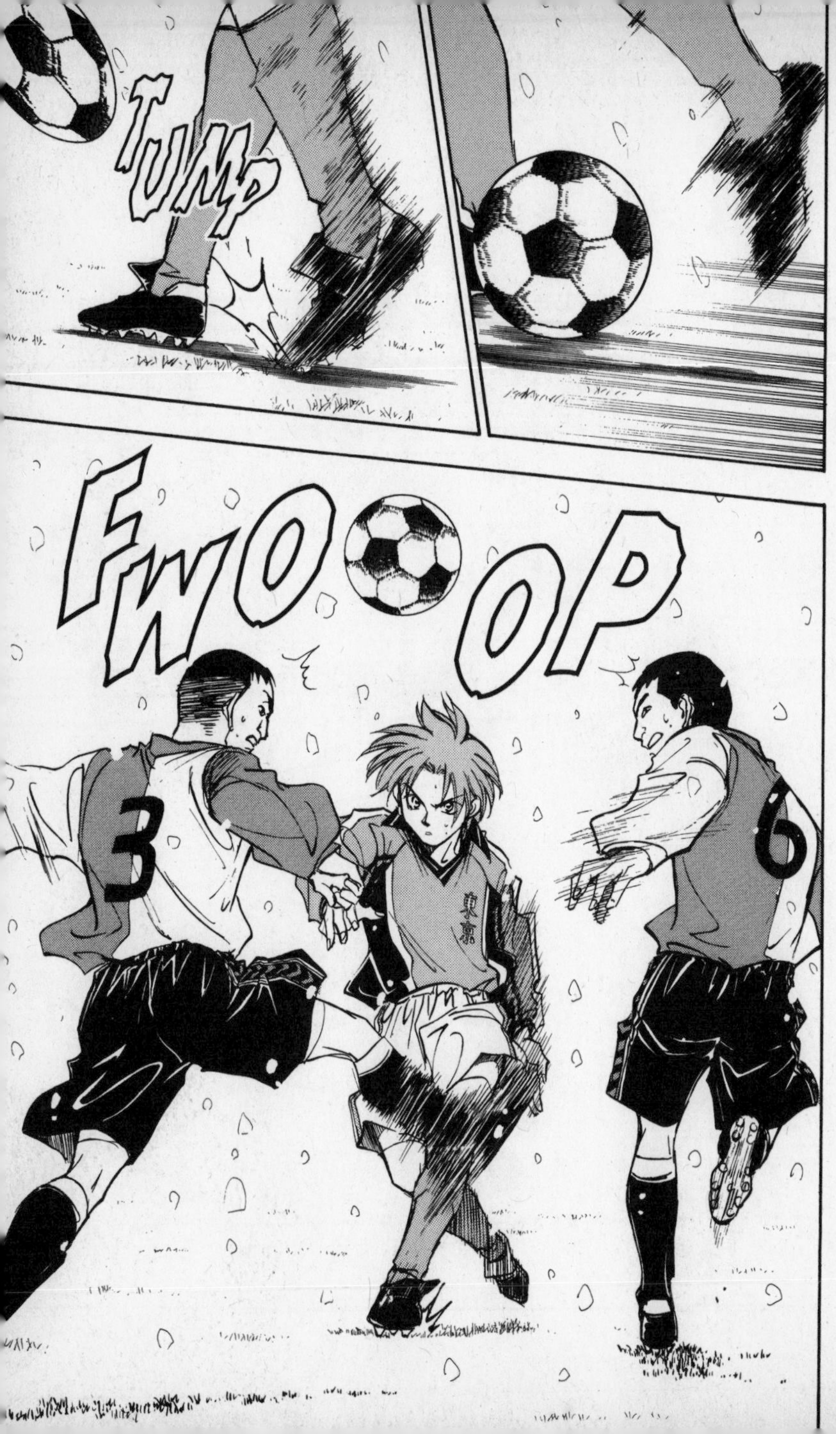
TUMP
FWOOP

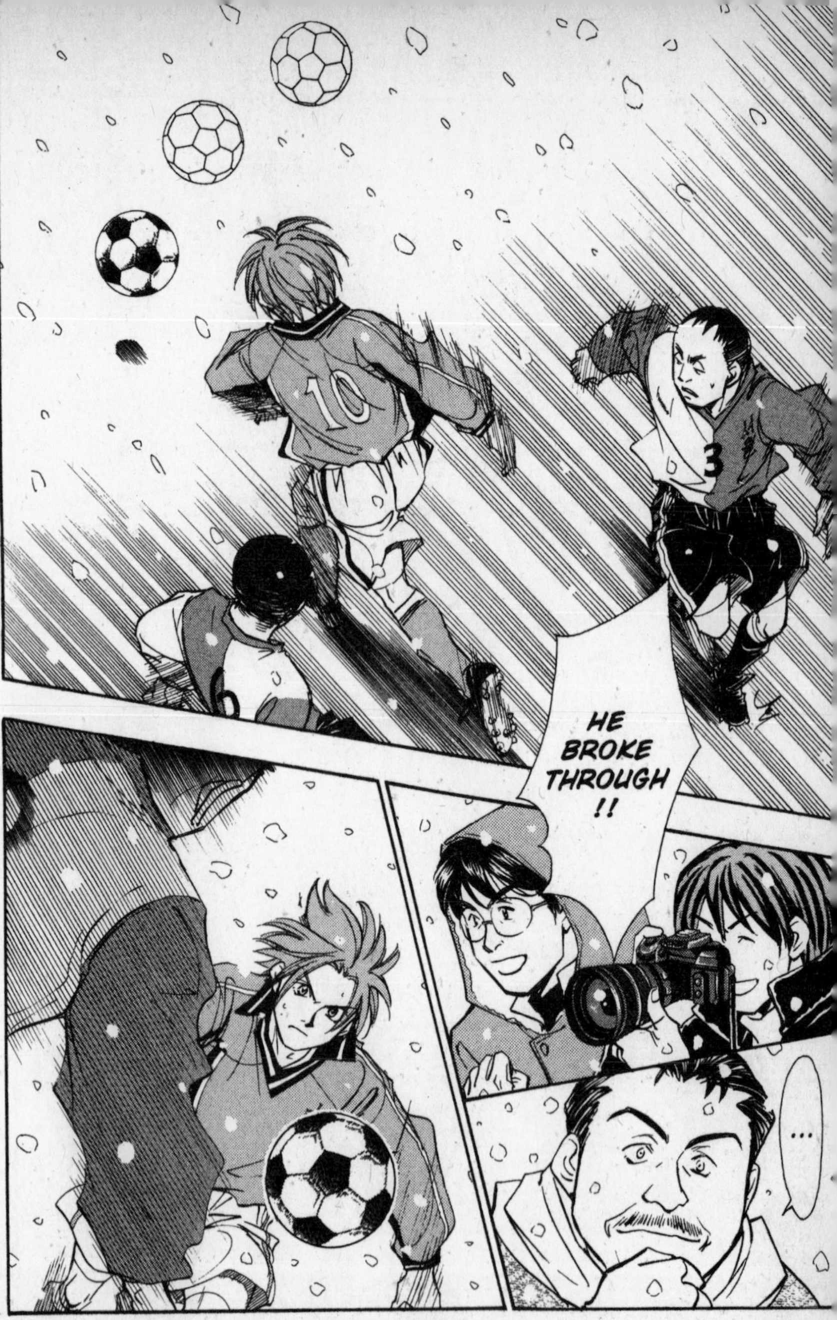
HE BROKE THROUGH !!
...

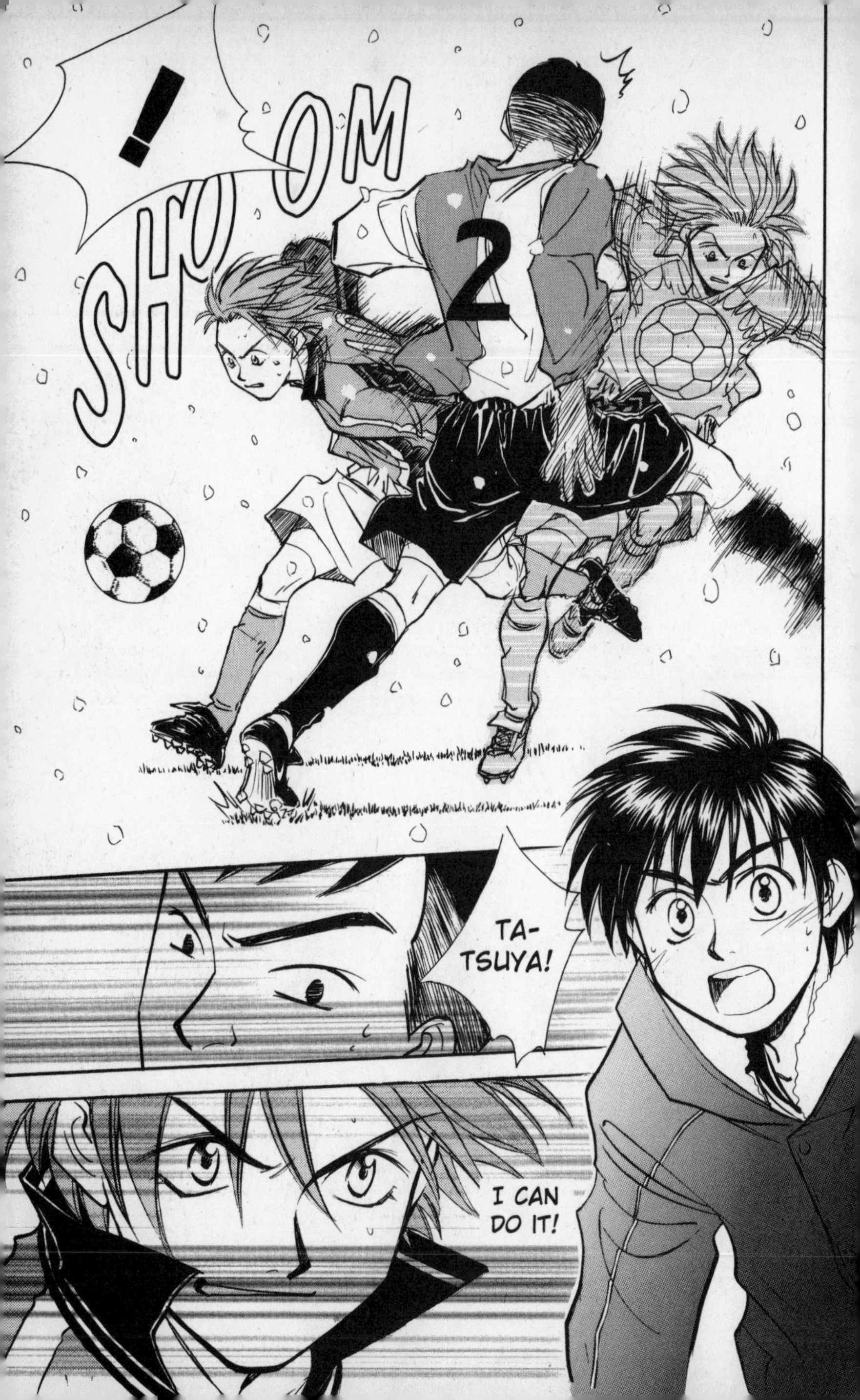
!
SHOOM
TA-TSUYA!
I CAN DO IT!

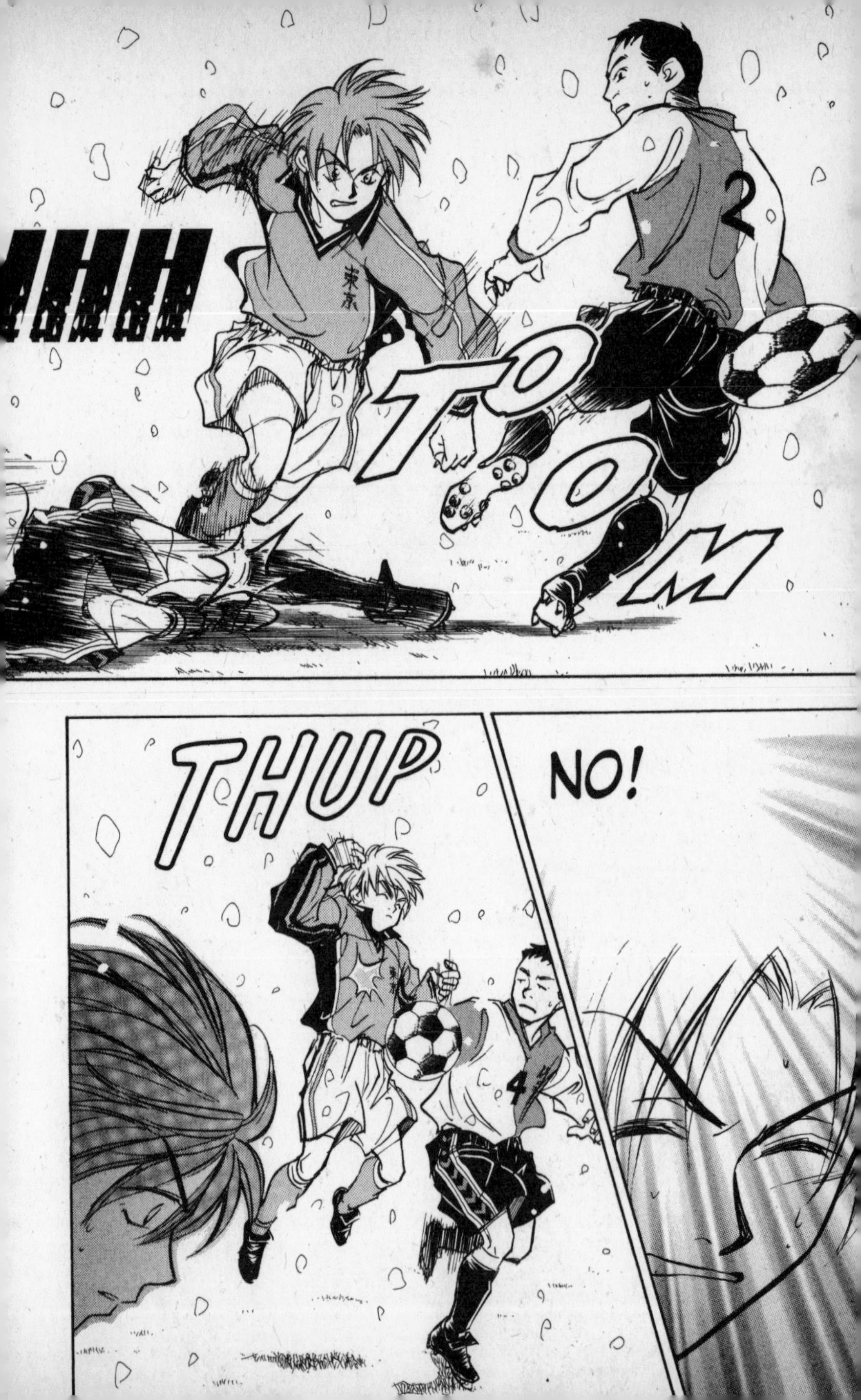
TOOM
NO!
THUP

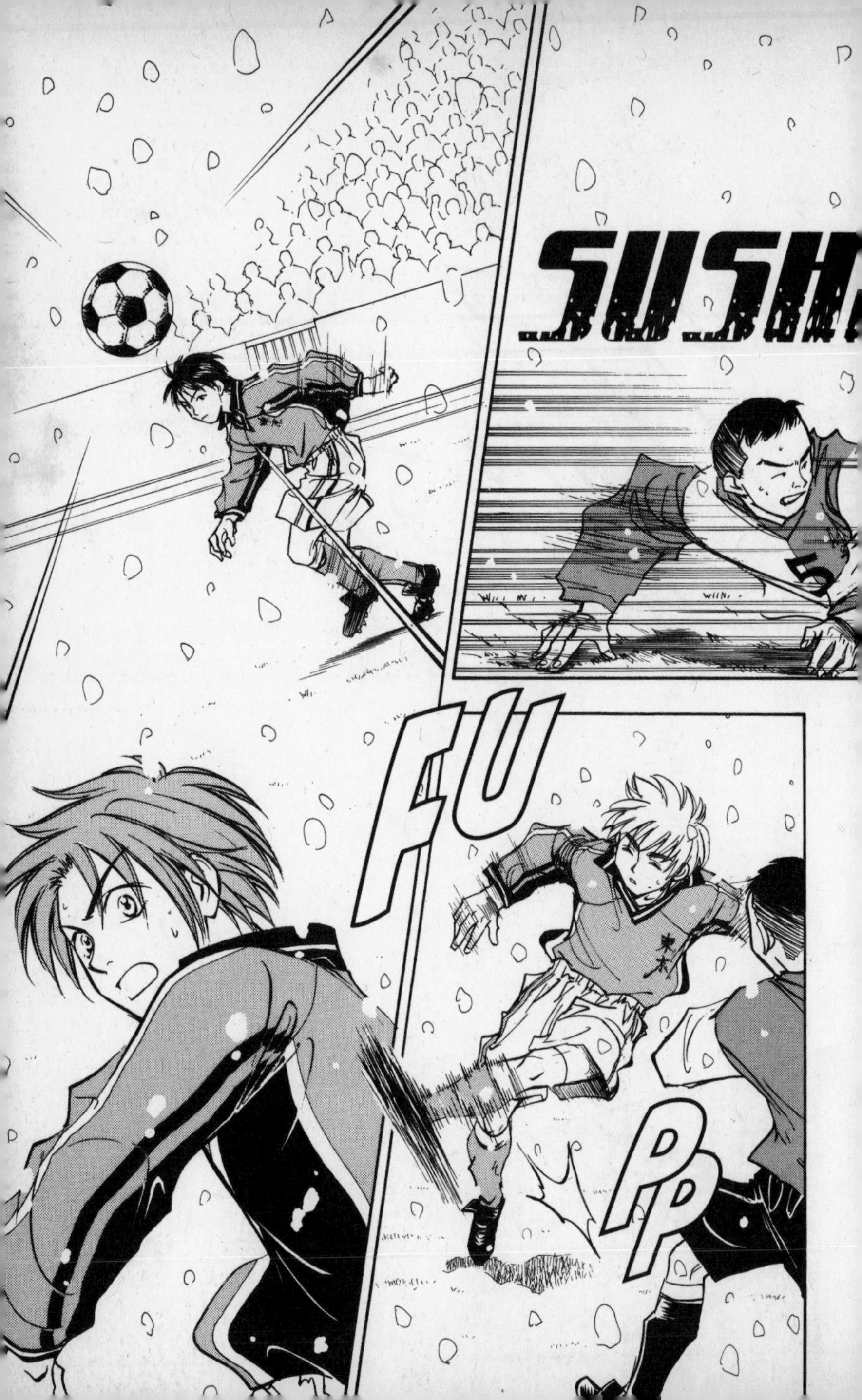
SUSH
FU
PP

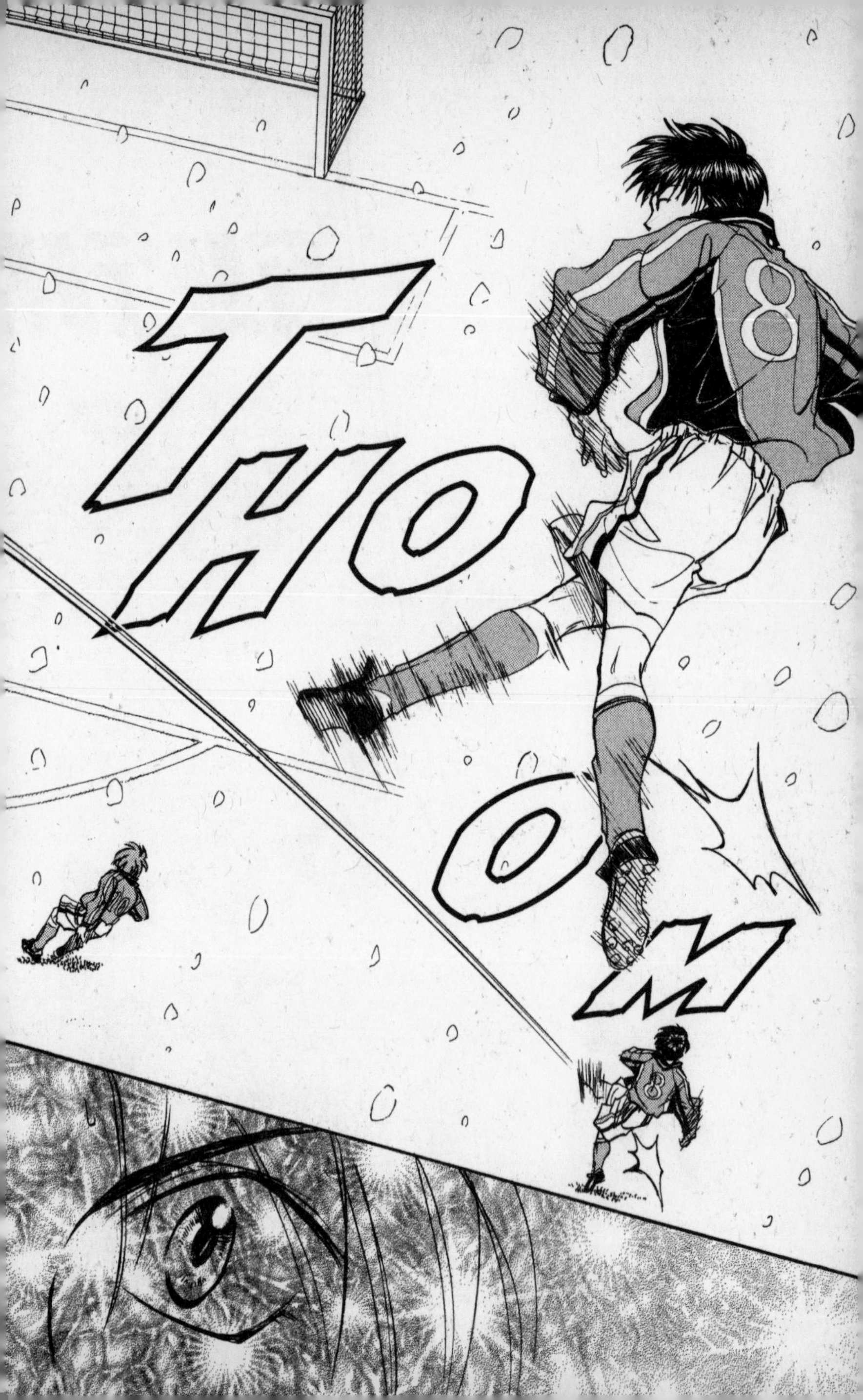
THOOM

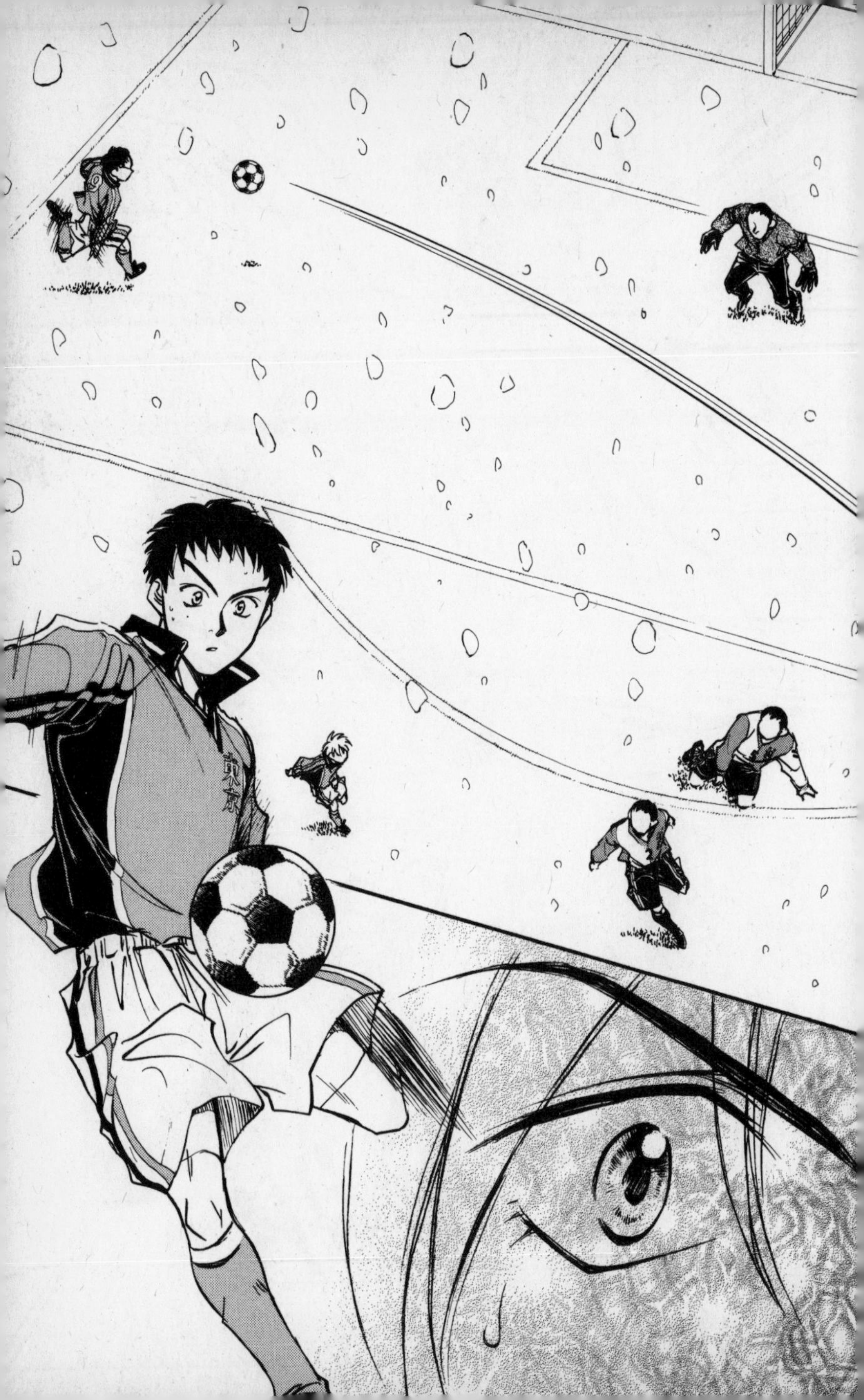
東京

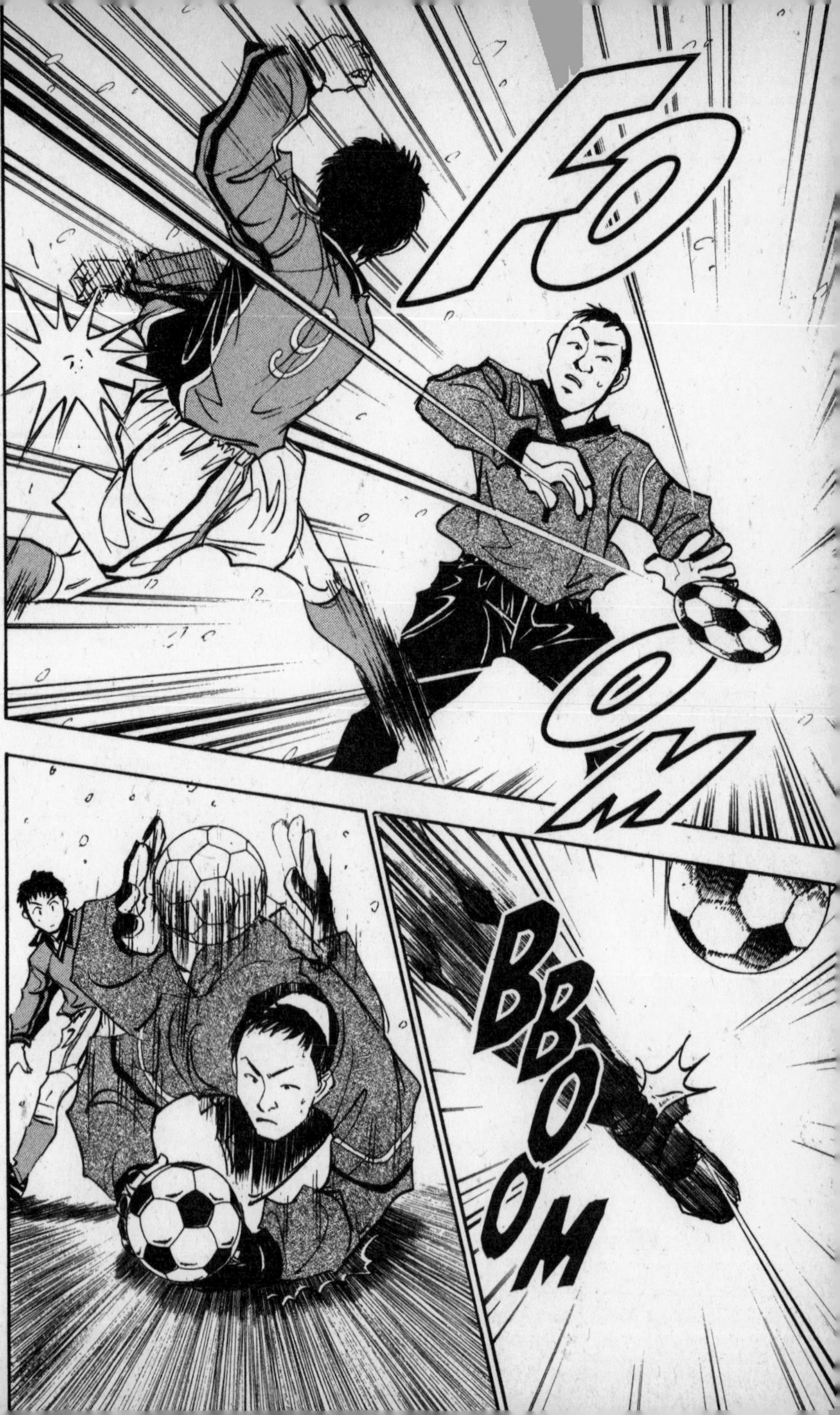
FOOM
BBOOOM

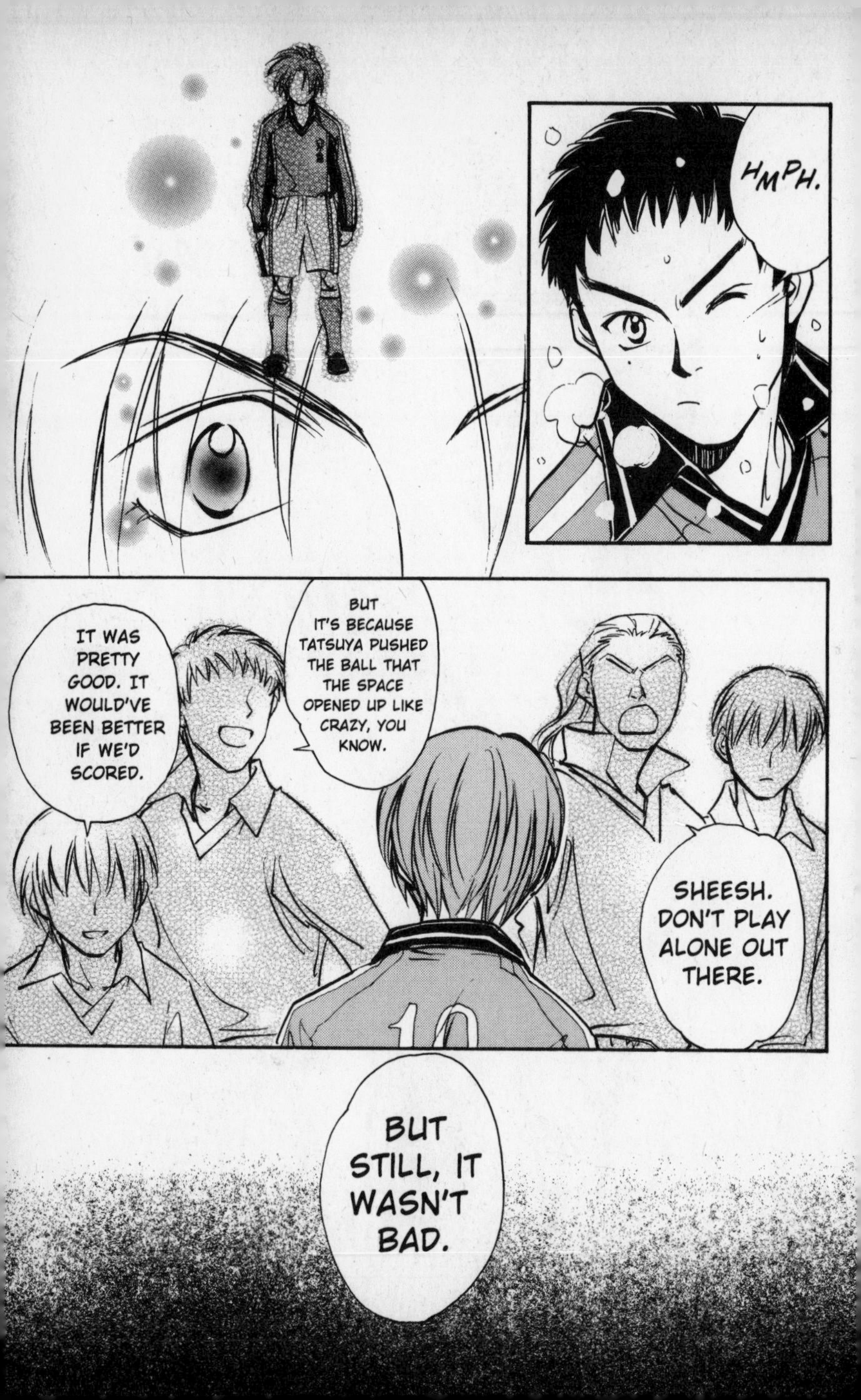
HMPH.
SHEESH. DON'T PLAY ALONE OUT THERE.
IT WAS PRETTY GOOD. IT WOULD'VE BEEN BETTER IF WE'D SCORED.
BUT IT'S BECAUSE TATSUYA PUSHED THE BALL THAT THE SPACE OPENED UP LIKE CRAZY, YOU KNOW.
BUT STILL, IT WASN'T BAD.

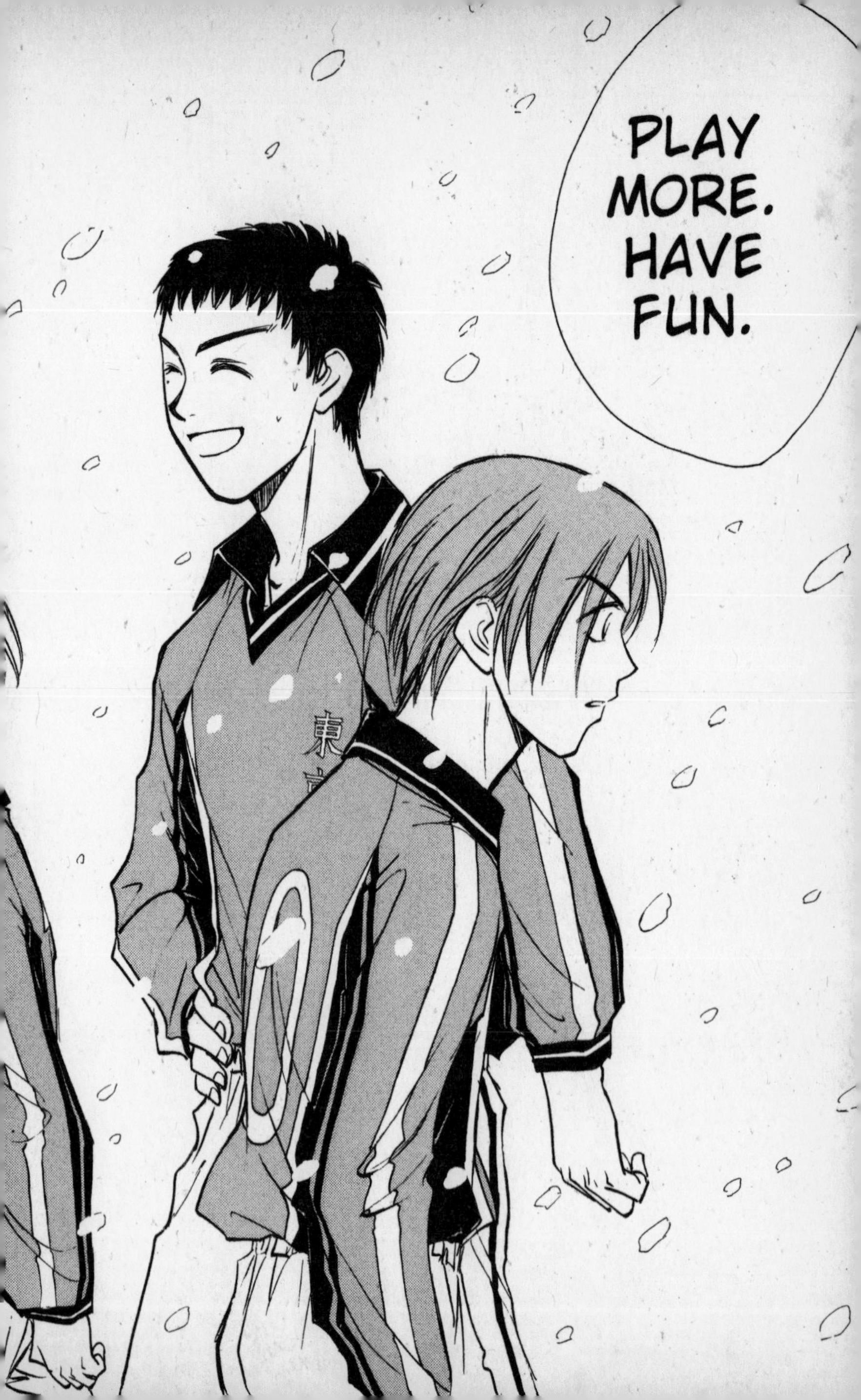
PLAY MORE. HAVE FUN.

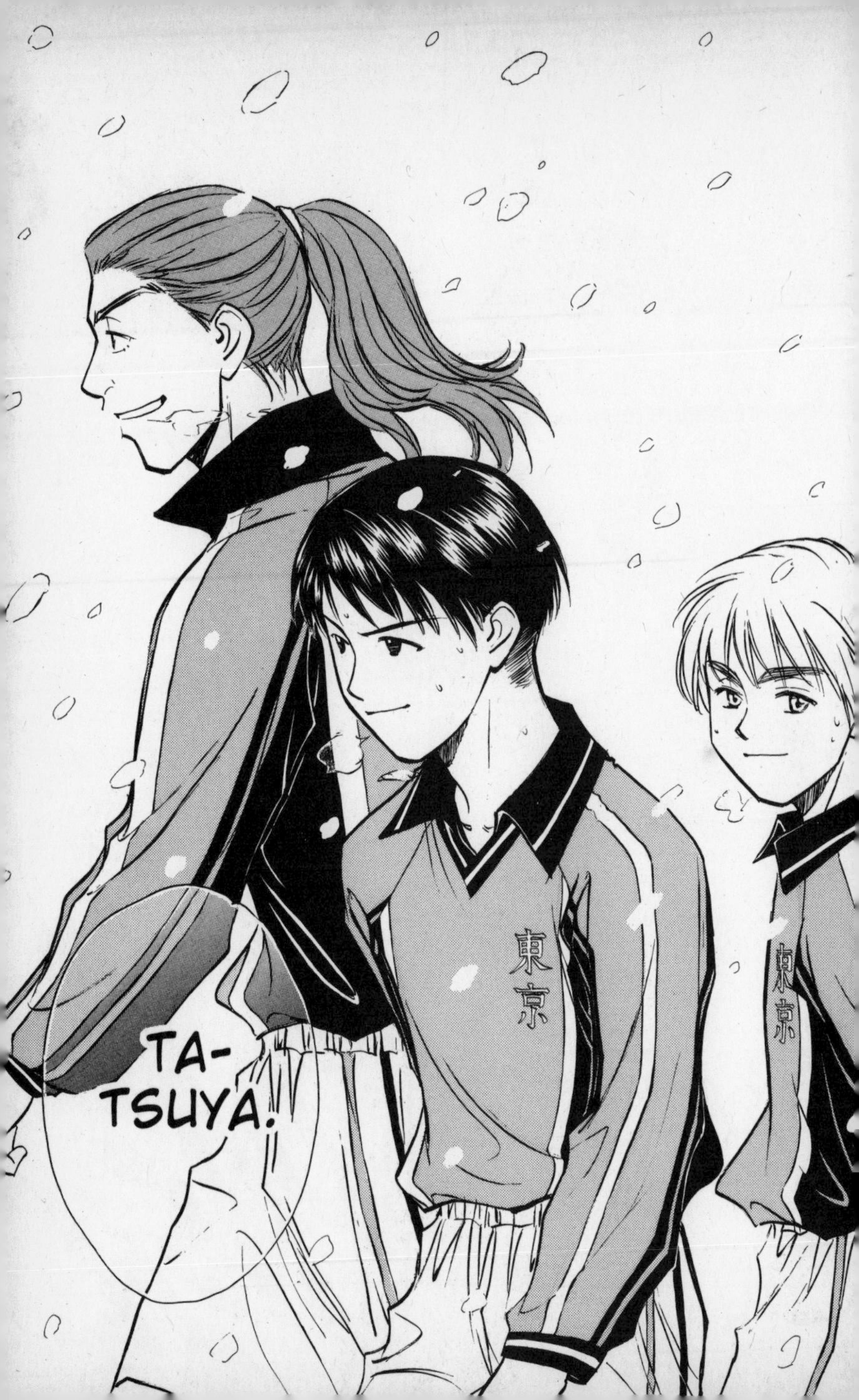
TA-
TSUYA!

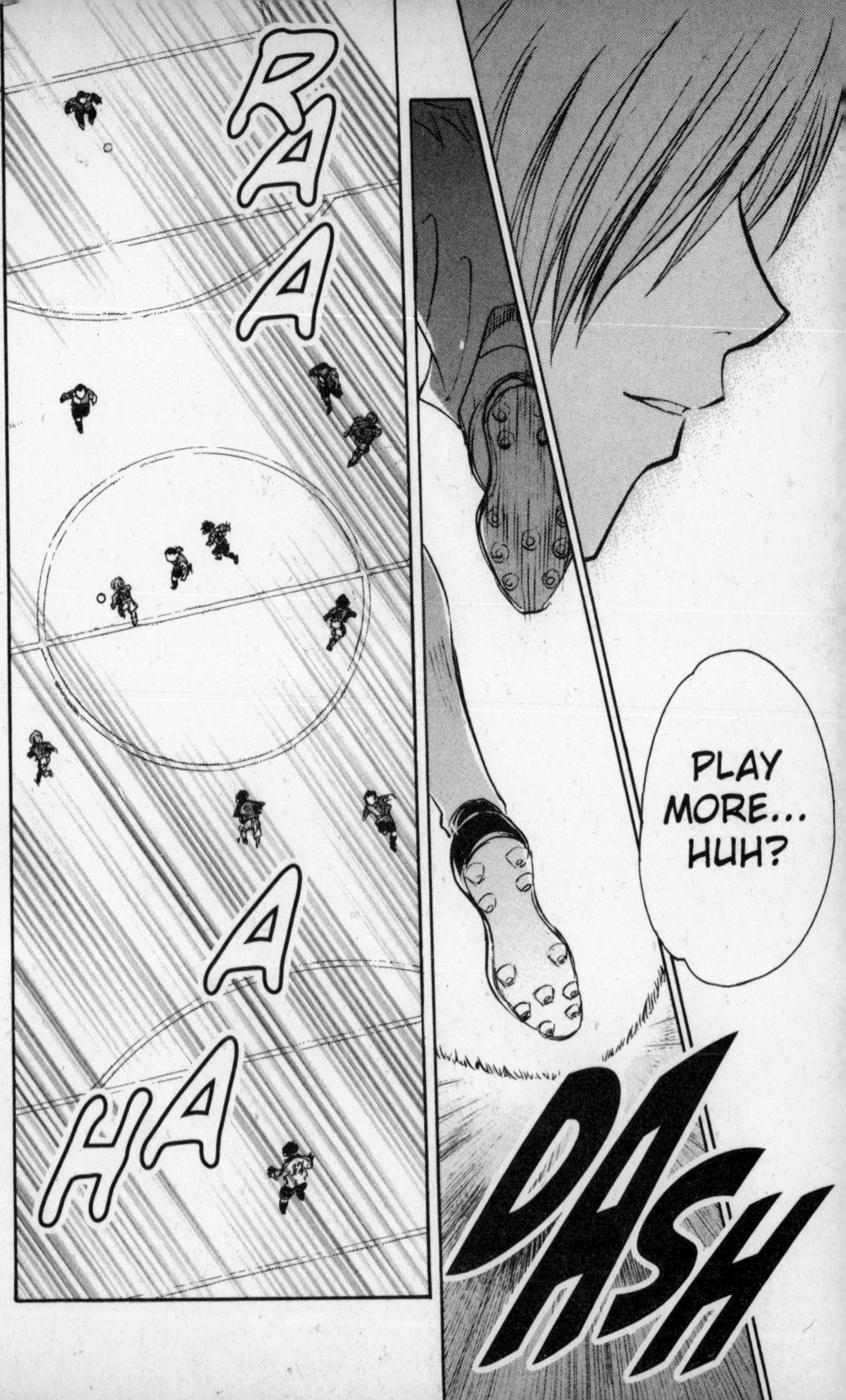
PLAY MORE... HUH?
DASH
RAA
AHA

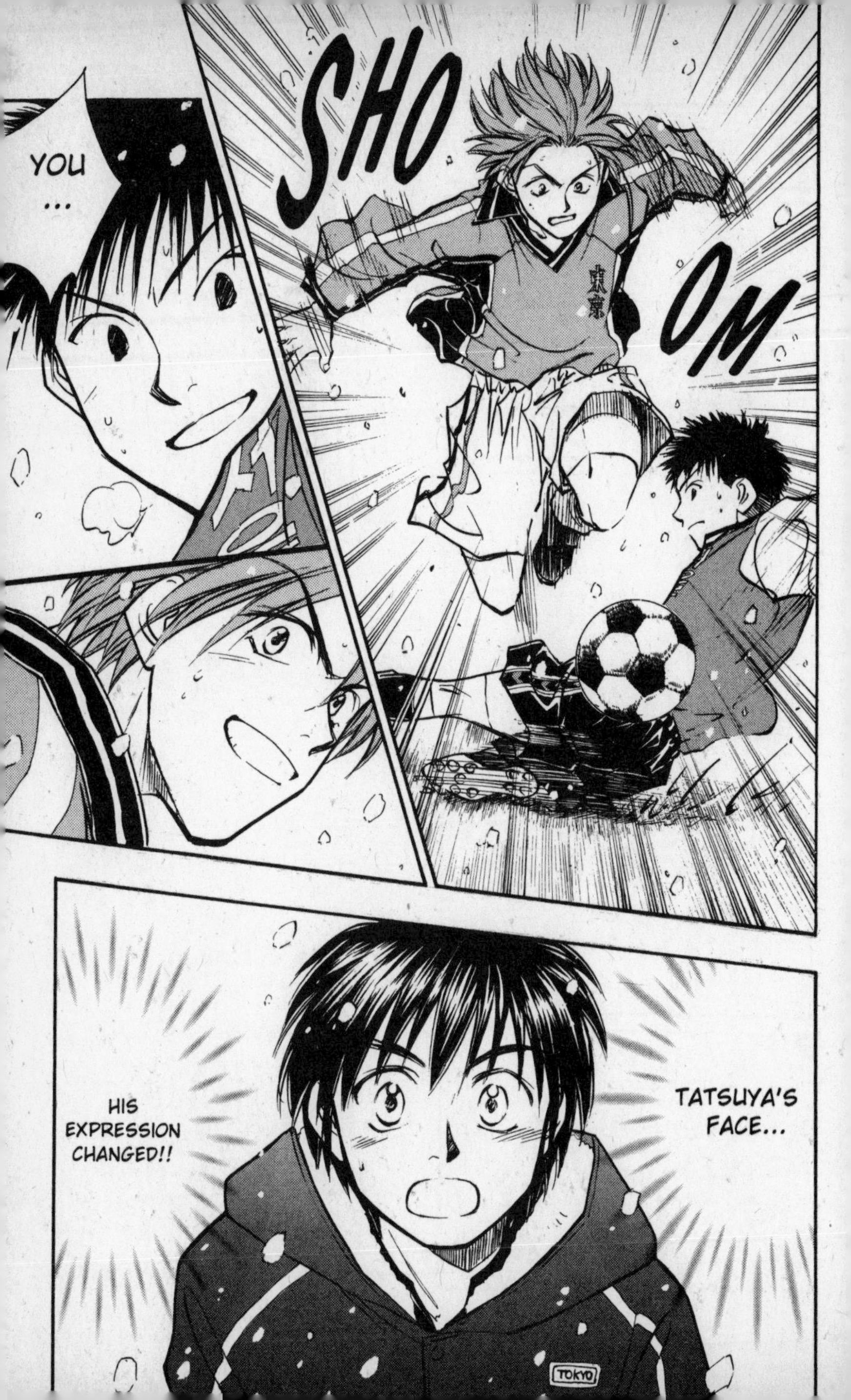
SHO
OM
YOU ...
TATSUYA'S FACE...
HIS EXPRESSION CHANGED!!
TOKYO

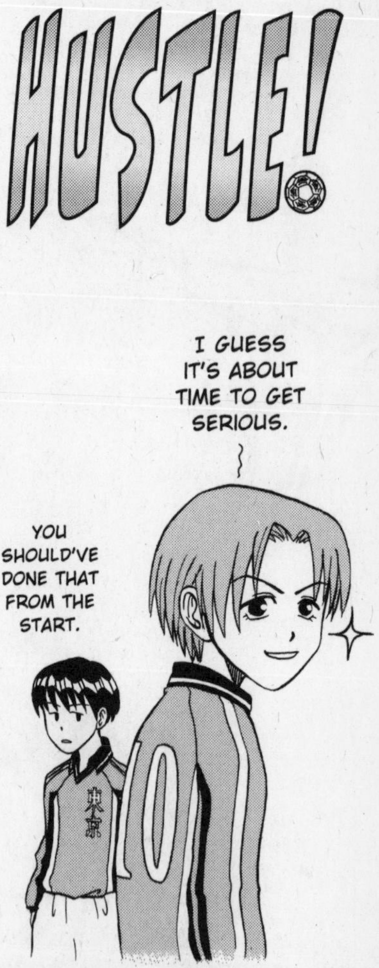
HUSTLE!
I GUESS IT'S ABOUT TIME TO GET SERIOUS.
YOU SHOULD'VE DONE THAT FROM THE START.

PRODUCED BY: ASSISTANT F. JAGUAR

A Familiar Scene

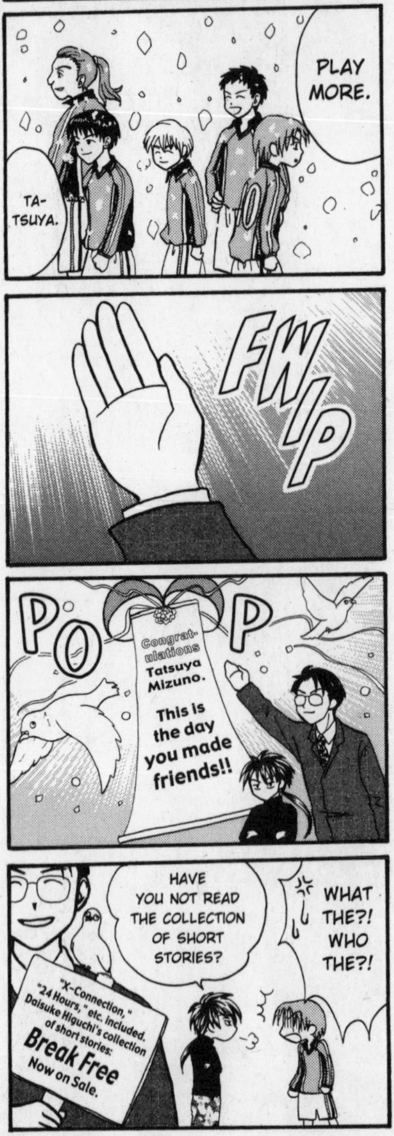
PLAY MORE.
TA-TSUYA.
FWIP
POP
Congrat-ulations Tatsuya Mizuno.
This is the day you made friends!!
WHAT THE?! WHO THE?!
HAVE YOU NOT READ THE COLLECTION OF SHORT STORIES?
"X-Connection," "24 Hours," etc. included. Daisuke Higuchi's collection of short stories:
Break Free
Now on Sale.

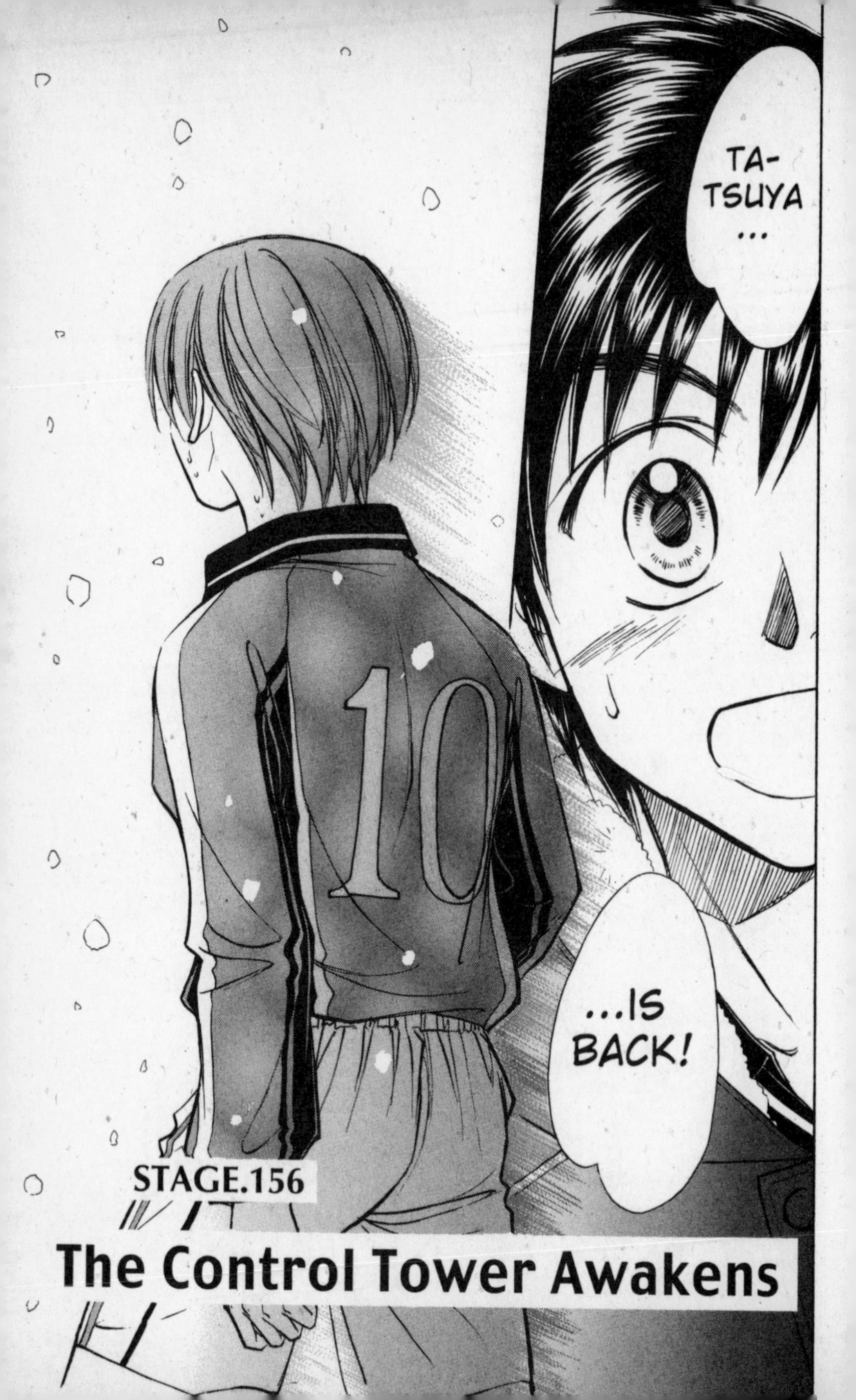
TA-TSUYA ...
...IS BACK!

STAGE.156

The Control Tower Awakens

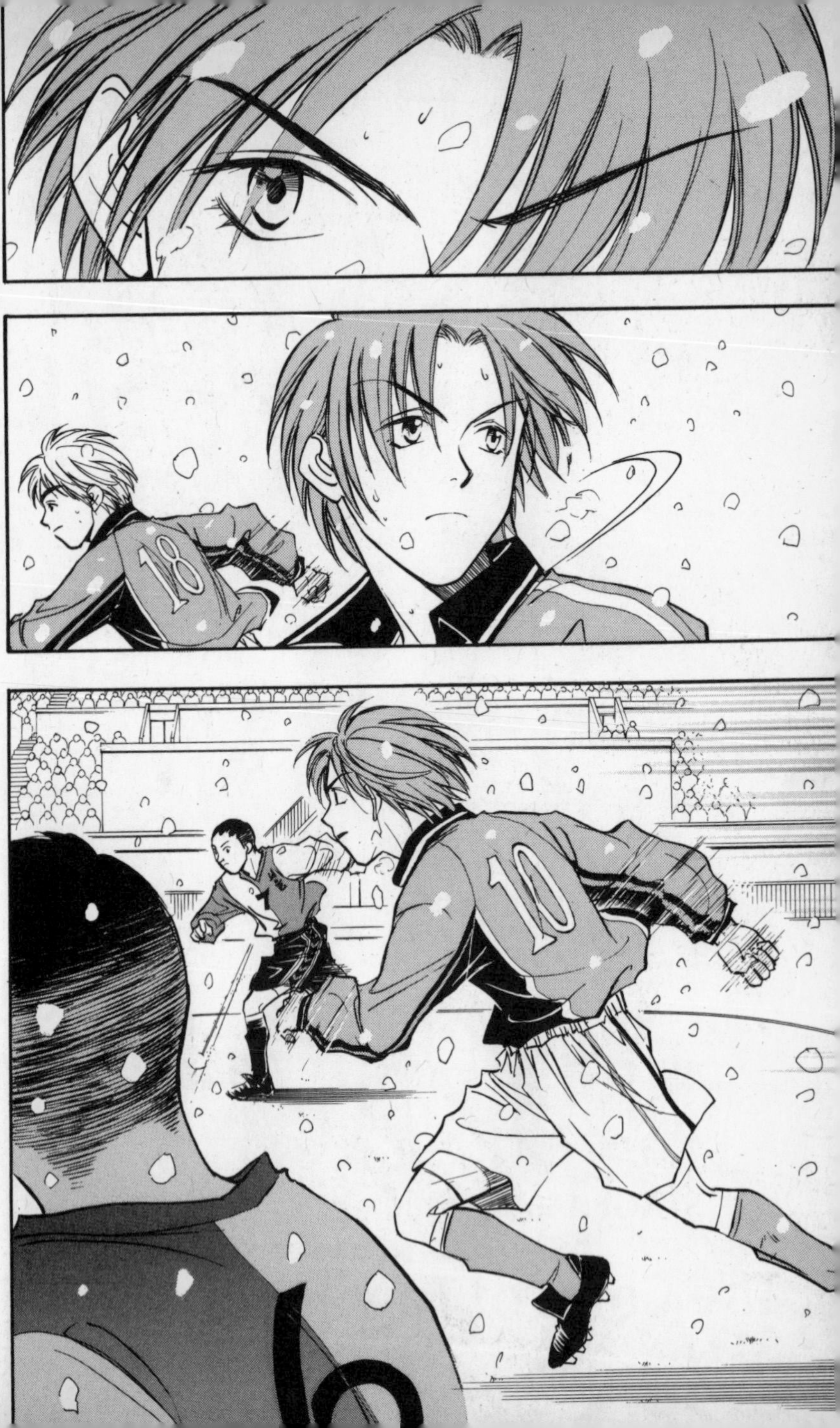

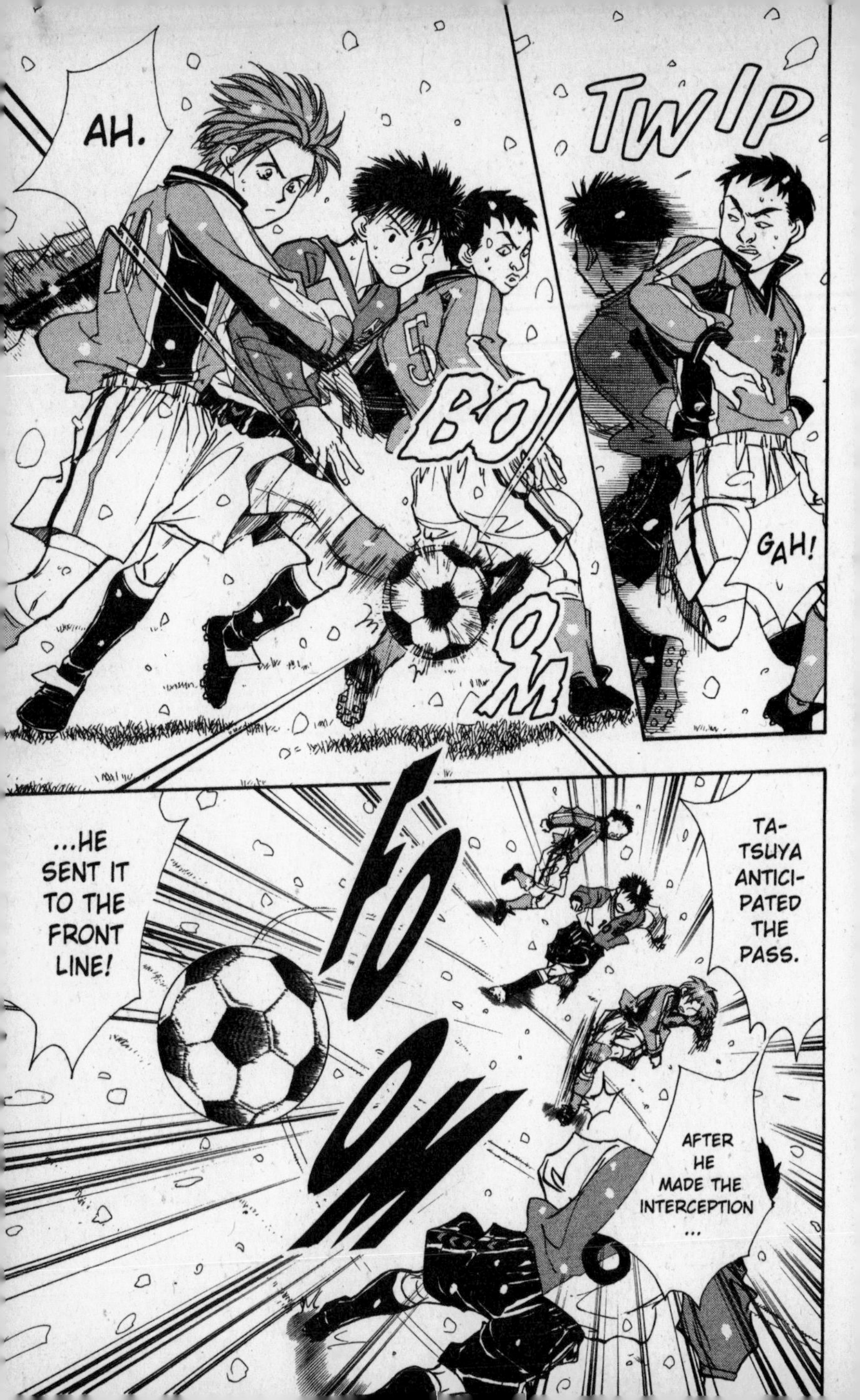
TWIP
GAH!
AH.
BOOM
TA-TSUYA ANTICI-PATED THE PASS.
AFTER HE MADE THE INTERCEPTION...
...HE SENT IT TO THE FRONT LINE!

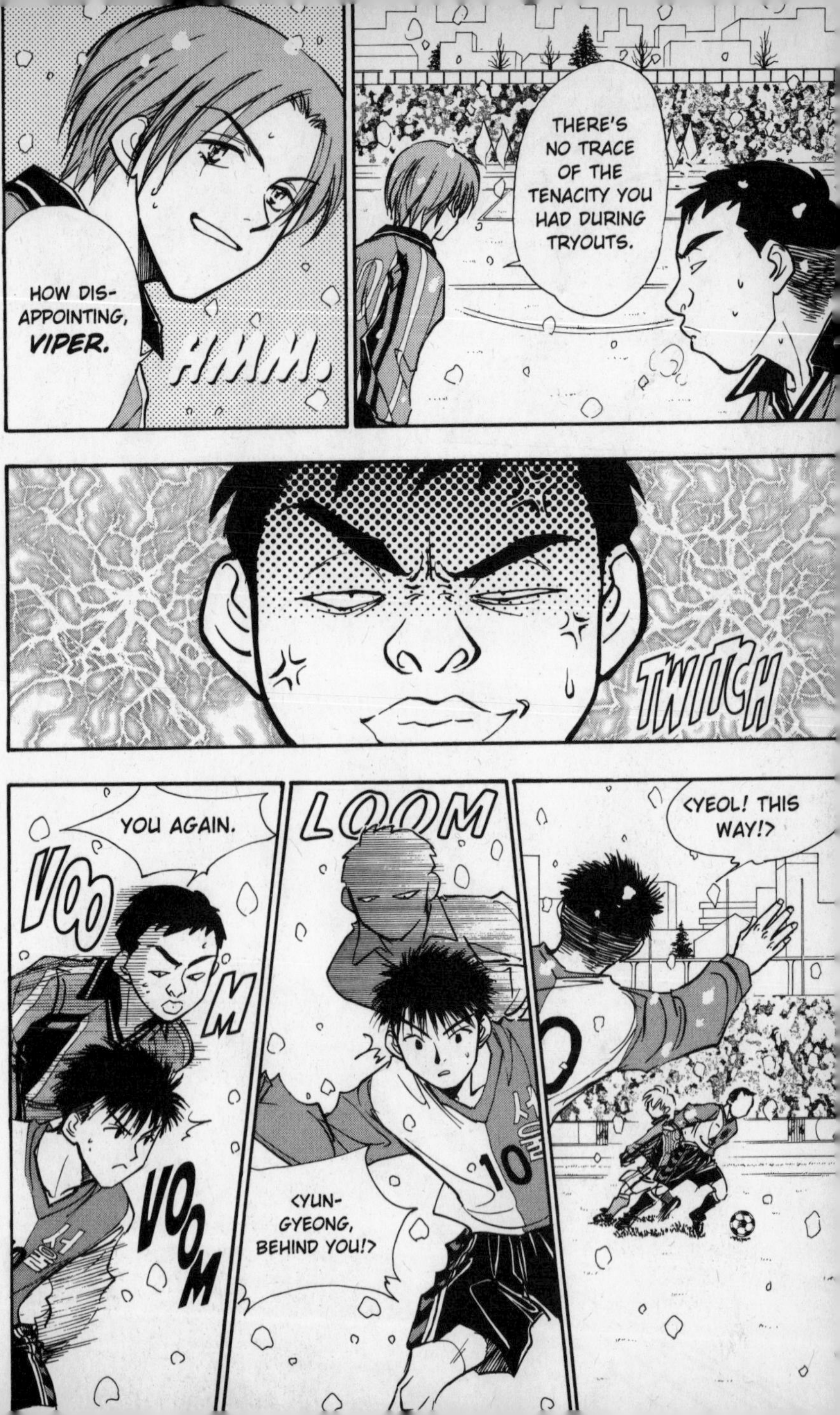
THERE'S NO TRACE OF THE TENACITY YOU HAD DURING TRYOUTS.
HMM.
HOW DIS-APPOINTING, VIPER.
TWITCH
<YEOL! THIS WAY!>
LOOM
<YUN-GYEONG, BEHIND YOU!>
YOU AGAIN.
VOOM
VOOM

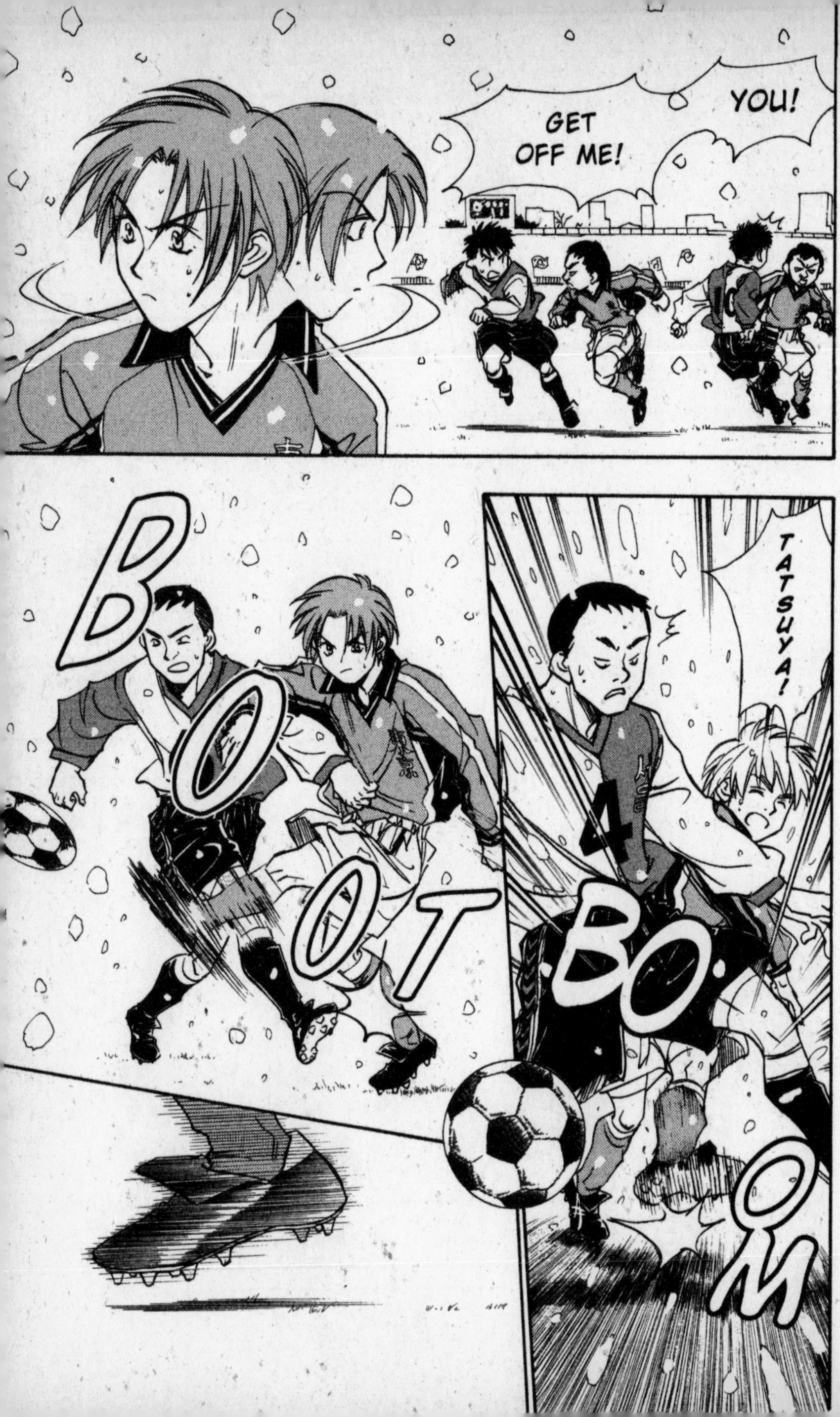
YOU!
GET OFF ME!
TATSUYA!
BOOM
BOOOT

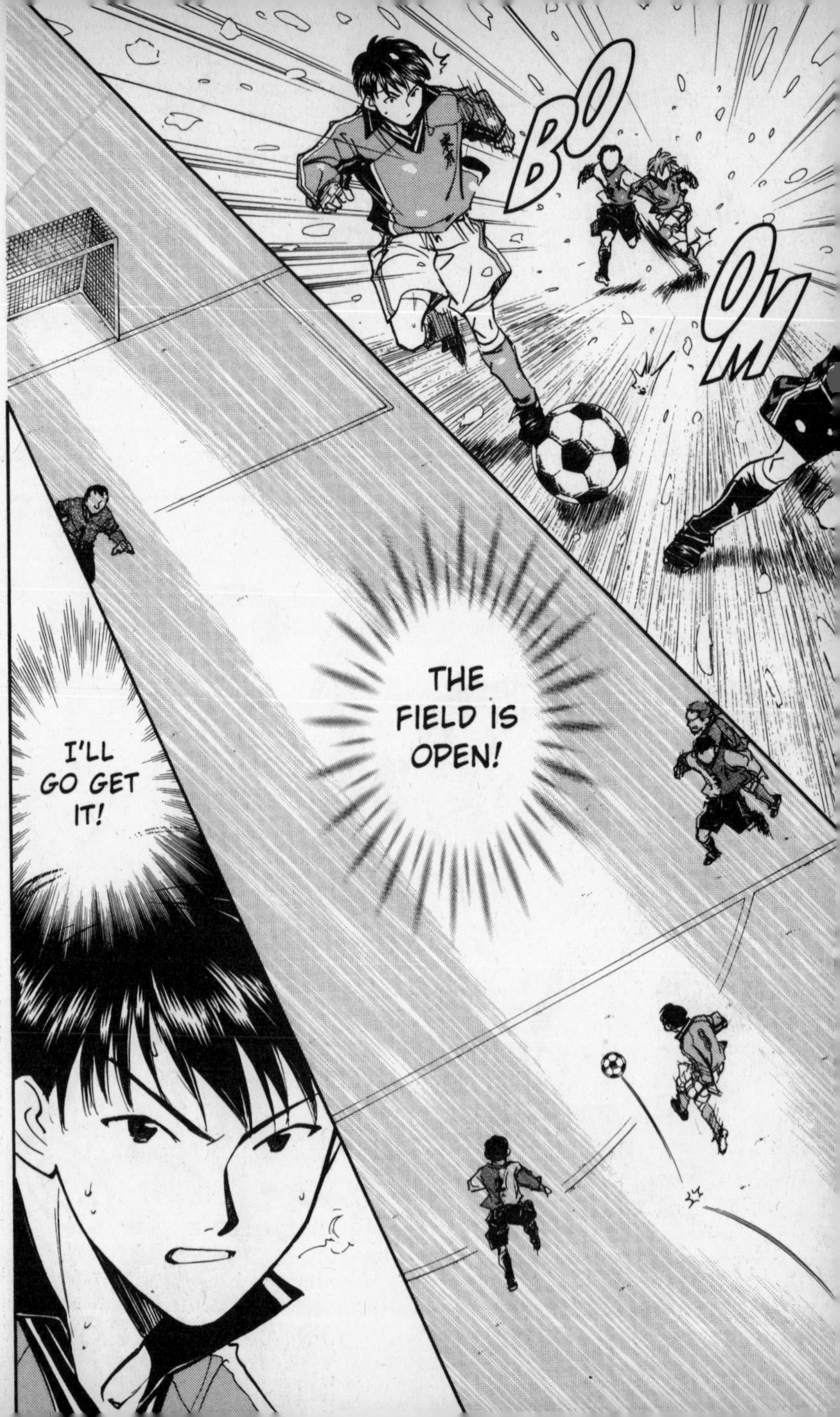
BOOOM
THE FIELD IS OPEN!
I'LL GO GET IT!

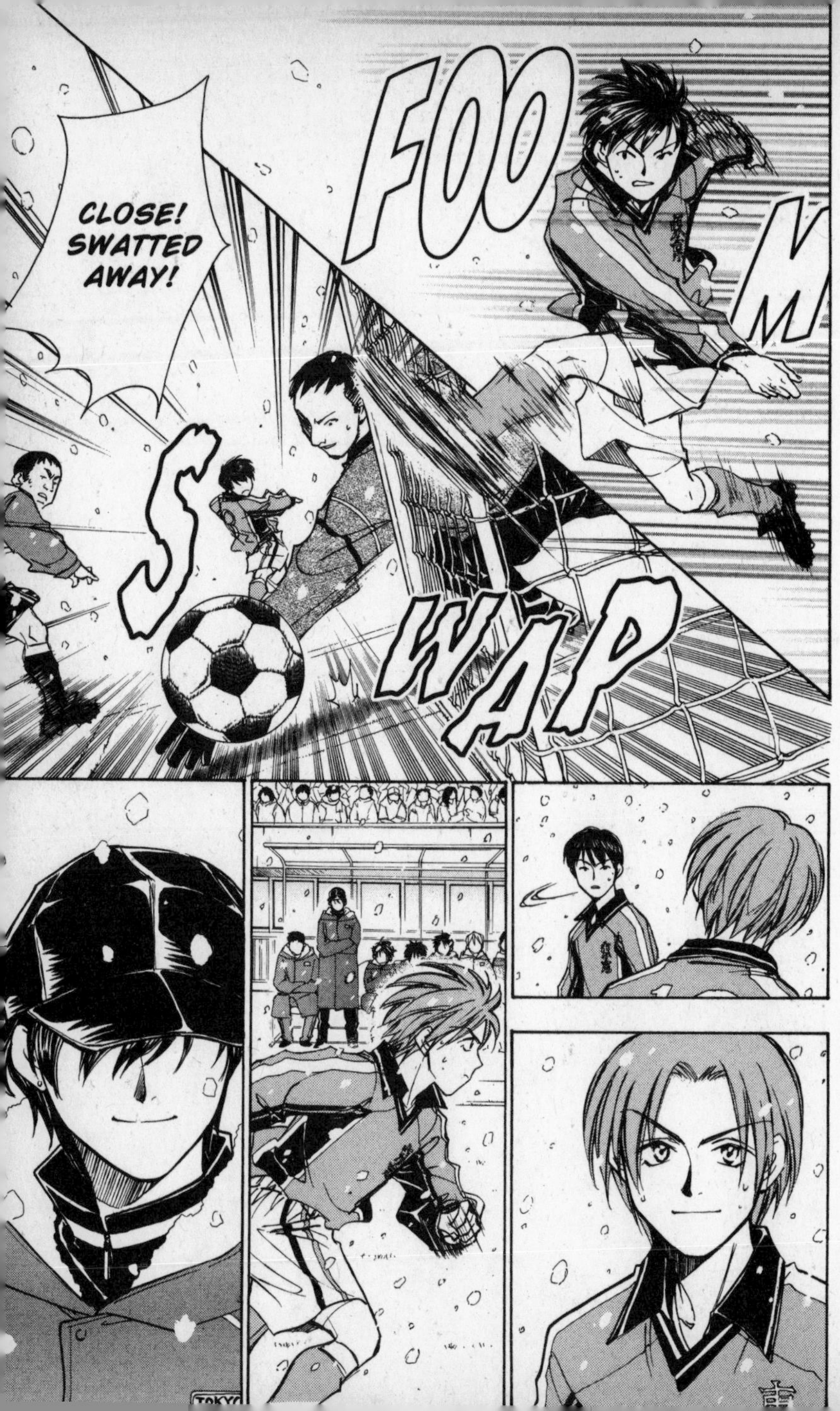
FOOM
CLOSE! SWATTED AWAY!
SWAP

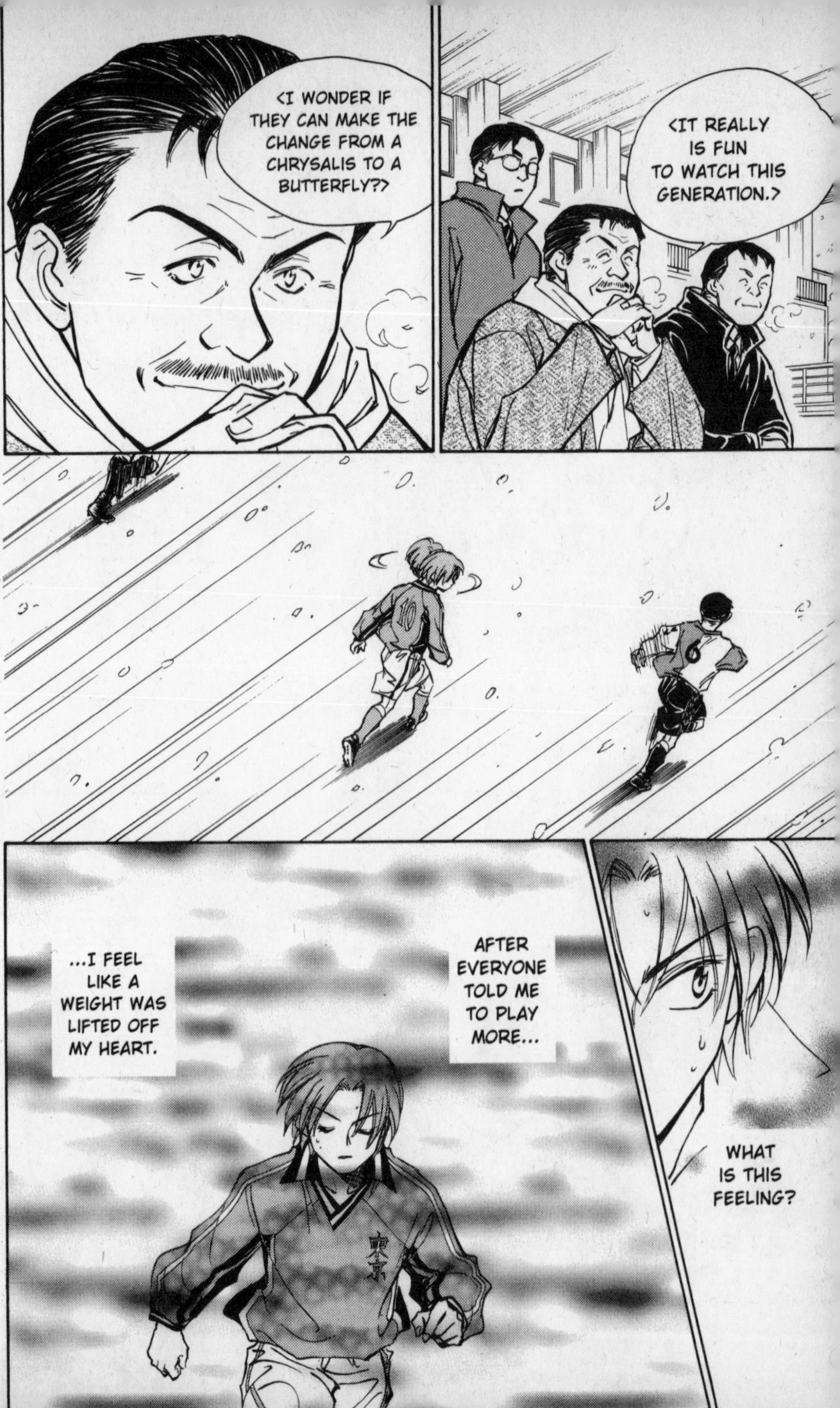
<IT REALLY IS FUN TO WATCH THIS GENERATION.>
<I WONDER IF THEY CAN MAKE THE CHANGE FROM A CHRYSALIS TO A BUTTERFLY?>
WHAT IS THIS FEELING?
AFTER EVERYONE TOLD ME TO PLAY MORE...
...I FEEL LIKE A WEIGHT WAS LIFTED OFF MY HEART.

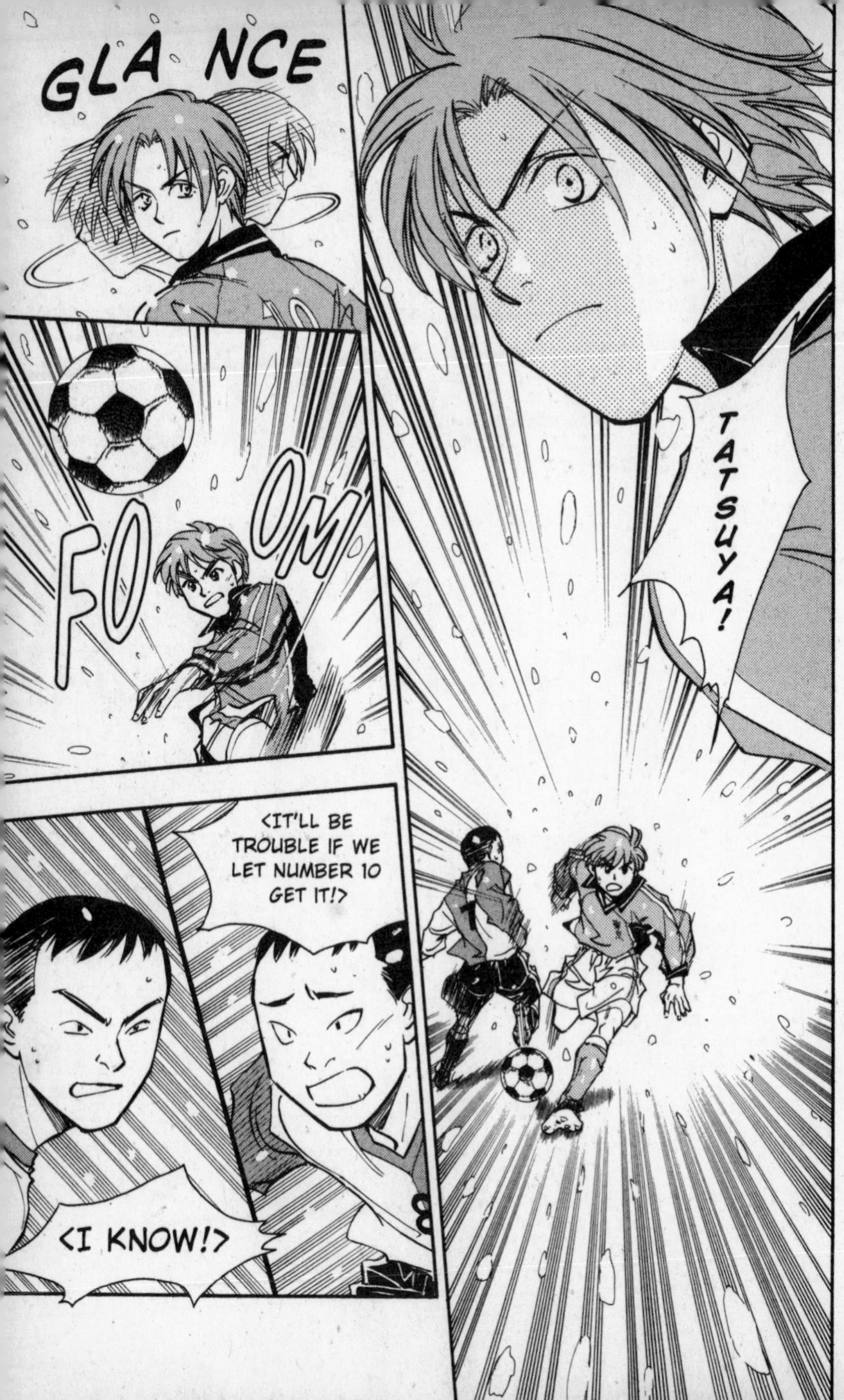
TATSUYA!
GLANCE
FOOM
<IT'LL BE TROUBLE IF WE LET NUMBER 10 GET IT!>
<I KNOW!>

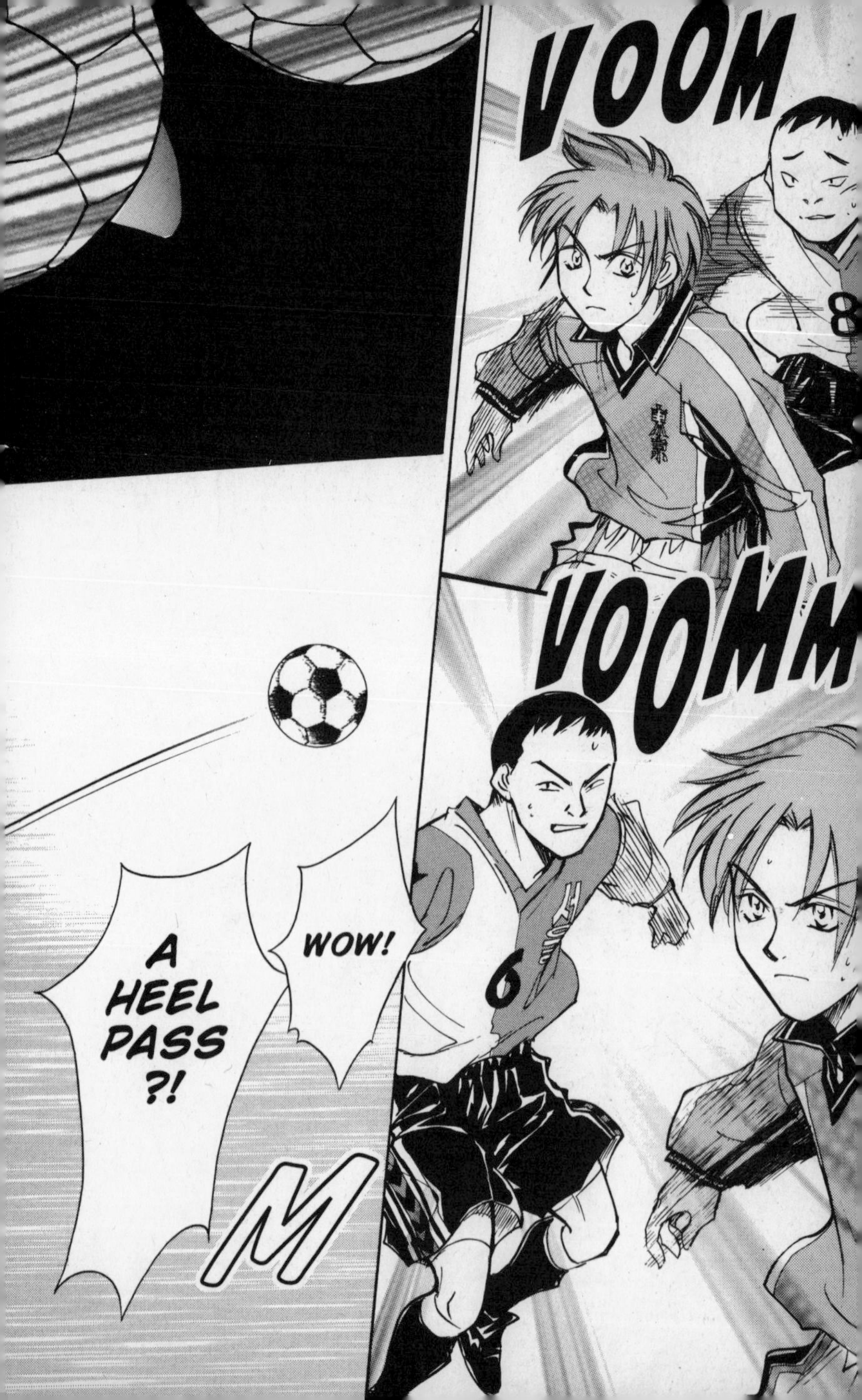
VOOM
VOOMM
WOW!
A HEEL PASS?!
M

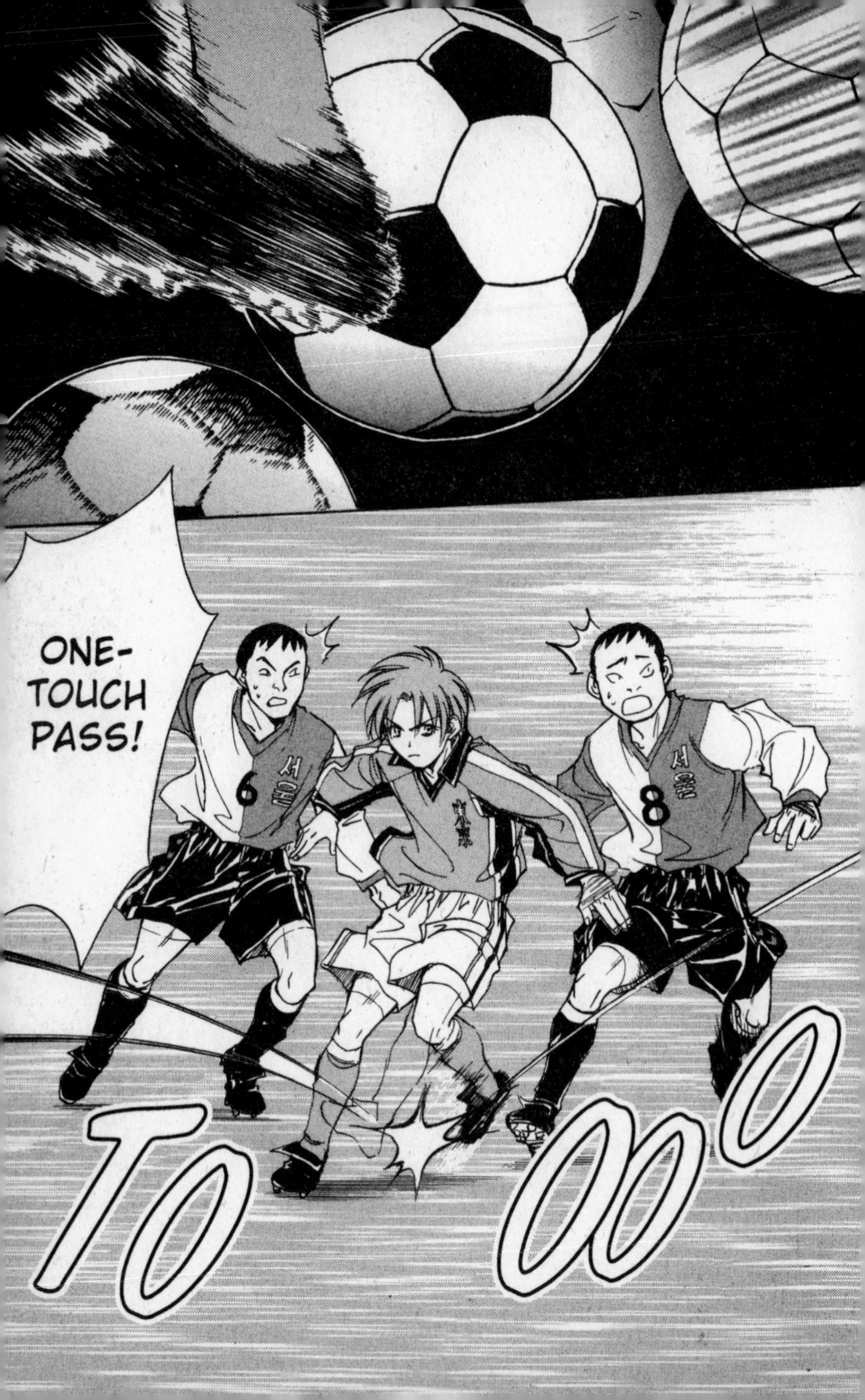
ONE-TOUCH PASS!
TOOOO

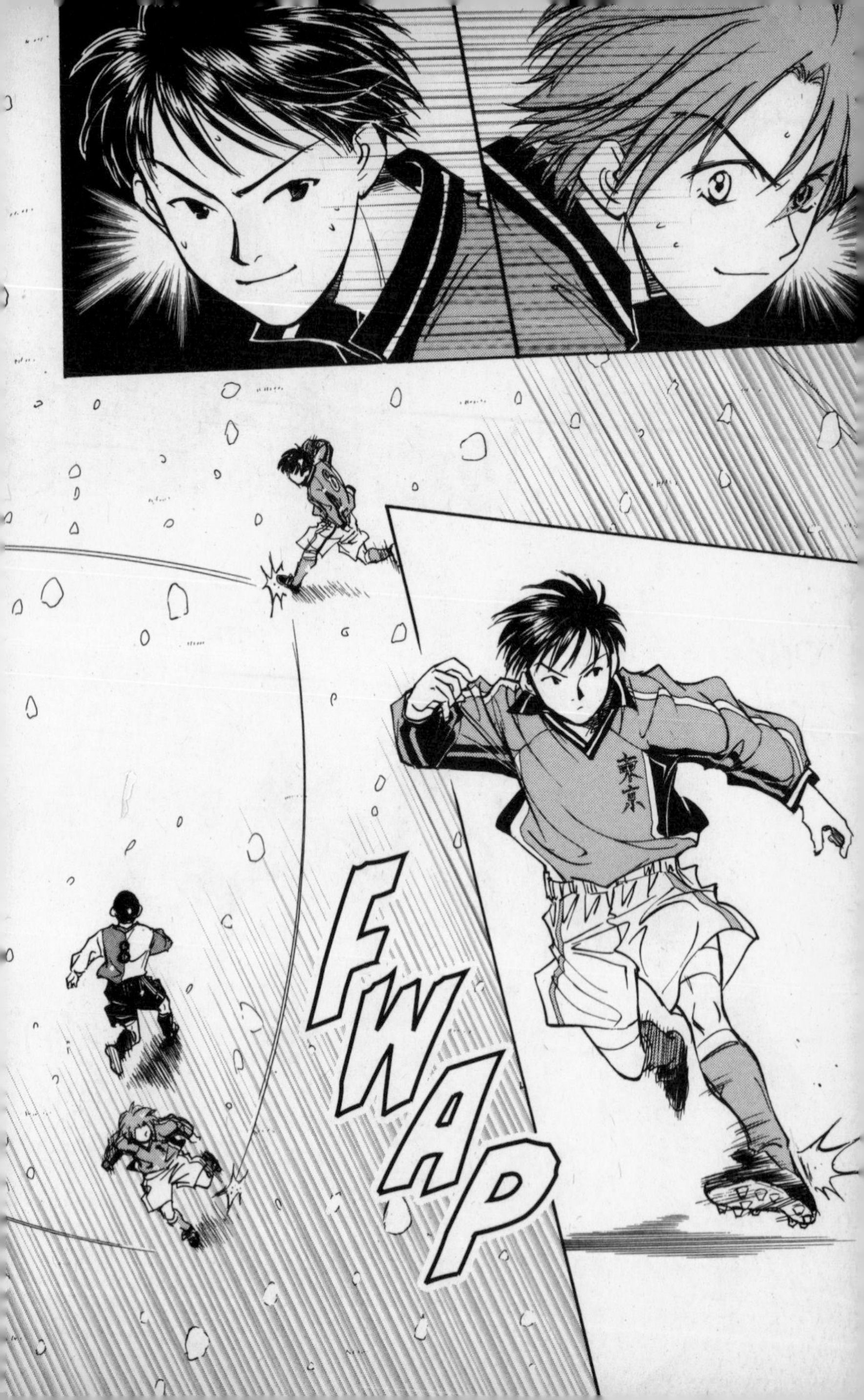
FWAP

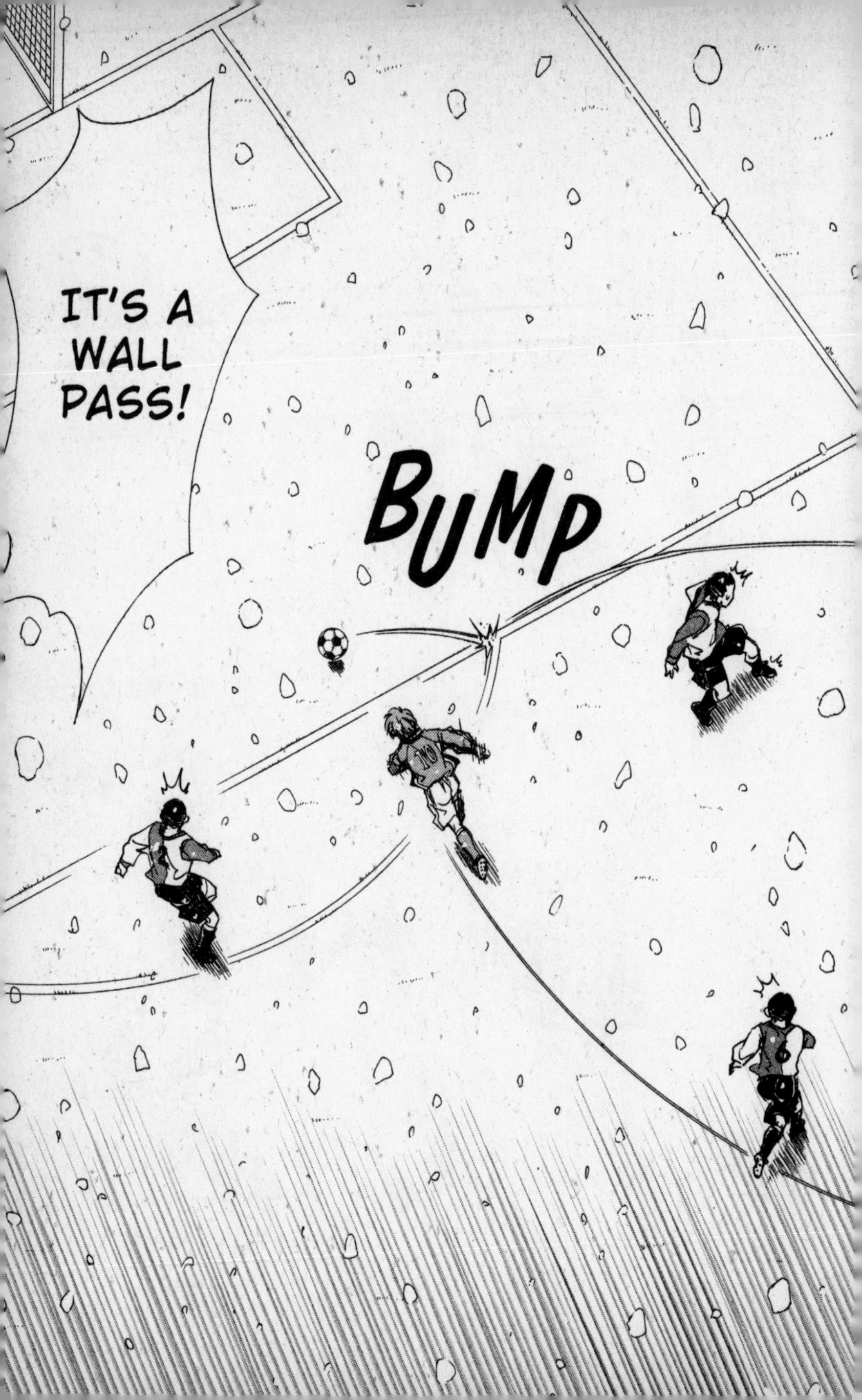
IT'S A WALL PASS!
BUMP

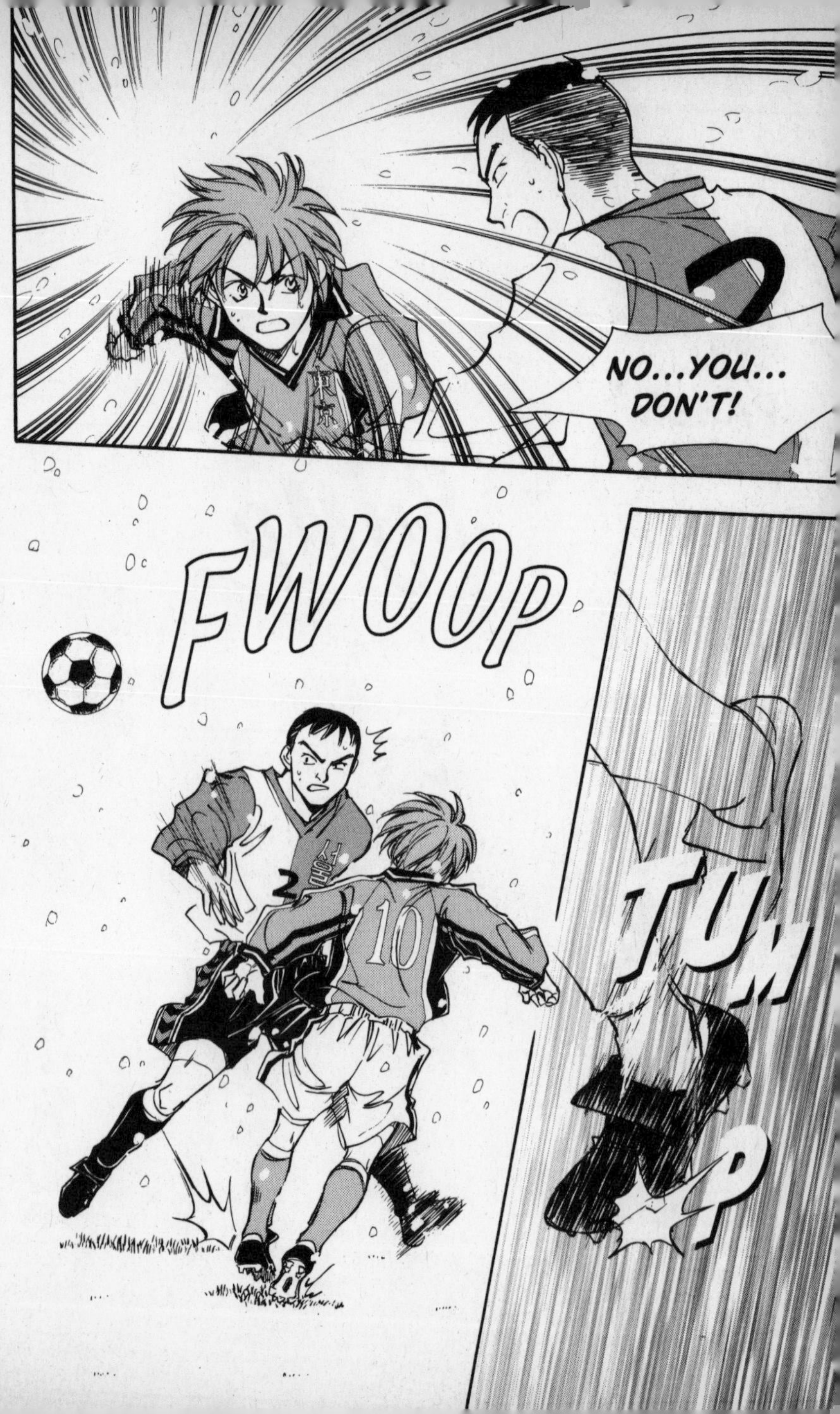
NO...YOU... DON'T!
TUMP
FWOOP

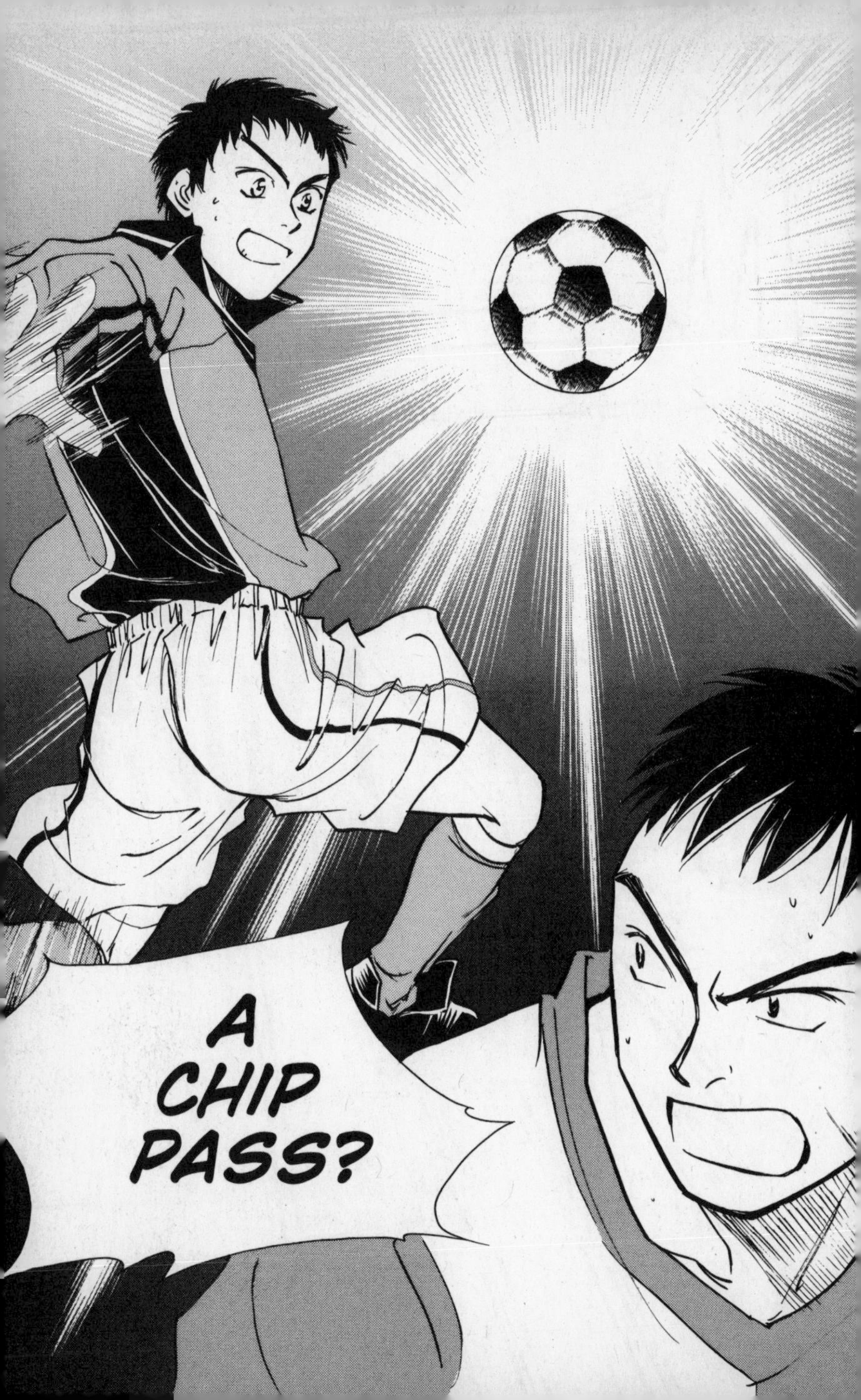
A CHIP PASS?

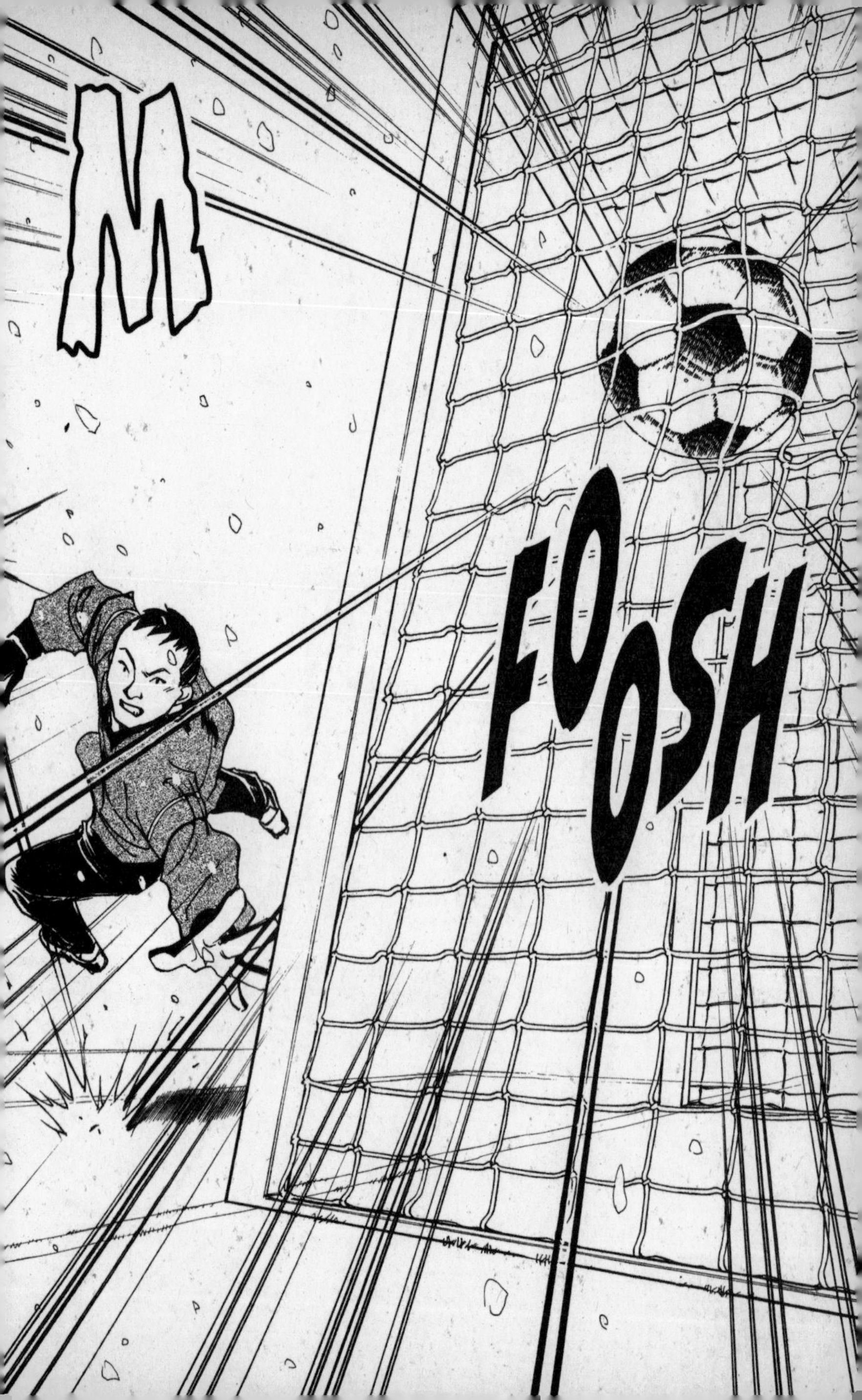
M
FOOSH

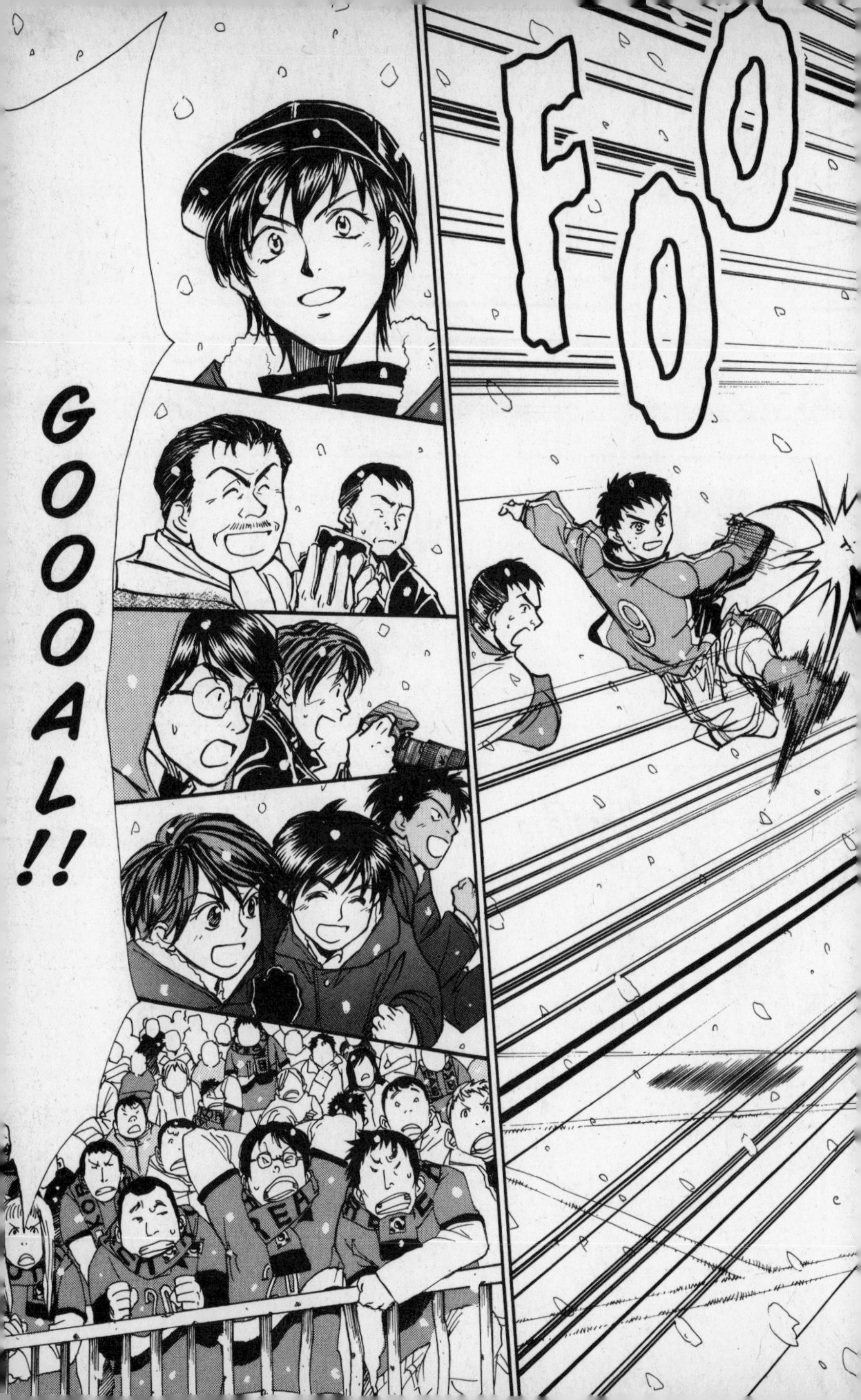
FOO
GOOOOAL!!

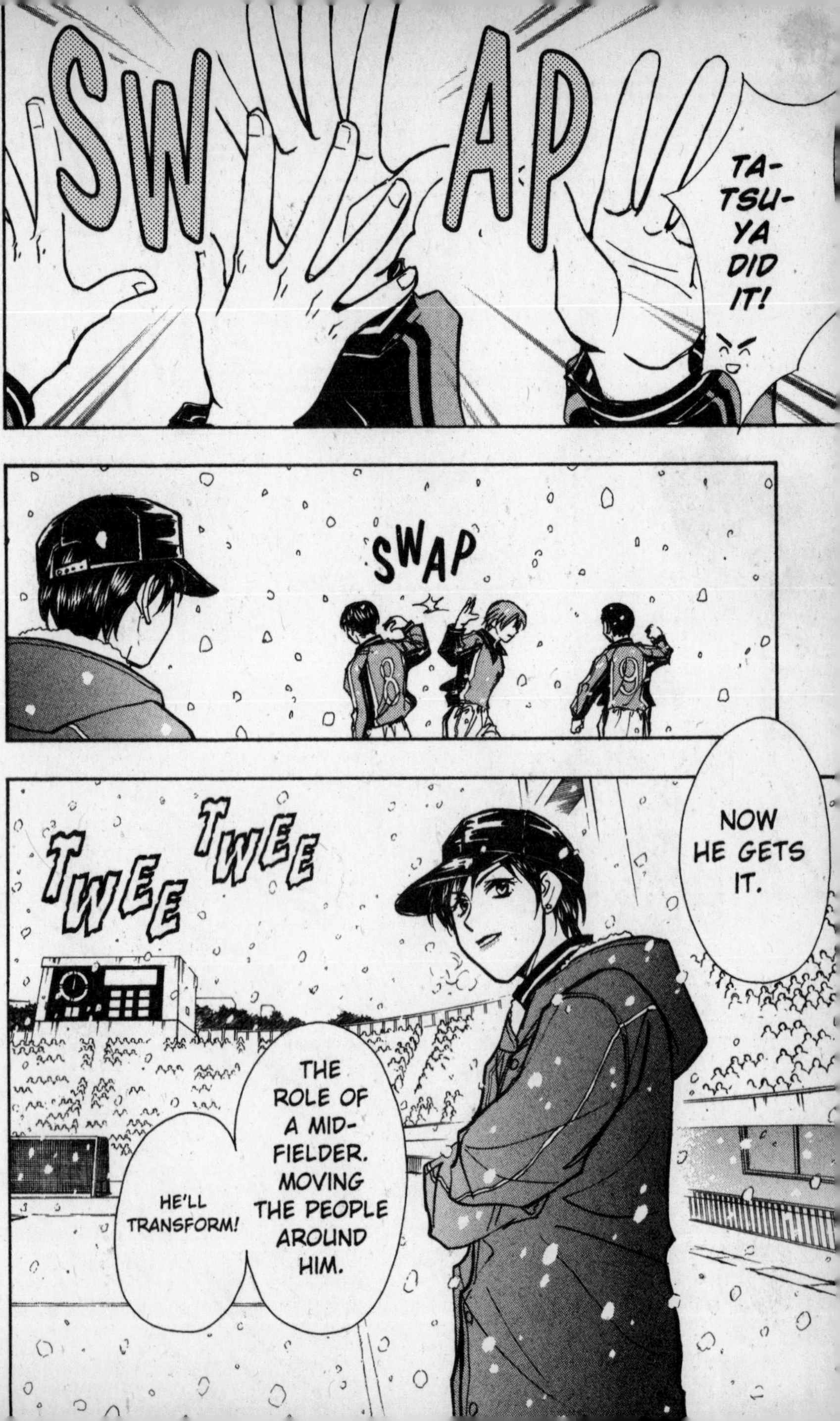
SWAP
TA-TSU-YA DID IT!
SWAP
NOW HE GETS IT.
THE ROLE OF A MID-FIELDER. MOVING THE PEOPLE AROUND HIM.
HE'LL TRANSFORM!
TWEE TWEE

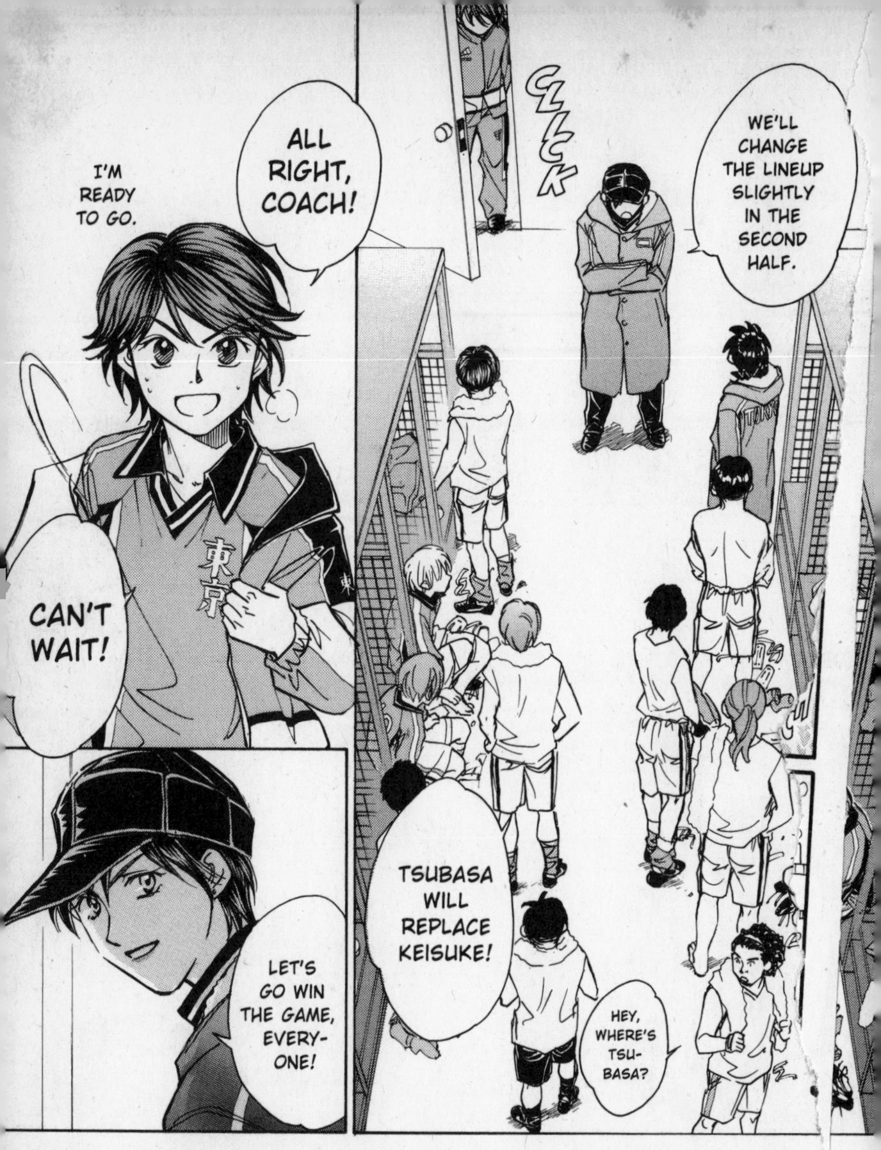
CLICK
WE'LL CHANGE THE LINEUP SLIGHTLY IN THE SECOND HALF.
TSUBASA WILL REPLACE KEISUKE!
HEY, WHERE'S TSU-BASA?
ALL RIGHT, COACH!
I'M READY TO GO.
CAN'T WAIT!
LET'S GO WIN THE GAME, EVERY-ONE!

STAGE.157

Under the Snowy Skies of Seoul

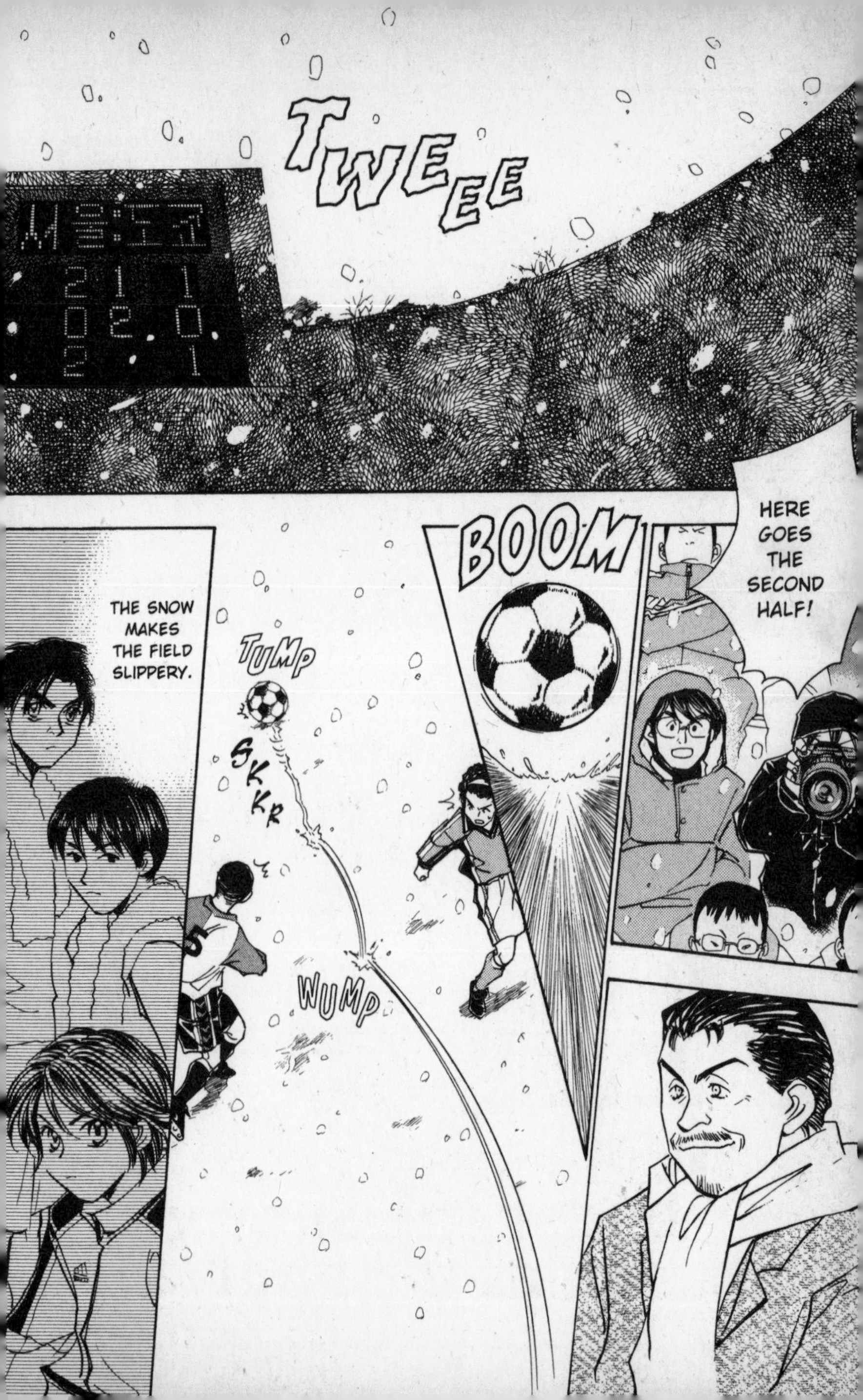
TWEEE
HERE GOES THE SECOND HALF!
BOOM
TUMP
SKKR
WUMP
THE SNOW MAKES THE FIELD SLIPPERY.

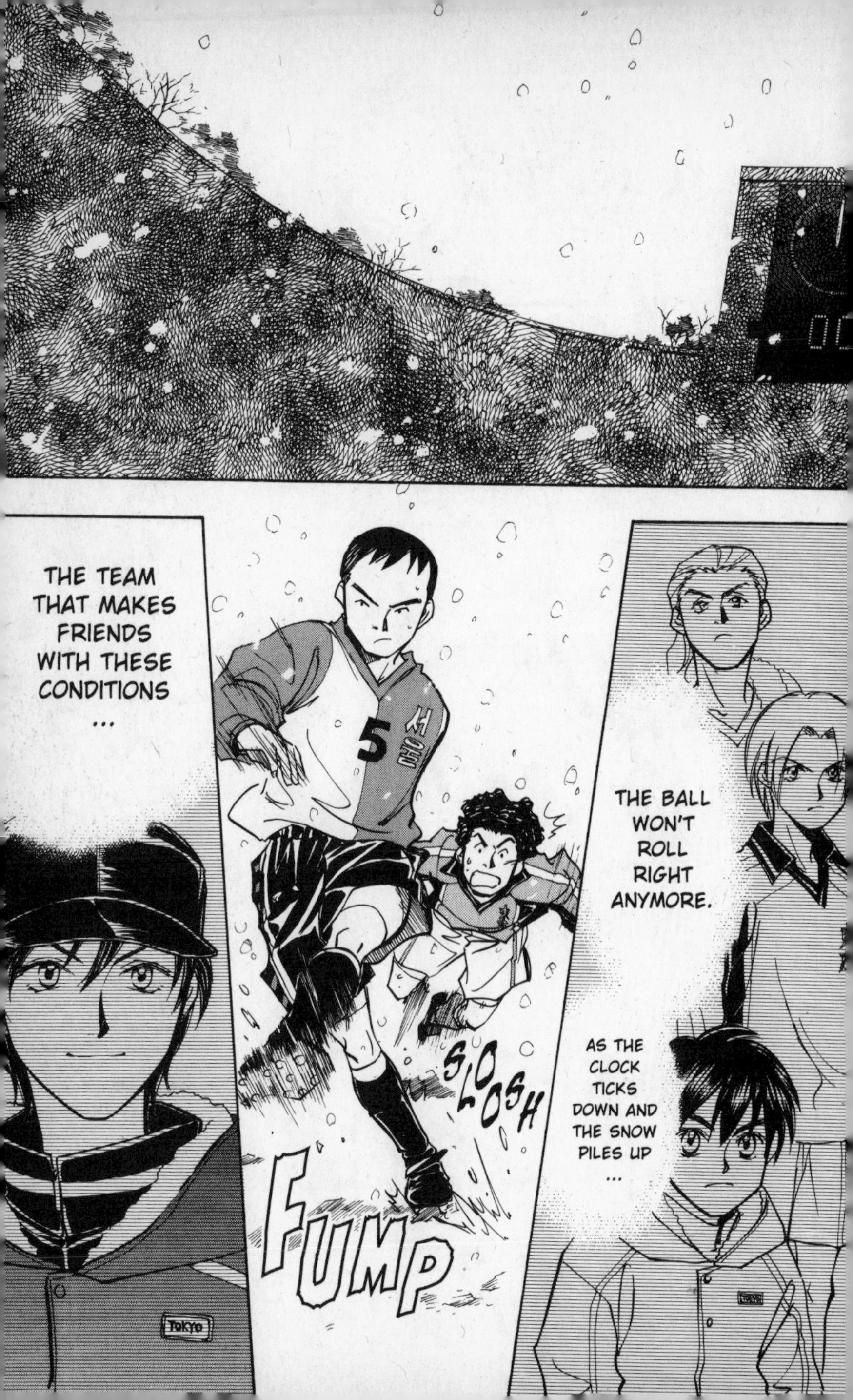
THE BALL WON'T ROLL RIGHT ANYMORE.
AS THE CLOCK TICKS DOWN AND THE SNOW PILES UP ...
SLOSH
FUMP
THE TEAM THAT MAKES FRIENDS WITH THESE CONDITIONS ...

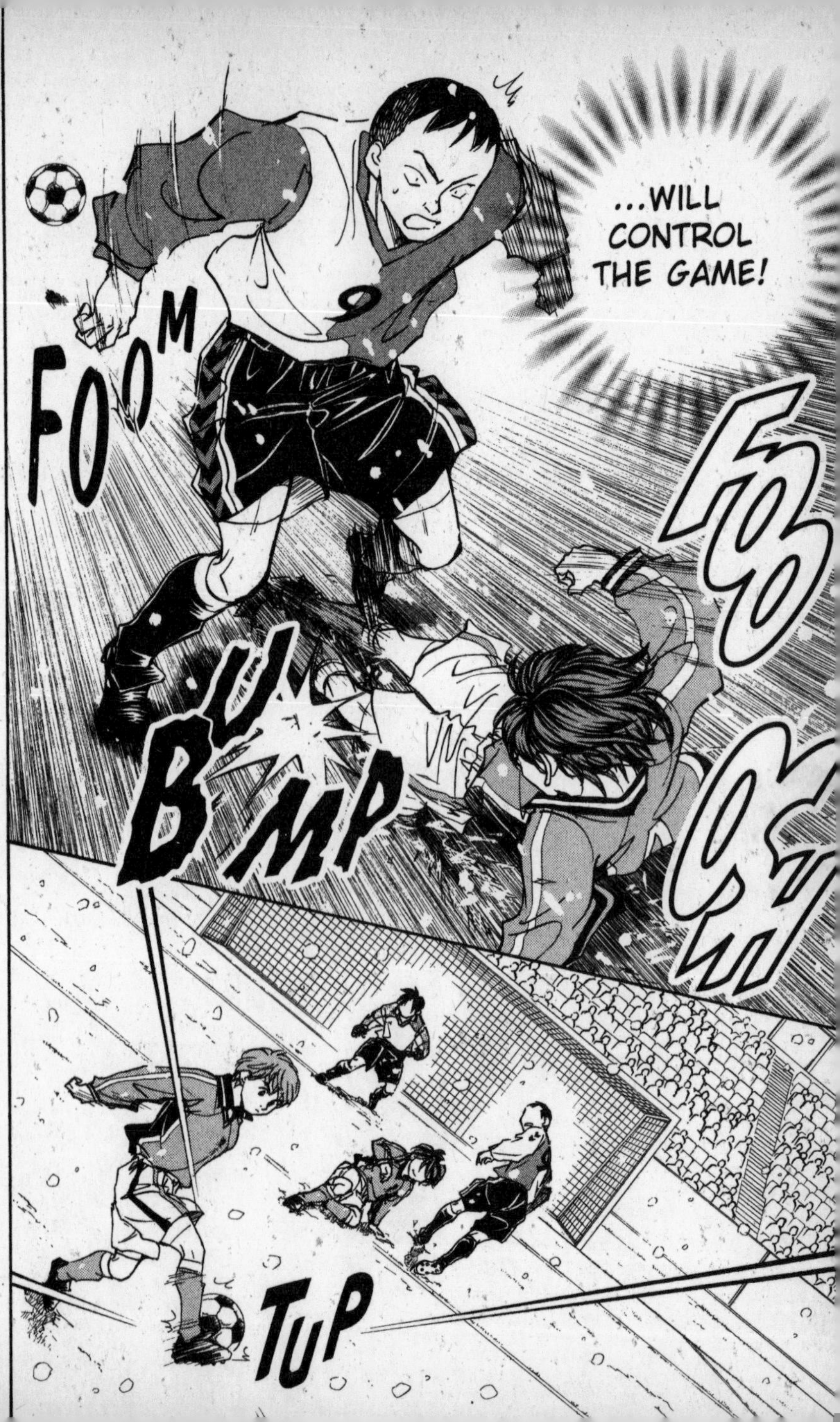
...WILL CONTROL THE GAME!
FOOM
BUMP
TUP

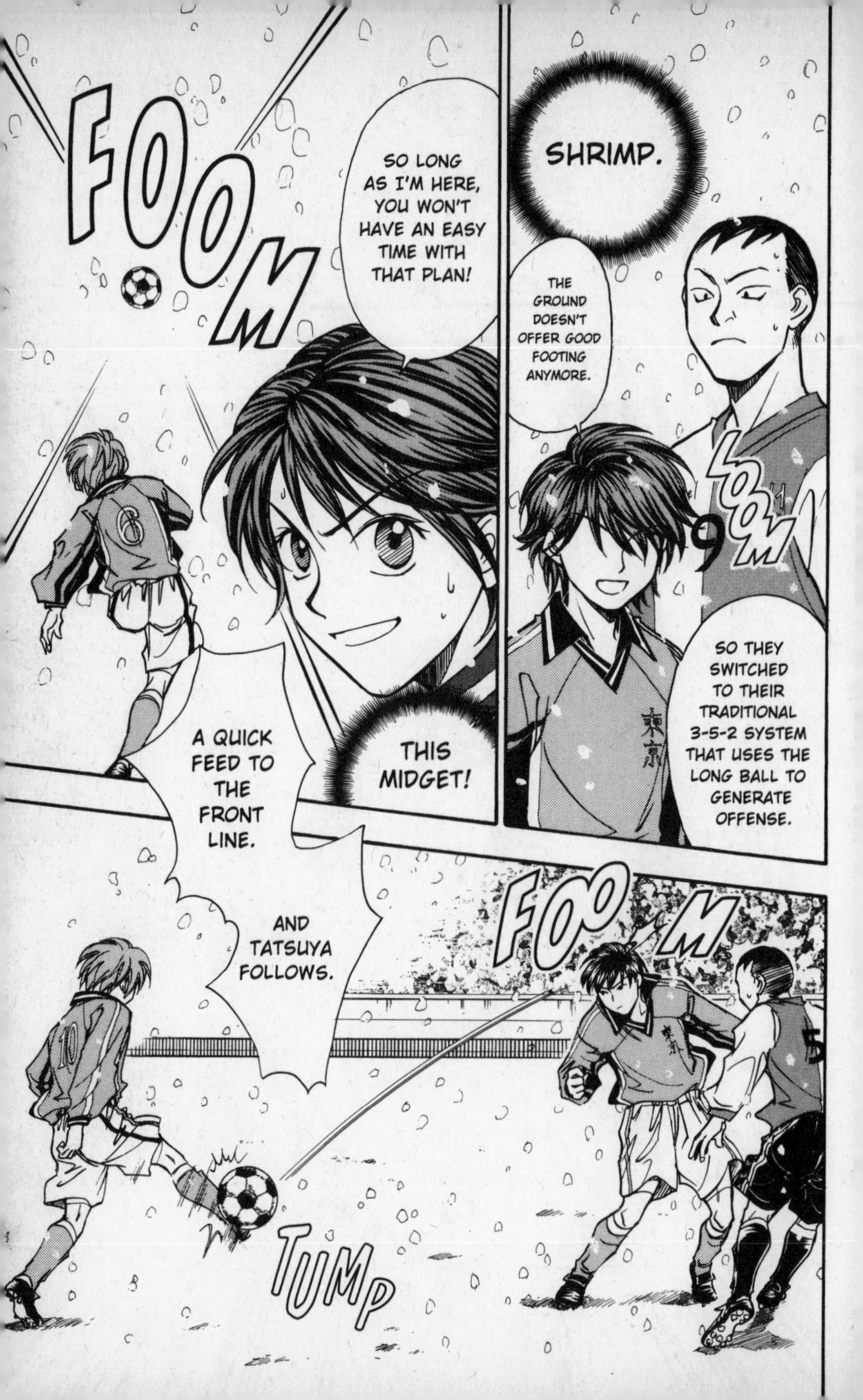
SHRIMP.
THE GROUND DOESN'T OFFER GOOD FOOTING ANYMORE.
LOOOM
SO THEY SWITCHED TO THEIR TRADITIONAL 3-5-2 SYSTEM THAT USES THE LONG BALL TO GENERATE OFFENSE.
FOOOM
SO LONG AS I'M HERE, YOU WON'T HAVE AN EASY TIME WITH THAT PLAN!
THIS MIDGET!
A QUICK FEED TO THE FRONT LINE.
AND TATSUYA FOLLOWS.
FOOOM
TUMP

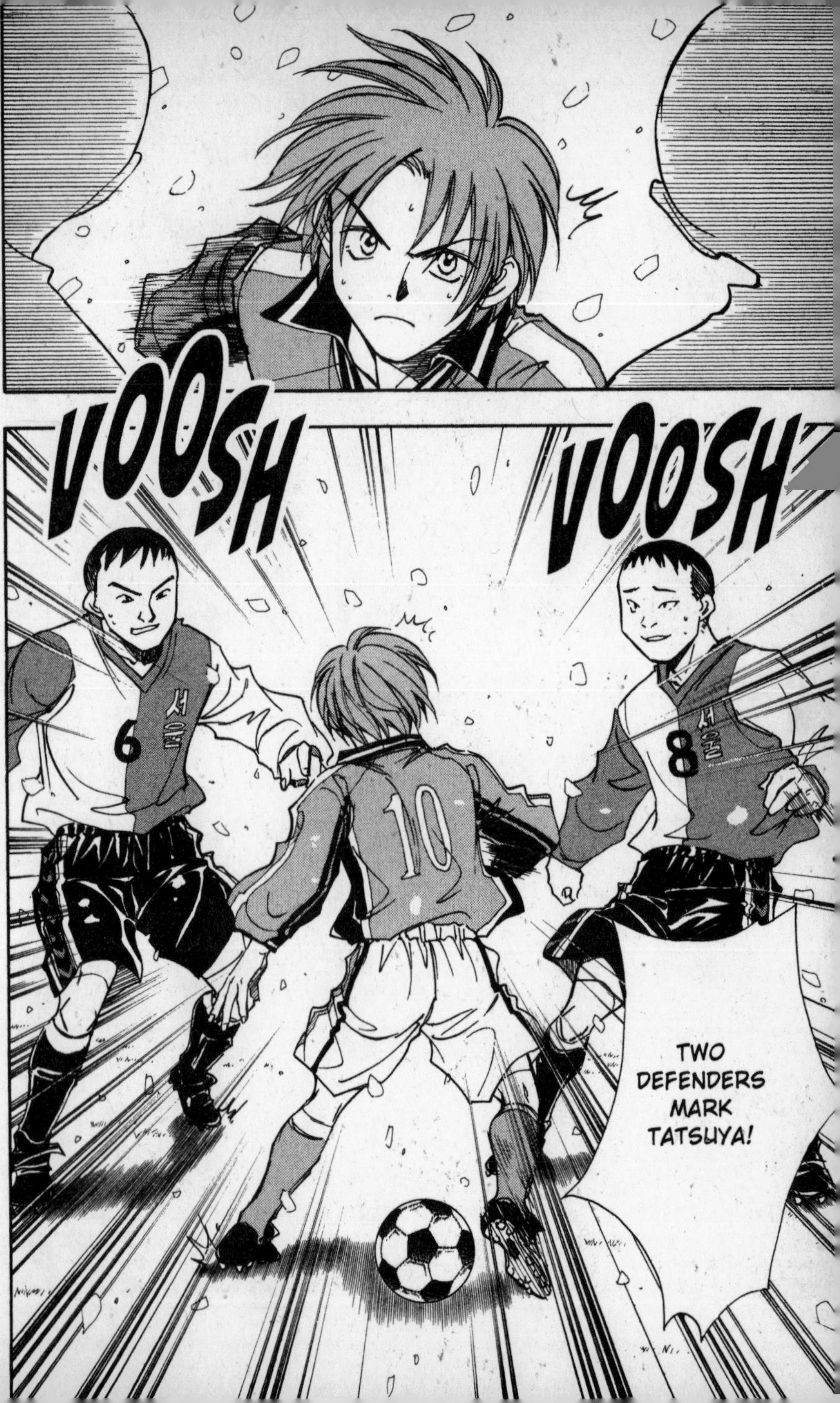
VOOSH
VOOSH
TWO DEFENDERS MARK TATSUYA!

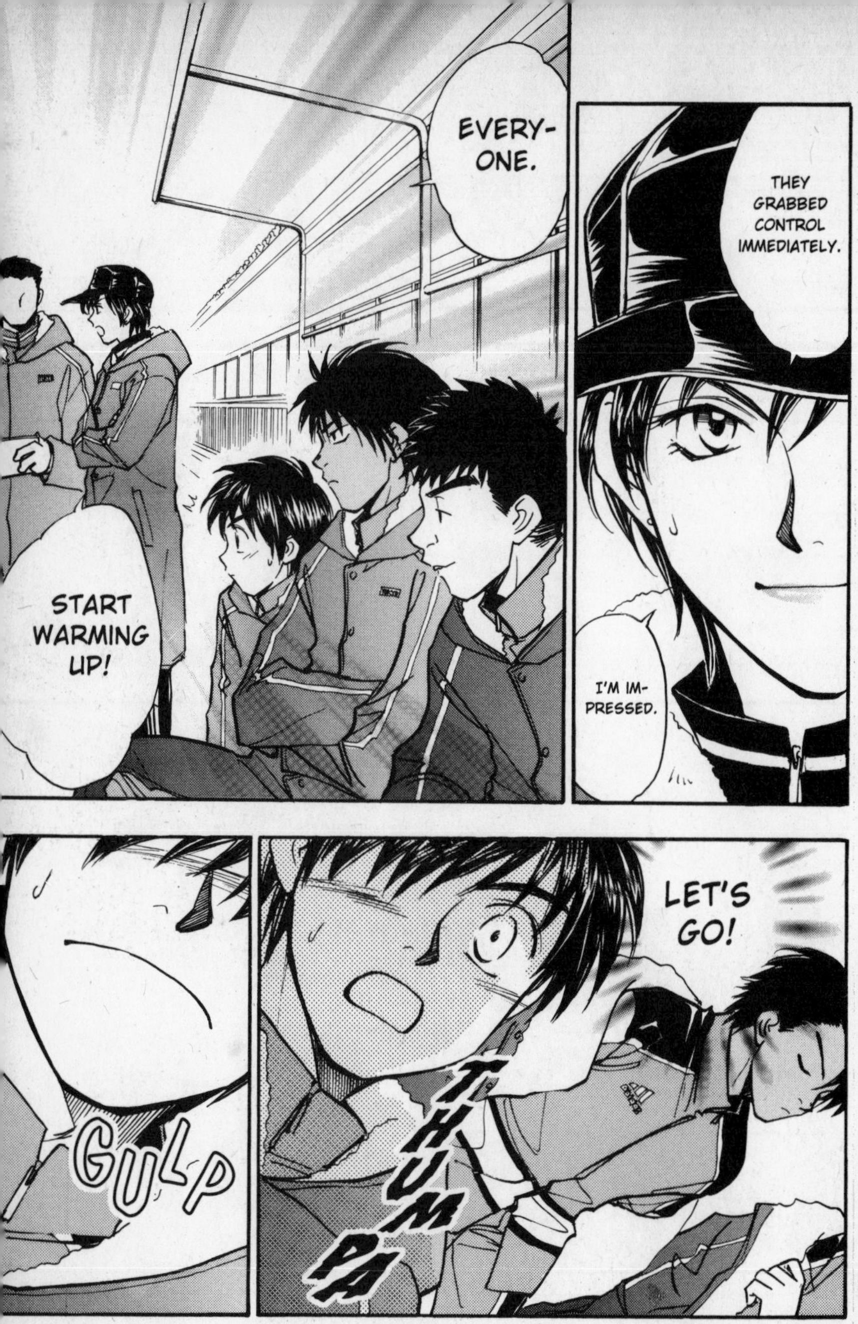
THEY GRABBED CONTROL IMMEDIATELY.
I'M IMPRESSED.
EVERY-ONE.
START WARMING UP!
LET'S GO!
THUMPA
GULP

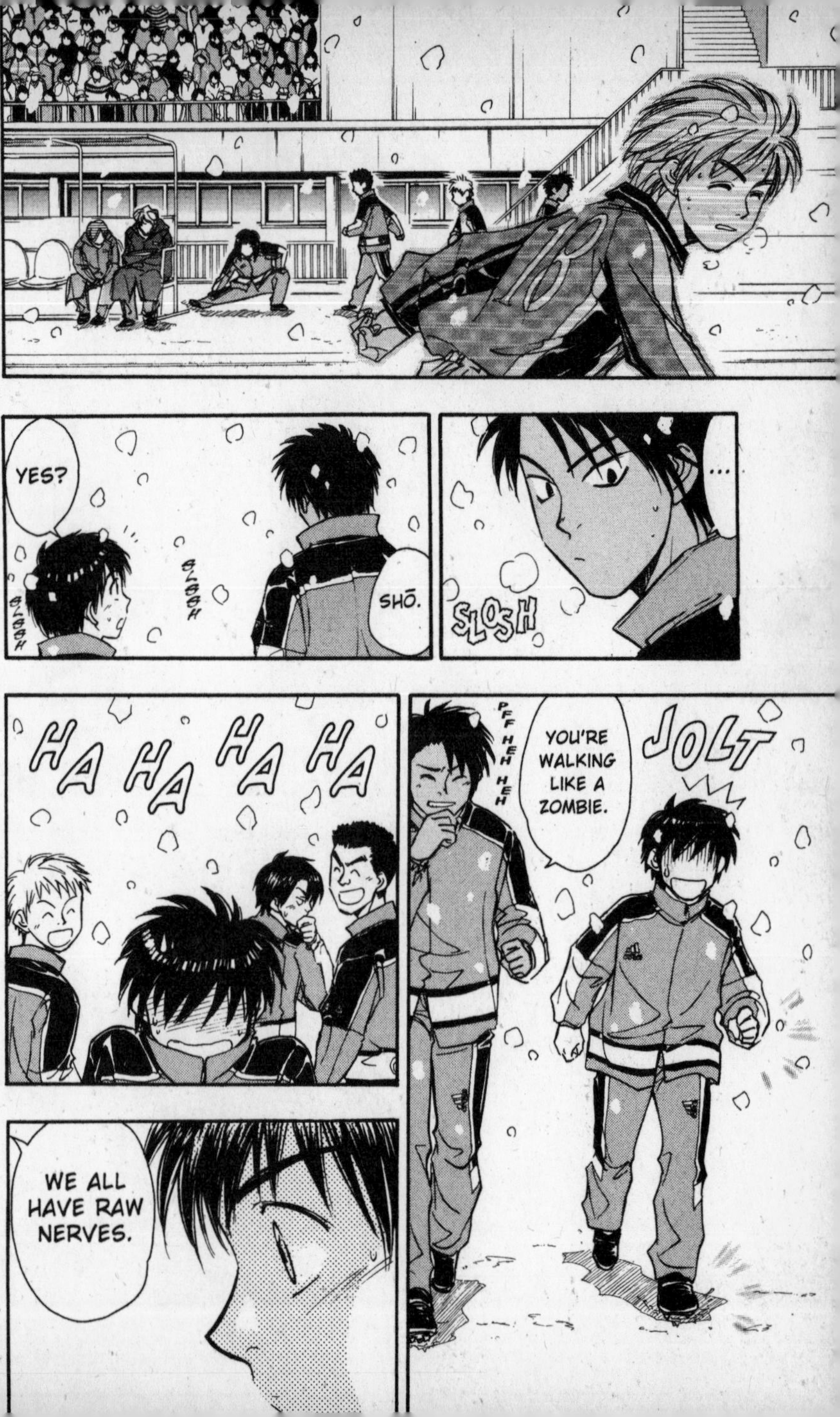
...
SLOSH
SHŌ.
YES?
SLOSH
SLOSH
JOLT
YOU'RE WALKING LIKE A ZOMBIE.
PFF HEH HEH HEH
HA HA HA HA HA HA
WE ALL HAVE RAW NERVES.

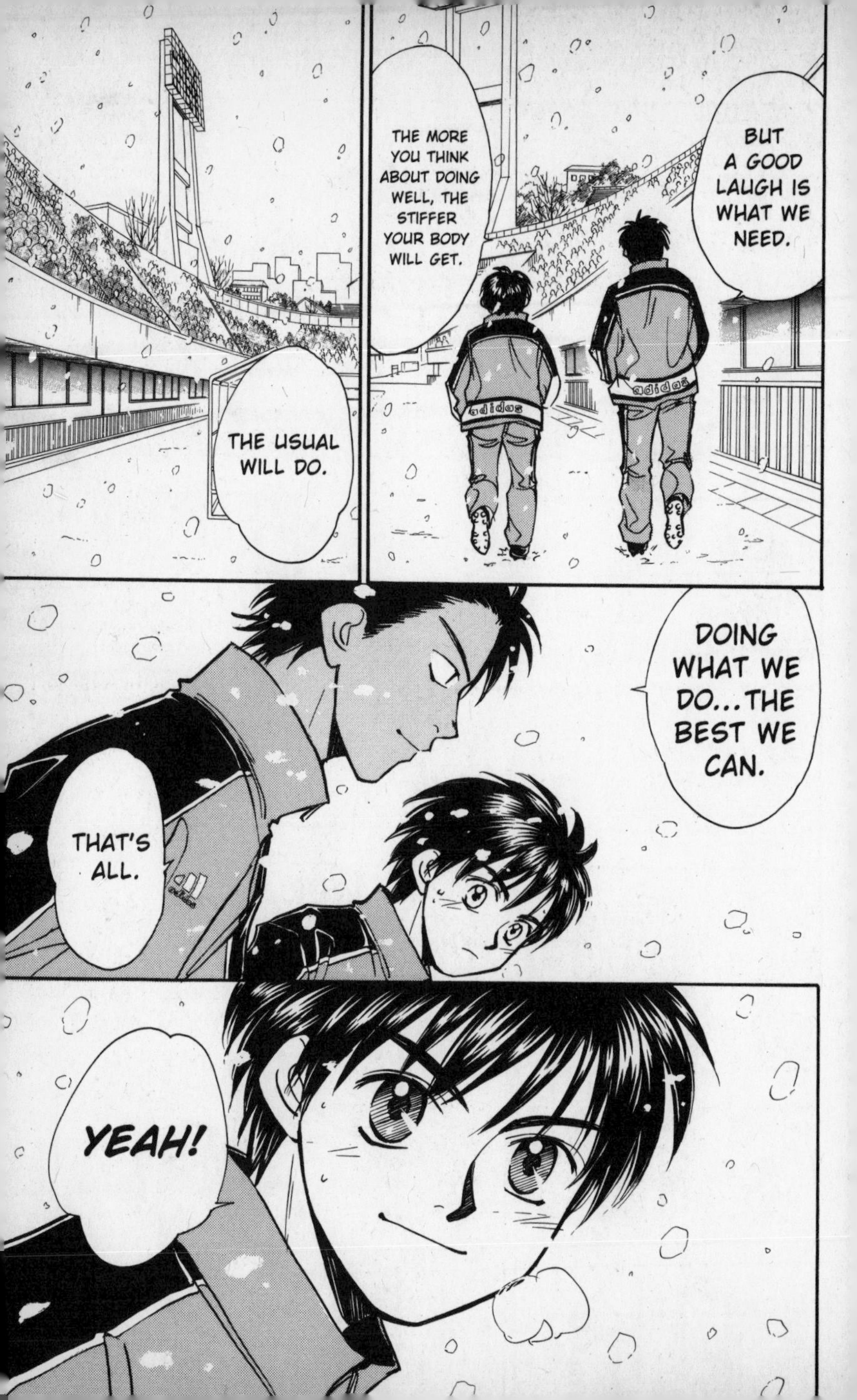
THE MORE YOU THINK ABOUT DOING WELL, THE STIFFER YOUR BODY WILL GET.
BUT A GOOD LAUGH IS WHAT WE NEED.
THE USUAL WILL DO.
DOING WHAT WE DO...THE BEST WE CAN.
THAT'S ALL.
YEAH!

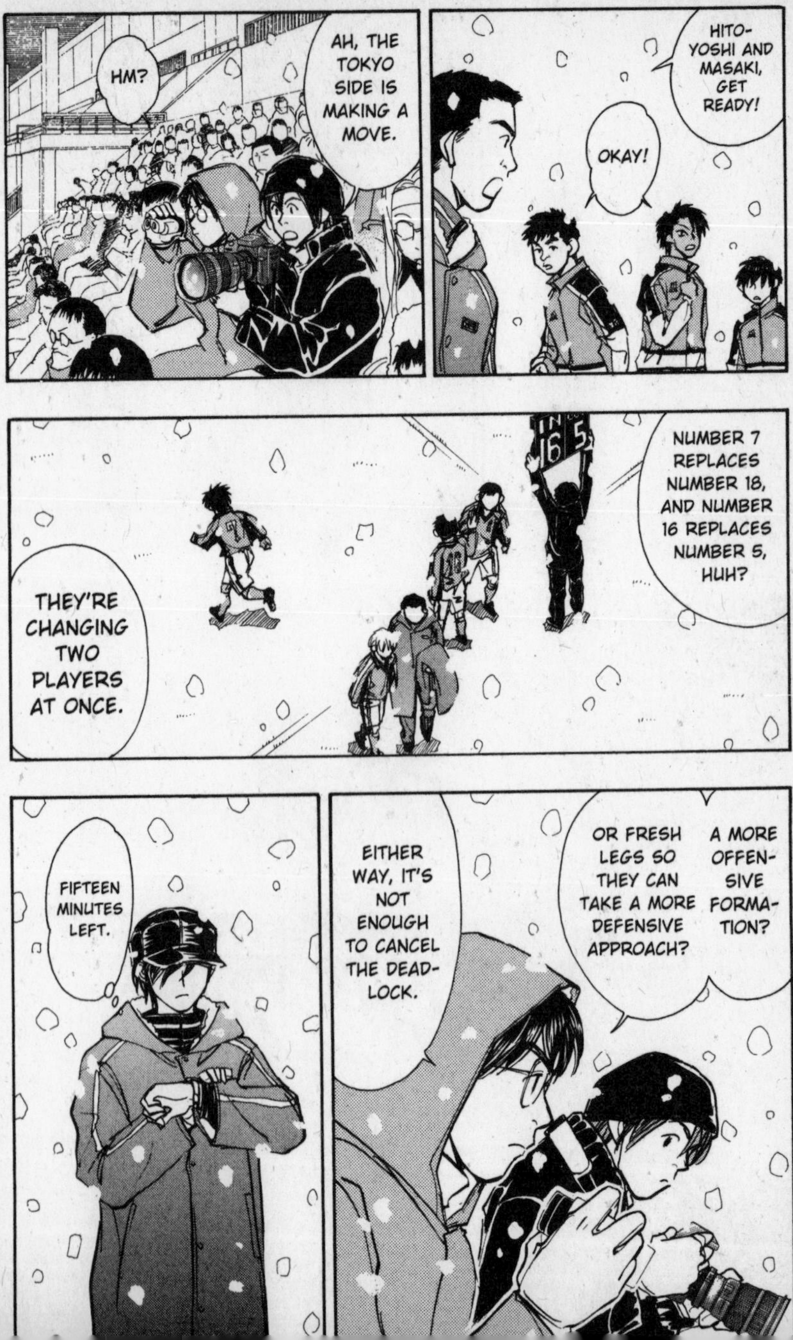
HITO-YOSHI AND MASAKI, GET READY!
OKAY!
AH, THE TOKYO SIDE IS MAKING A MOVE.
HM?
NUMBER 7 REPLACES NUMBER 18, AND NUMBER 16 REPLACES NUMBER 5, HUH?
THEY'RE CHANGING TWO PLAYERS AT ONCE.
A MORE OFFEN-SIVE FORMA-TION?
OR FRESH LEGS SO THEY CAN TAKE A MORE DEFENSIVE APPROACH?
EITHER WAY, IT'S NOT ENOUGH TO CANCEL THE DEAD-LOCK.
FIFTEEN MINUTES LEFT.

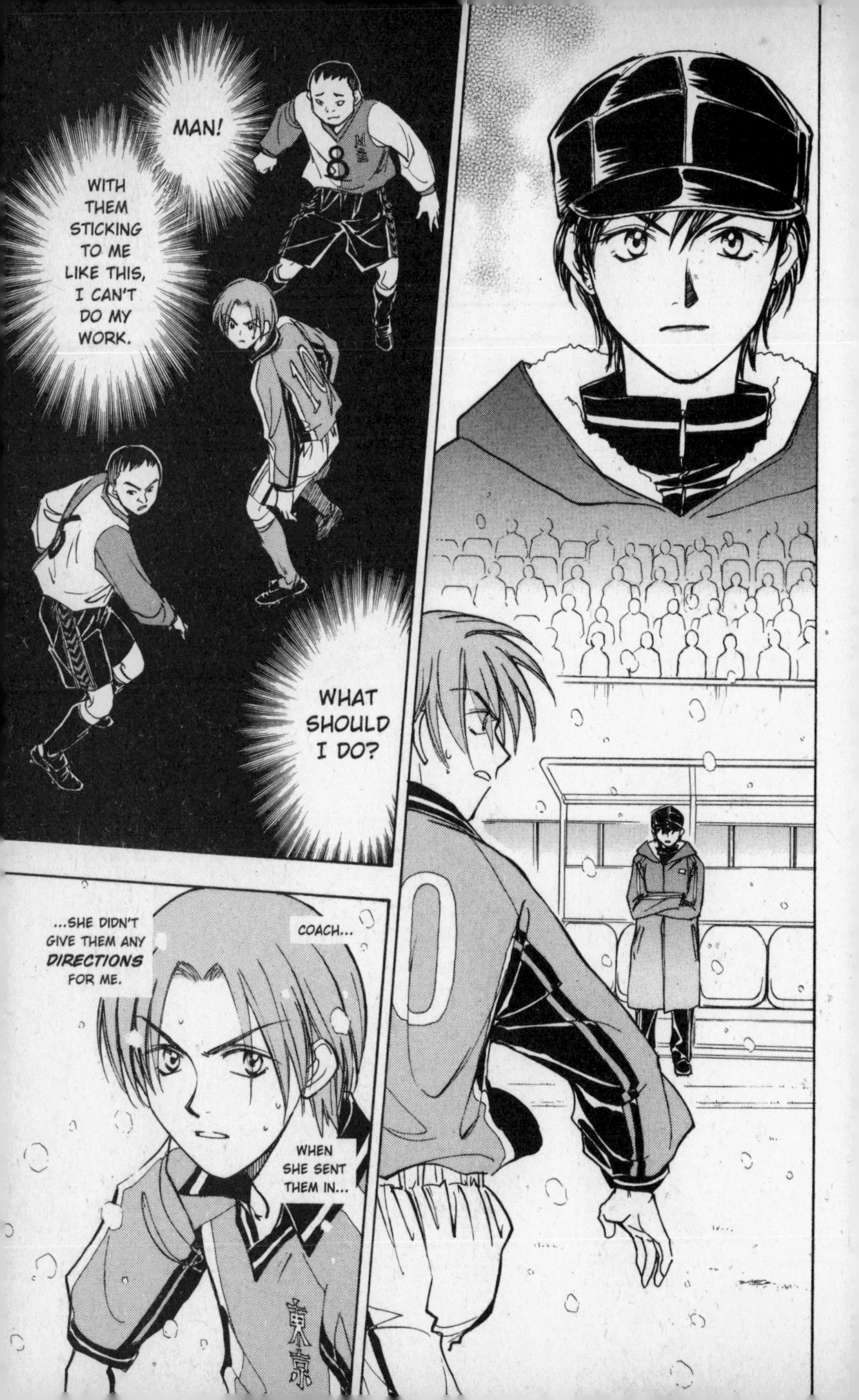
MAN!
WITH THEM STICKING TO ME LIKE THIS, I CAN'T DO MY WORK.
WHAT SHOULD I DO?
COACH...
WHEN SHE SENT THEM IN...
...SHE DIDN'T GIVE THEM ANY *DIRECTIONS* FOR ME.

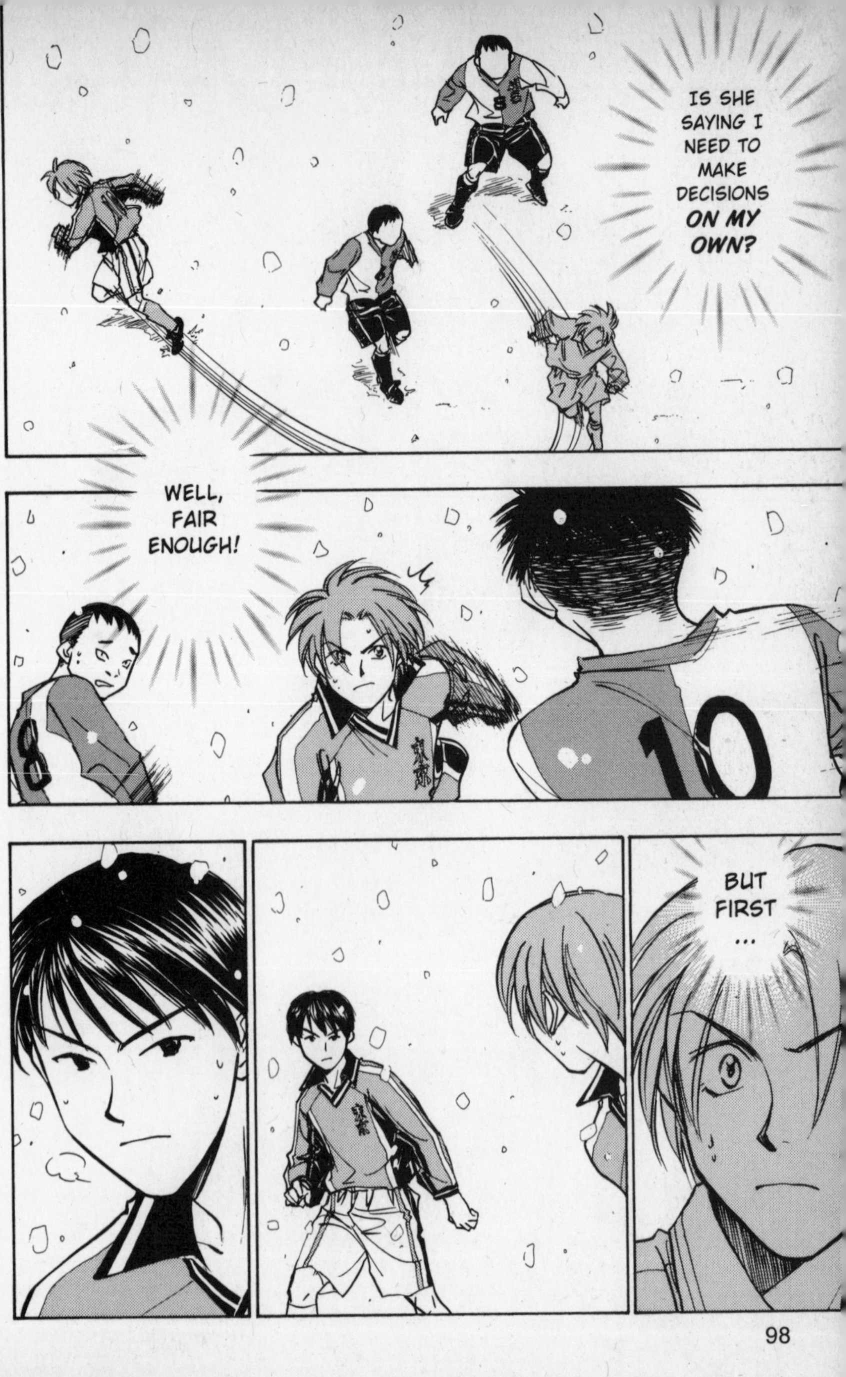
IS SHE SAYING I NEED TO MAKE DECISIONS ON MY OWN?
WELL, FAIR ENOUGH!
BUT FIRST ...

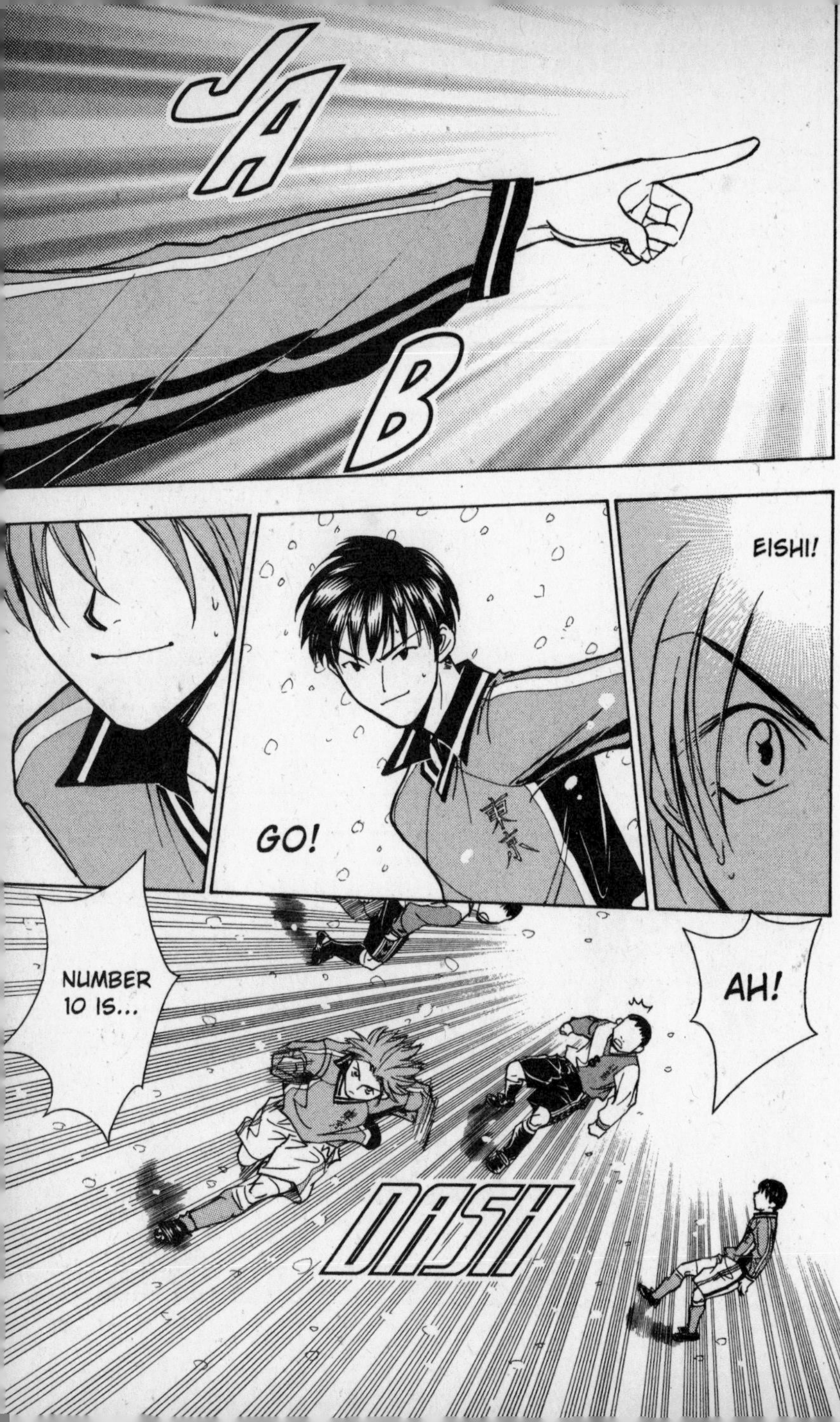
JAB
EISHI!
GO!
AH!
NUMBER 10 IS...
DASH

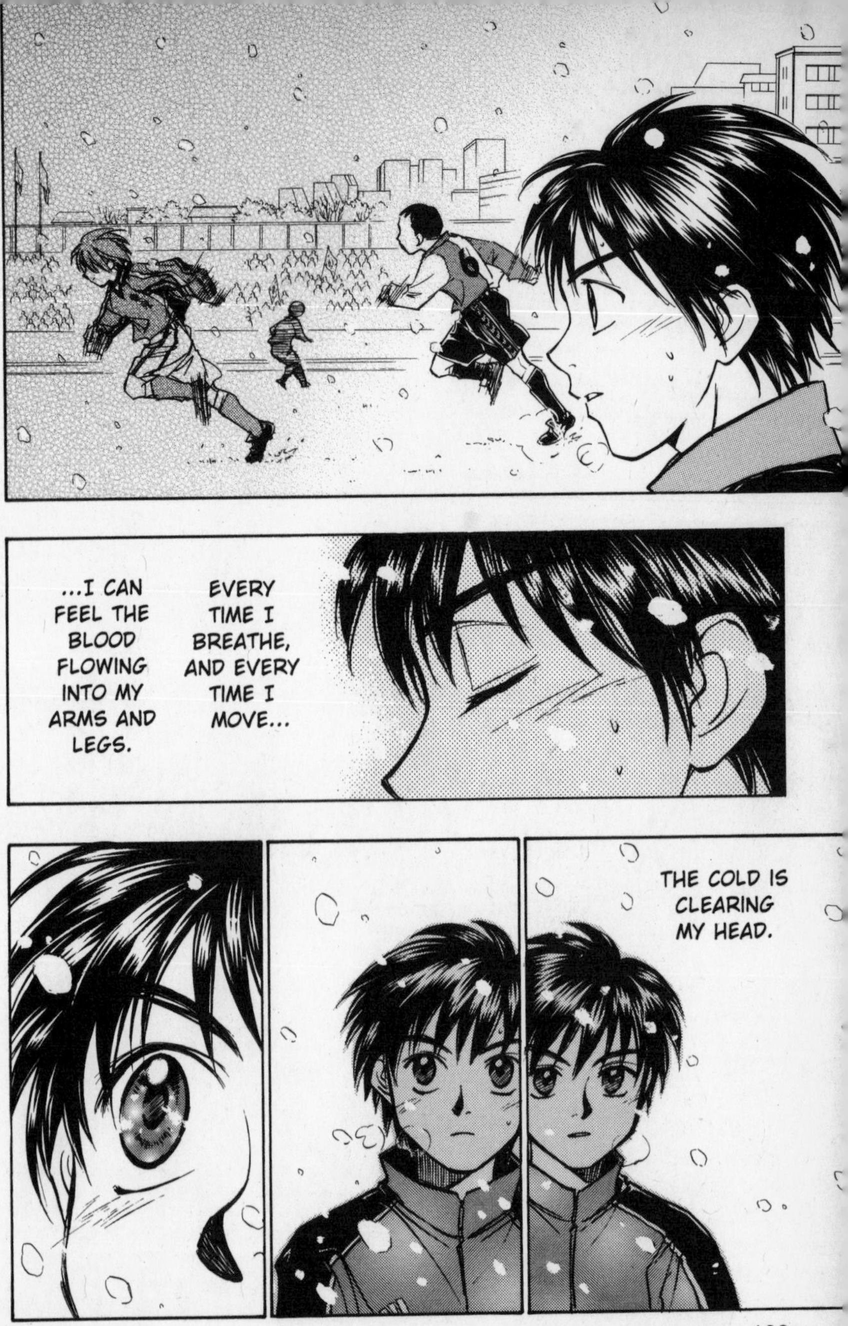
EVERY TIME I BREATHE, AND EVERY TIME I MOVE...
...I CAN FEEL THE BLOOD FLOWING INTO MY ARMS AND LEGS.
THE COLD IS CLEARING MY HEAD.

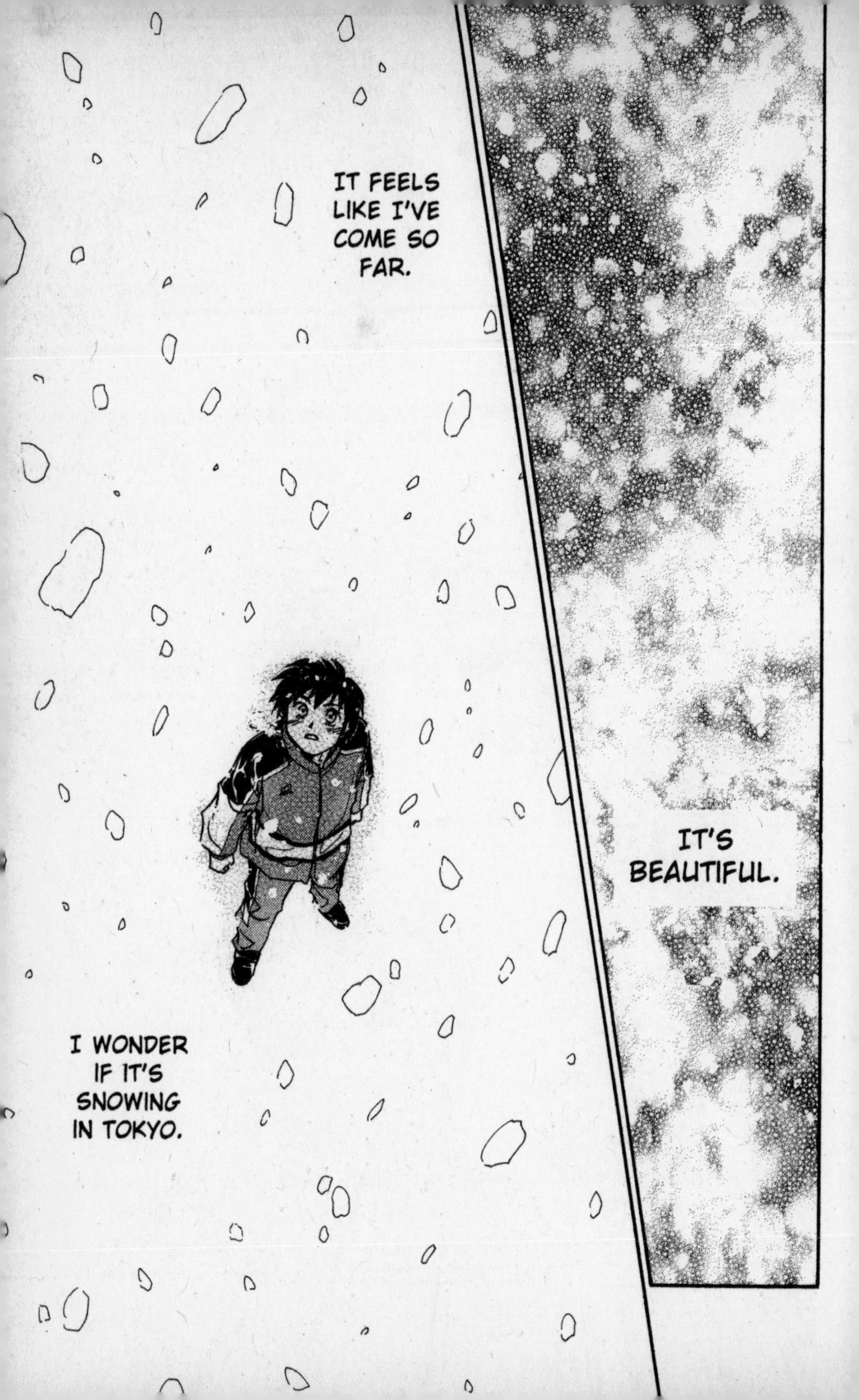
IT'S BEAUTIFUL.
IT FEELS LIKE I'VE COME SO FAR.
I WONDER IF IT'S SNOWING IN TOKYO.

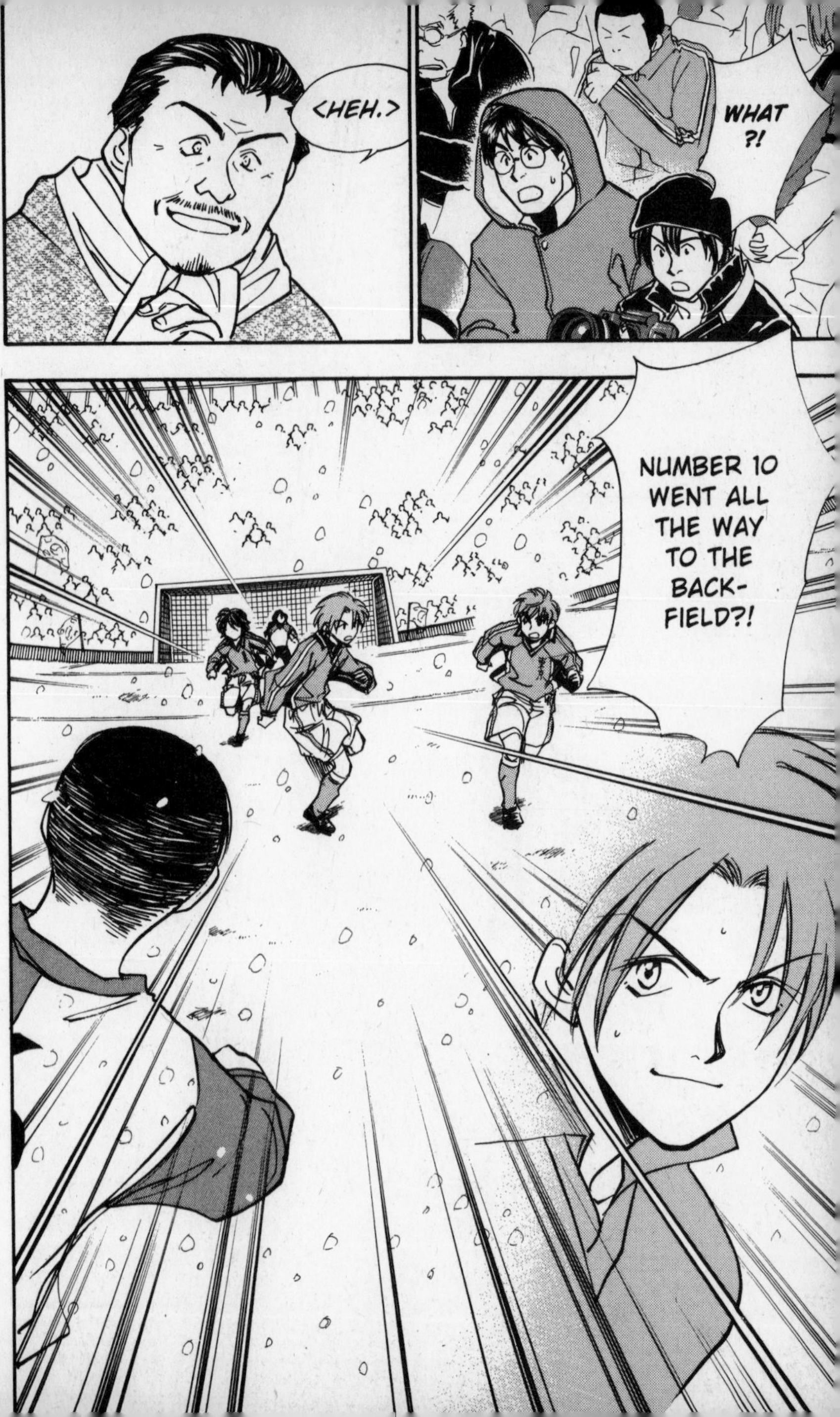
WHAT ?!
<HEH.>
NUMBER 10 WENT ALL THE WAY TO THE BACK-FIELD?!

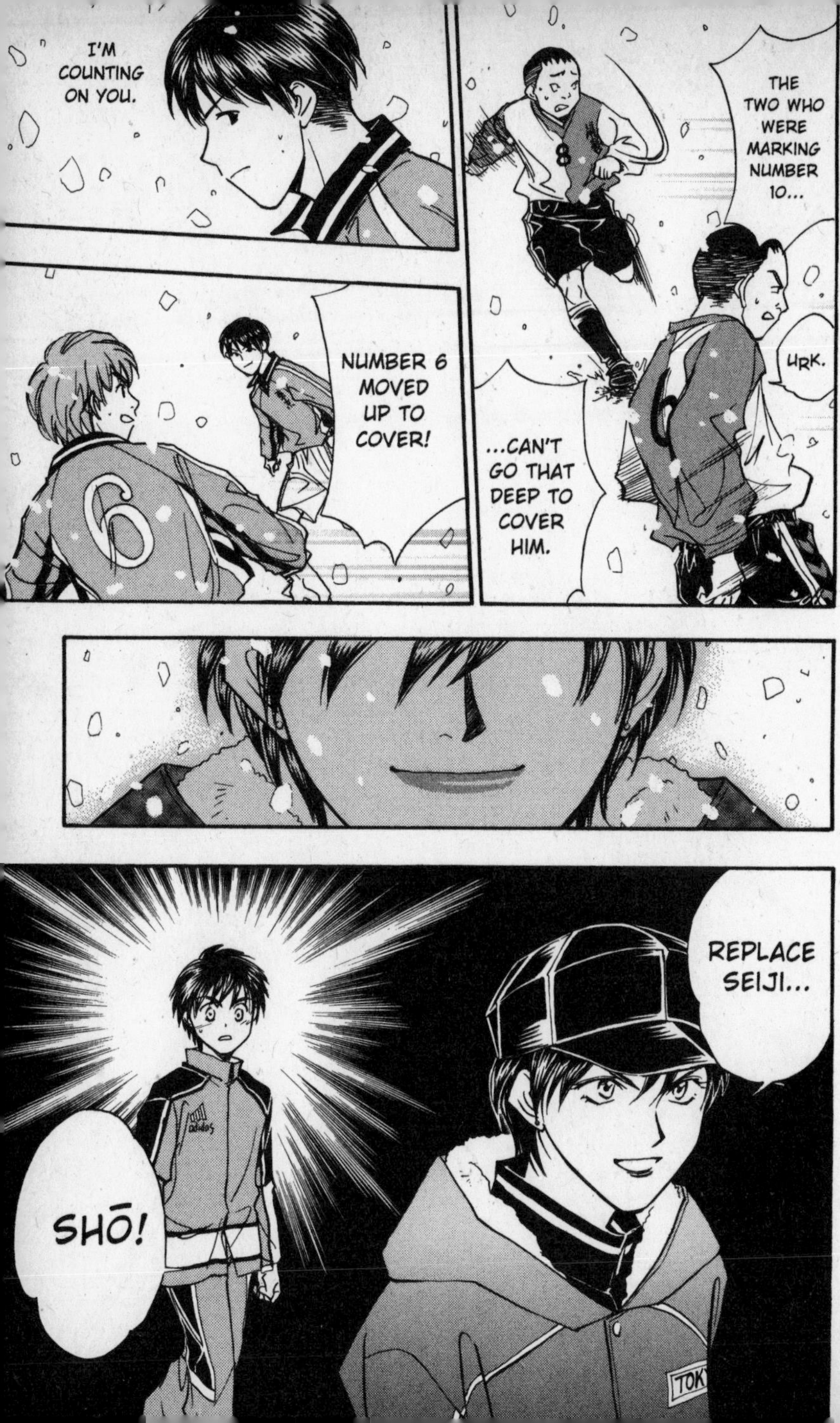
THE TWO WHO WERE MARKING NUMBER 10...
URK.
...CAN'T GO THAT DEEP TO COVER HIM.
I'M COUNTING ON YOU.
NUMBER 6 MOVED UP TO COVER!
REPLACE SEIJI...
SHŌ!

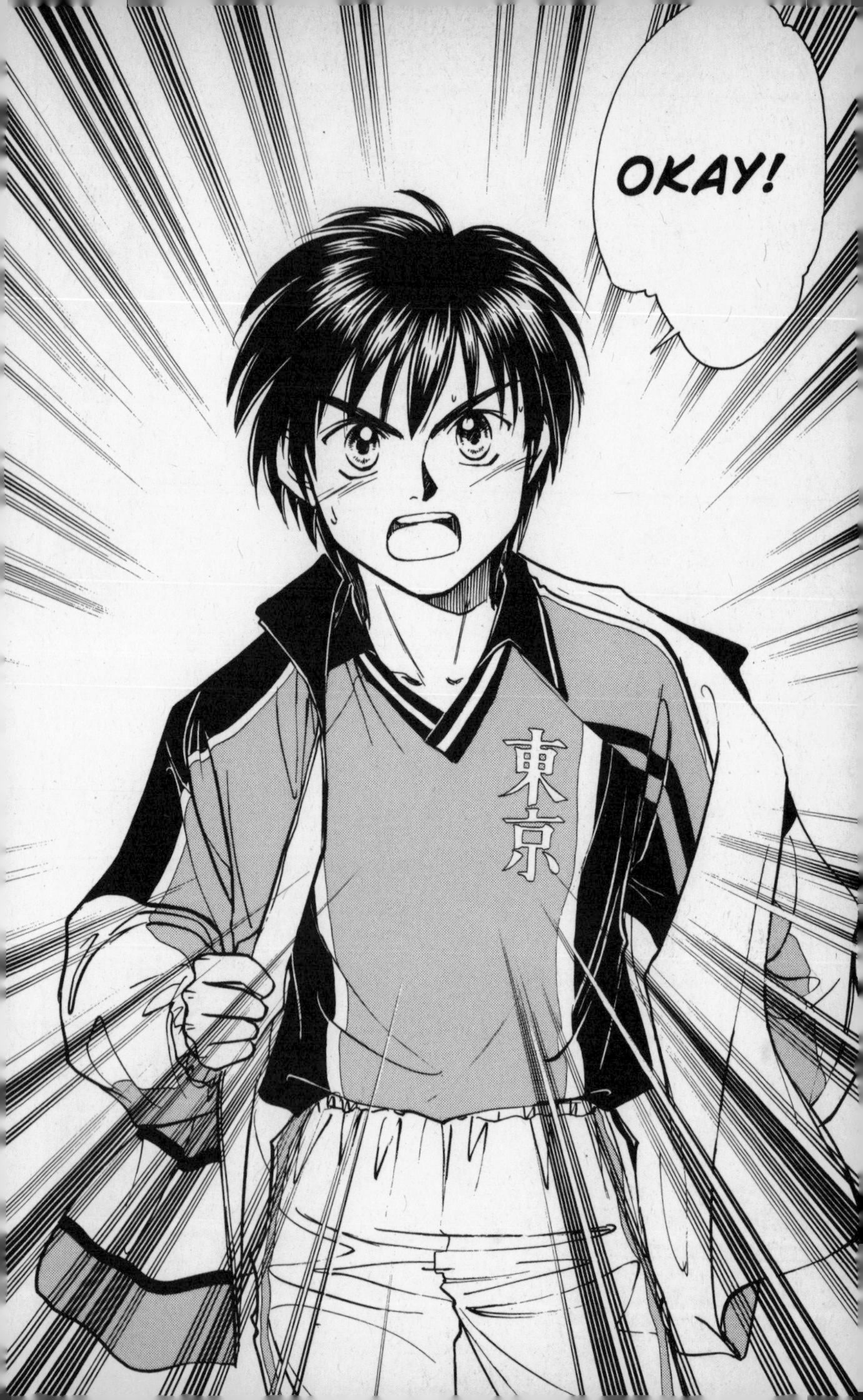
OKAY!
東京

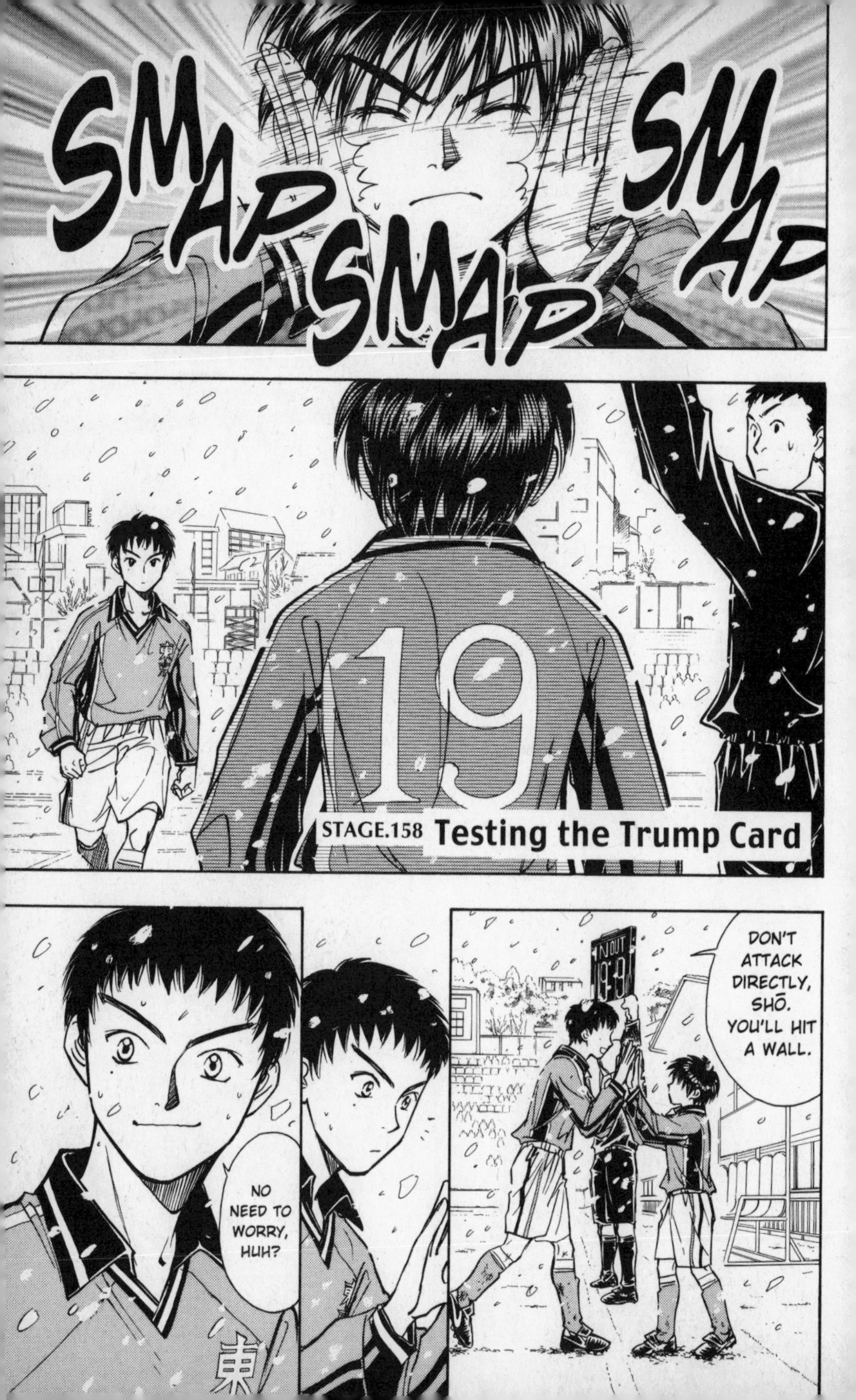
SMAP
SMAP
SMAP
STAGE.158 Testing the Trump Card
DON'T ATTACK DIRECTLY, SHŌ. YOU'LL HIT A WALL.
NO NEED TO WORRY, HUH?

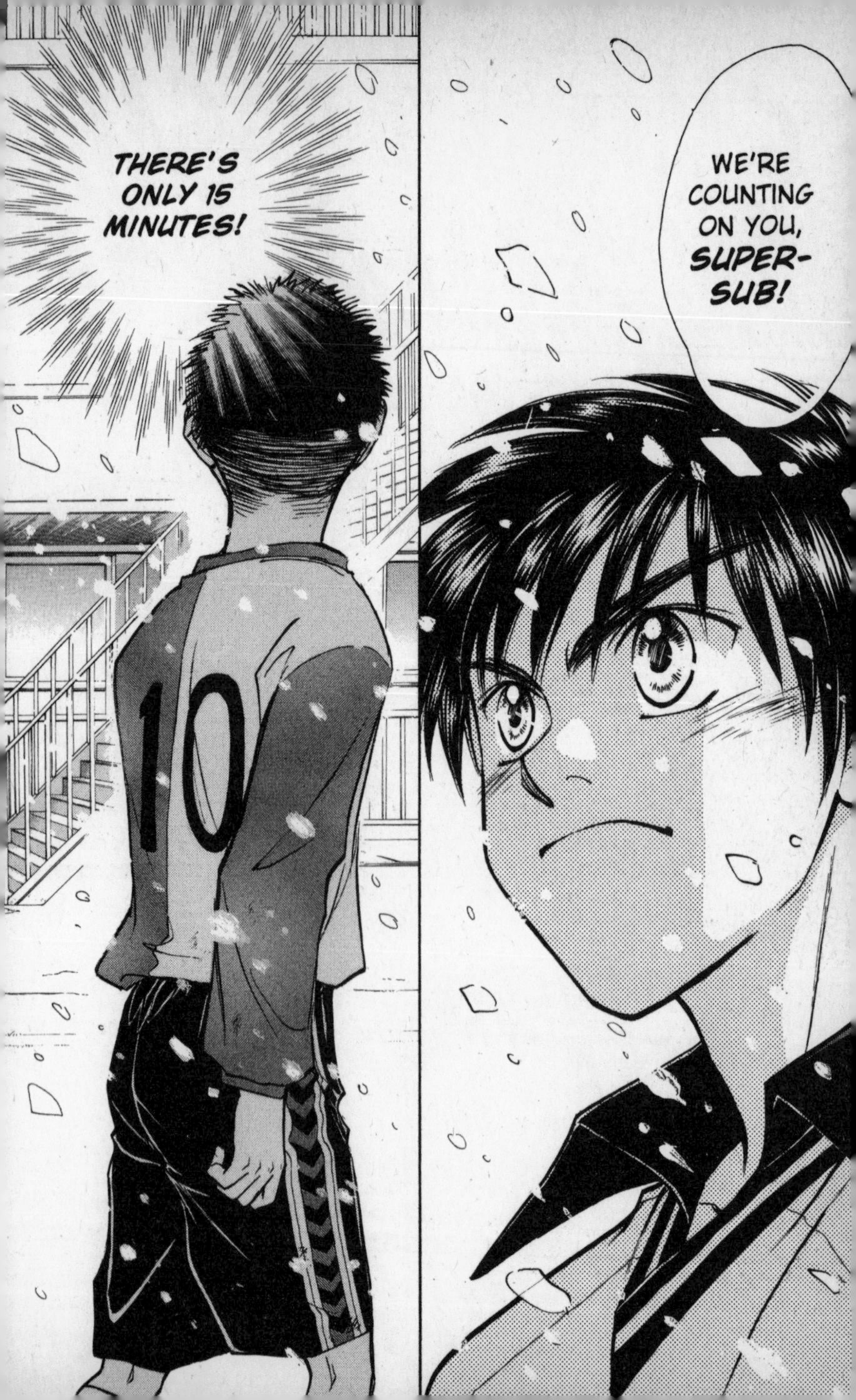
WE'RE COUNTING ON YOU, SUPER-SUB!
THERE'S ONLY 15 MINUTES!

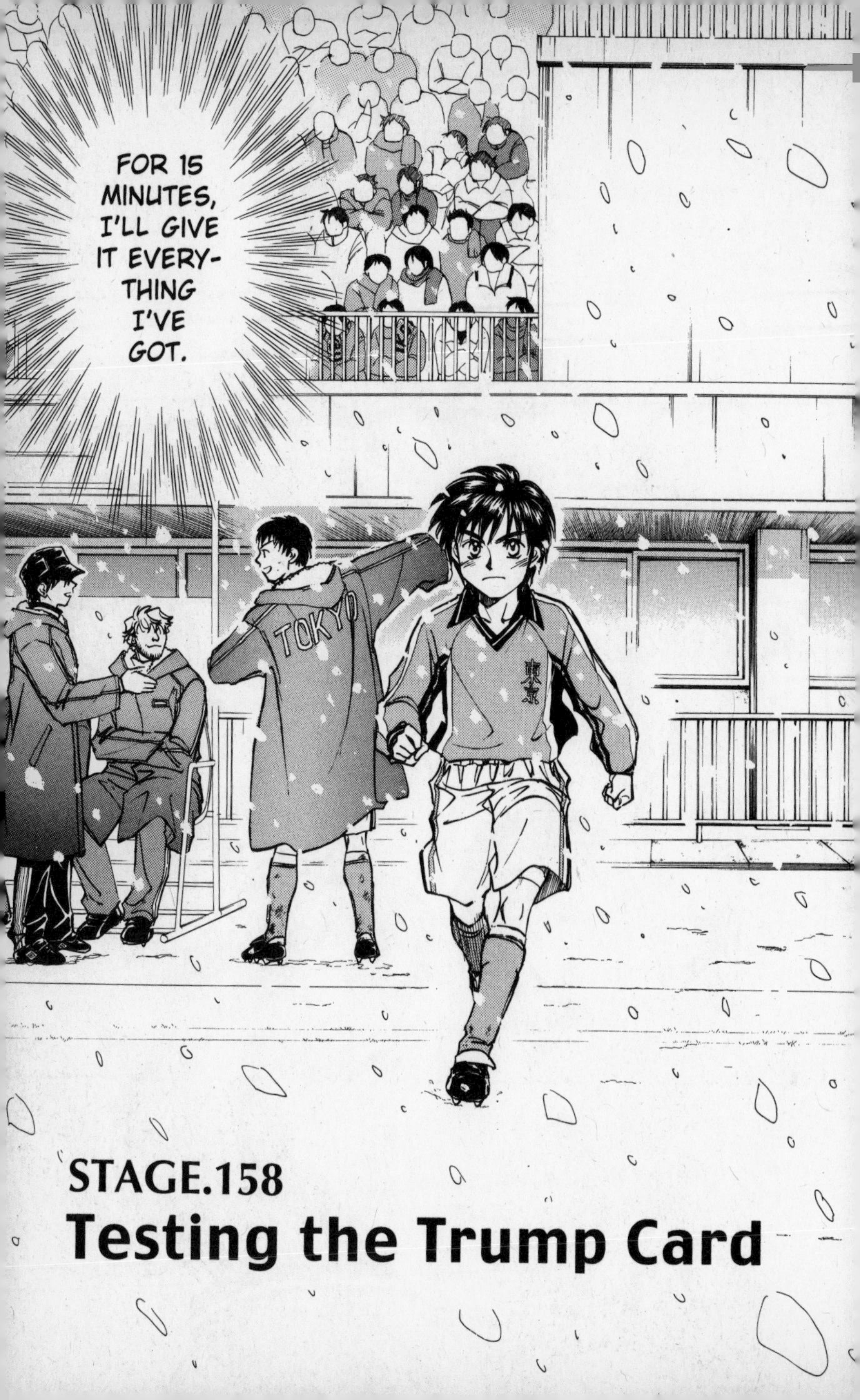
FOR 15 MINUTES, I'LL GIVE IT EVERYTHING I'VE GOT.

STAGE.158
Testing the Trump Card

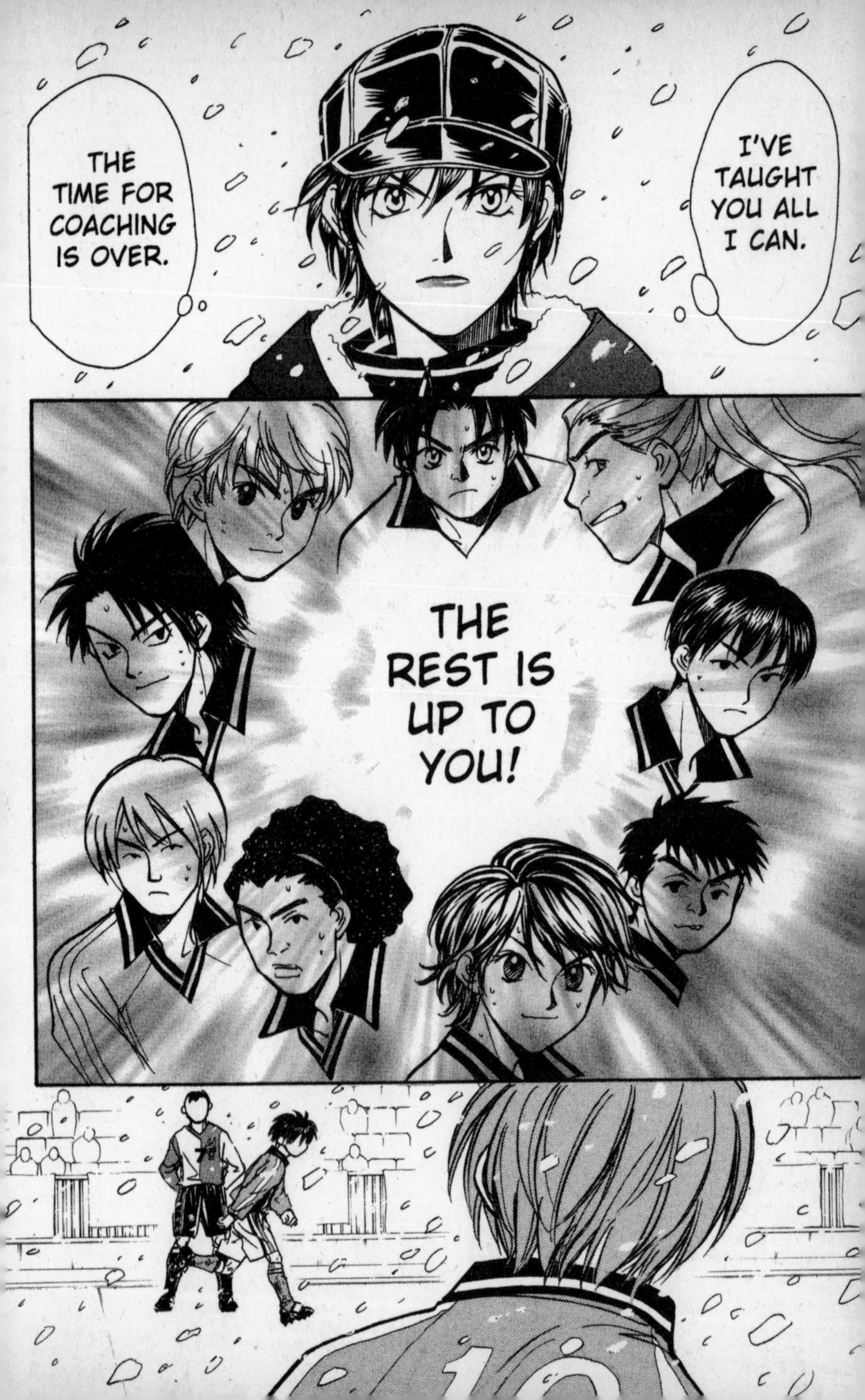
I'VE TAUGHT YOU ALL I CAN.
THE TIME FOR COACHING IS OVER.
THE REST IS UP TO YOU!

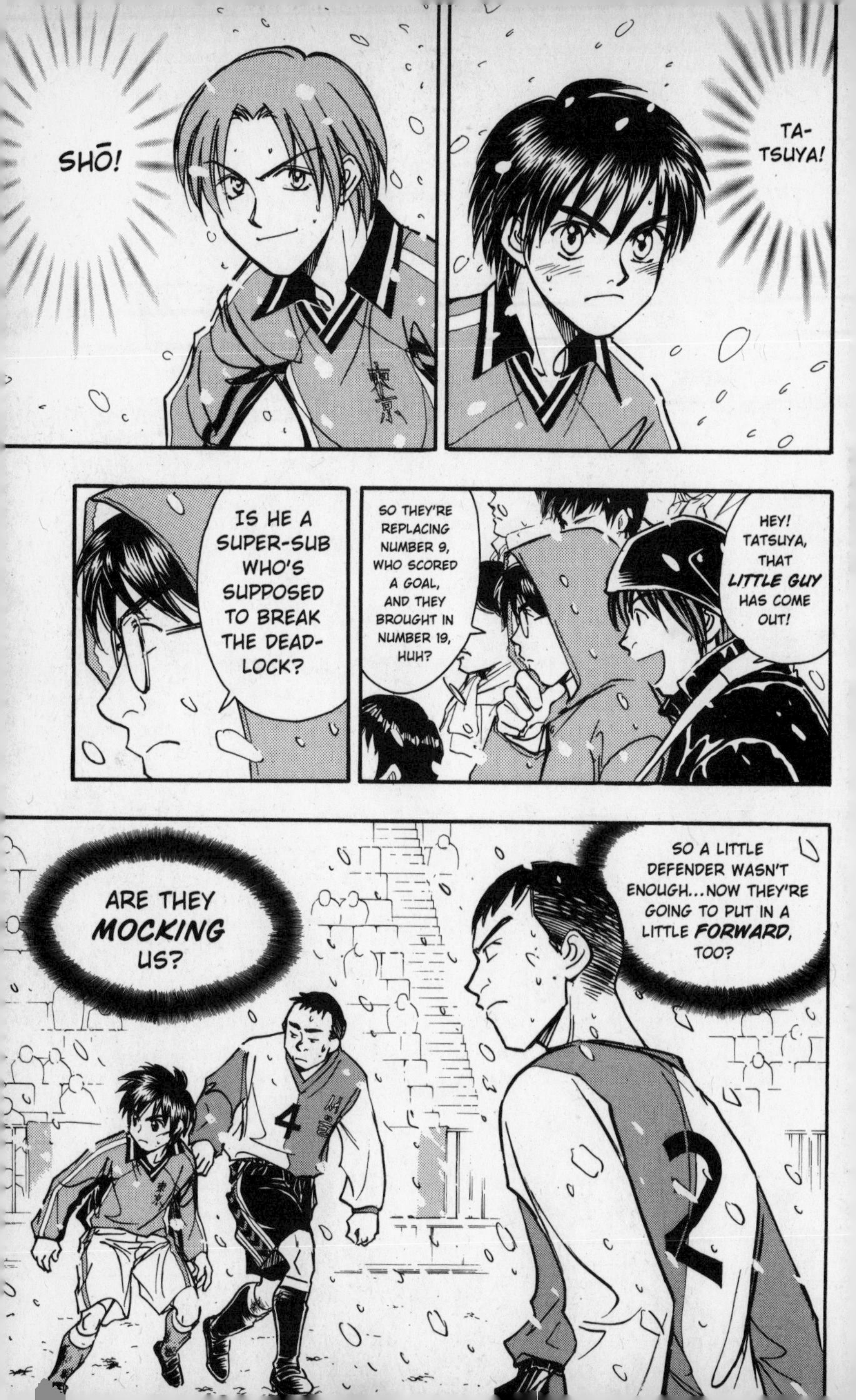
TA-TSUYA!
SHŌ!
HEY! TATSUYA, THAT LITTLE GUY HAS COME OUT!
SO THEY'RE REPLACING NUMBER 9, WHO SCORED A GOAL, AND THEY BROUGHT IN NUMBER 19, HUH?
IS HE A SUPER-SUB WHO'S SUPPOSED TO BREAK THE DEAD-LOCK?
SO A LITTLE DEFENDER WASN'T ENOUGH...NOW THEY'RE GOING TO PUT IN A LITTLE FORWARD, TOO?
ARE THEY MOCKING US?

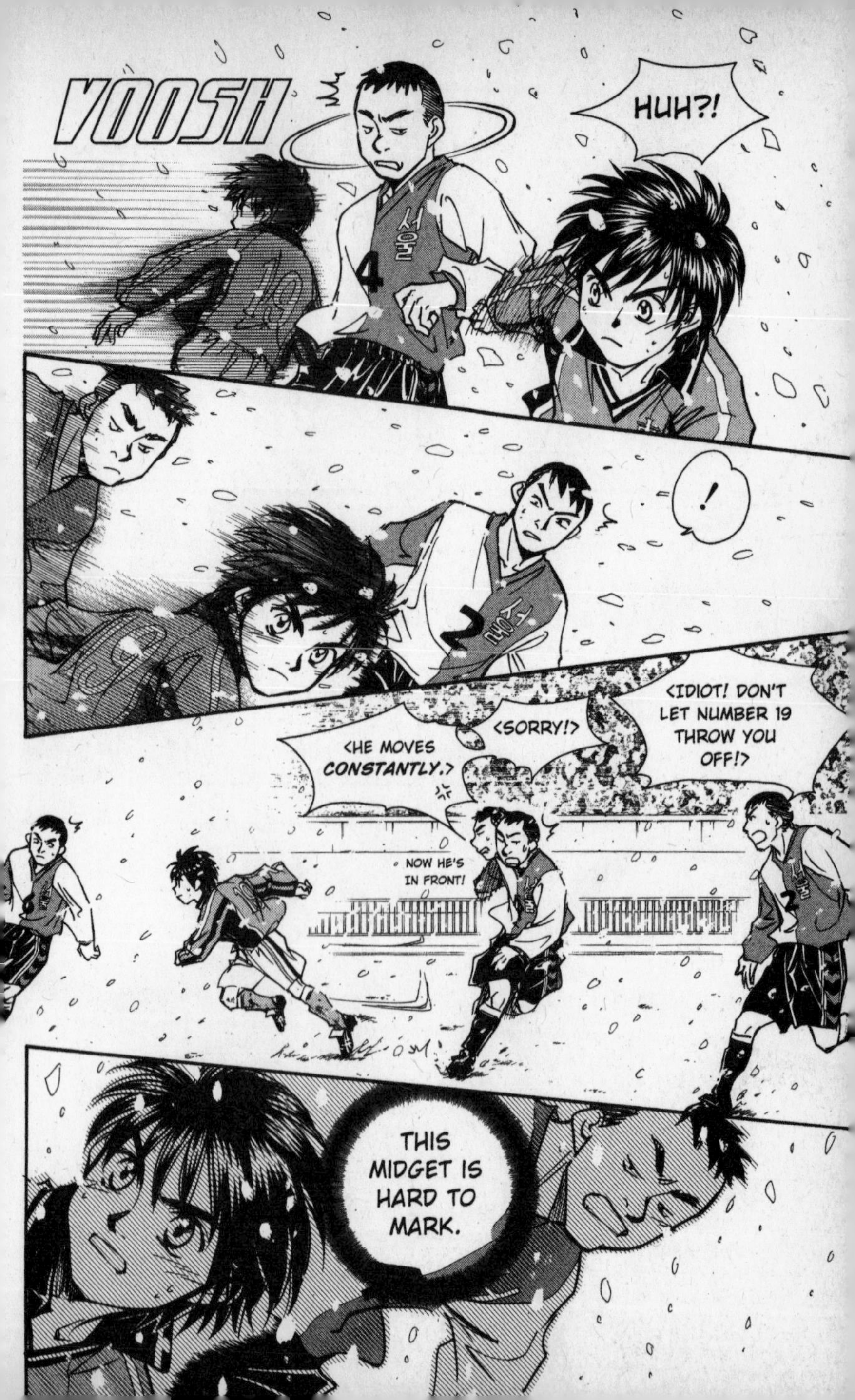
HUH?!
VOOSH
!
<IDIOT! DON'T LET NUMBER 19 THROW YOU OFF!>
<SORRY!>
<HE MOVES CONSTANTLY.>
NOW HE'S IN FRONT!
THIS MIDGET IS HARD TO MARK.

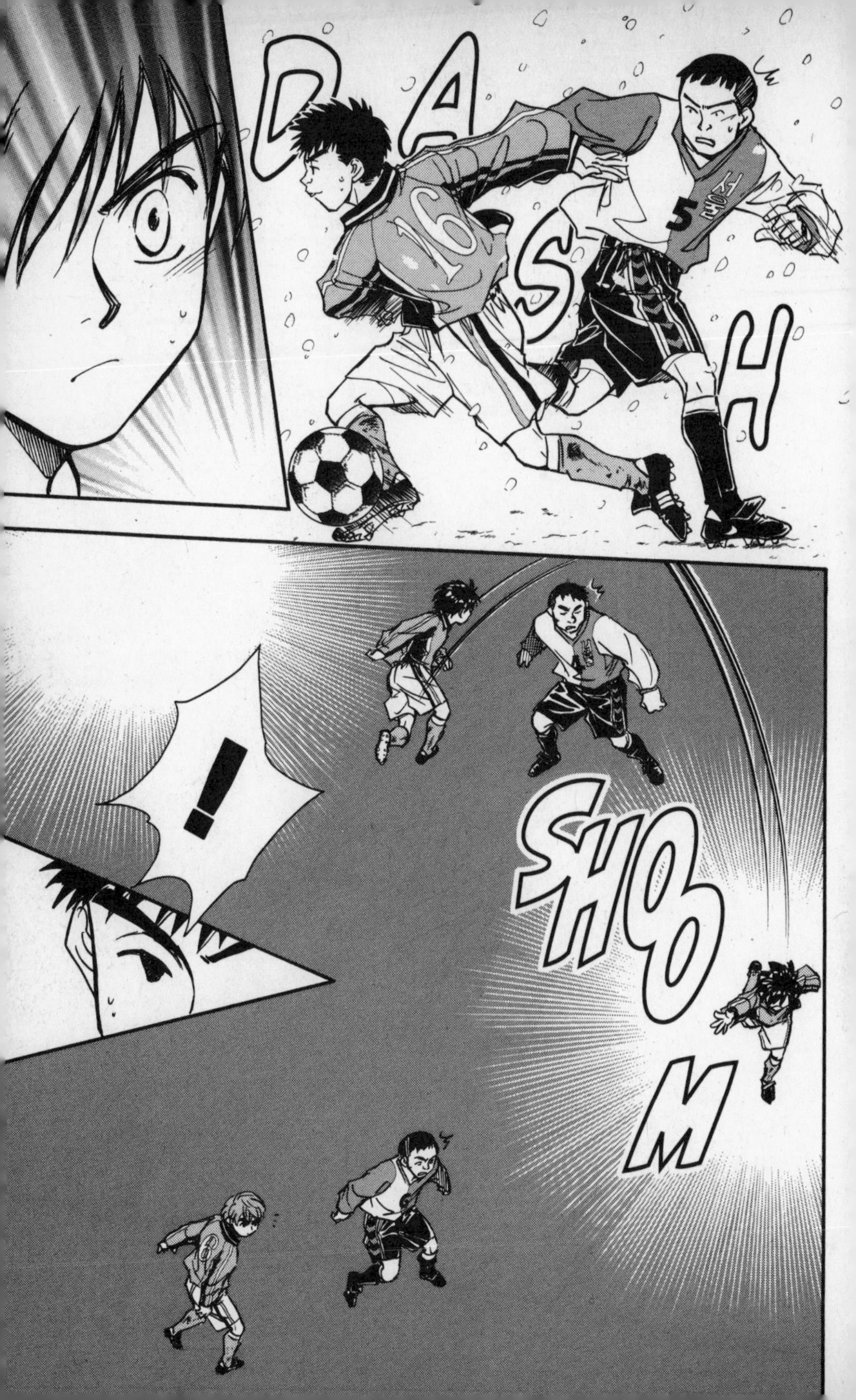
DASH
SHOOM
!

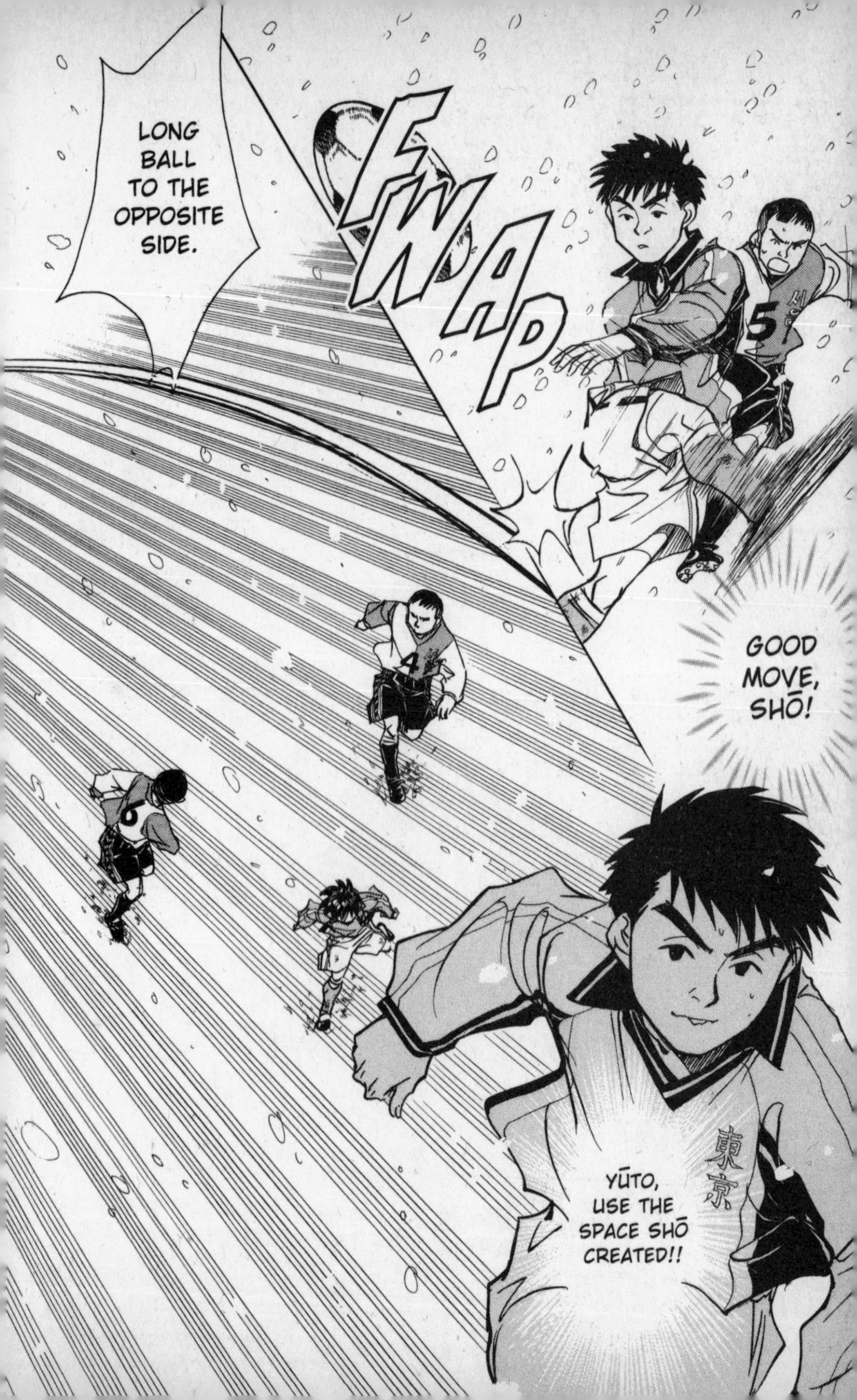
FWAP
LONG BALL TO THE OPPOSITE SIDE.
GOOD MOVE, SHŌ!
YŪTO, USE THE SPACE SHŌ CREATED!!

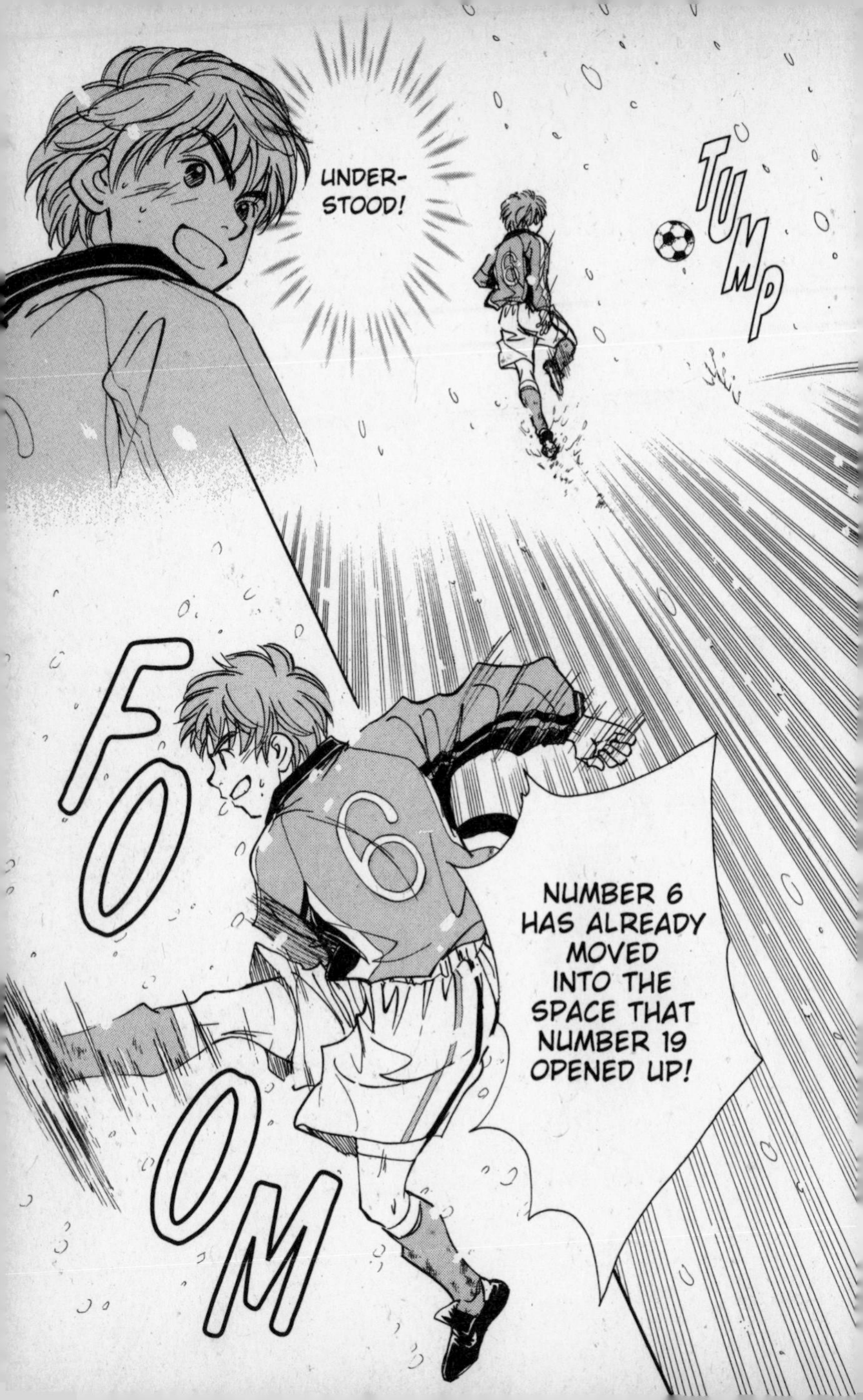
TUMP
UNDER-STOOD!
NUMBER 6 HAS ALREADY MOVED INTO THE SPACE THAT NUMBER 19 OPENED UP!
FOOM

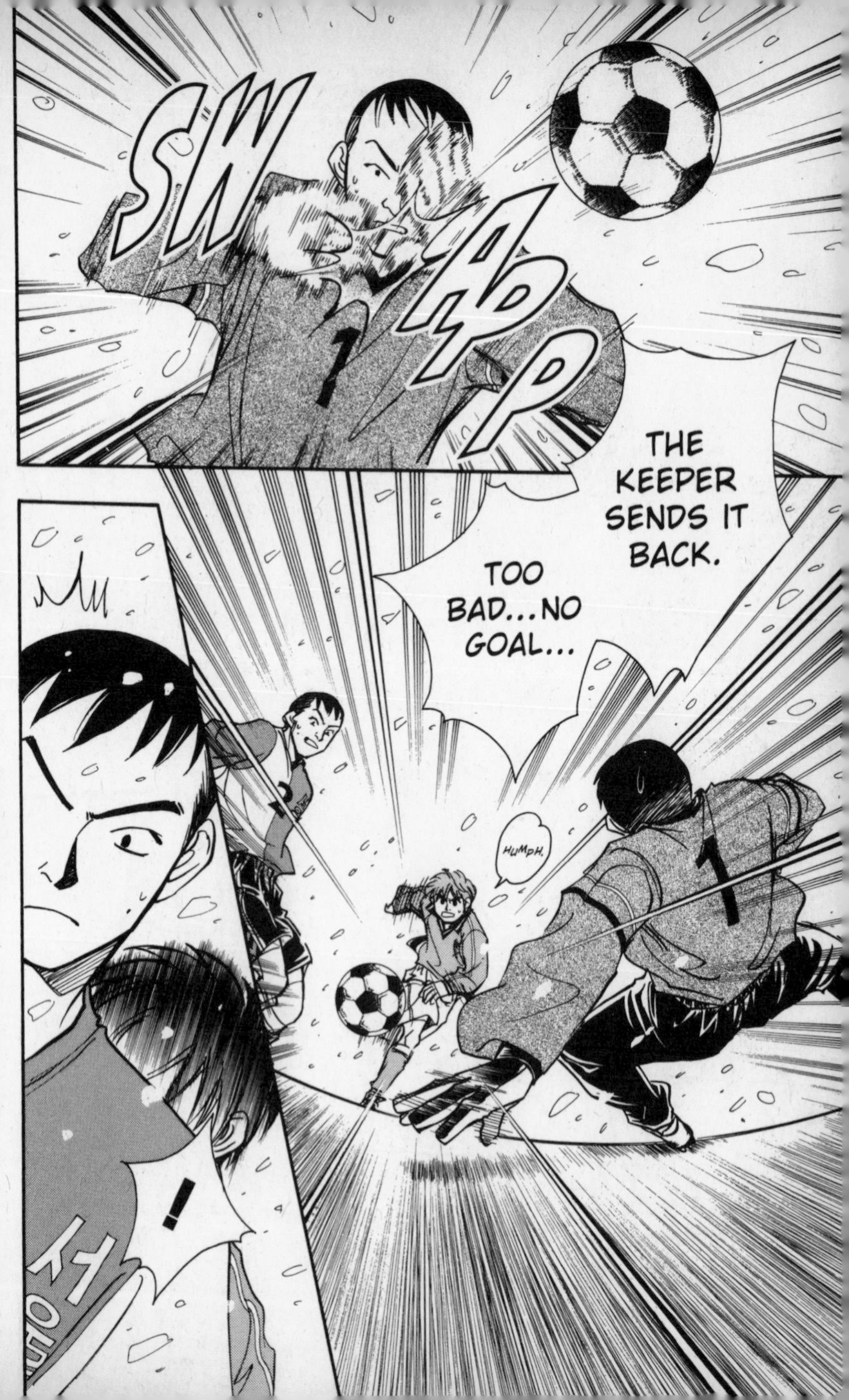
SHWAPP
THE KEEPER SENDS IT BACK.
TOO BAD...NO GOAL...
HUMPH.
!

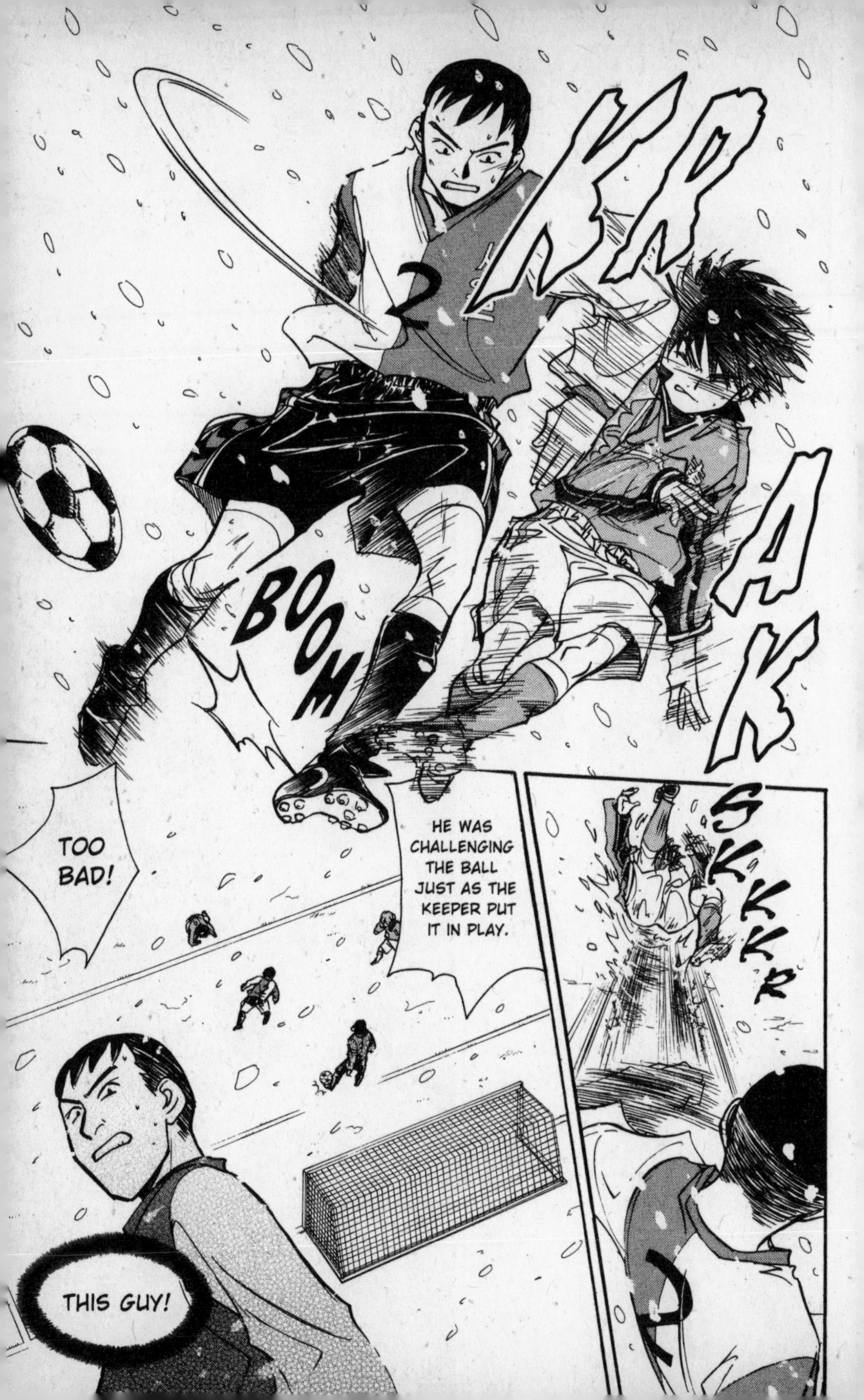
KRAK
BOOM
SKKKR
HE WAS CHALLENGING THE BALL JUST AS THE KEEPER PUT IT IN PLAY.
TOO BAD!
THIS GUY!

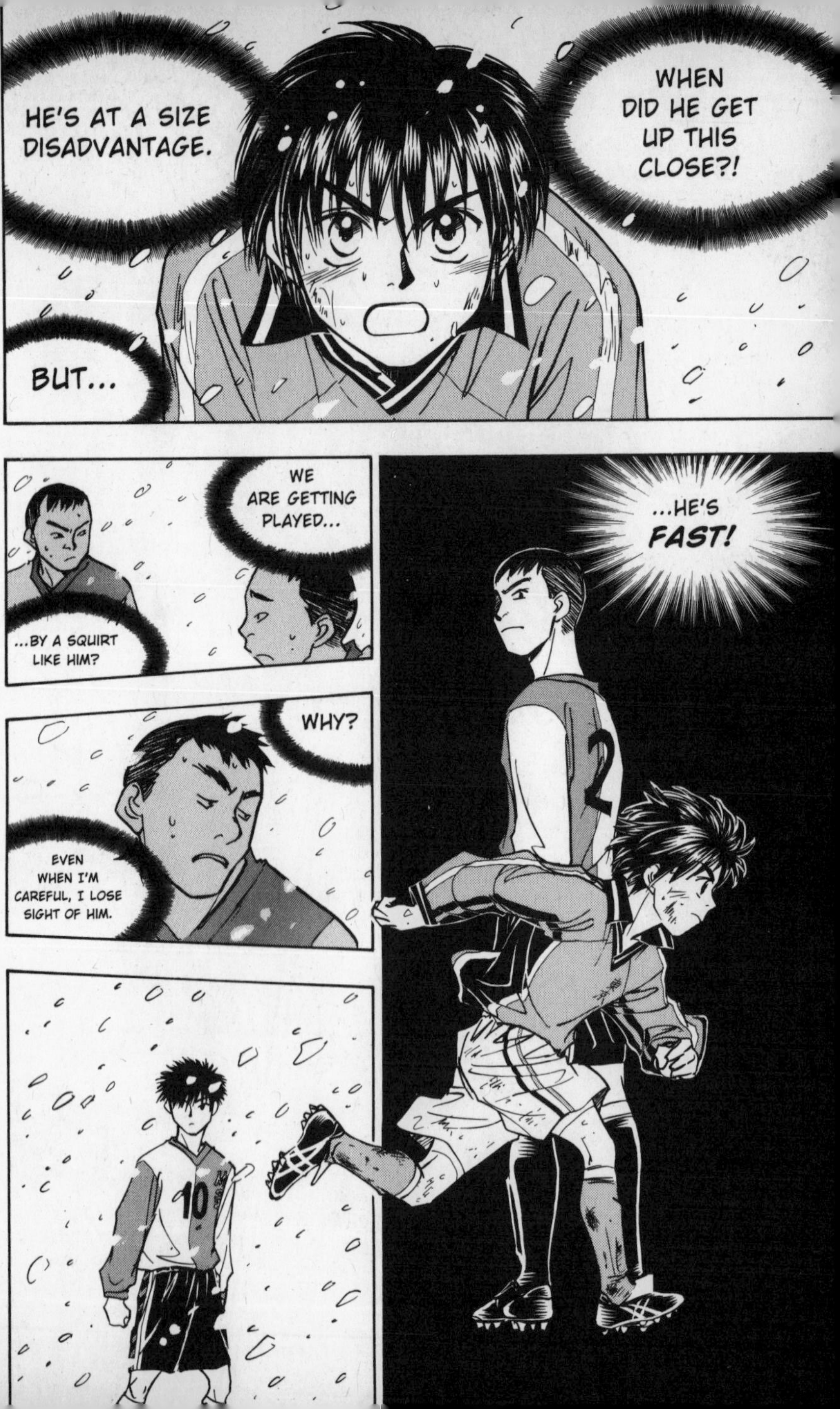
WHEN DID HE GET UP THIS CLOSE?!
HE'S AT A SIZE DISADVANTAGE.
BUT...
...HE'S FAST!
WE ARE GETTING PLAYED...
...BY A SQUIRT LIKE HIM?
WHY?
EVEN WHEN I'M CAREFUL, I LOSE SIGHT OF HIM.

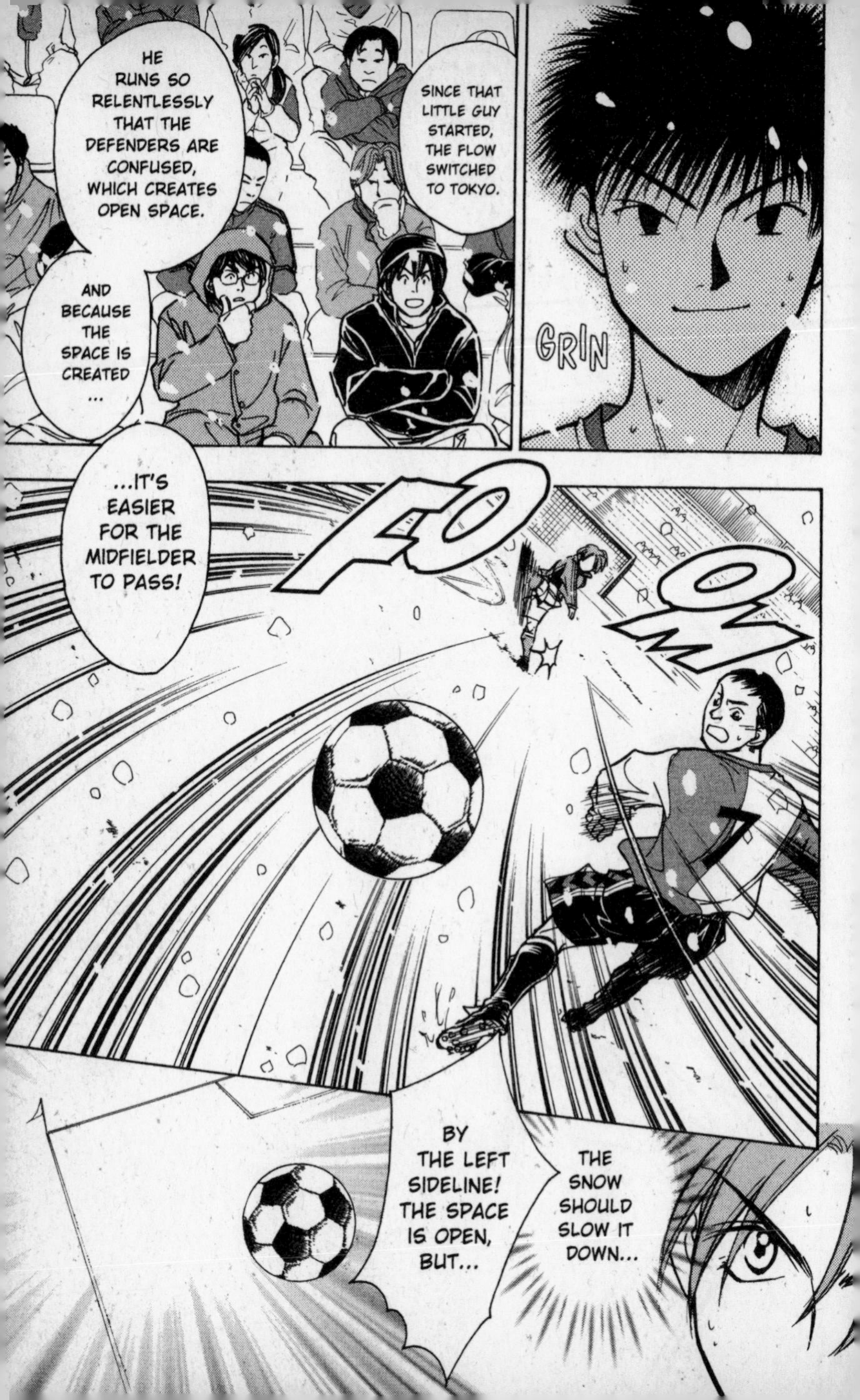
GRIN
SINCE THAT LITTLE GUY STARTED, THE FLOW SWITCHED TO TOKYO.
HE RUNS SO RELENTLESSLY THAT THE DEFENDERS ARE CONFUSED, WHICH CREATES OPEN SPACE.
AND BECAUSE THE SPACE IS CREATED ...
...IT'S EASIER FOR THE MIDFIELDER TO PASS!
FOOM
BY THE LEFT SIDELINE! THE SPACE IS OPEN, BUT...
THE SNOW SHOULD SLOW IT DOWN...

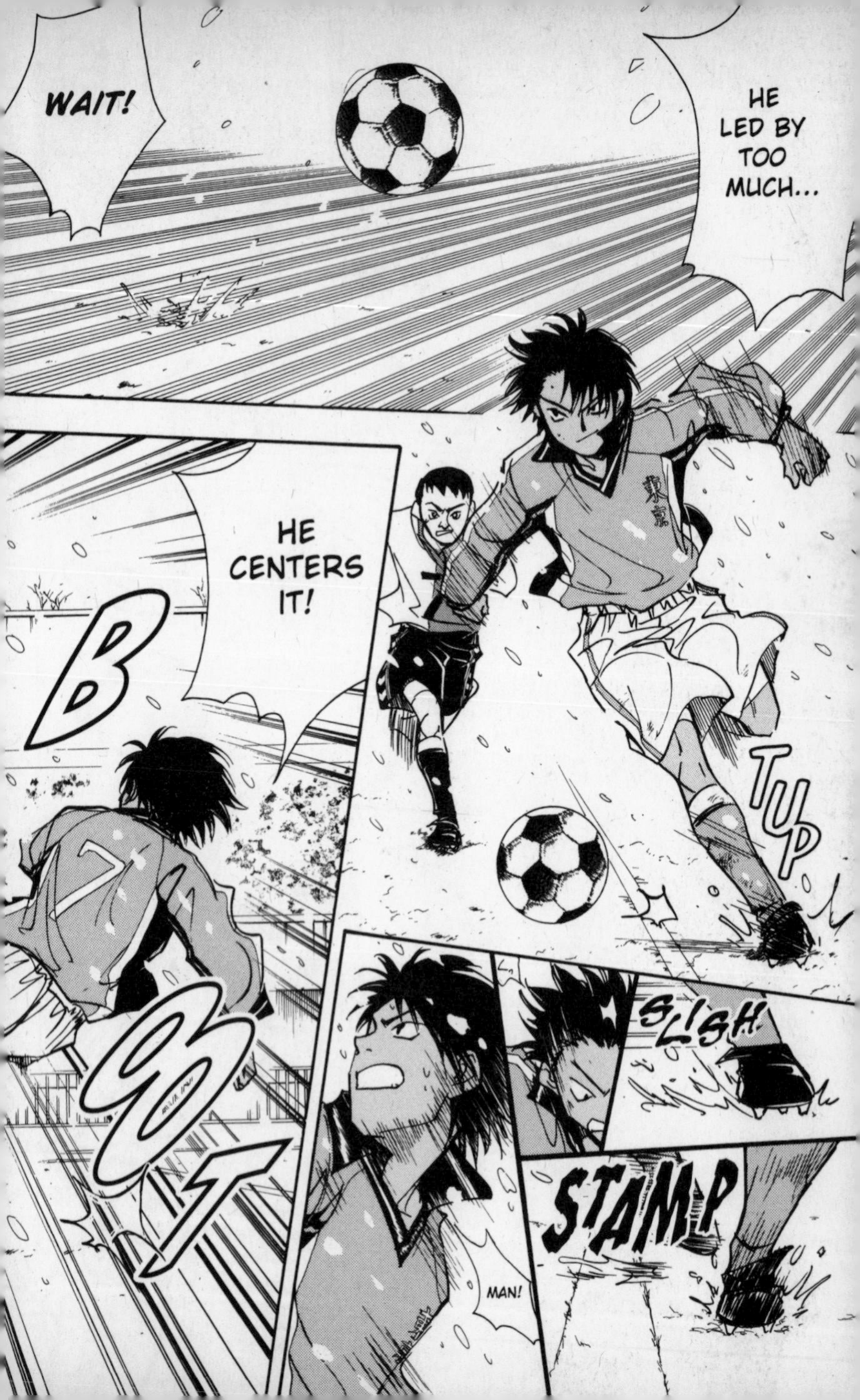
HE LED BY TOO MUCH...
WAIT!
TUP
HE CENTERS IT!
SLISH
STAMP
MAN!

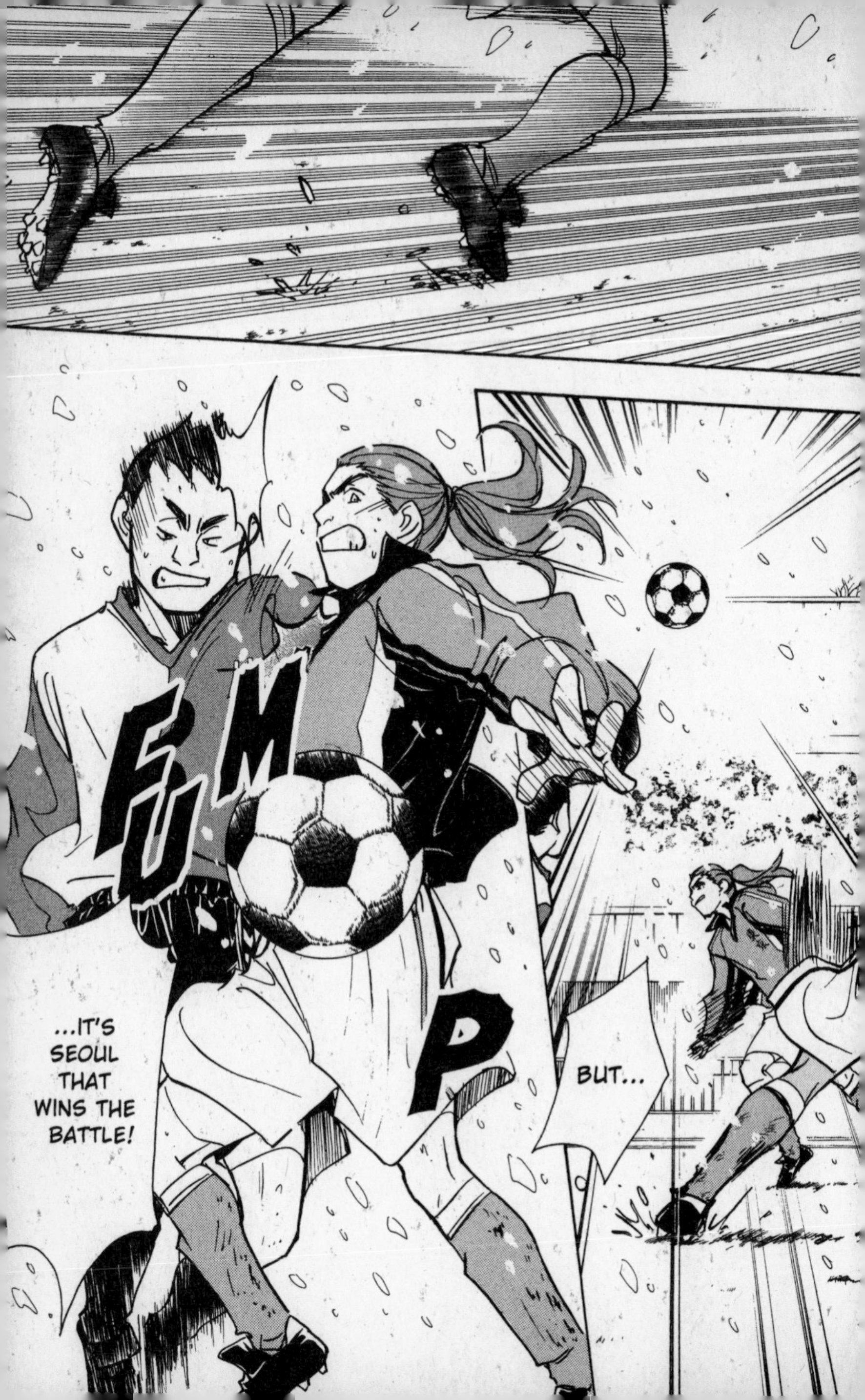
BUT...
...IT'S SEOUL THAT WINS THE BATTLE!

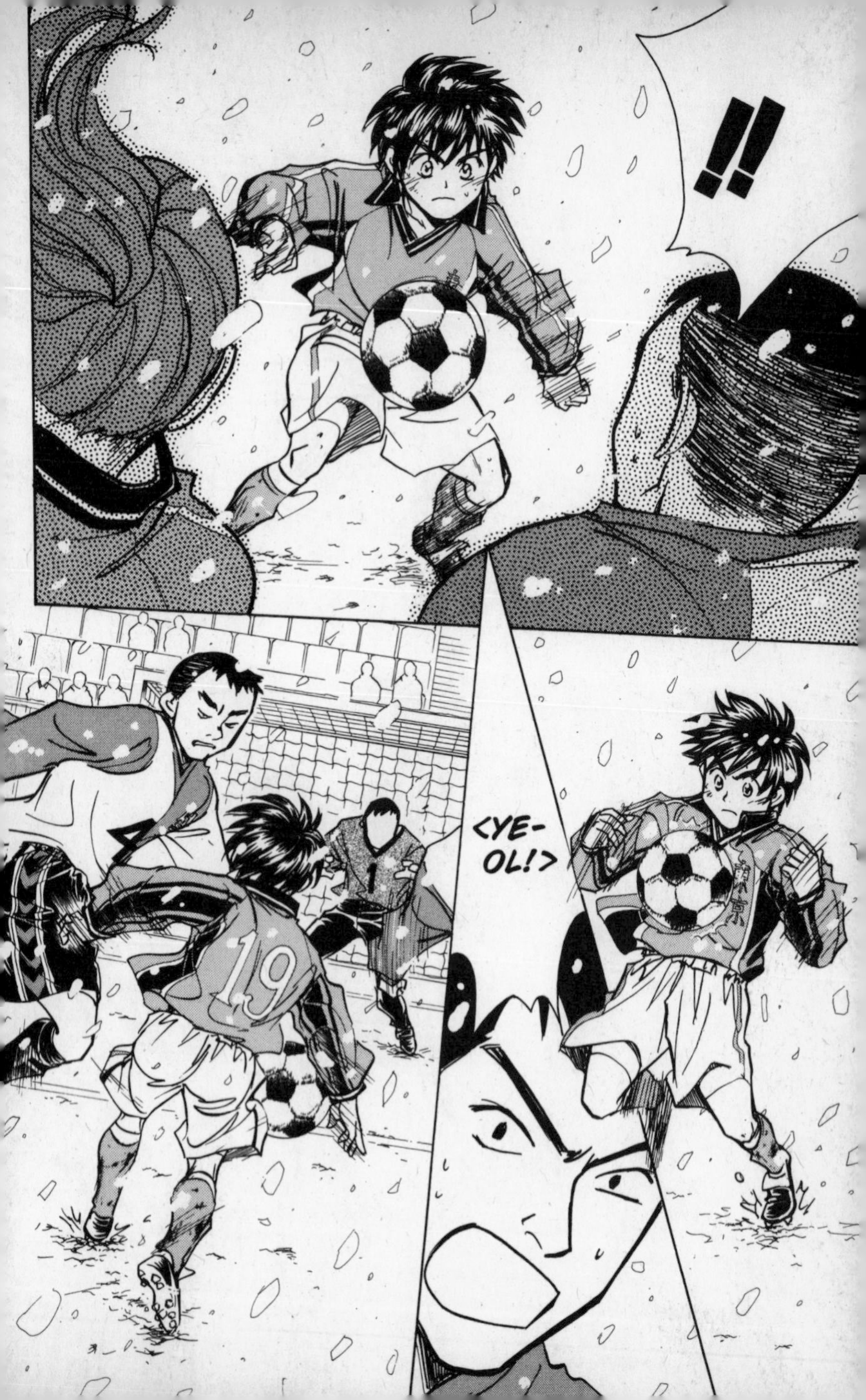
!!
<YE-
OL!>

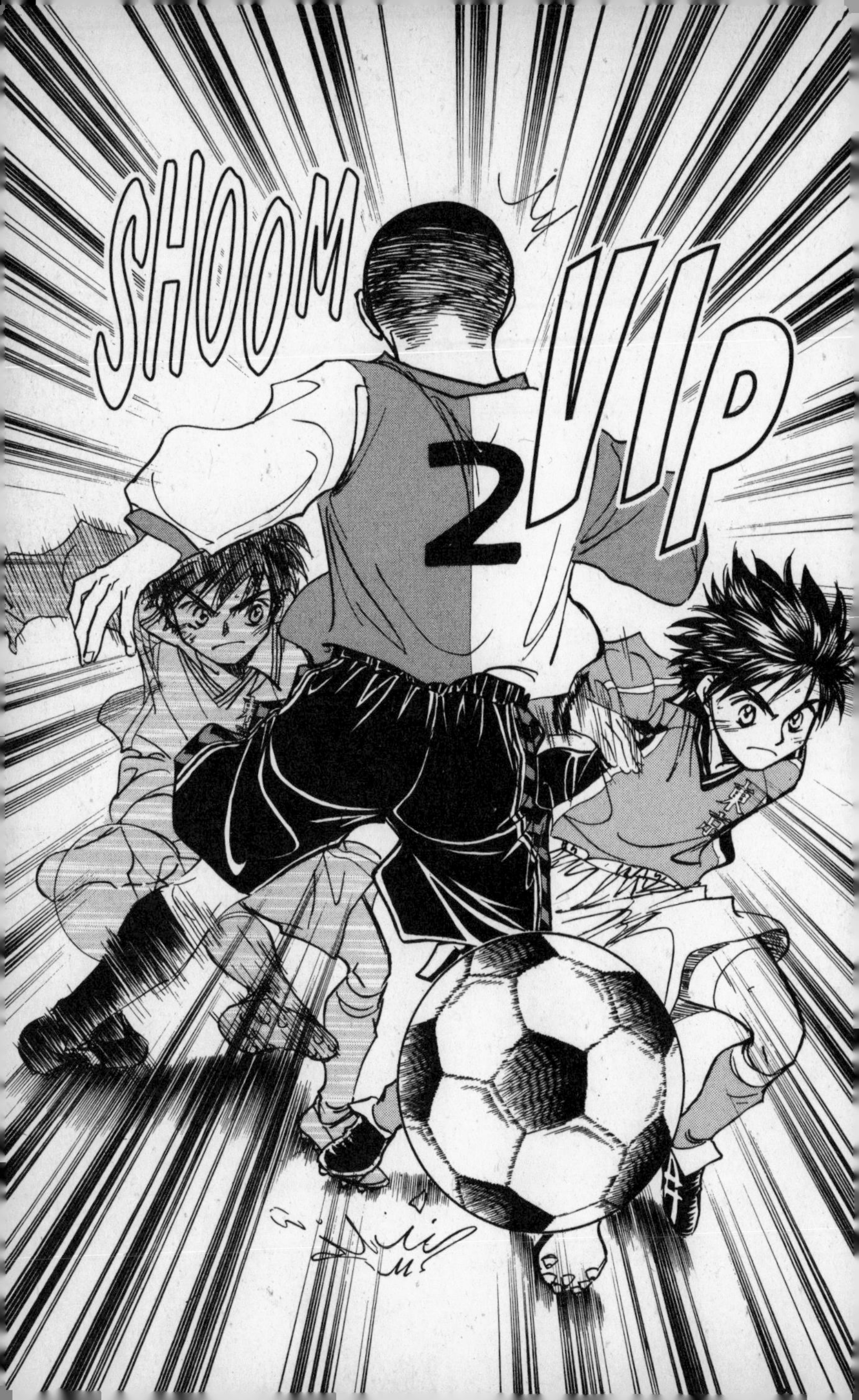
SHOOM
VIP

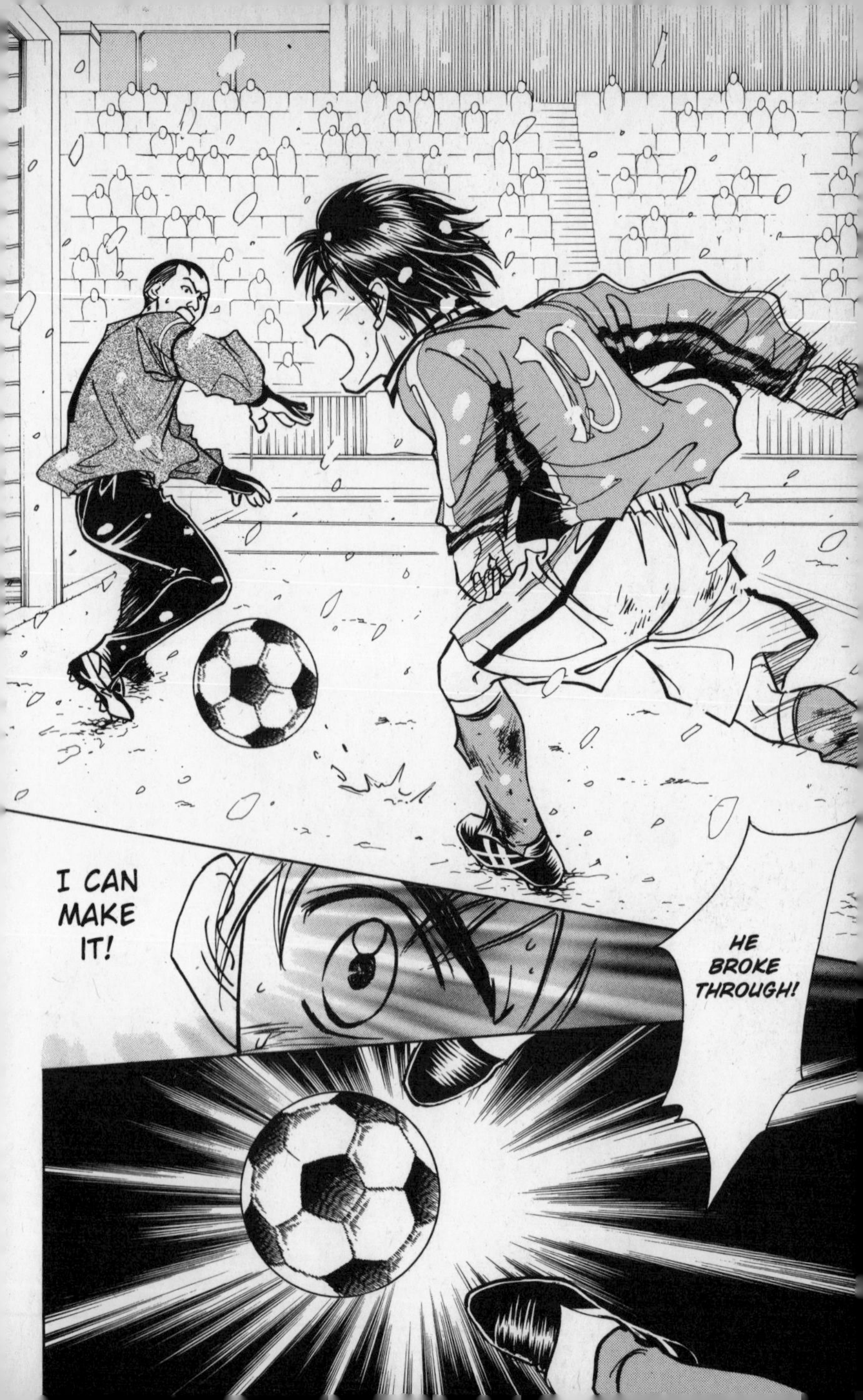
HE BROKE THROUGH!
I CAN MAKE IT!

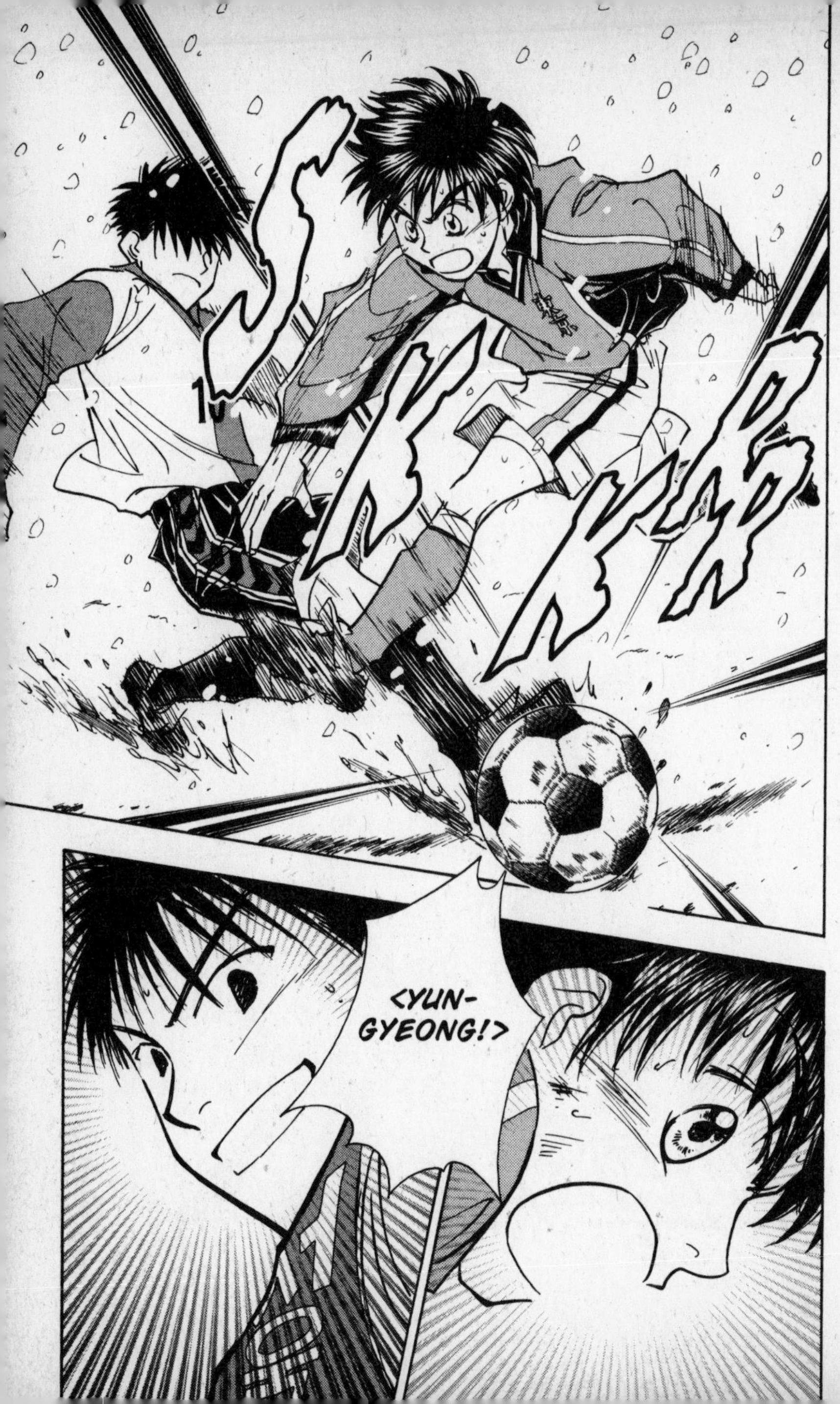
<YUN-
GYEONG!>

WHISTLE!™

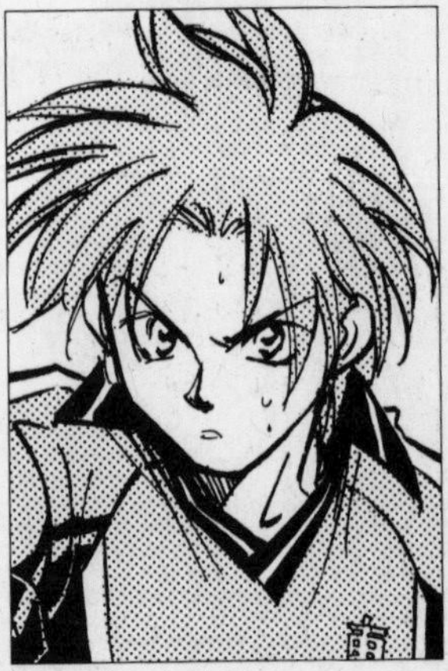

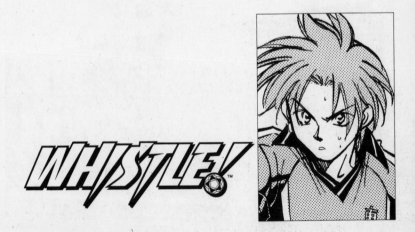

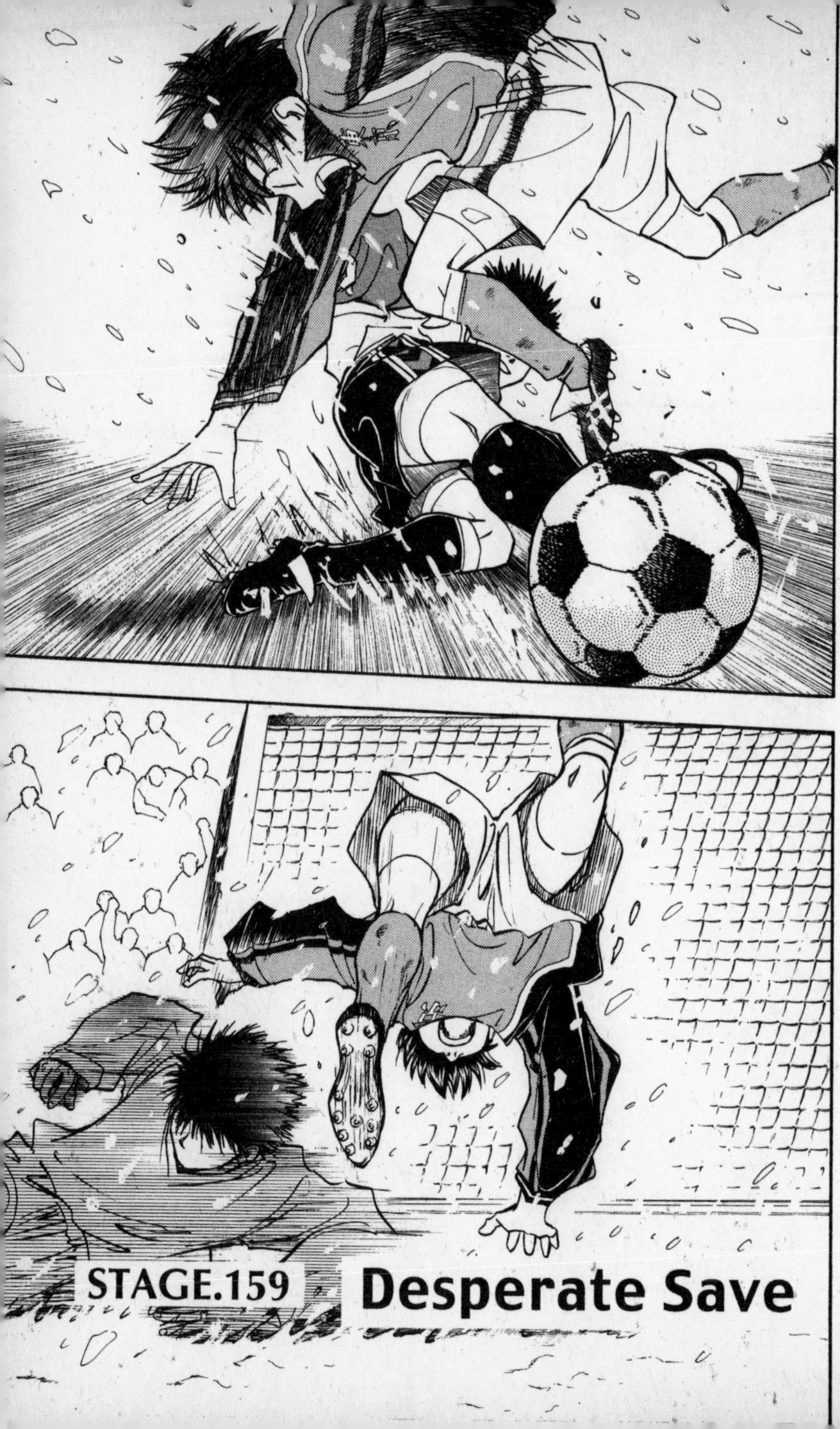
STAGE.159
Desperate Save

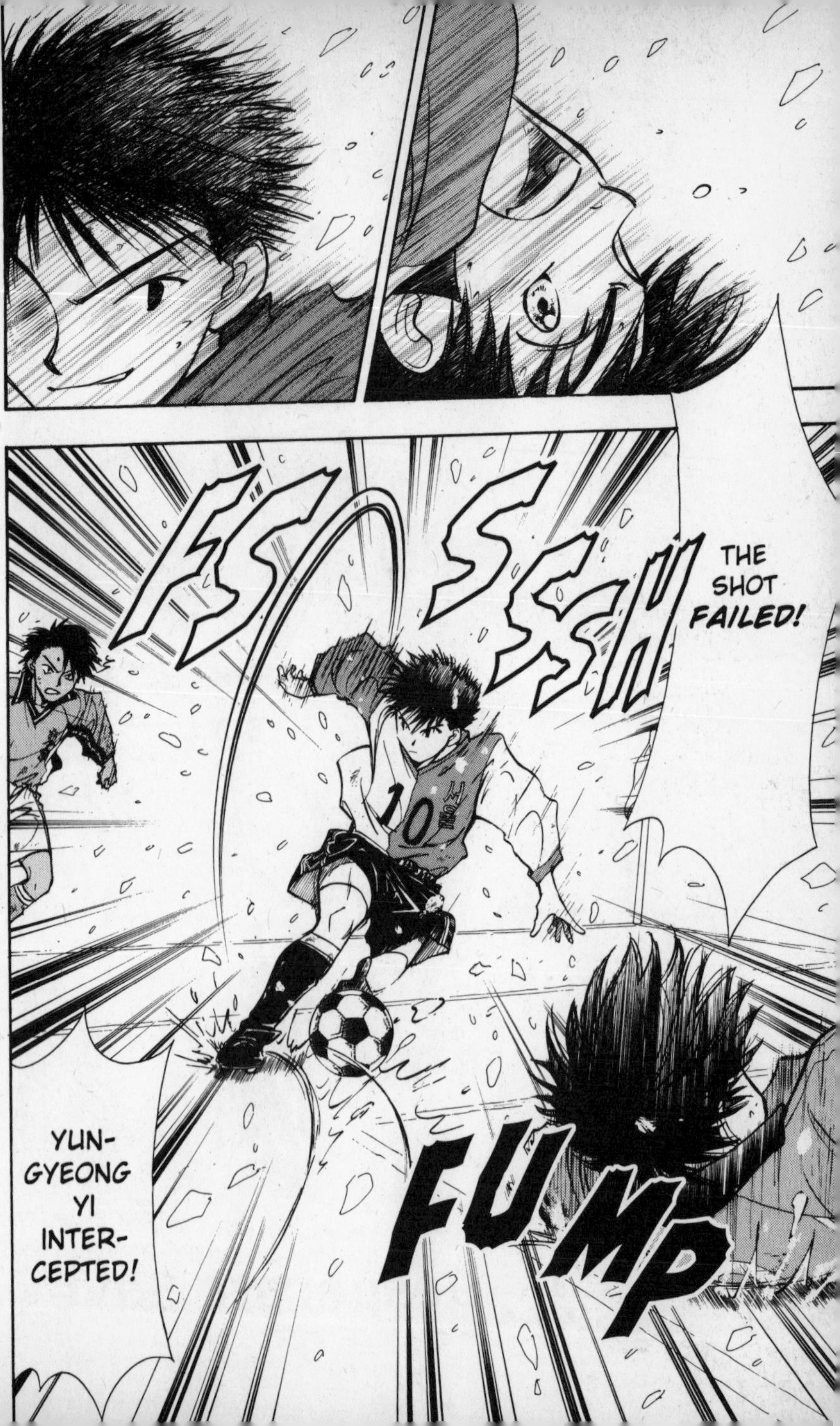
FSSSH
THE SHOT FAILED!
FUMP
YUN-GYEONG YI INTER-CEPTED!

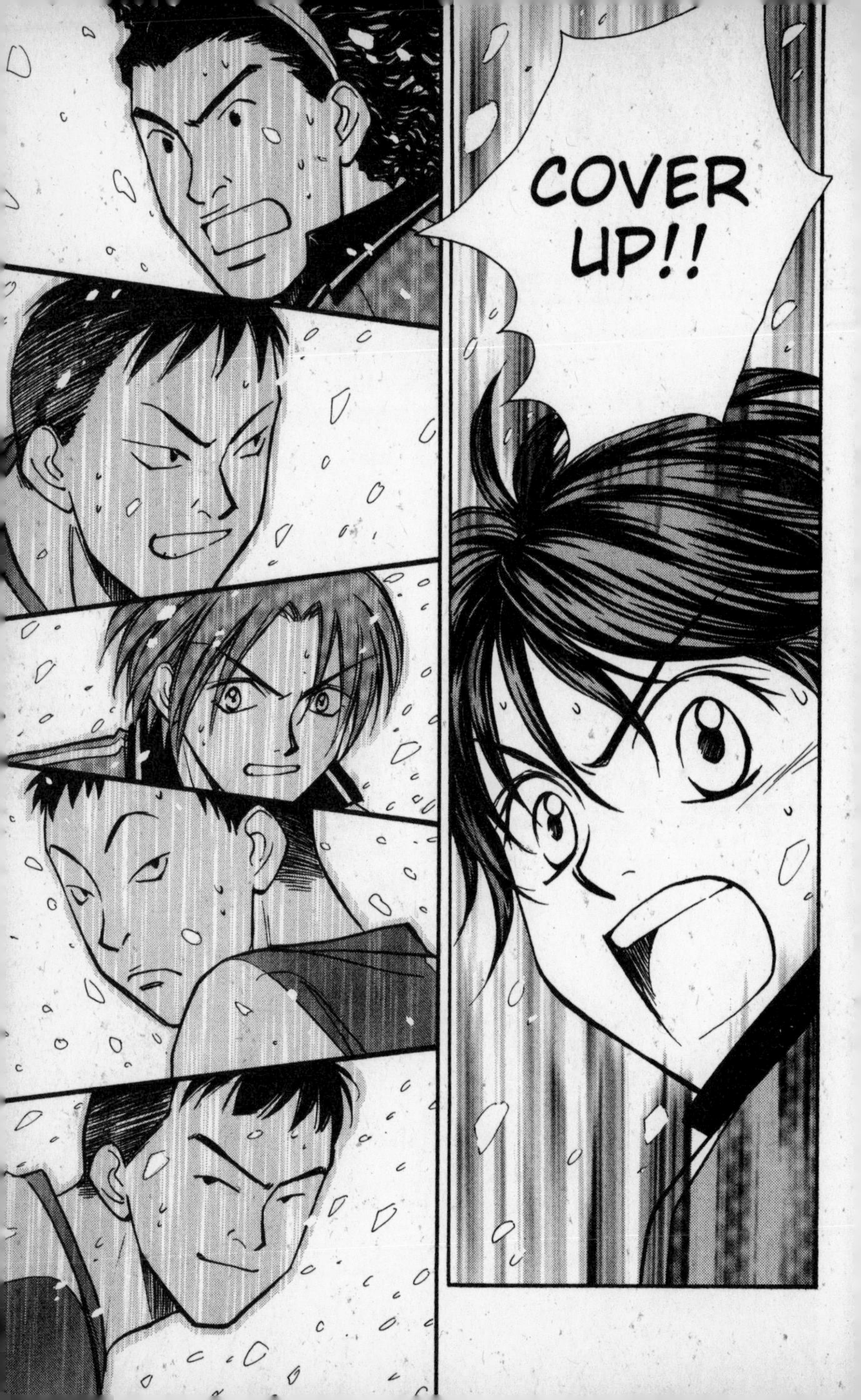
COVER UP!!

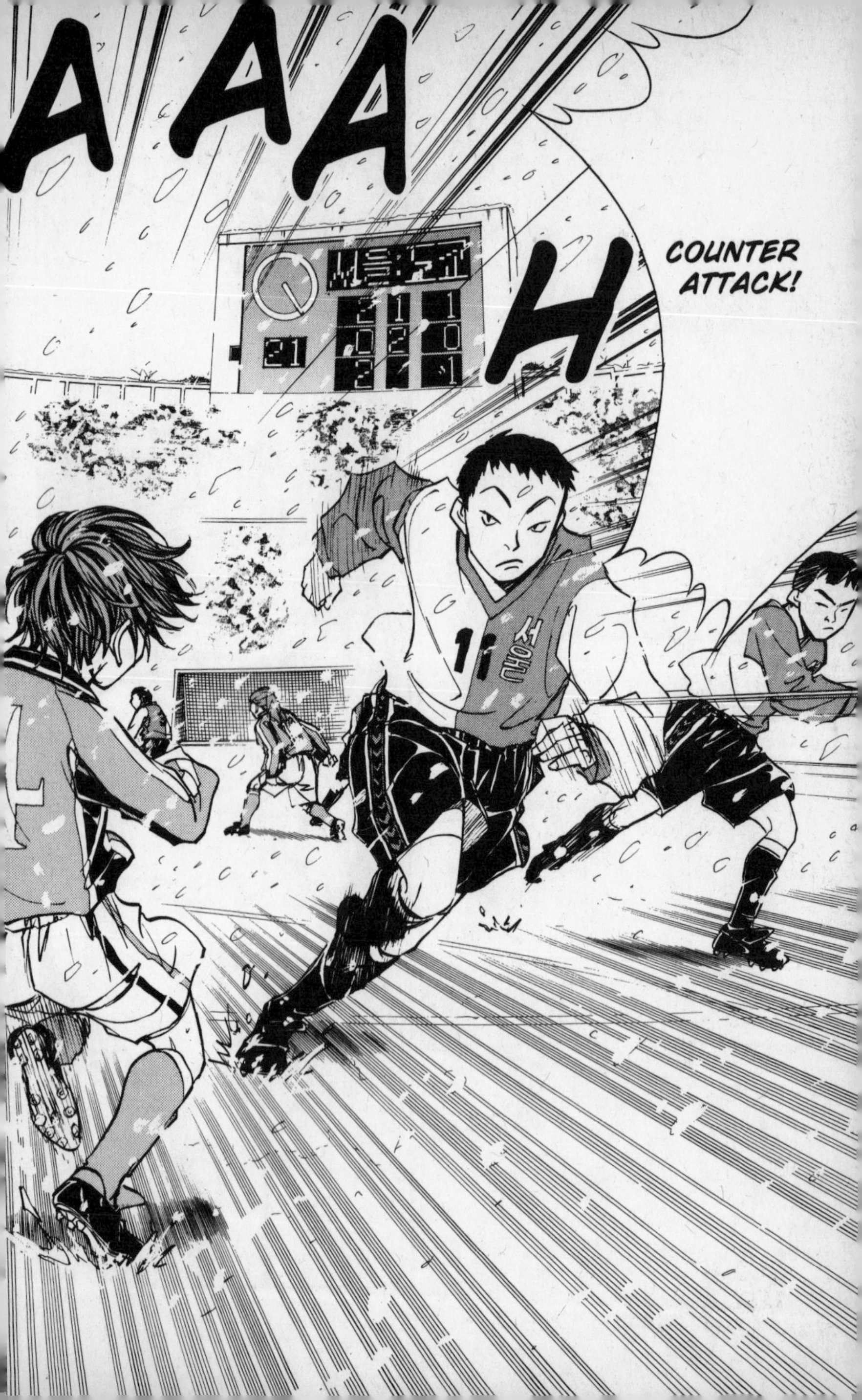
AAAAH
COUNTER ATTACK!

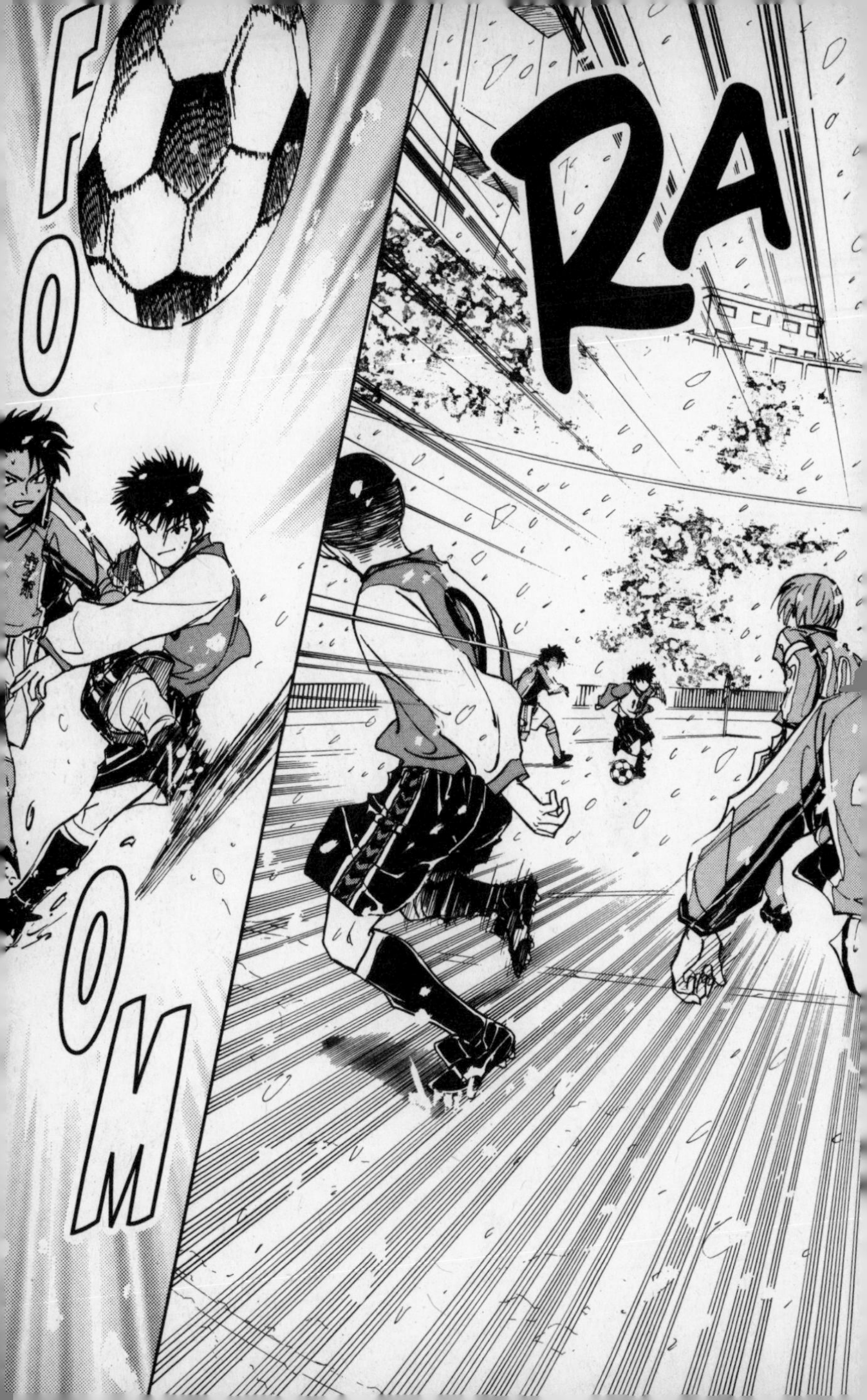
RA
FOOM

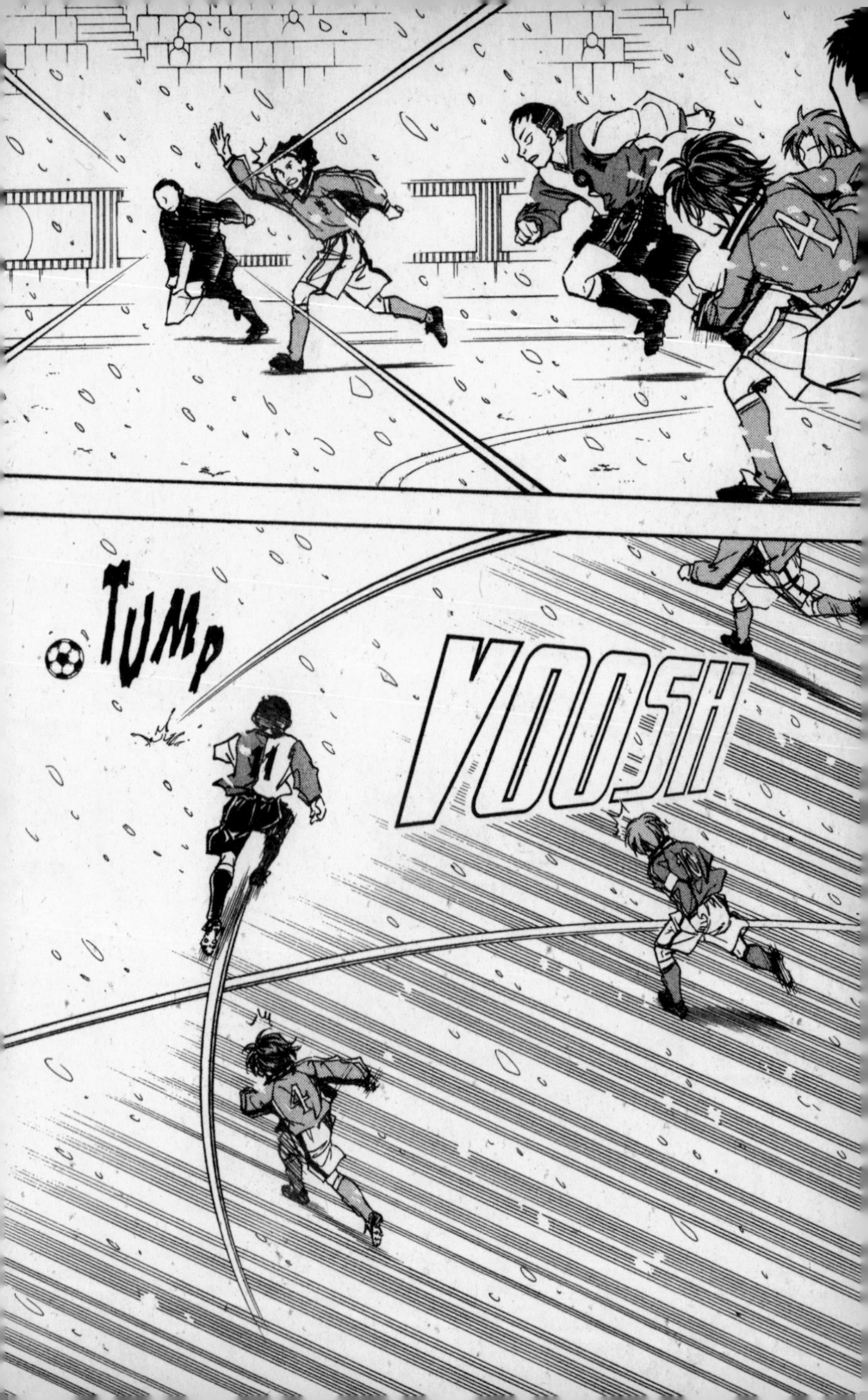
VOOSH
TUMP

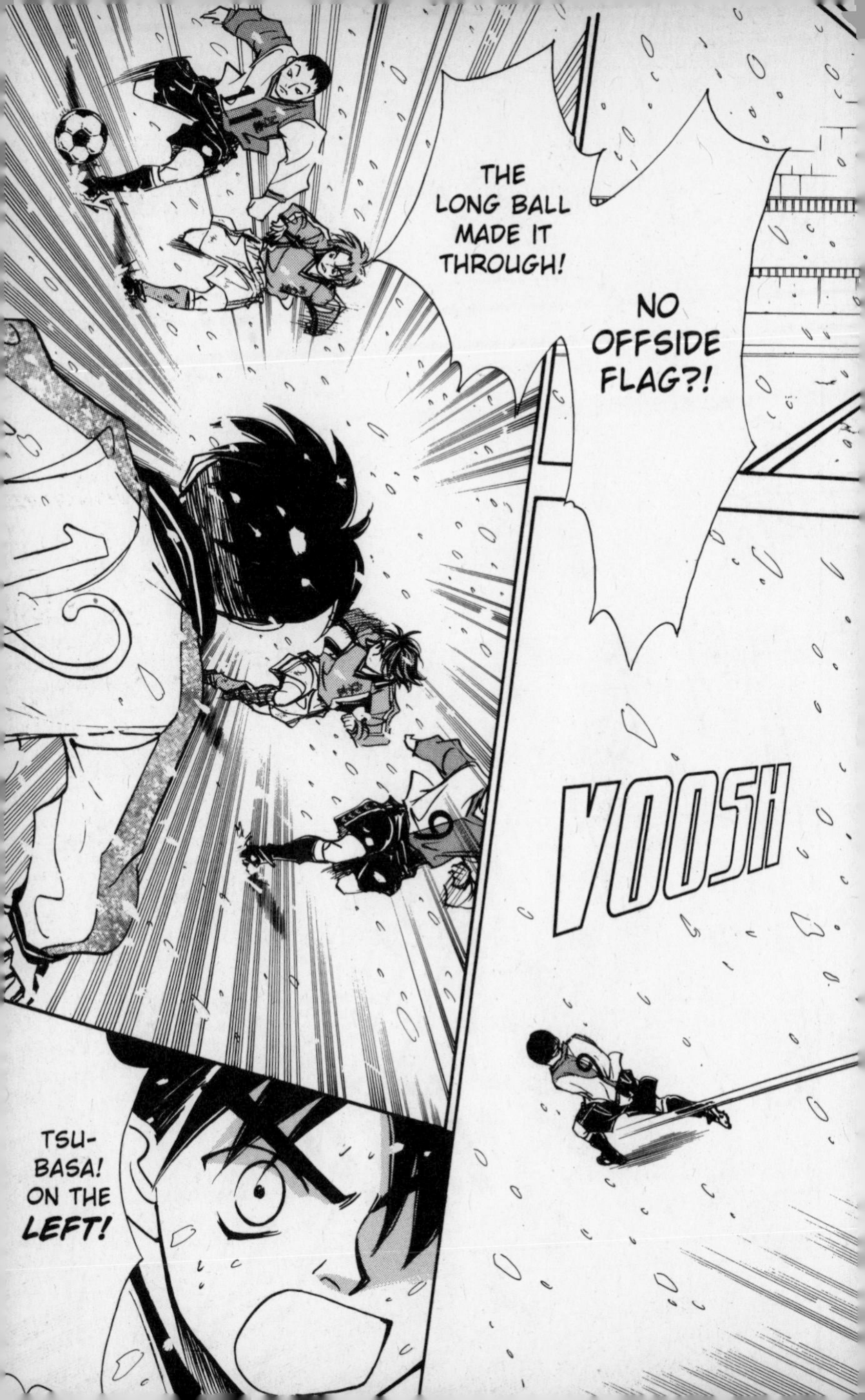
NO OFFSIDE FLAG?!
THE LONG BALL MADE IT THROUGH!
VOOSH
TSU-BASA! ON THE LEFT!

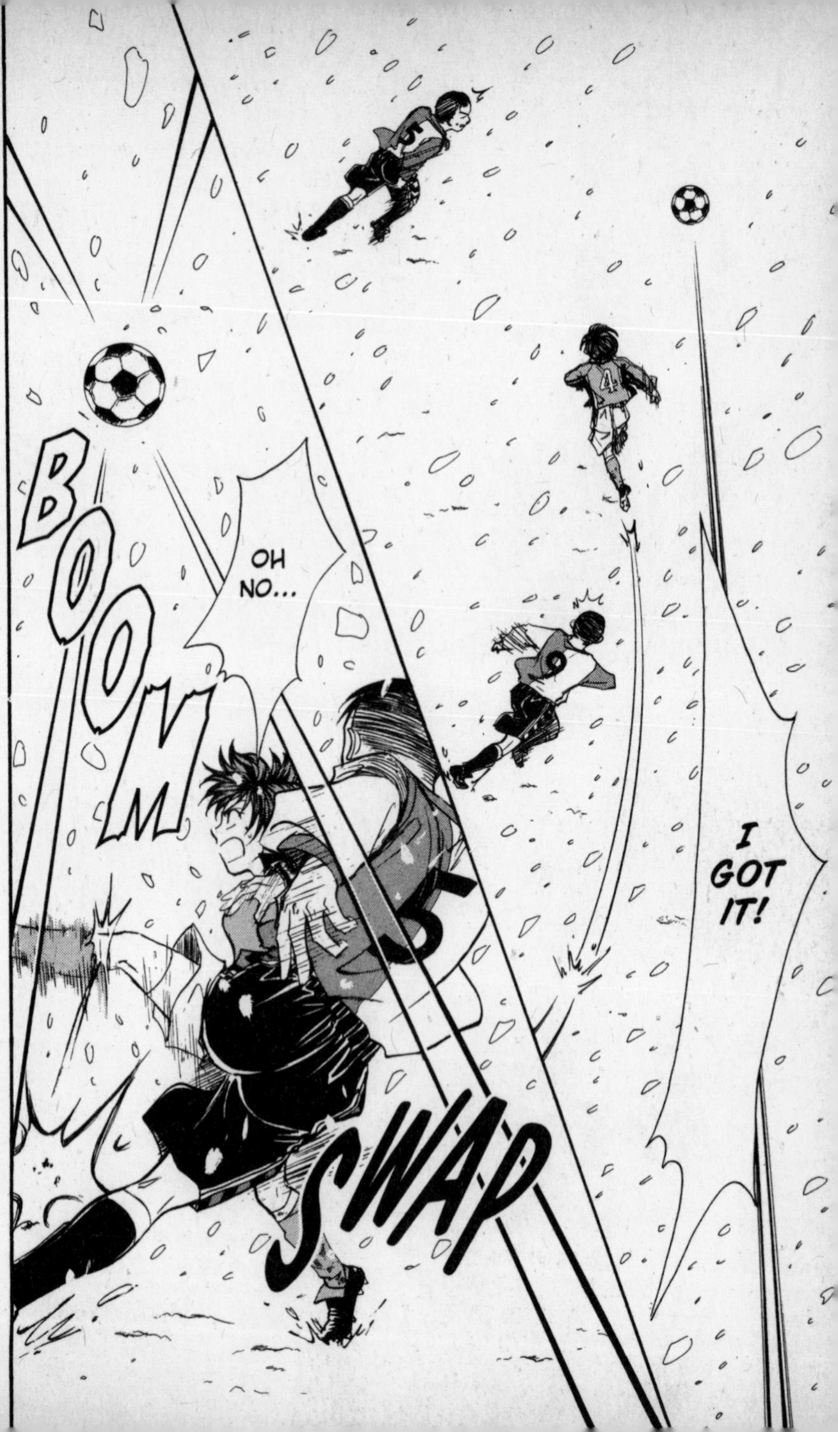
I GOT IT!
BOOM
OH NO...
SWAP

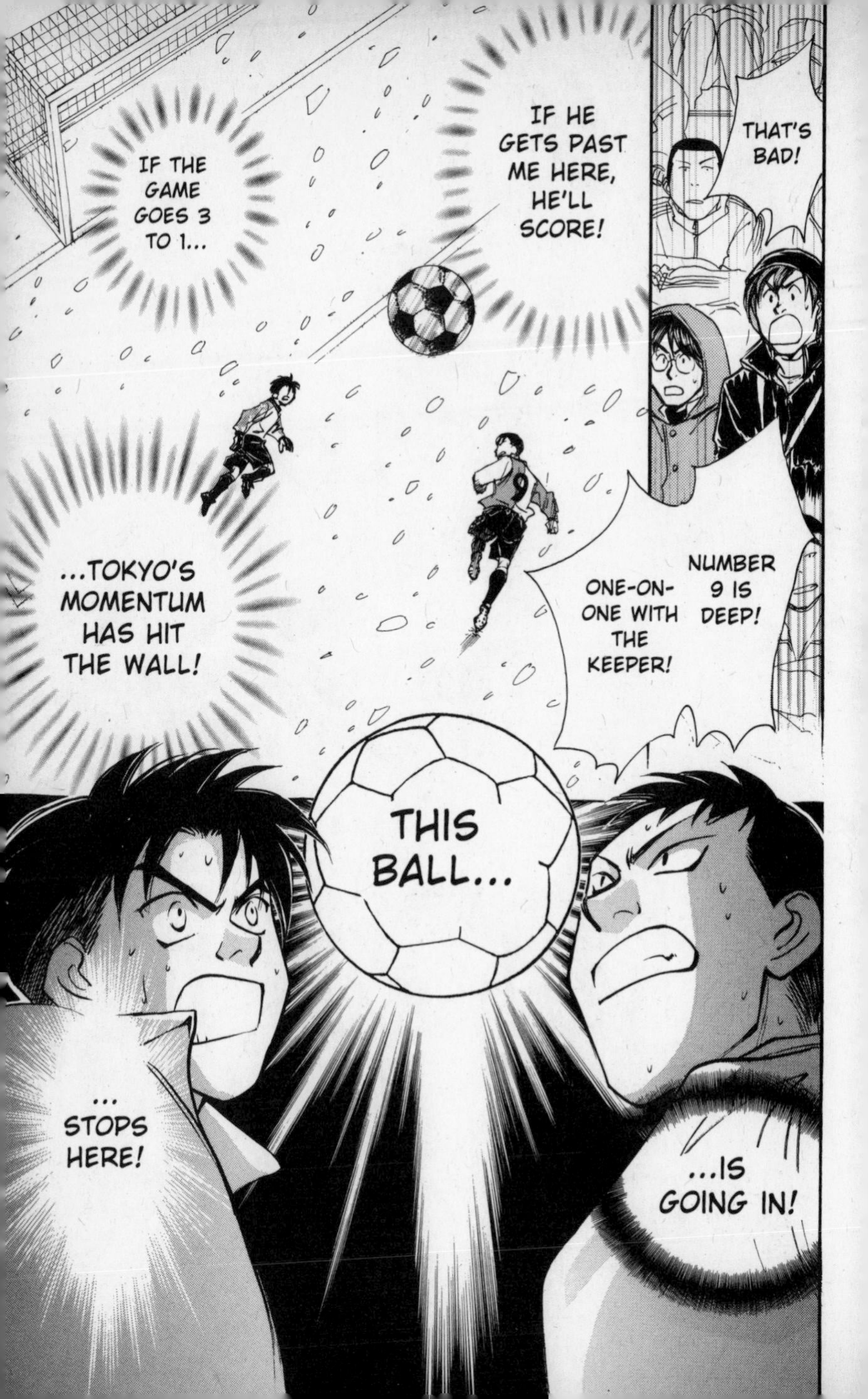
THAT'S BAD!
IF HE GETS PAST ME HERE, HE'LL SCORE!
NUMBER 9 IS DEEP!
ONE-ON-ONE WITH THE KEEPER!
IF THE GAME GOES 3 TO 1...
...TOKYO'S MOMENTUM HAS HIT THE WALL!
THIS BALL...
...IS GOING IN!
... STOPS HERE!

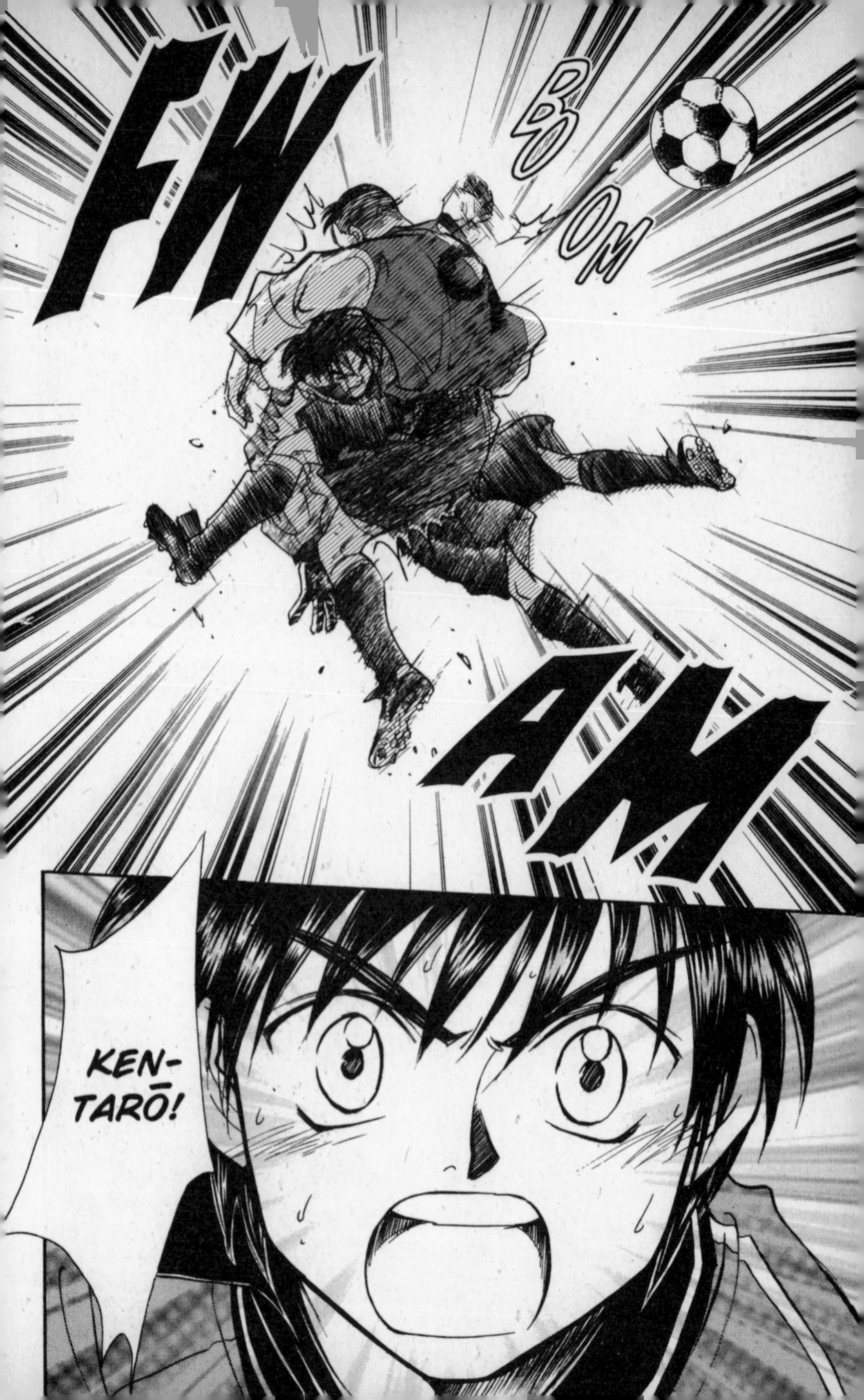
FW
BOOM
AM
KEN-
TARŌ!

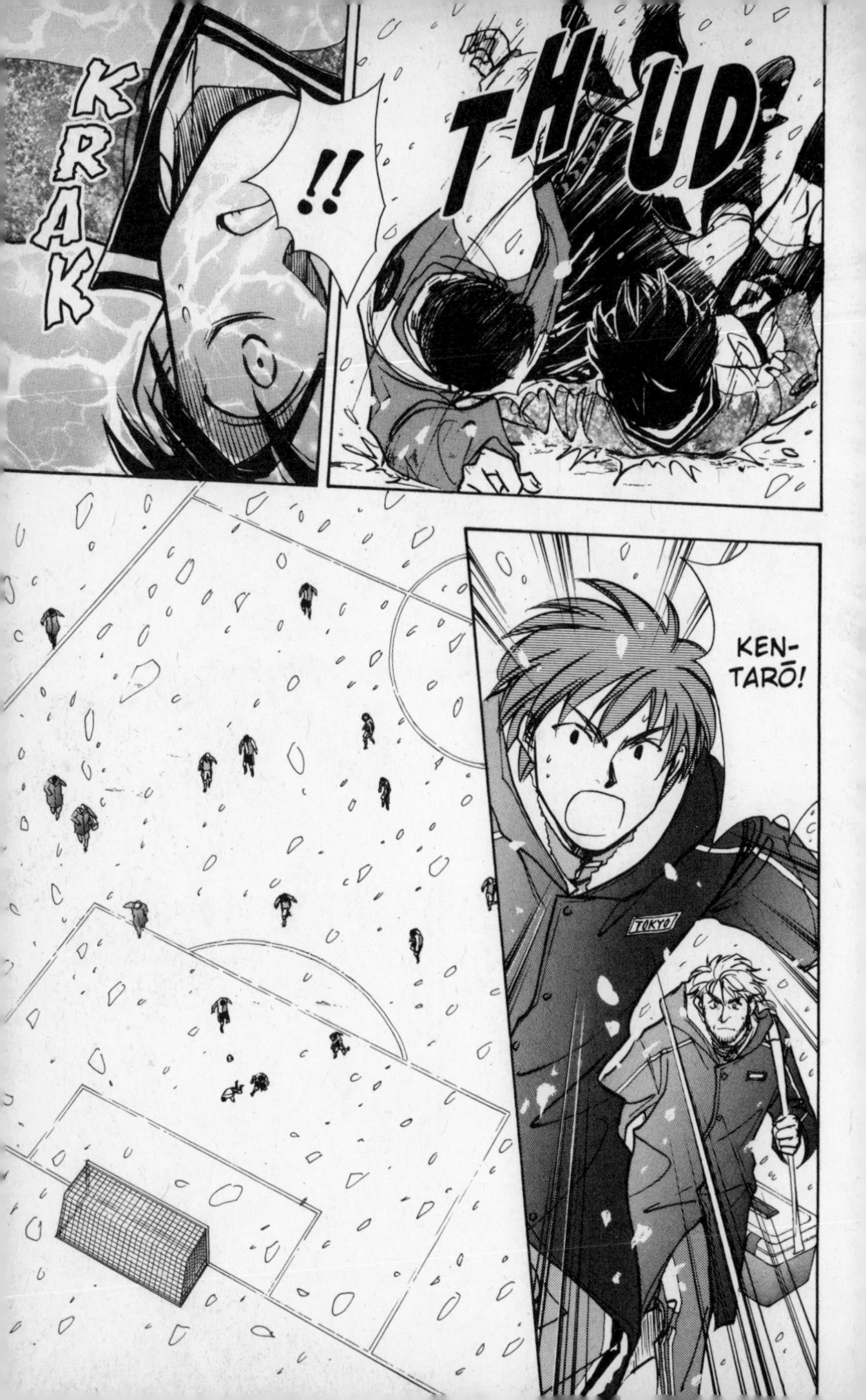
THUD
!!
KRAK
KEN-
TARŌ!

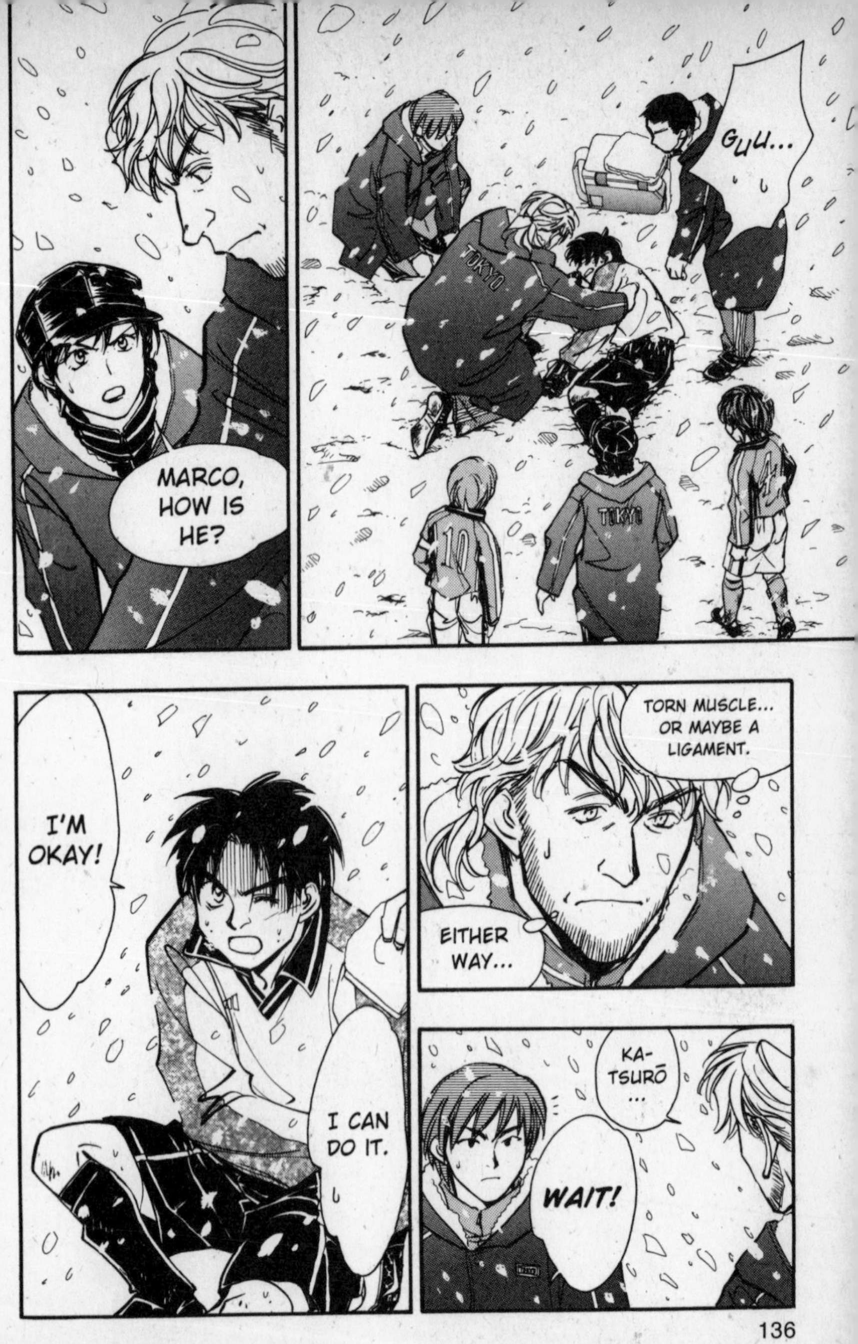
GUU...
MARCO, HOW IS HE?
TORN MUSCLE... OR MAYBE A LIGAMENT.
EITHER WAY...
KA-TSURŌ ...
WAIT!
I'M OKAY!
I CAN DO IT.

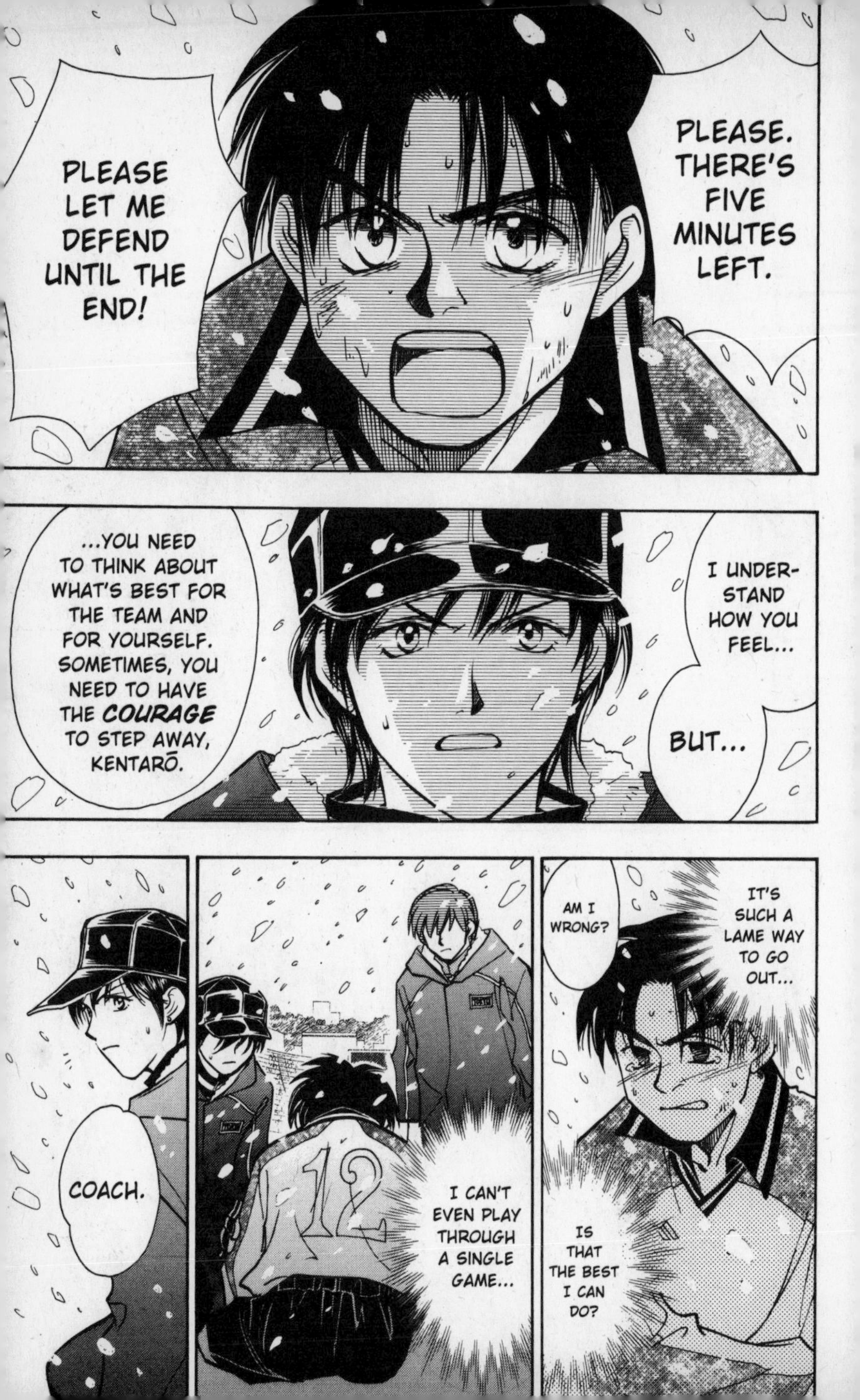
PLEASE. THERE'S FIVE MINUTES LEFT.
PLEASE LET ME DEFEND UNTIL THE END!
I UNDER-STAND HOW YOU FEEL...
BUT...
...YOU NEED TO THINK ABOUT WHAT'S BEST FOR THE TEAM AND FOR YOURSELF. SOMETIMES, YOU NEED TO HAVE THE COURAGE TO STEP AWAY, KENTARŌ.
IT'S SUCH A LAME WAY TO GO OUT...
AM I WRONG?
IS THAT THE BEST I CAN DO?
I CAN'T EVEN PLAY THROUGH A SINGLE GAME...
COACH.

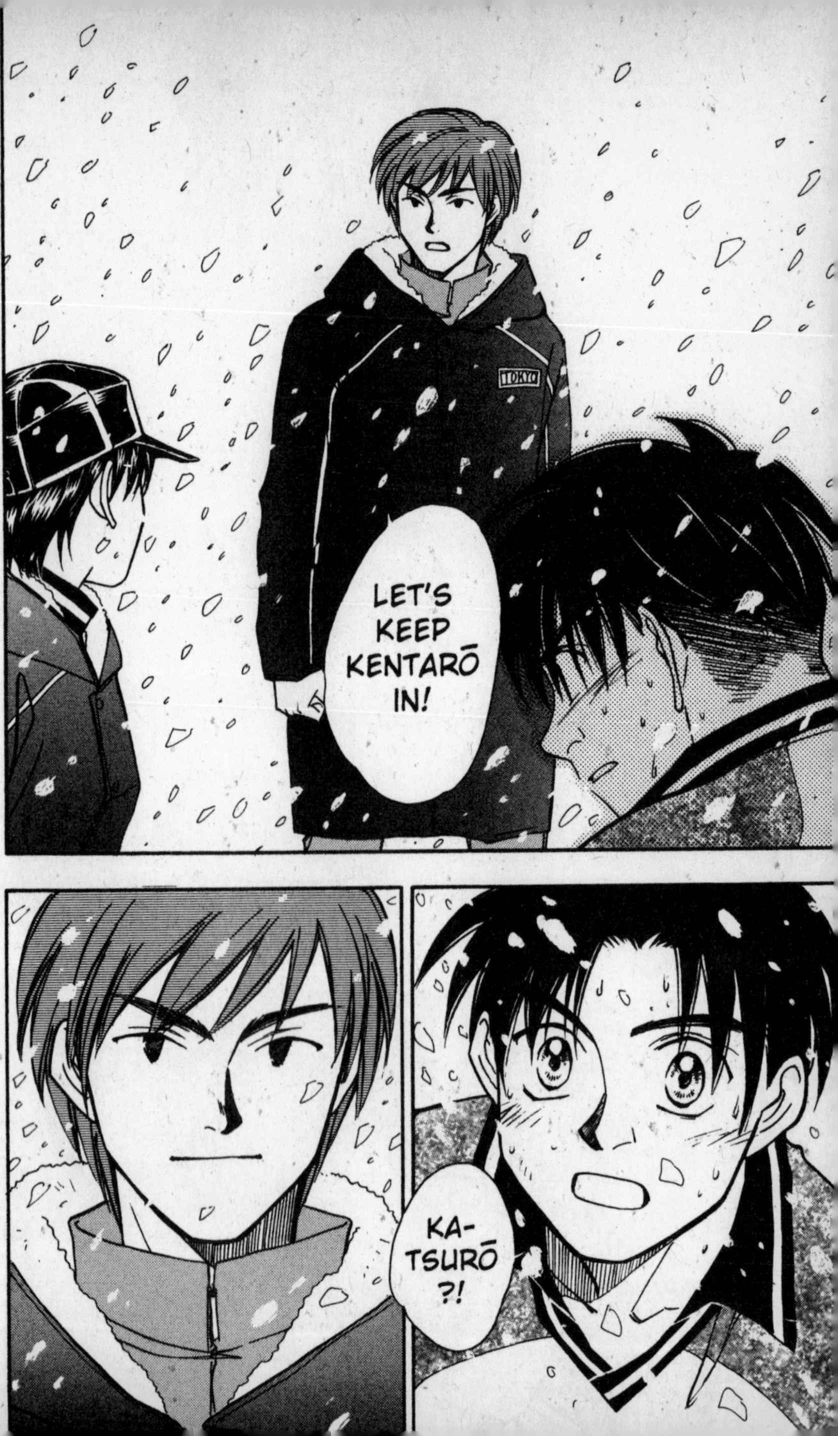
LET'S KEEP KENTARŌ IN!
KA-TSURŌ ?!

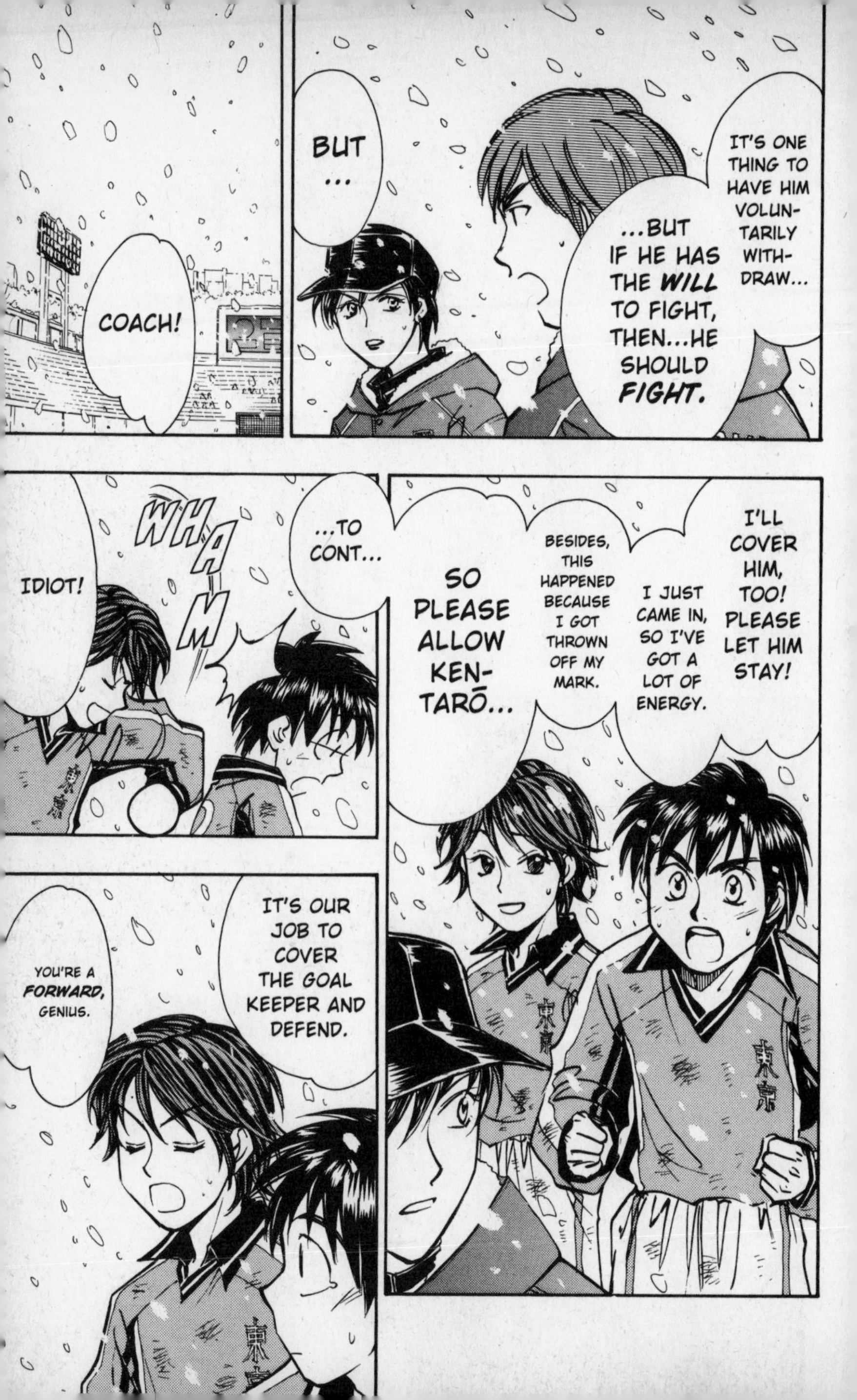
IT'S ONE THING TO HAVE HIM VOLUNTARILY WITHDRAW...
...BUT IF HE HAS THE *WILL* TO FIGHT, THEN...HE SHOULD *FIGHT.*
BUT...
COACH!
I'LL COVER HIM, TOO! PLEASE LET HIM STAY!
I JUST CAME IN, SO I'VE GOT A LOT OF ENERGY.
BESIDES, THIS HAPPENED BECAUSE I GOT THROWN OFF MY MARK.
SO PLEASE ALLOW KENTARŌ...
...TO CONT...
WHAMM
IDIOT!
IT'S OUR JOB TO COVER THE GOAL KEEPER AND DEFEND.
YOU'RE A *FORWARD,* GENIUS.

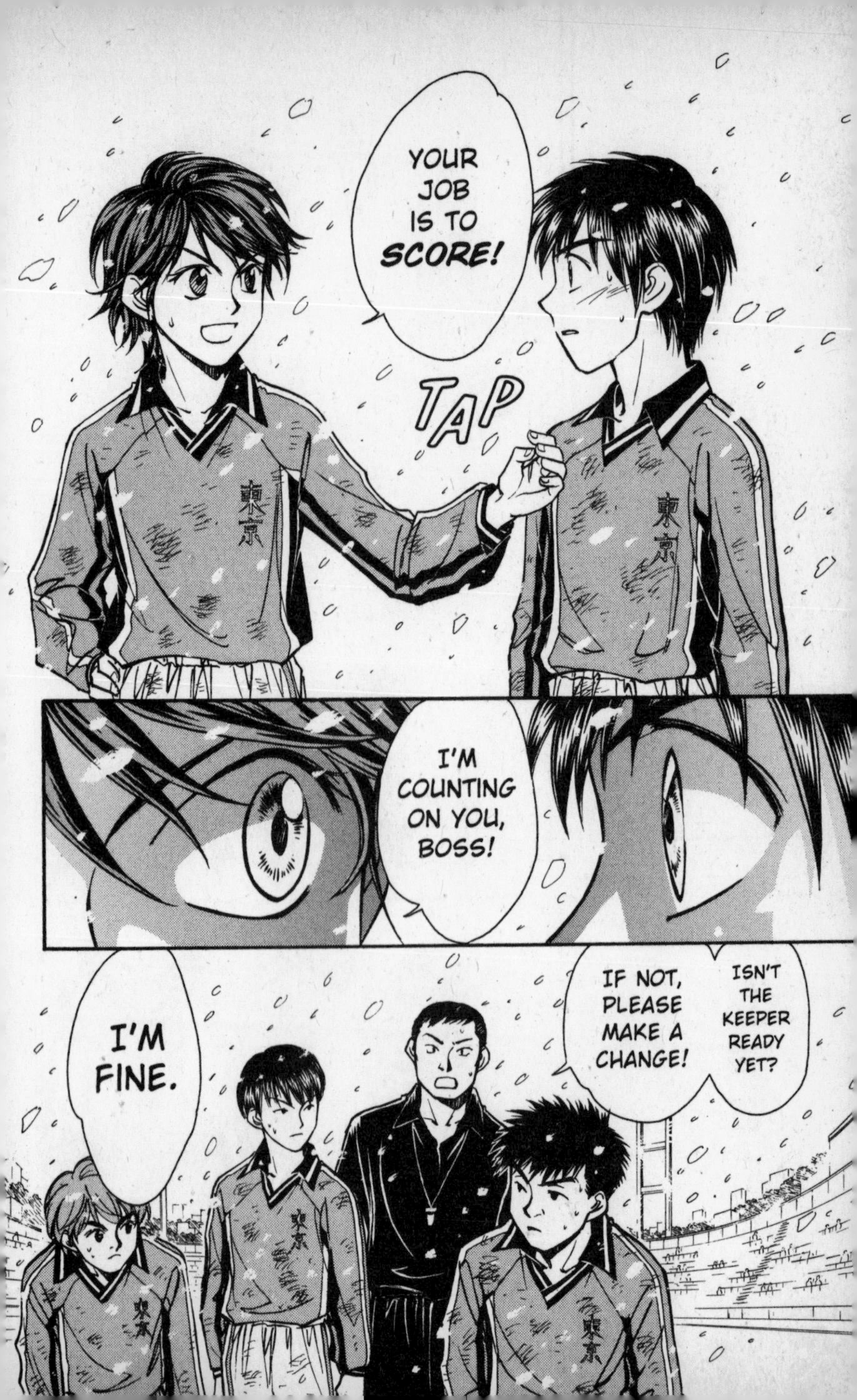
YOUR JOB IS TO SCORE!
TAP
I'M COUNTING ON YOU, BOSS!
ISN'T THE KEEPER READY YET?
IF NOT, PLEASE MAKE A CHANGE!
I'M FINE.

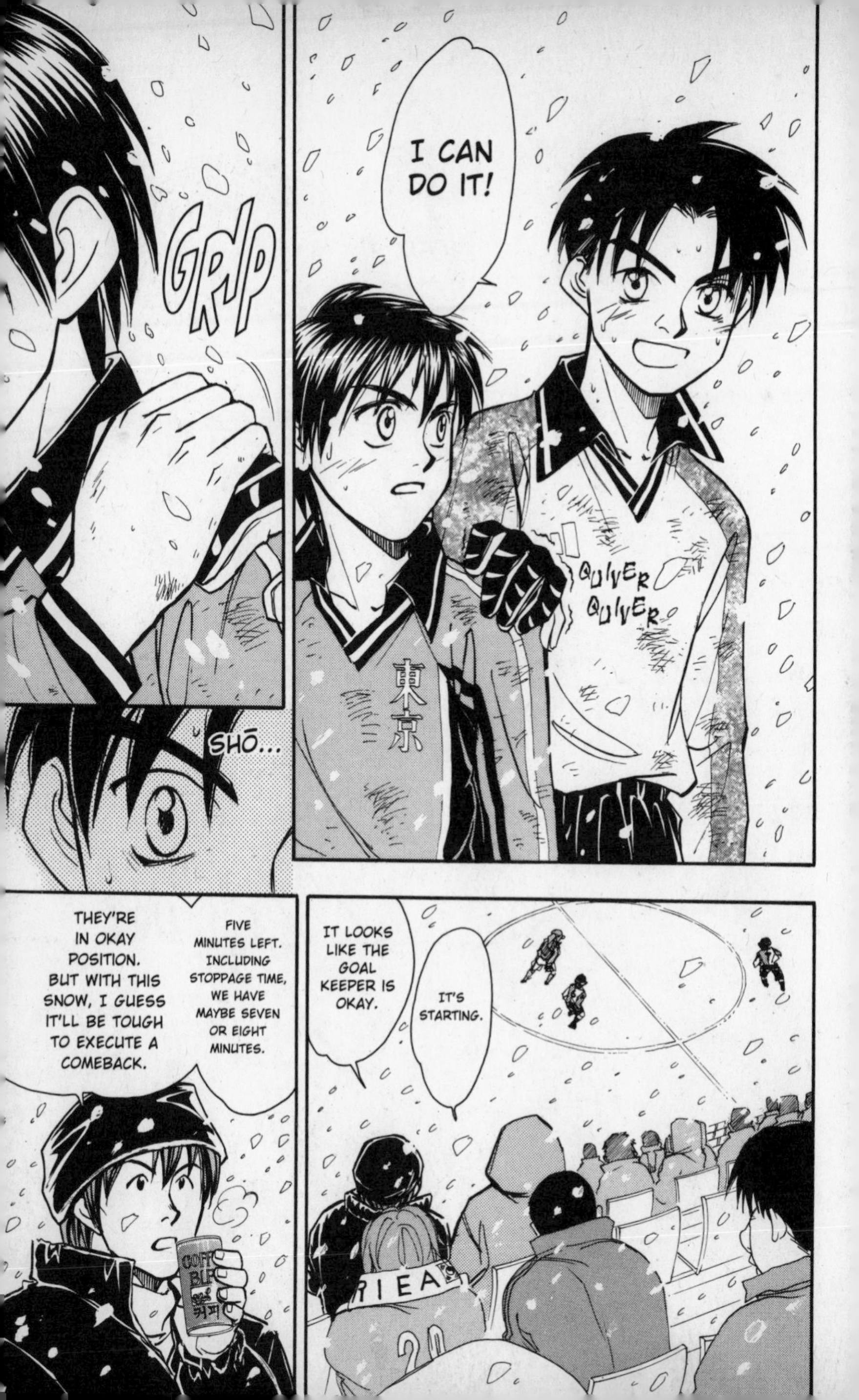
I CAN DO IT!
QUIVER QUIVER
GRIP
SHŌ...
IT'S STARTING.
IT LOOKS LIKE THE GOAL KEEPER IS OKAY.
FIVE MINUTES LEFT. INCLUDING STOPPAGE TIME, WE HAVE MAYBE SEVEN OR EIGHT MINUTES.
THEY'RE IN OKAY POSITION. BUT WITH THIS SNOW, I GUESS IT'LL BE TOUGH TO EXECUTE A COMEBACK.

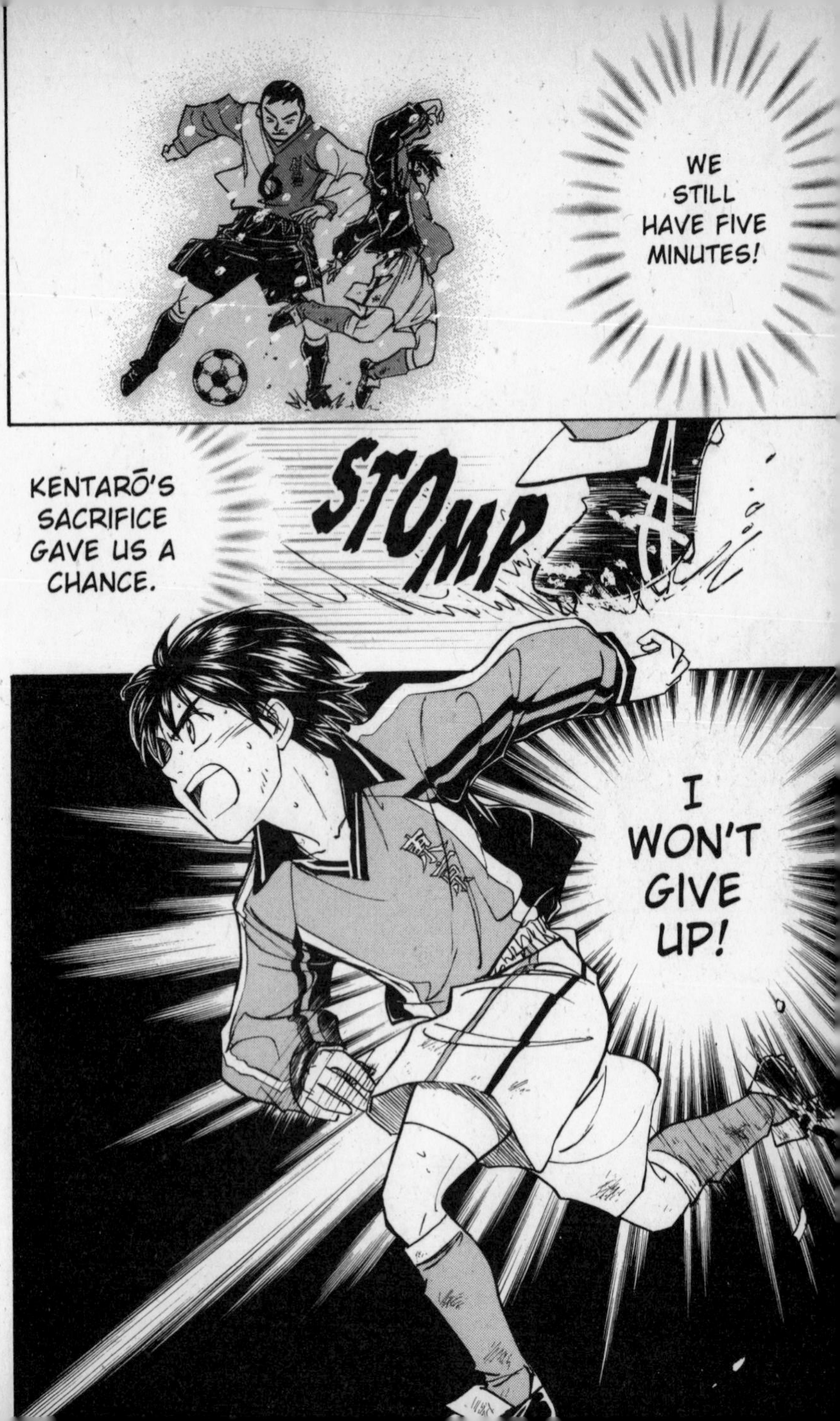
WE STILL HAVE FIVE MINUTES!
STOMP
KENTARŌ'S SACRIFICE GAVE US A CHANCE.
I WON'T GIVE UP!

STAGE.160 Reliable Back

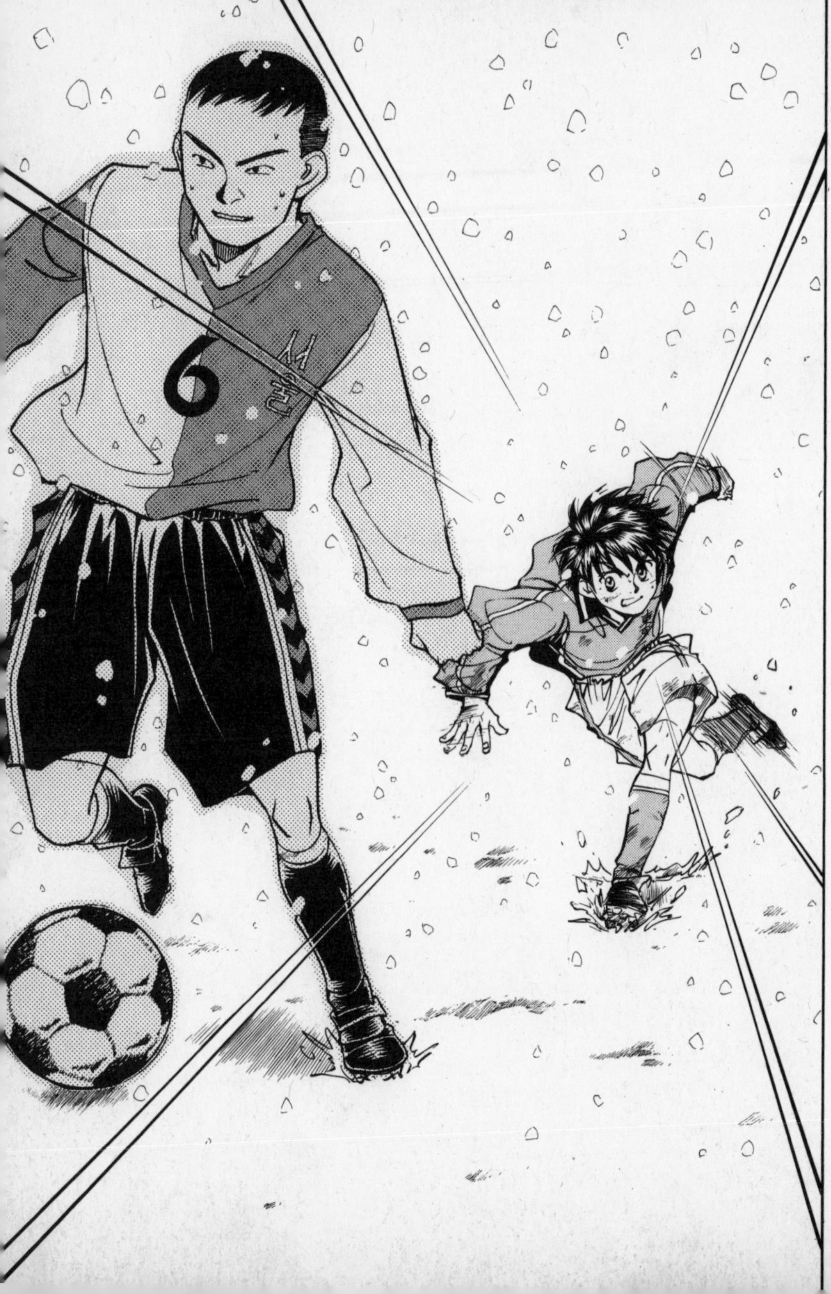

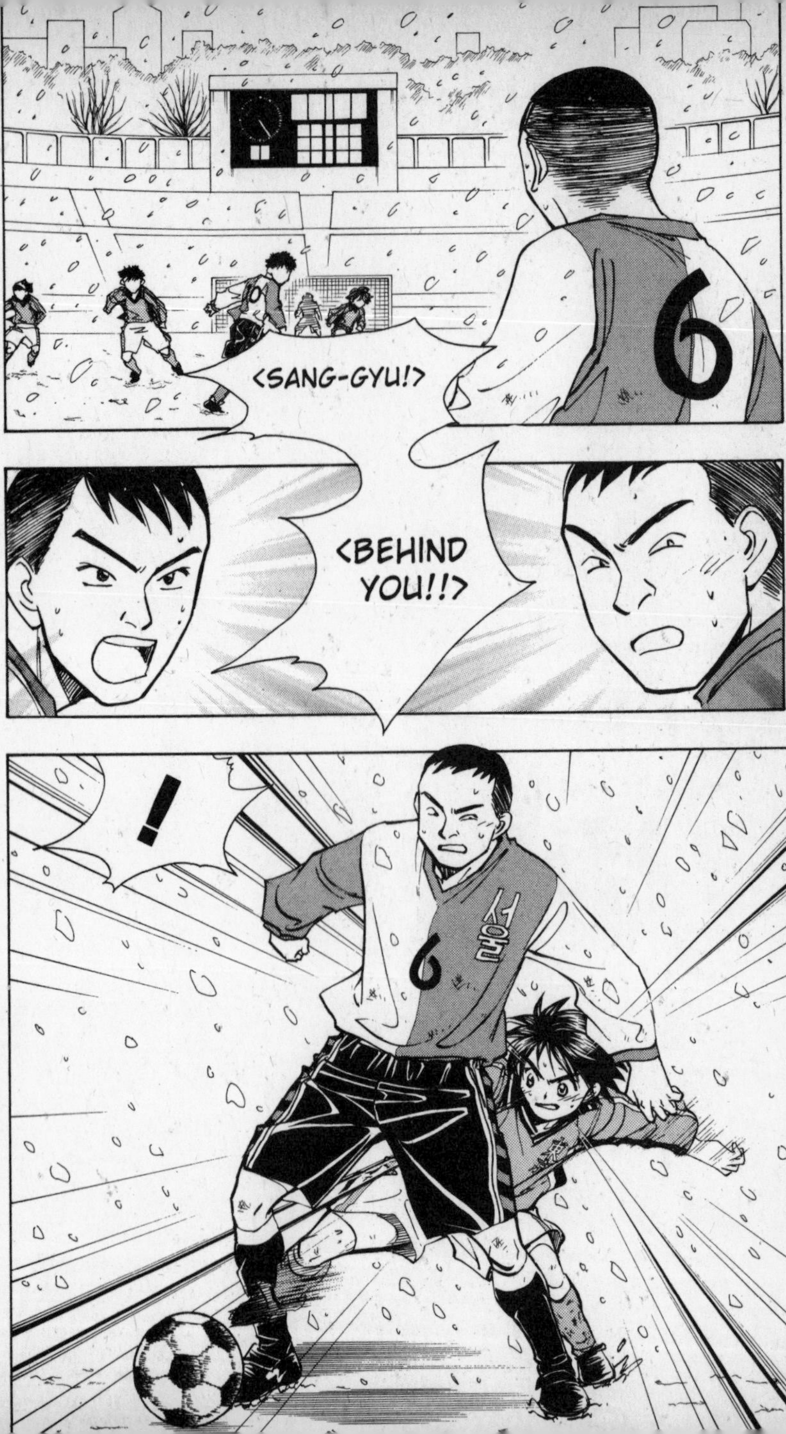
<SANG-GYU!>
<BEHIND YOU!!>
!
서울

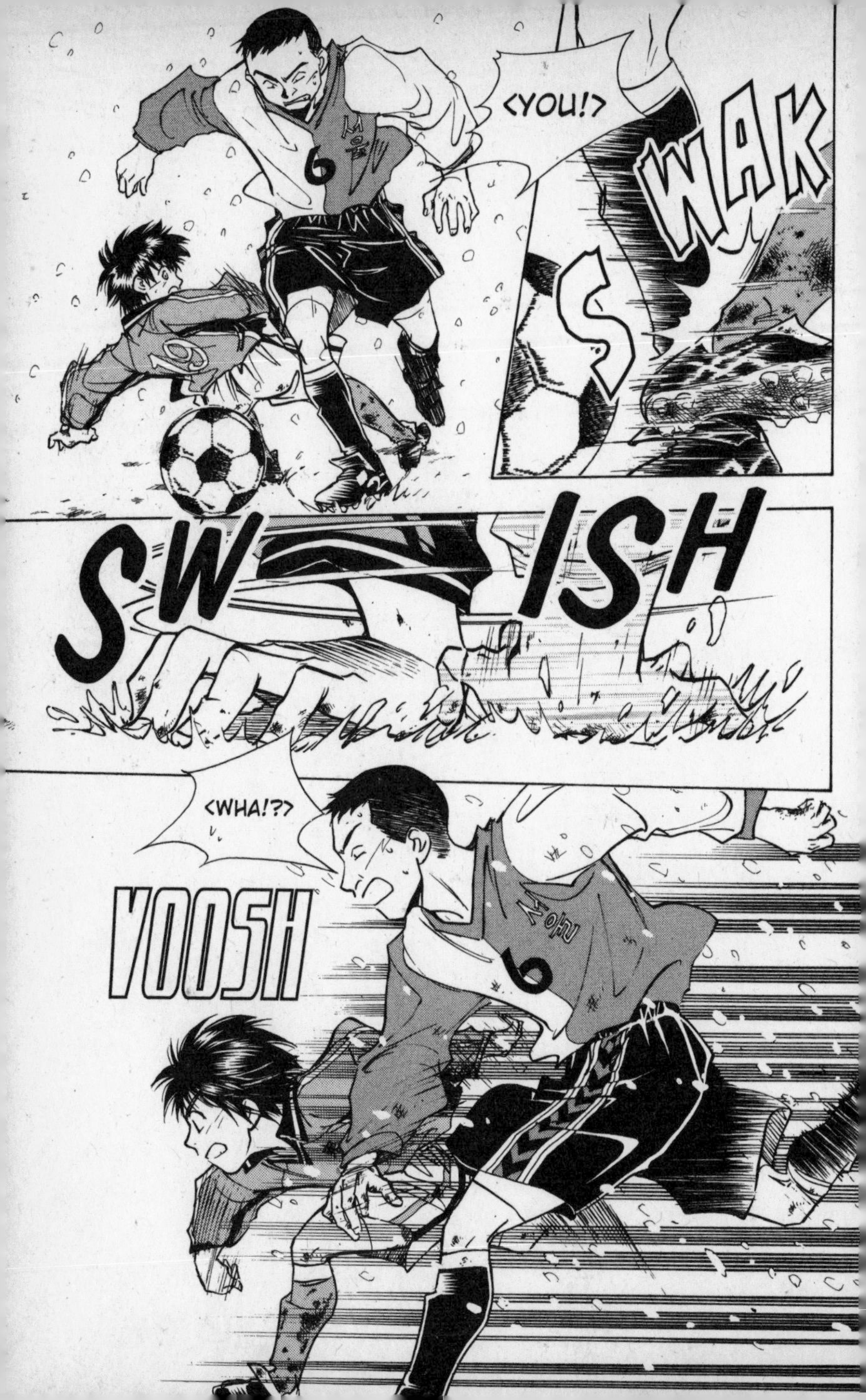

<YOU!?>
SWAK
S
SW ISH
<WHA!?>
VOOSH

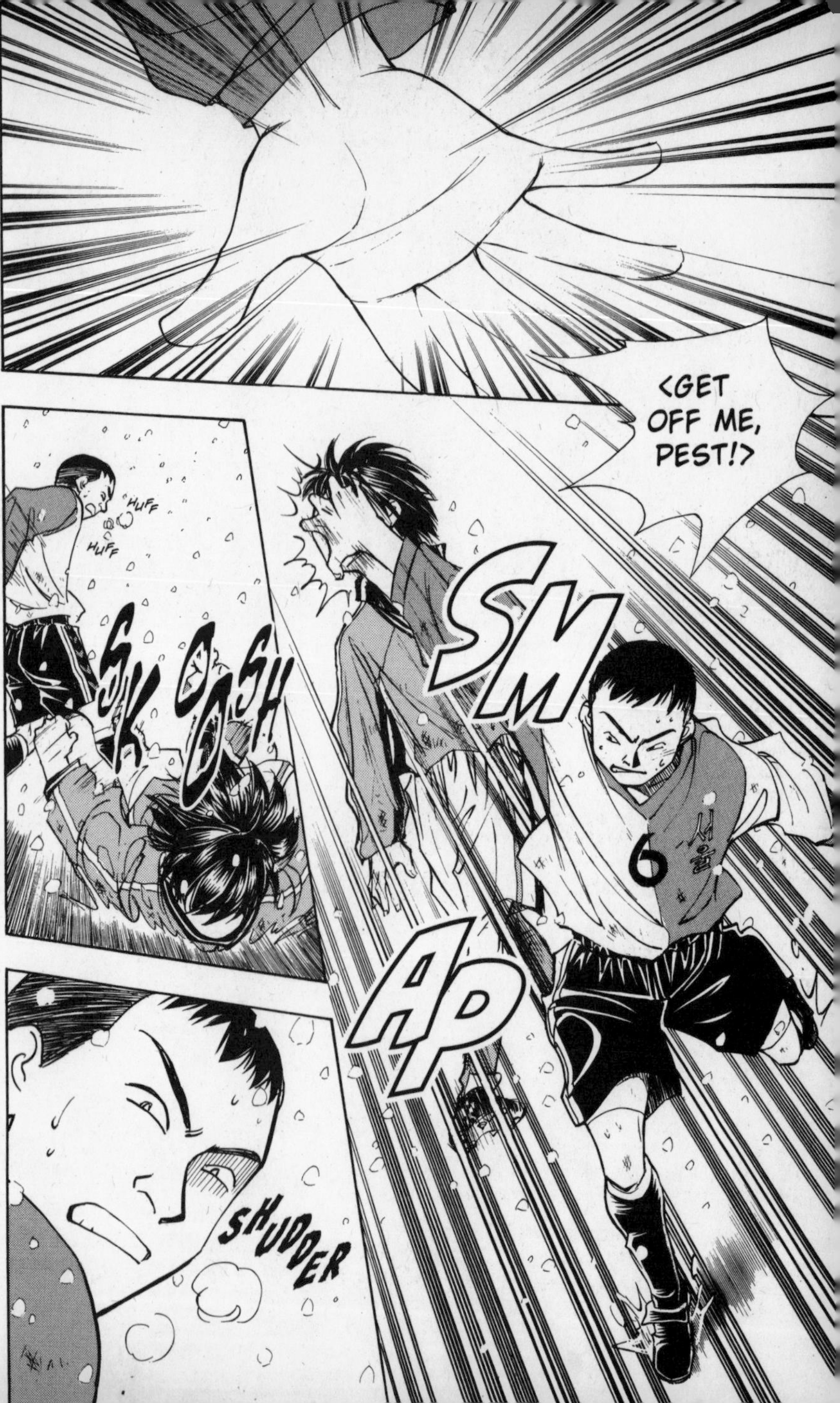
<GET OFF ME, PEST!>
SMAP
HUFF HUFF
SKOOSH!
SHUDDER

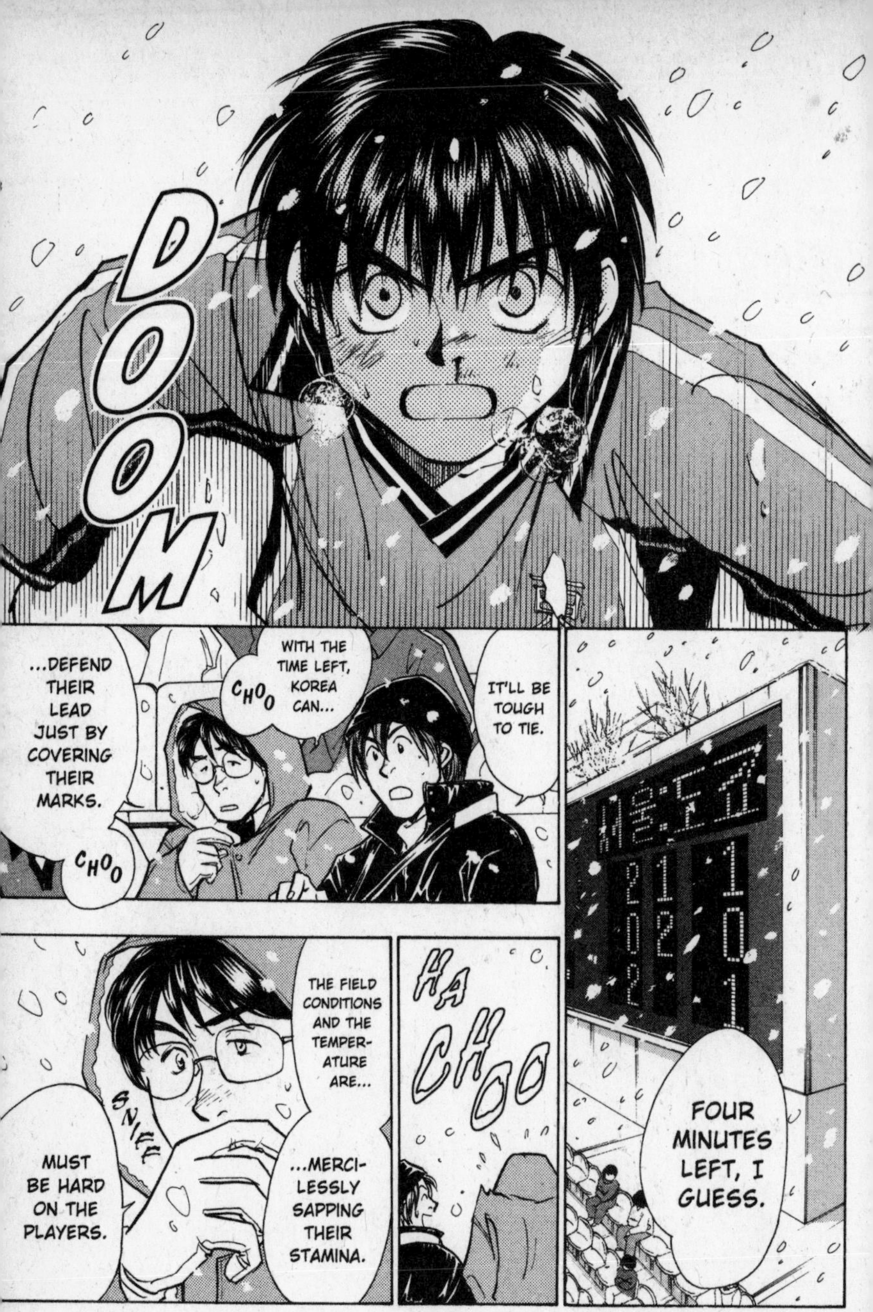
DOOOM
FOUR MINUTES LEFT, I GUESS.
IT'LL BE TOUGH TO TIE.
WITH THE TIME LEFT, KOREA CAN...
CHOO
...DEFEND THEIR LEAD JUST BY COVERING THEIR MARKS.
CHOO
HACHOO
THE FIELD CONDITIONS AND THE TEMPER-ATURE ARE...
...MERCI-LESSLY SAPPING THEIR STAMINA.
SNIFF
MUST BE HARD ON THE PLAYERS.

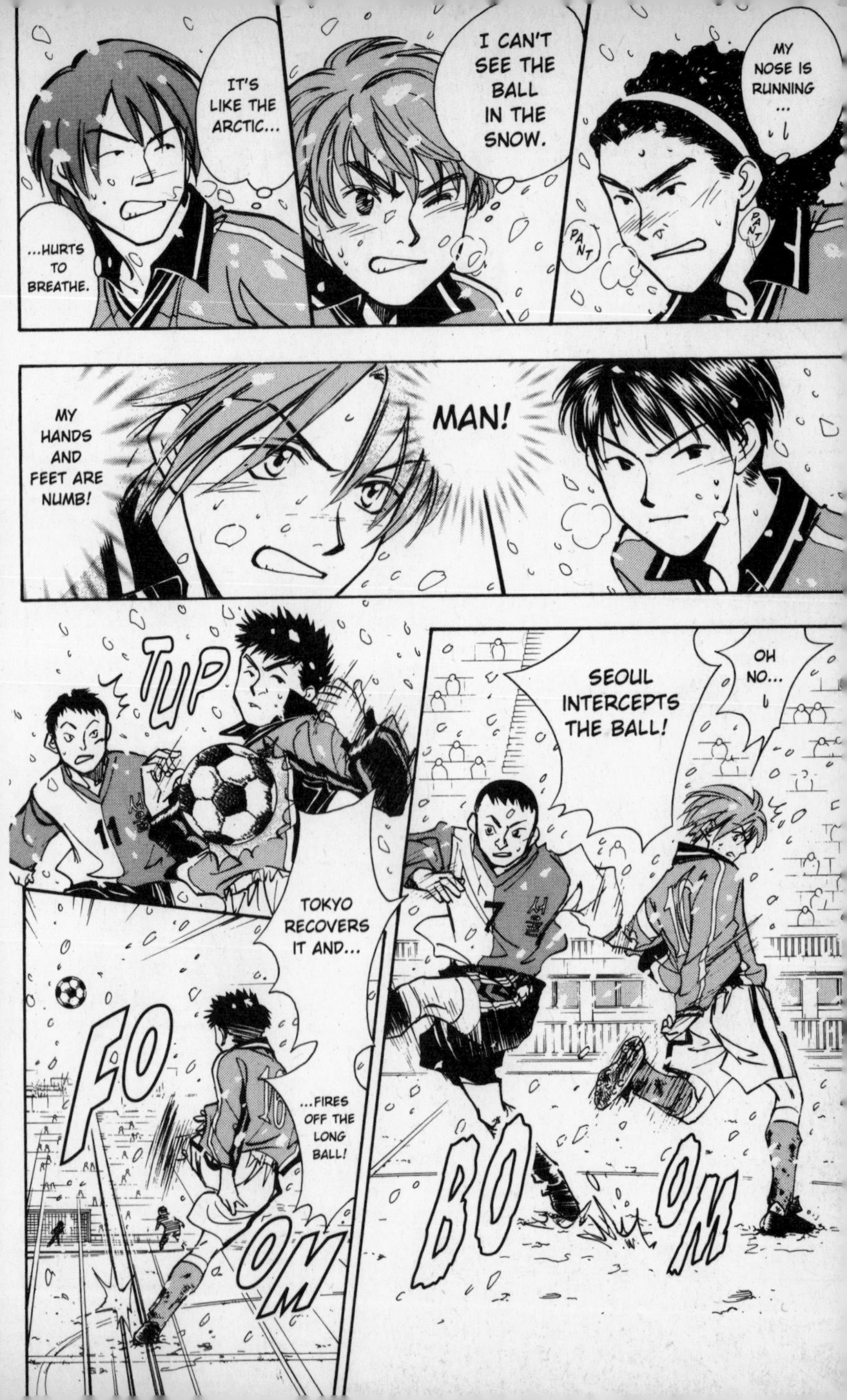
MY NOSE IS RUNNING ...
PANT
PANT
I CAN'T SEE THE BALL IN THE SNOW.
IT'S LIKE THE ARCTIC...
...HURTS TO BREATHE.
MAN!
MY HANDS AND FEET ARE NUMB!
OH NO...
SEOUL INTERCEPTS THE BALL!
BOOM
TUP
TOKYO RECOVERS IT AND...
...FIRES OFF THE LONG BALL!
FOOM

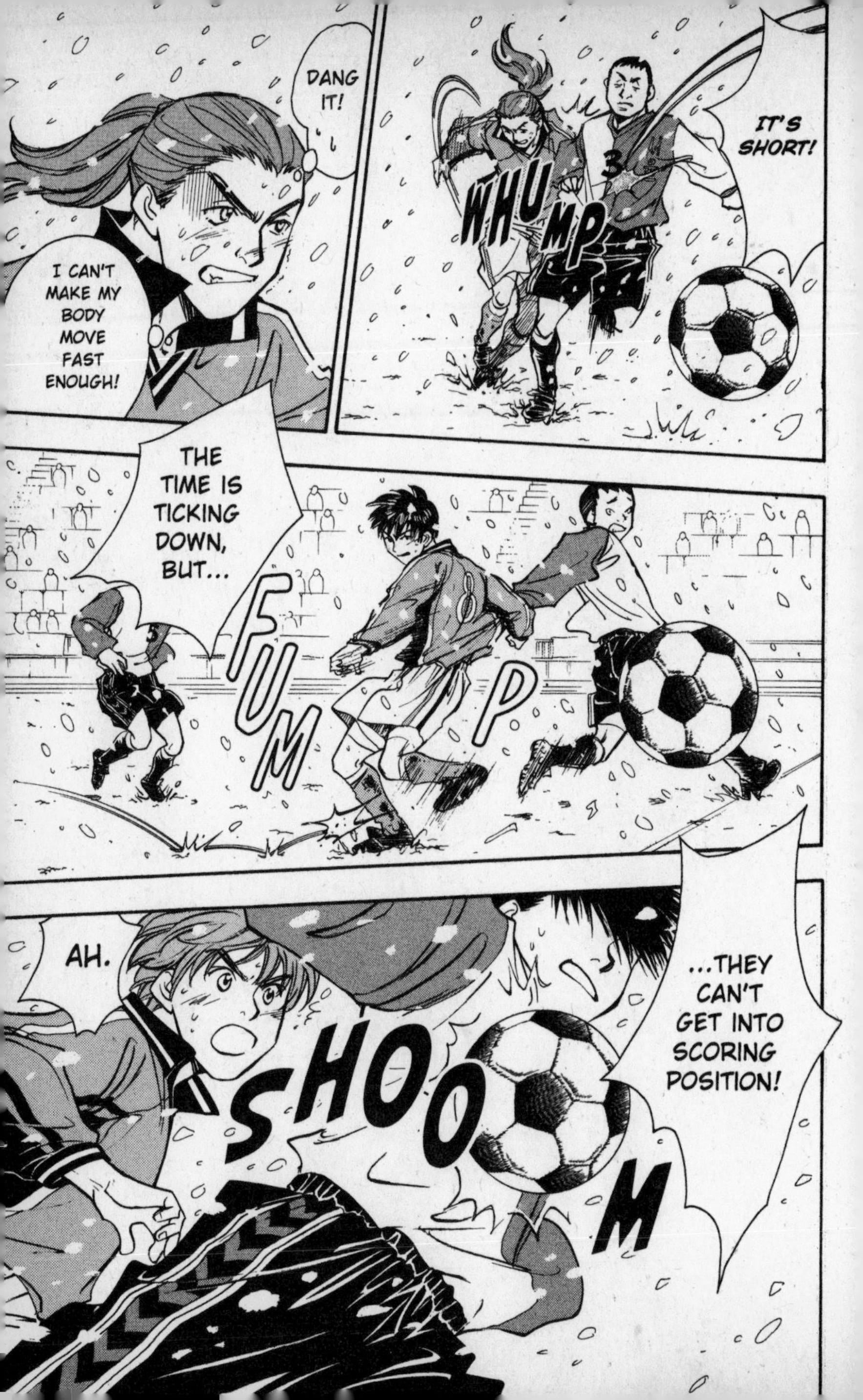
IT'S SHORT!
WHUMP
DANG IT!
I CAN'T MAKE MY BODY MOVE FAST ENOUGH!
FUMP
THE TIME IS TICKING DOWN, BUT...
...THEY CAN'T GET INTO SCORING POSITION!
SHOOOM
AH.

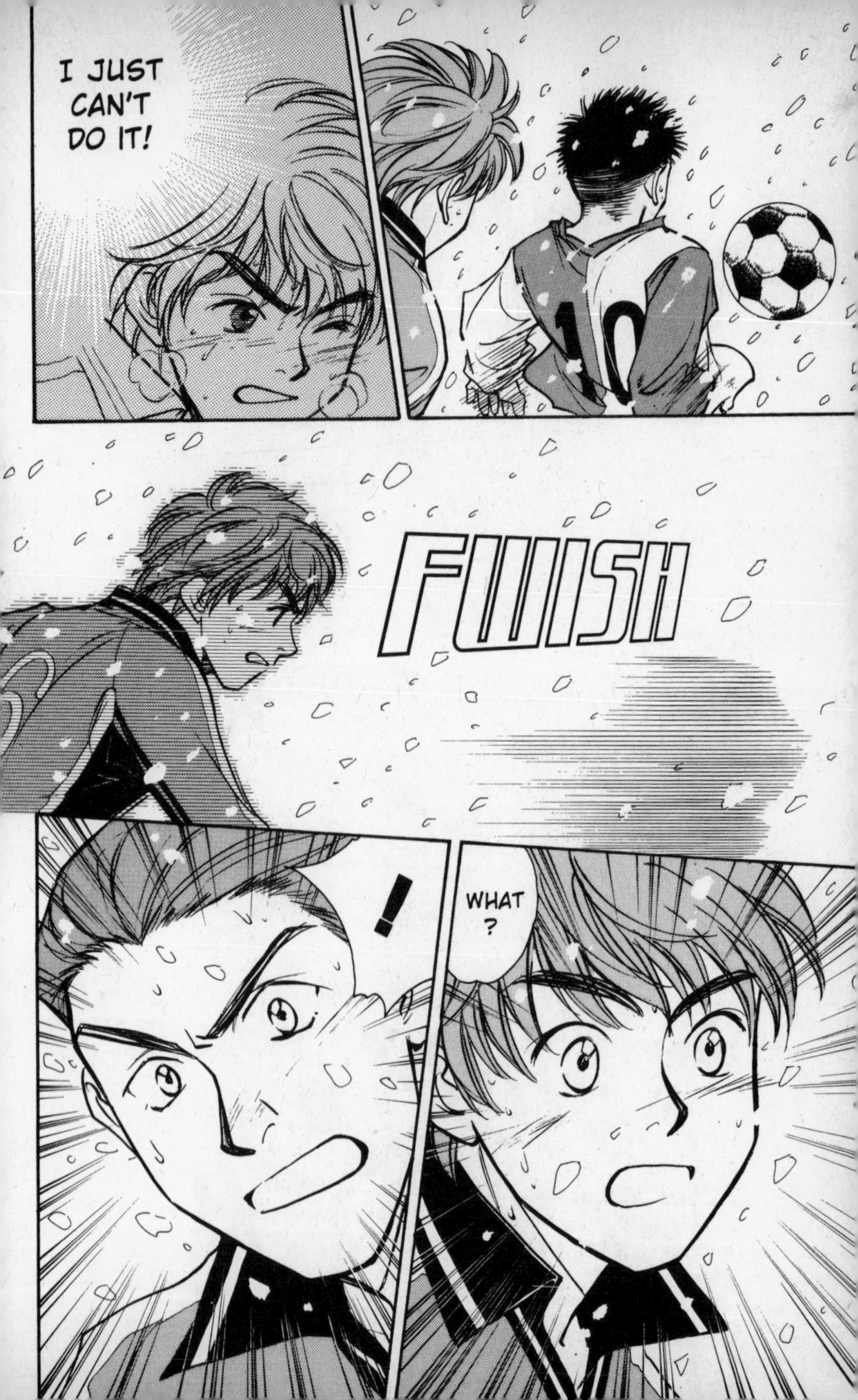
I JUST CAN'T DO IT!
FWISH
WHAT?
!

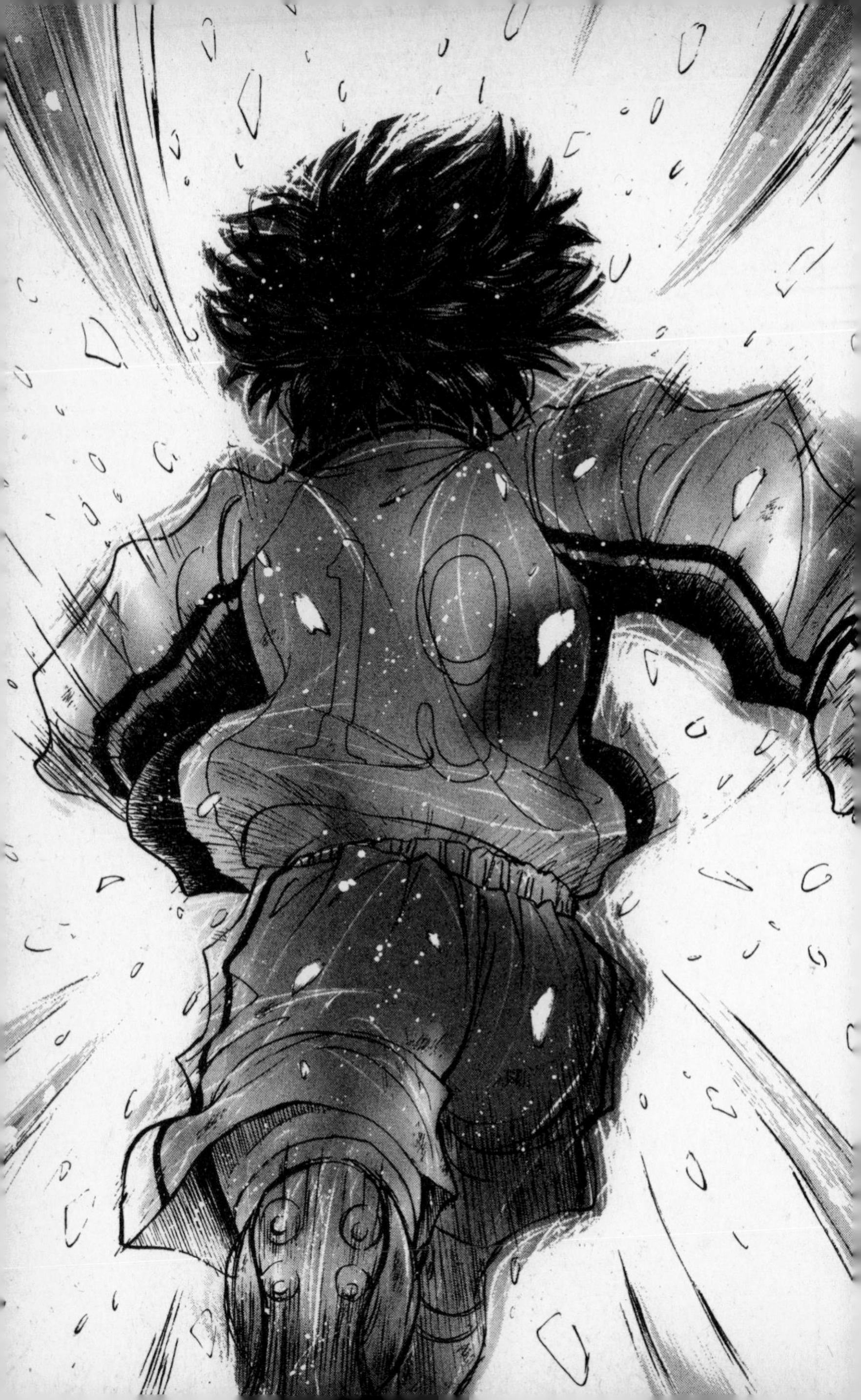

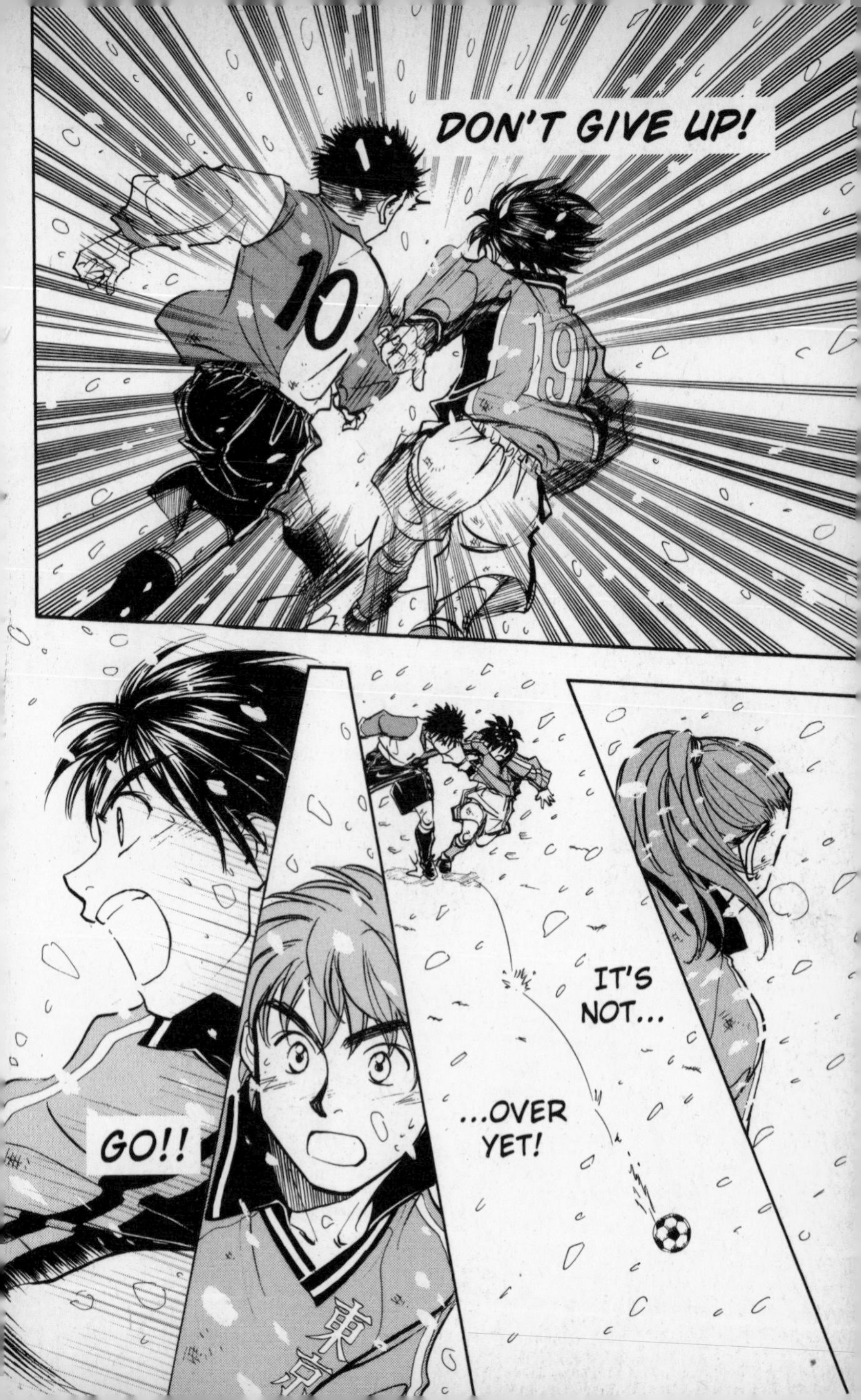
DON'T GIVE UP!
IT'S NOT...
...OVER YET!
GO!!

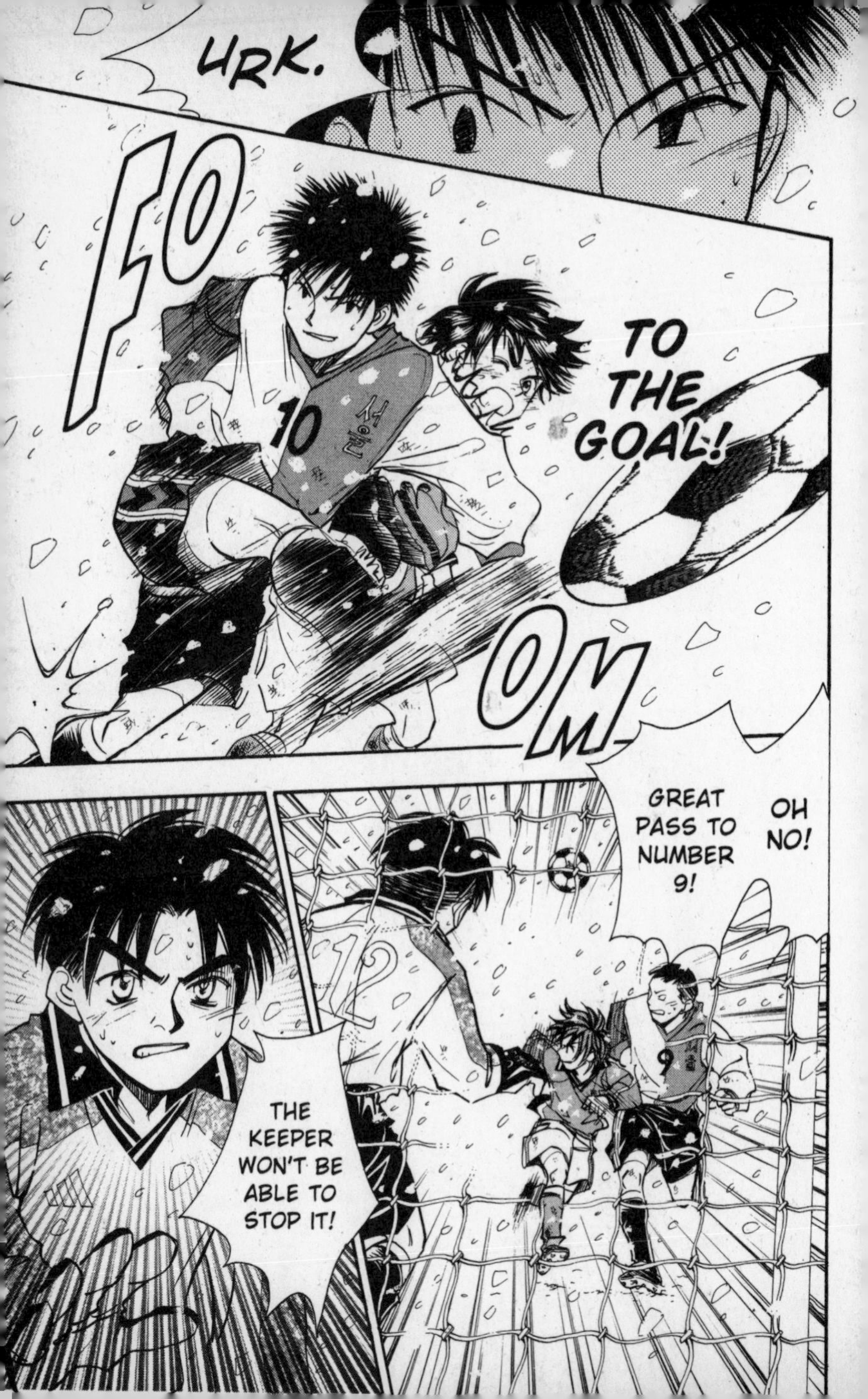
URK.
FOOM
TO THE GOAL!
OH NO!
GREAT PASS TO NUMBER 9!
THE KEEPER WON'T BE ABLE TO STOP IT!

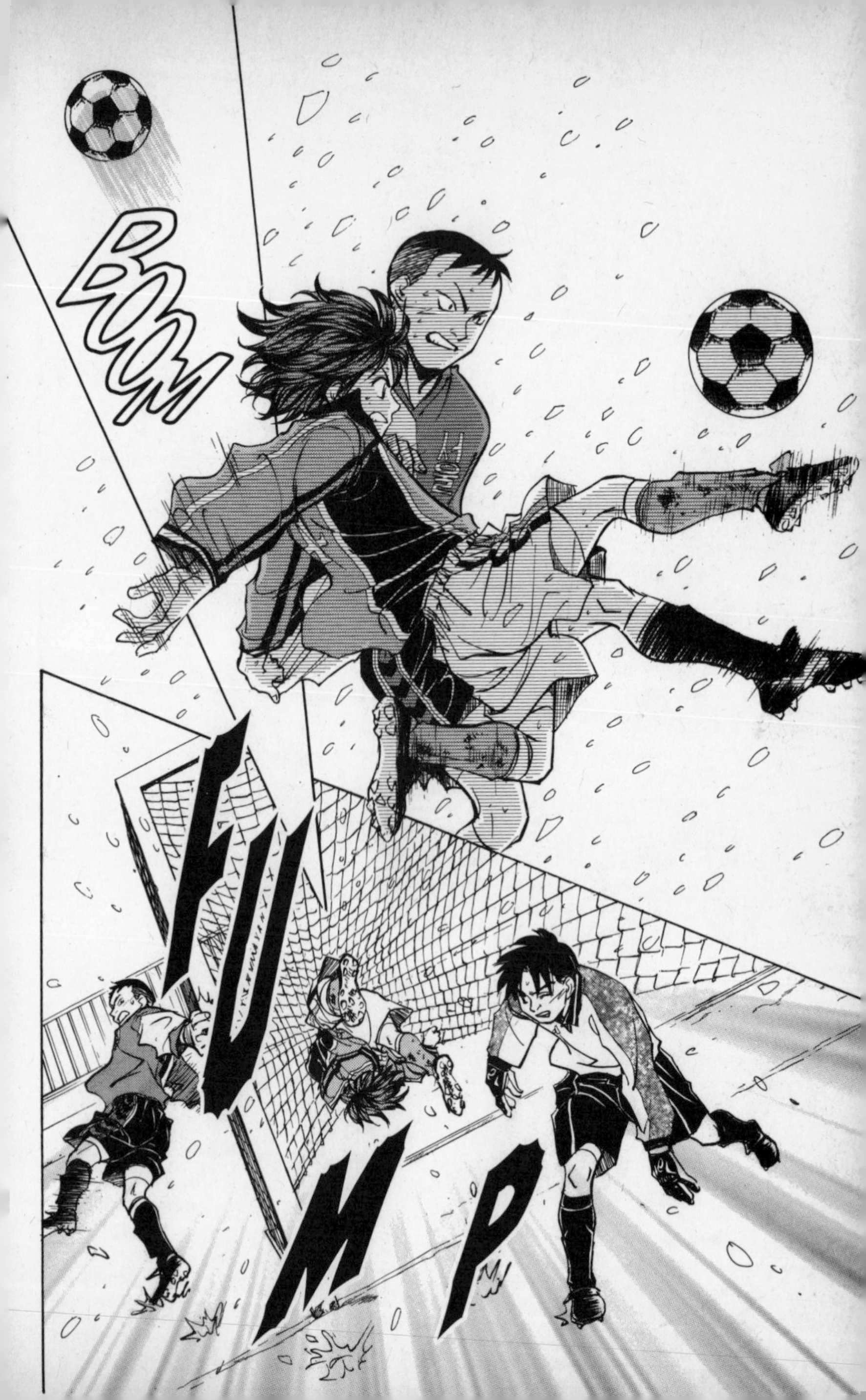
BOOM
FUMP

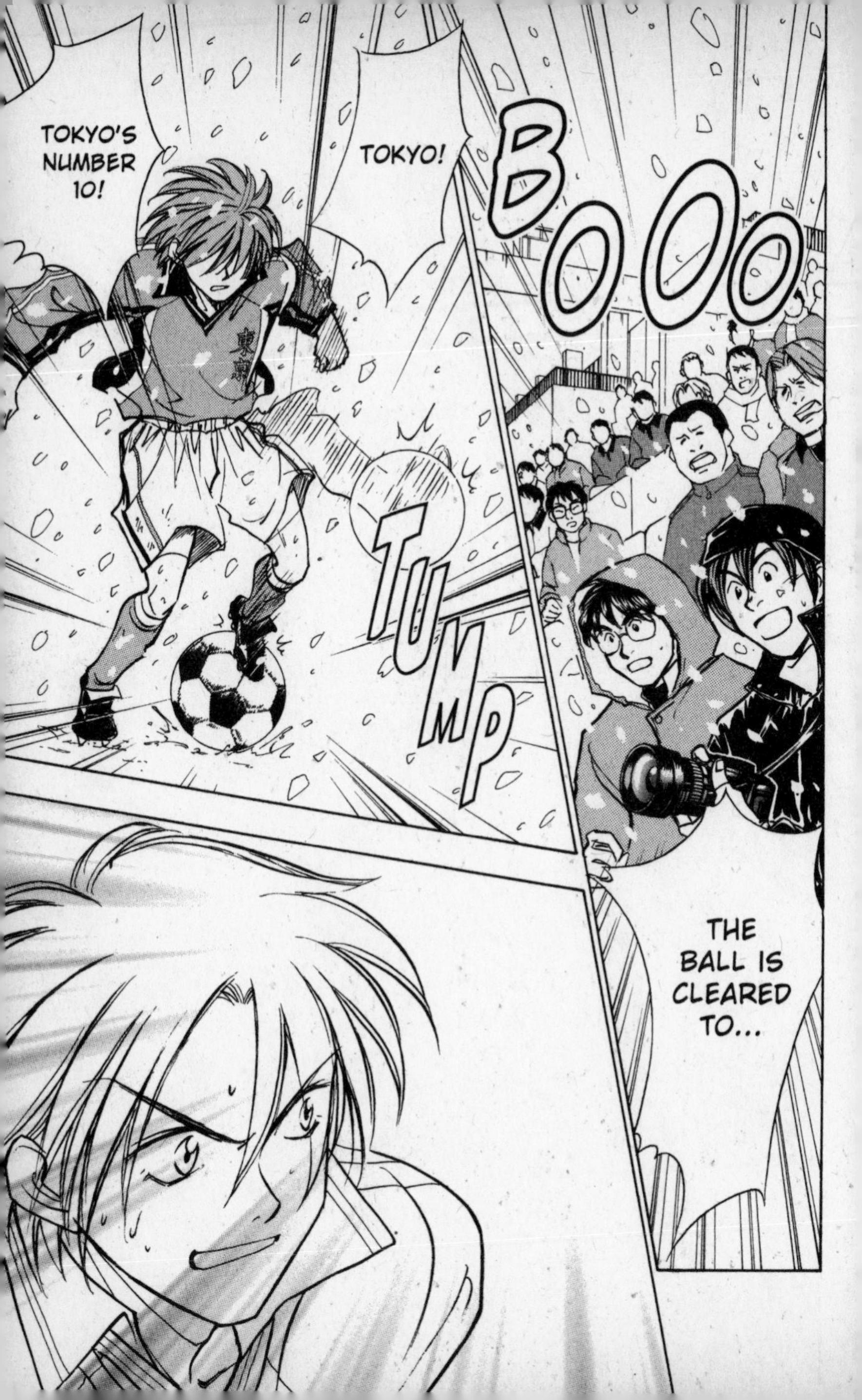
BOOOO
TOKYO!
TOKYO'S NUMBER 10!
TUMP
THE BALL IS CLEARED TO...

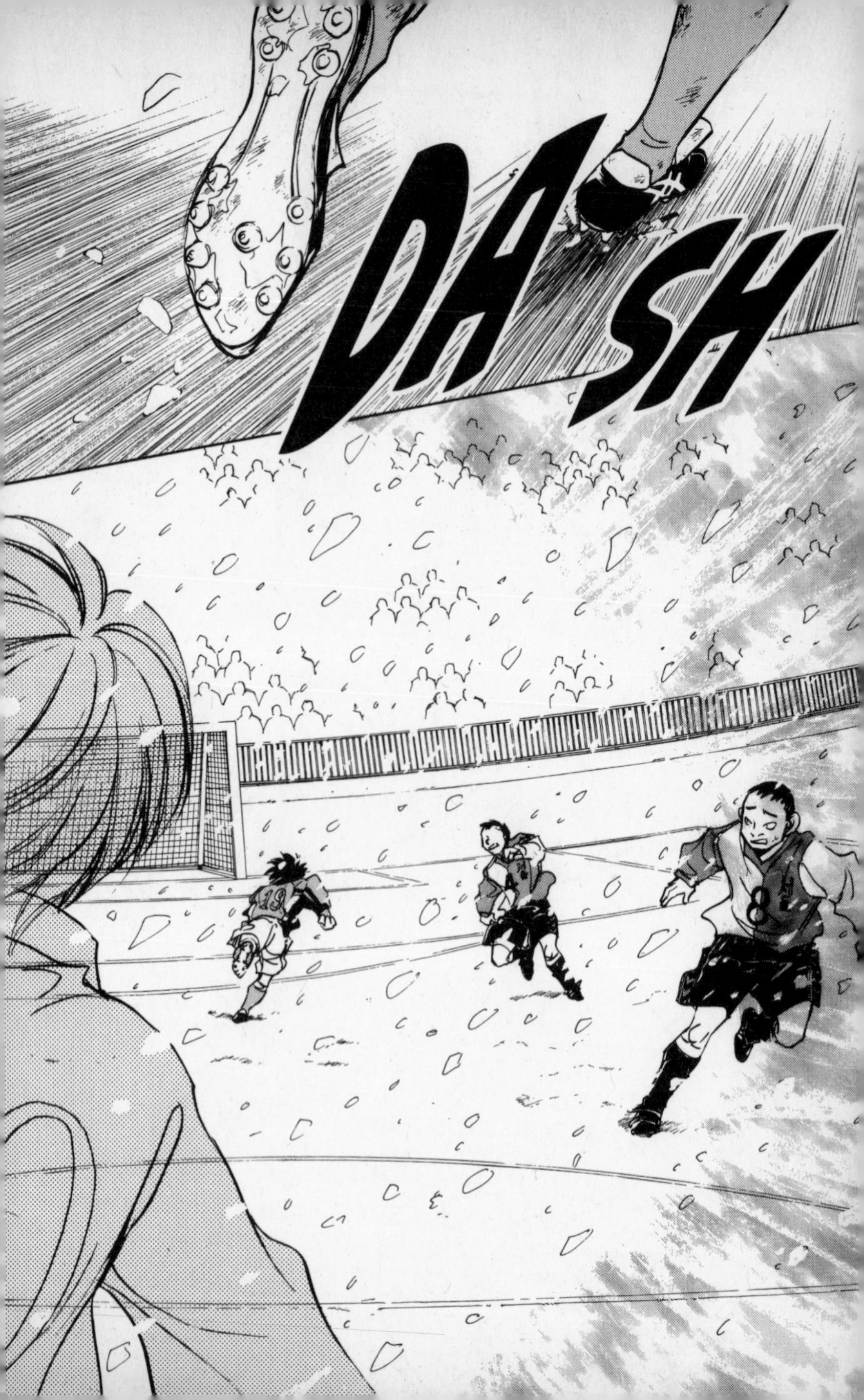
DASH

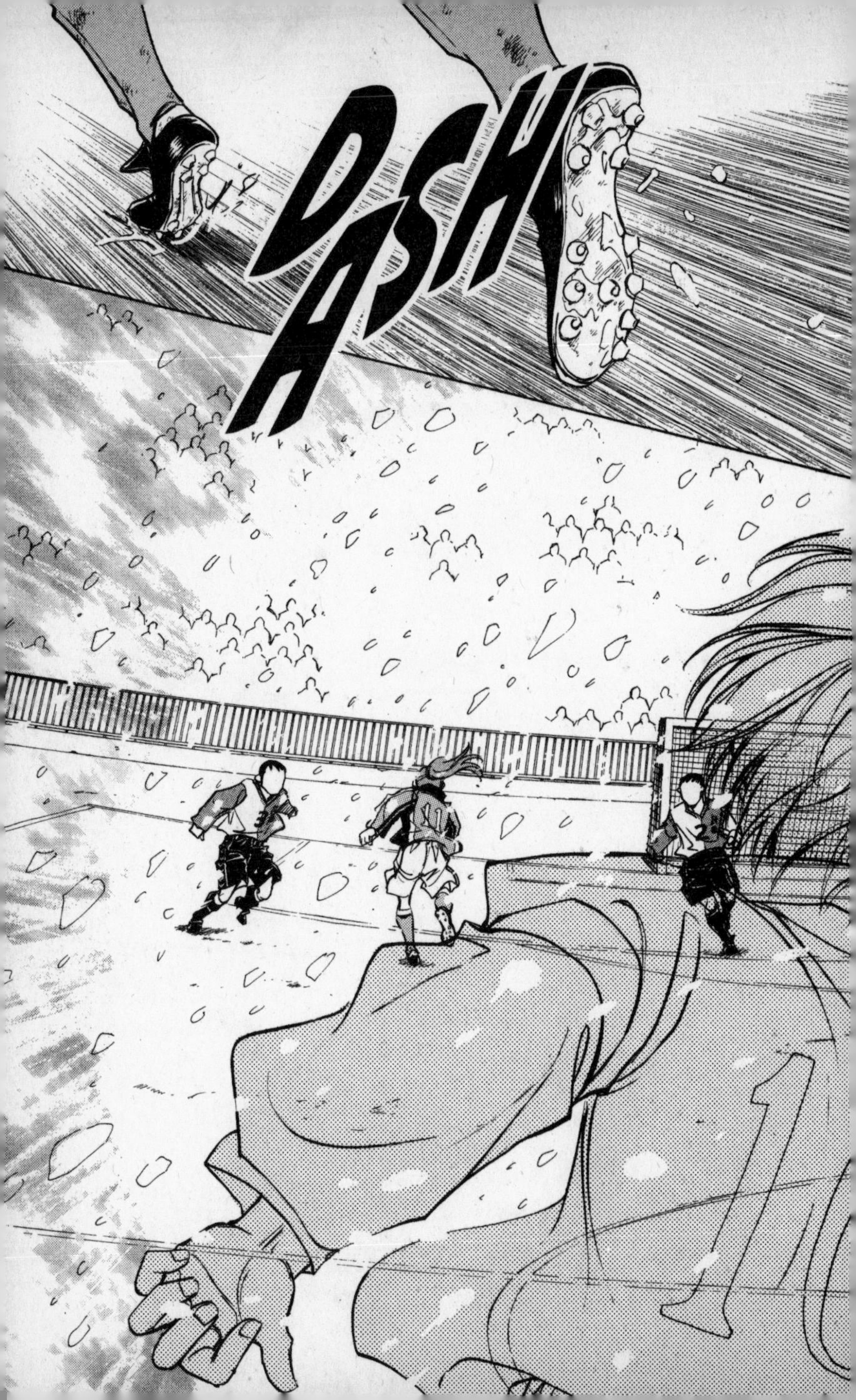
DASH

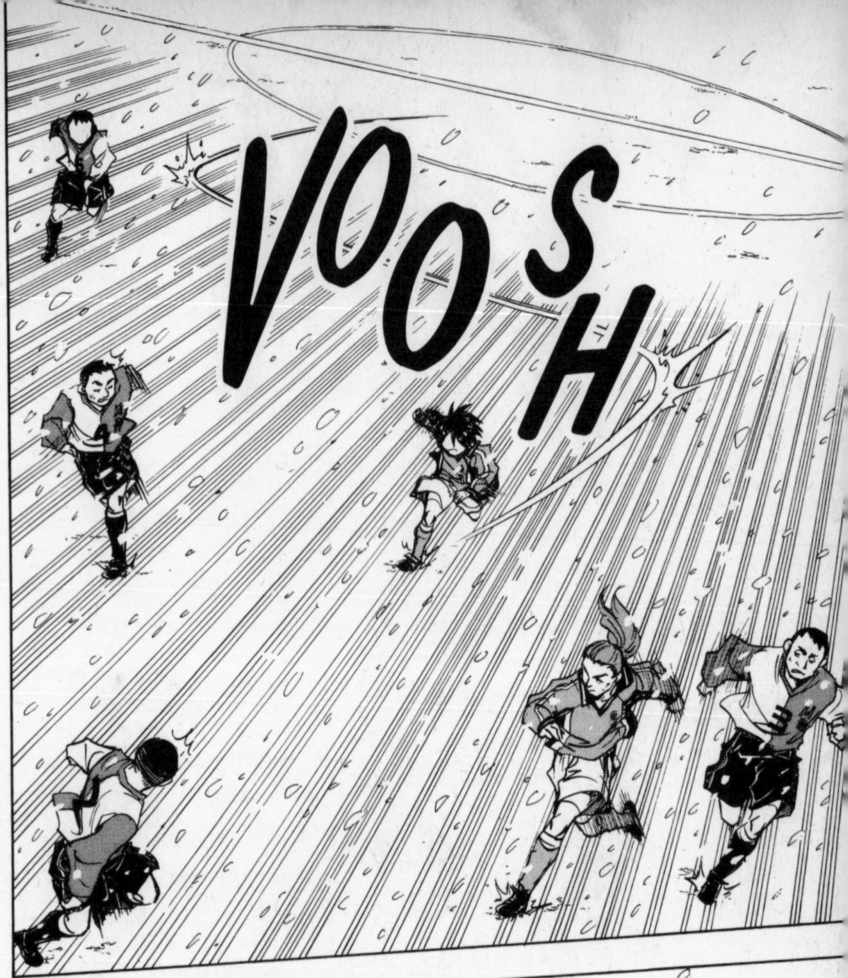
VOOSH

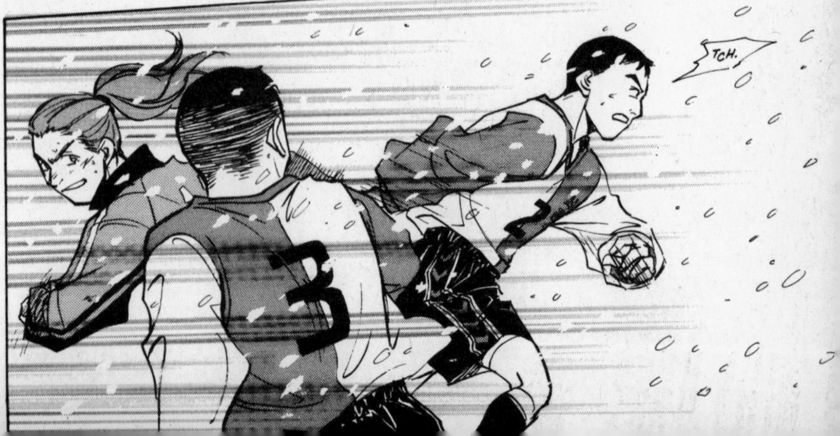
TCH.

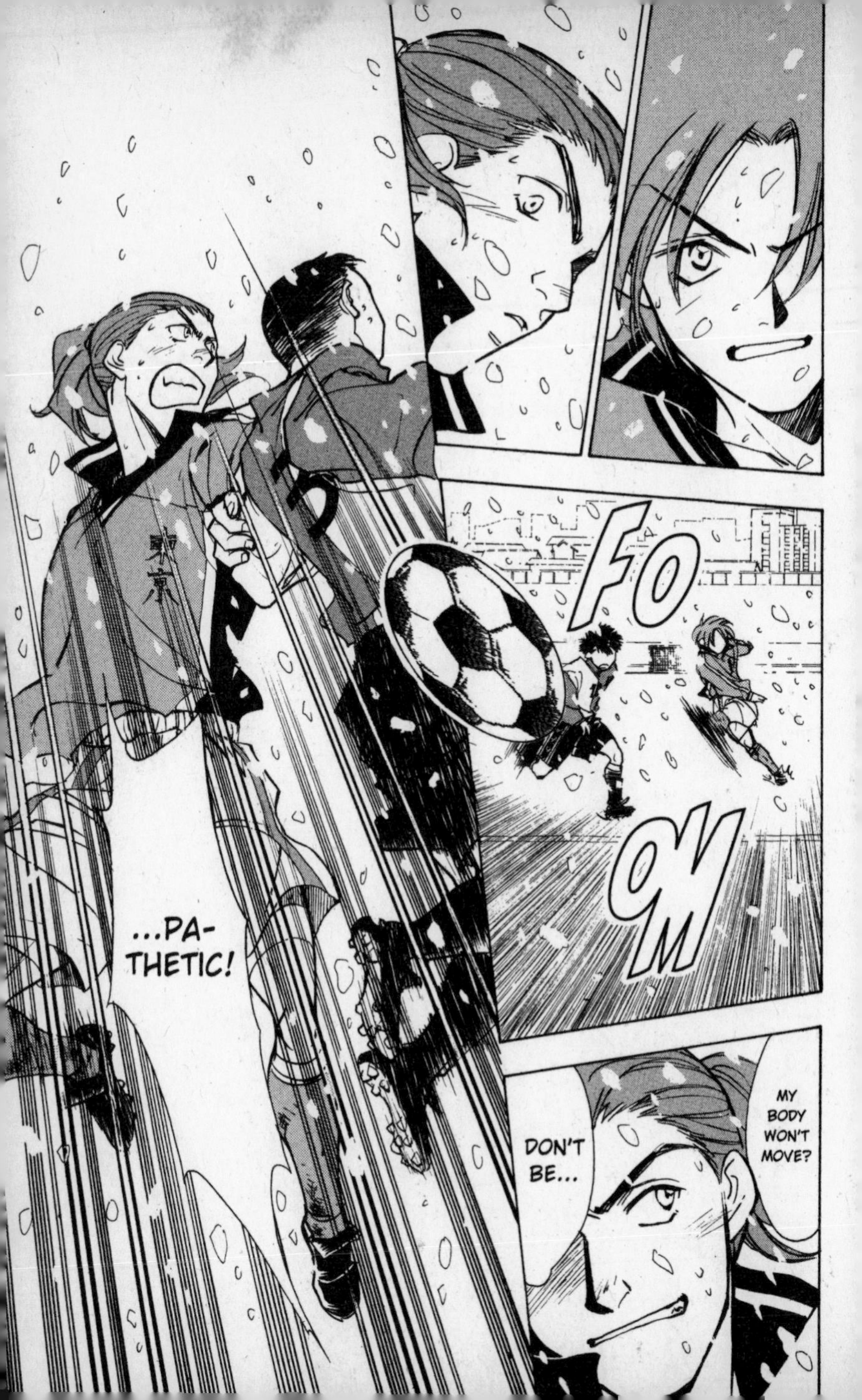
FOOM
MY BODY WON'T MOVE?
DON'T BE...
...PA-THETIC!

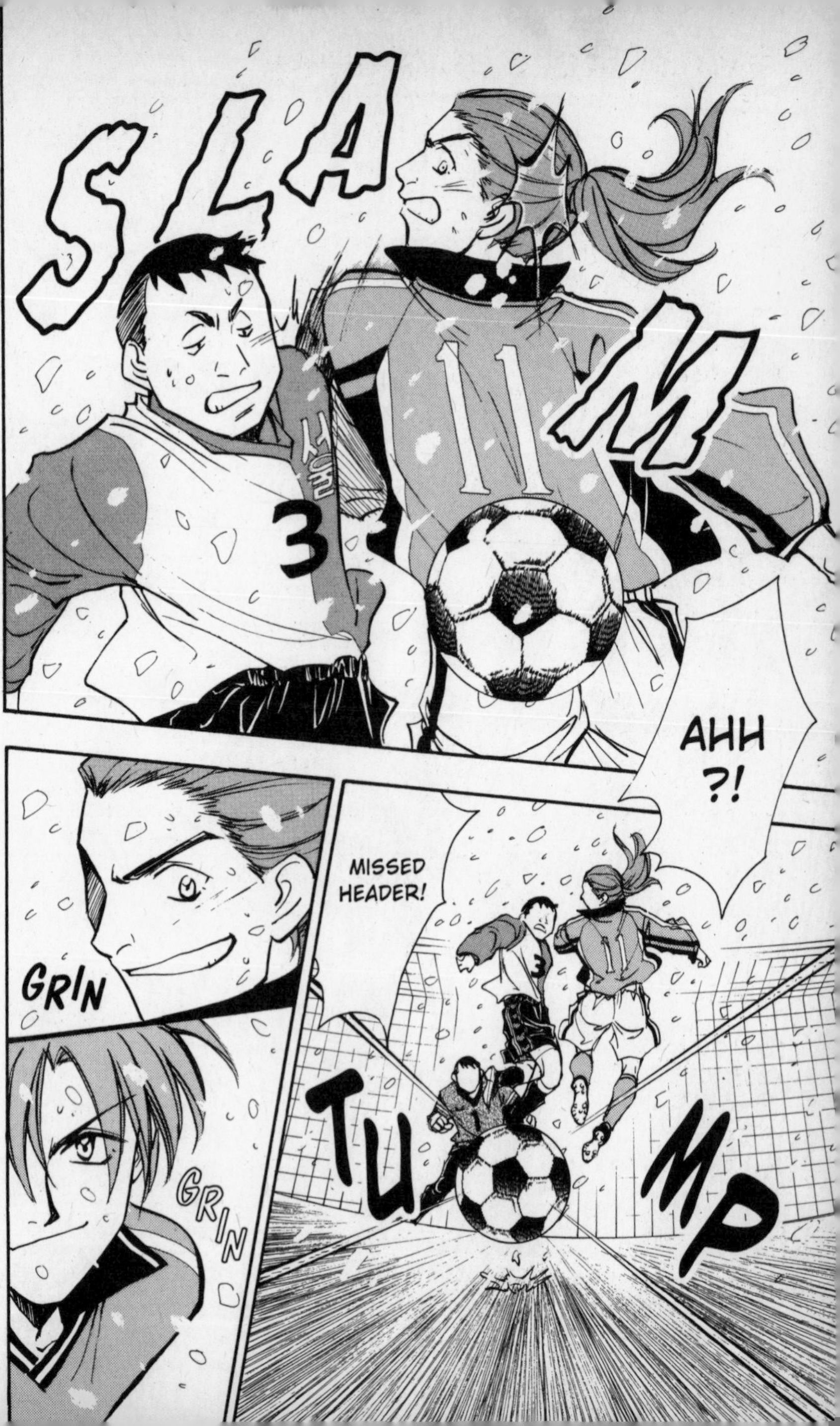
SLAM
AHH ?!
MISSED HEADER!
TU MP
GRIN
GRIN

STAGE.161 Stare in Wonder

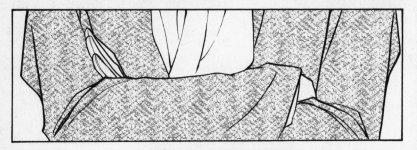

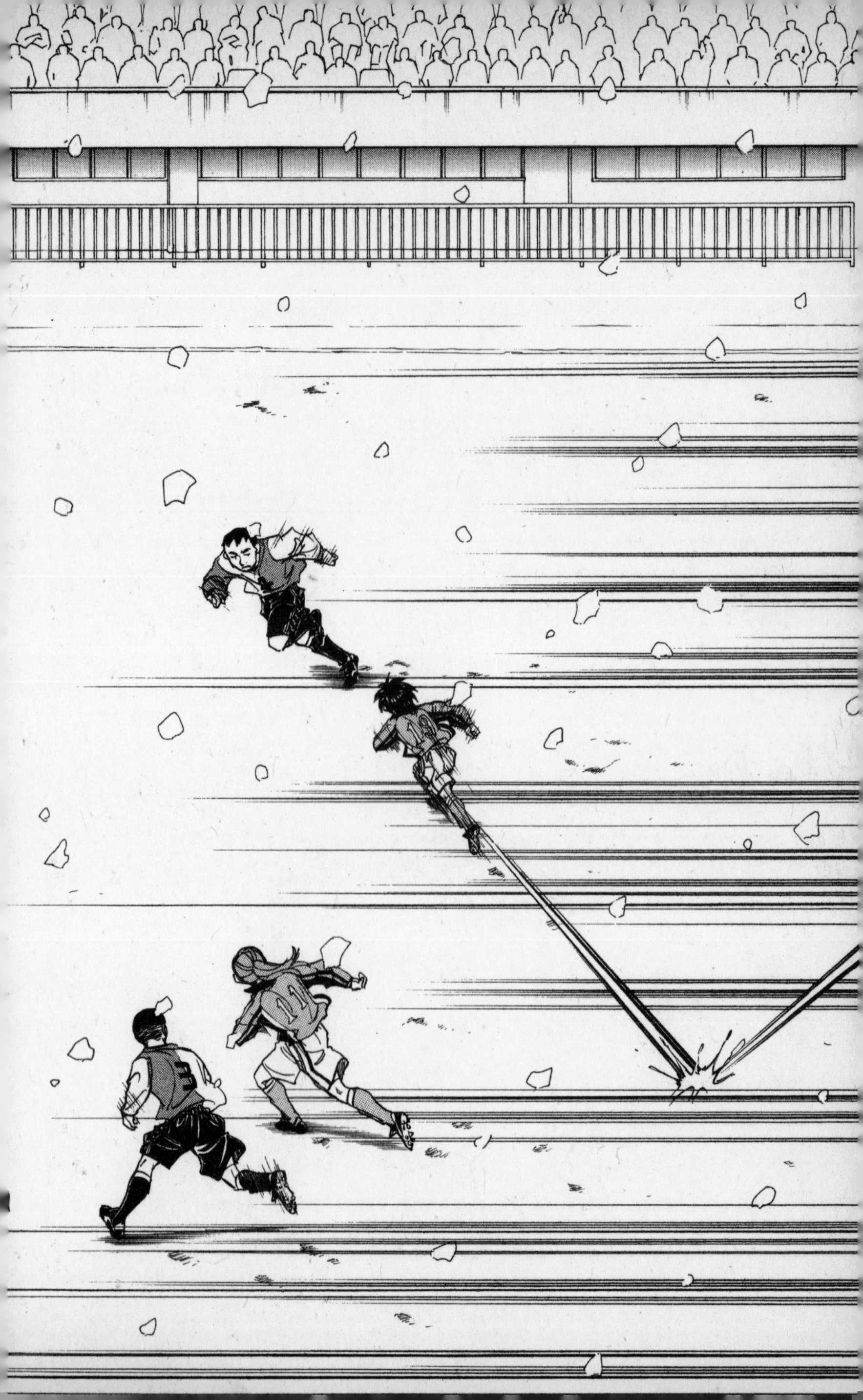

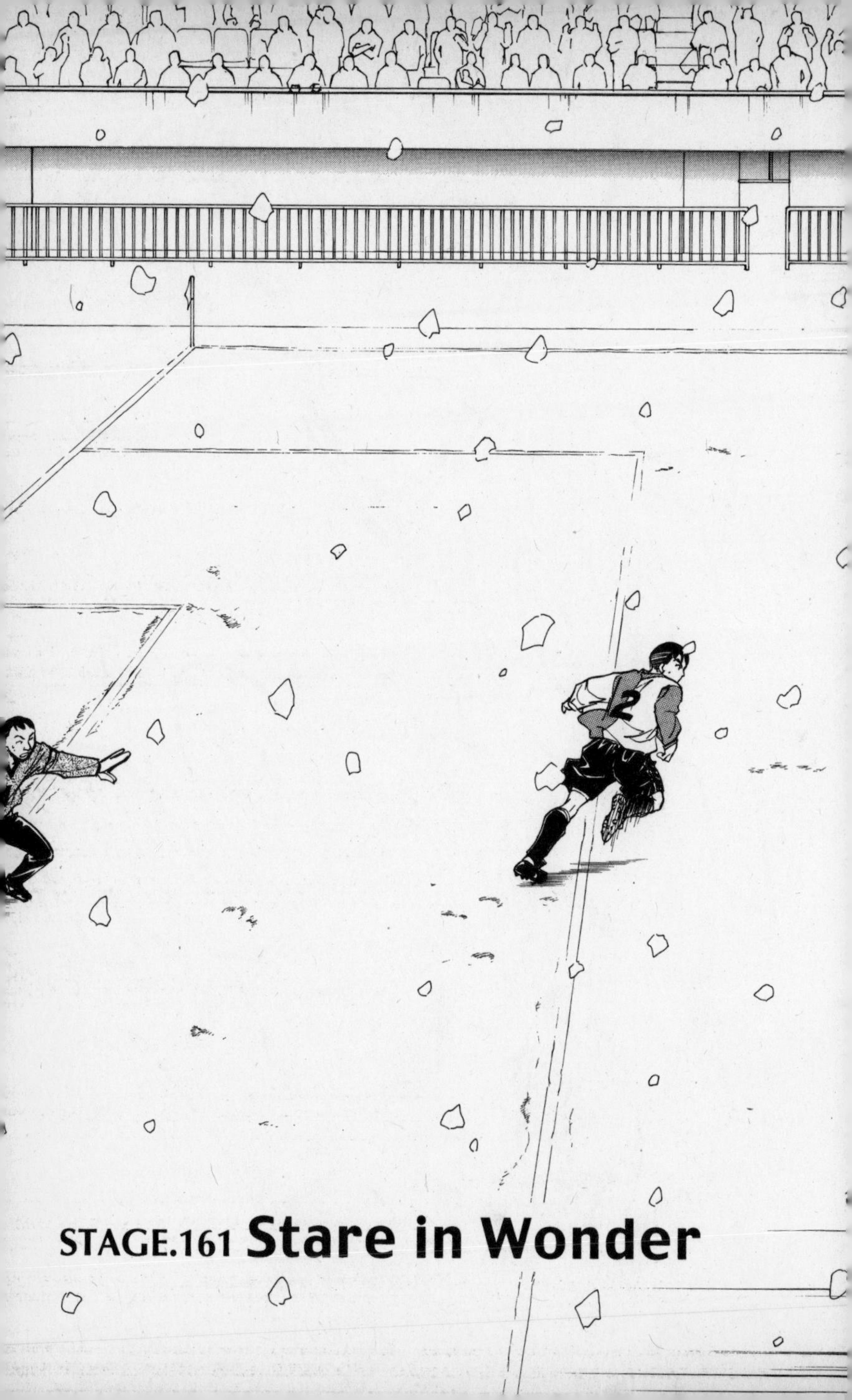

STAGE.161 Stare in Wonder

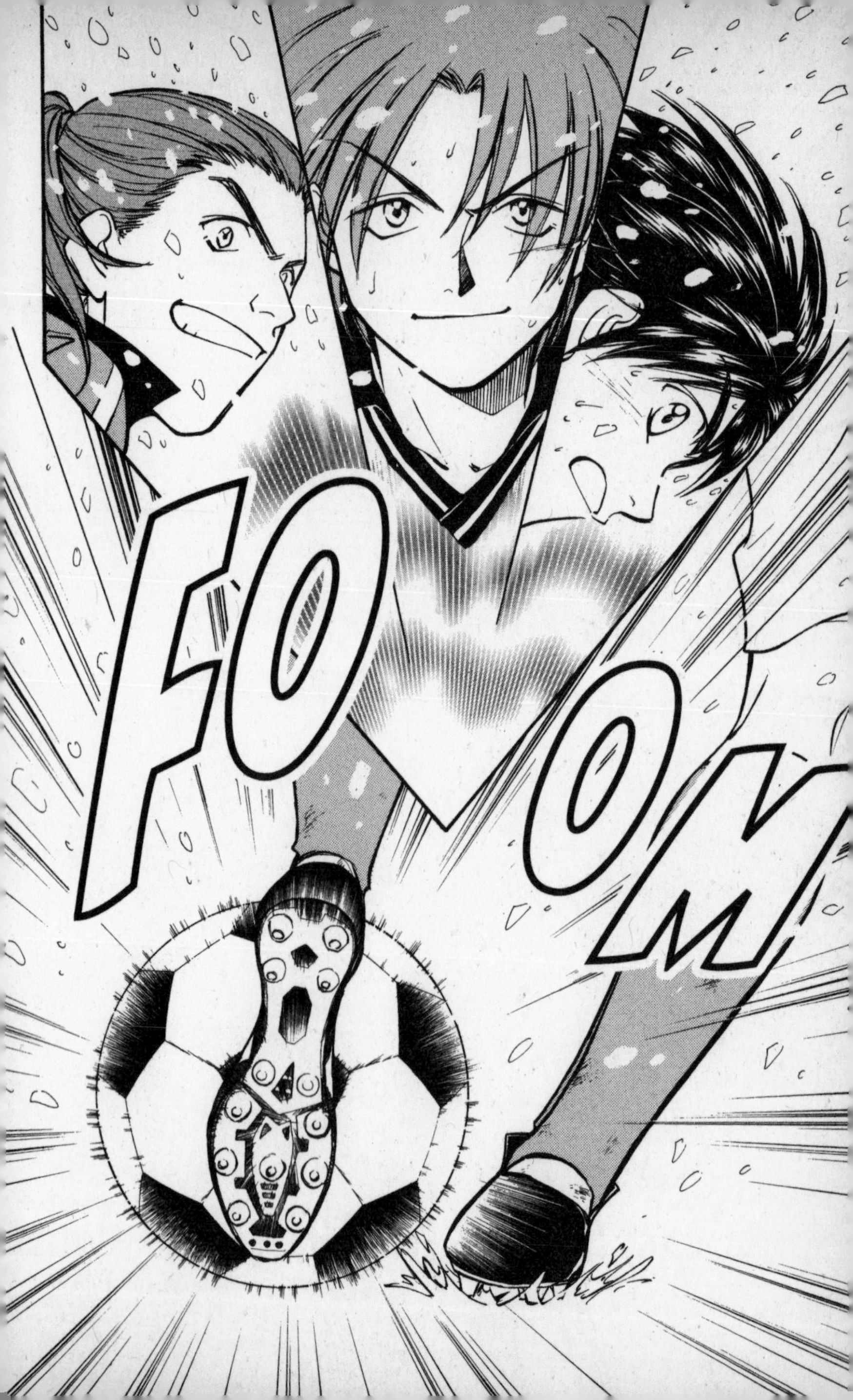
FOOM

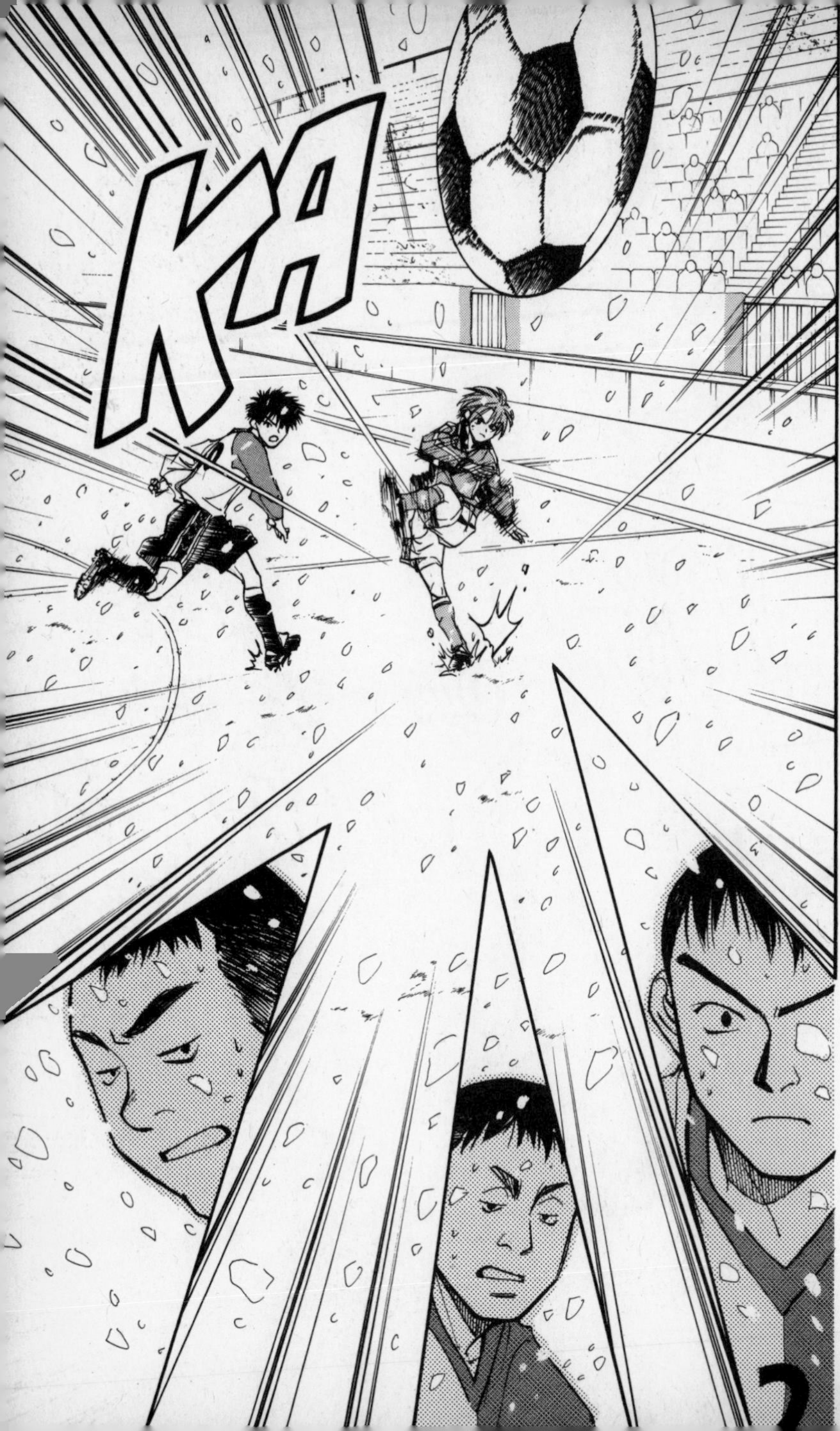
KA

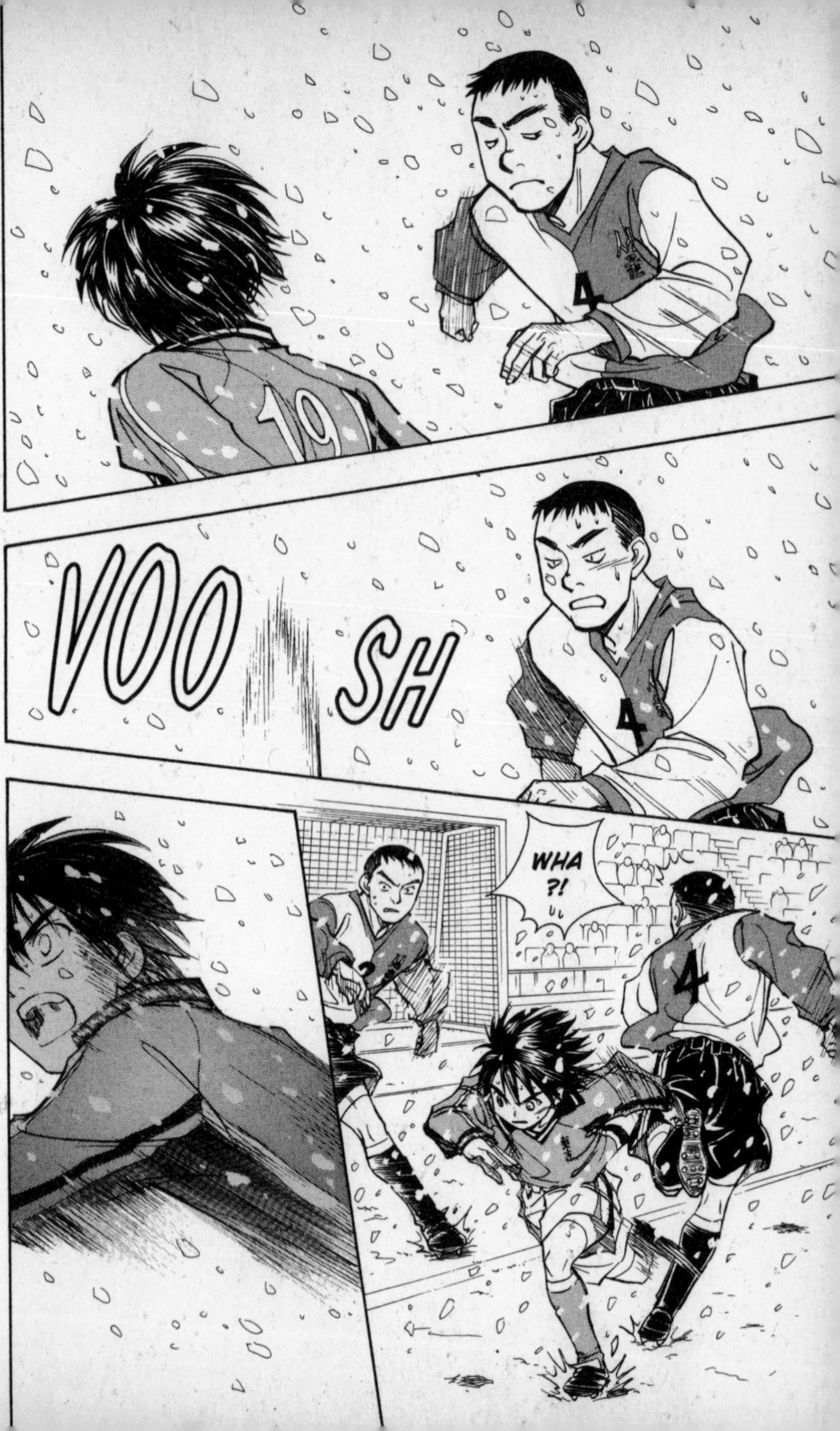
VOOSH
WHA?!

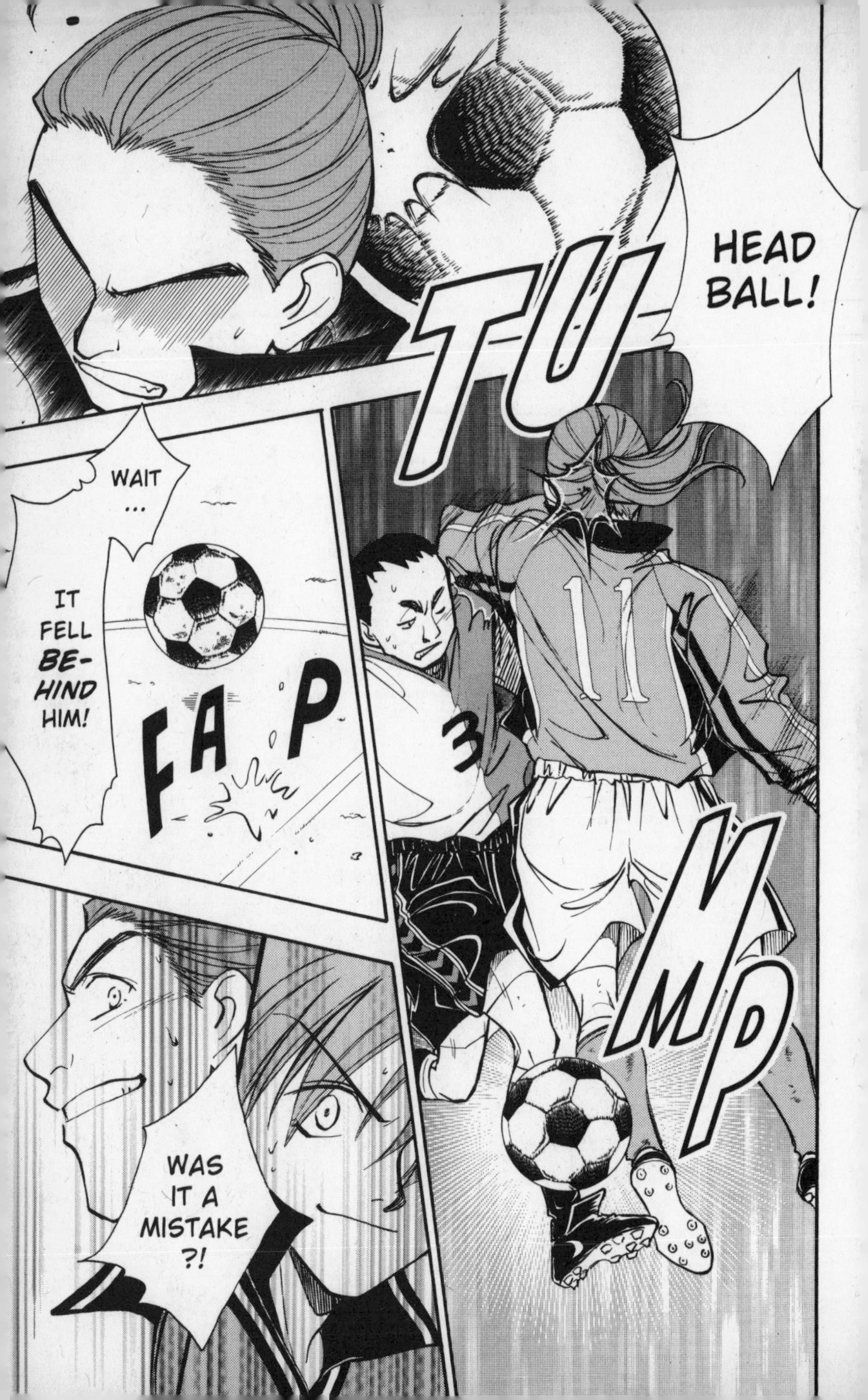
HEAD BALL!
TU
MP
WAIT...
IT FELL BE-HIND HIM!
FAP
WAS IT A MISTAKE?!

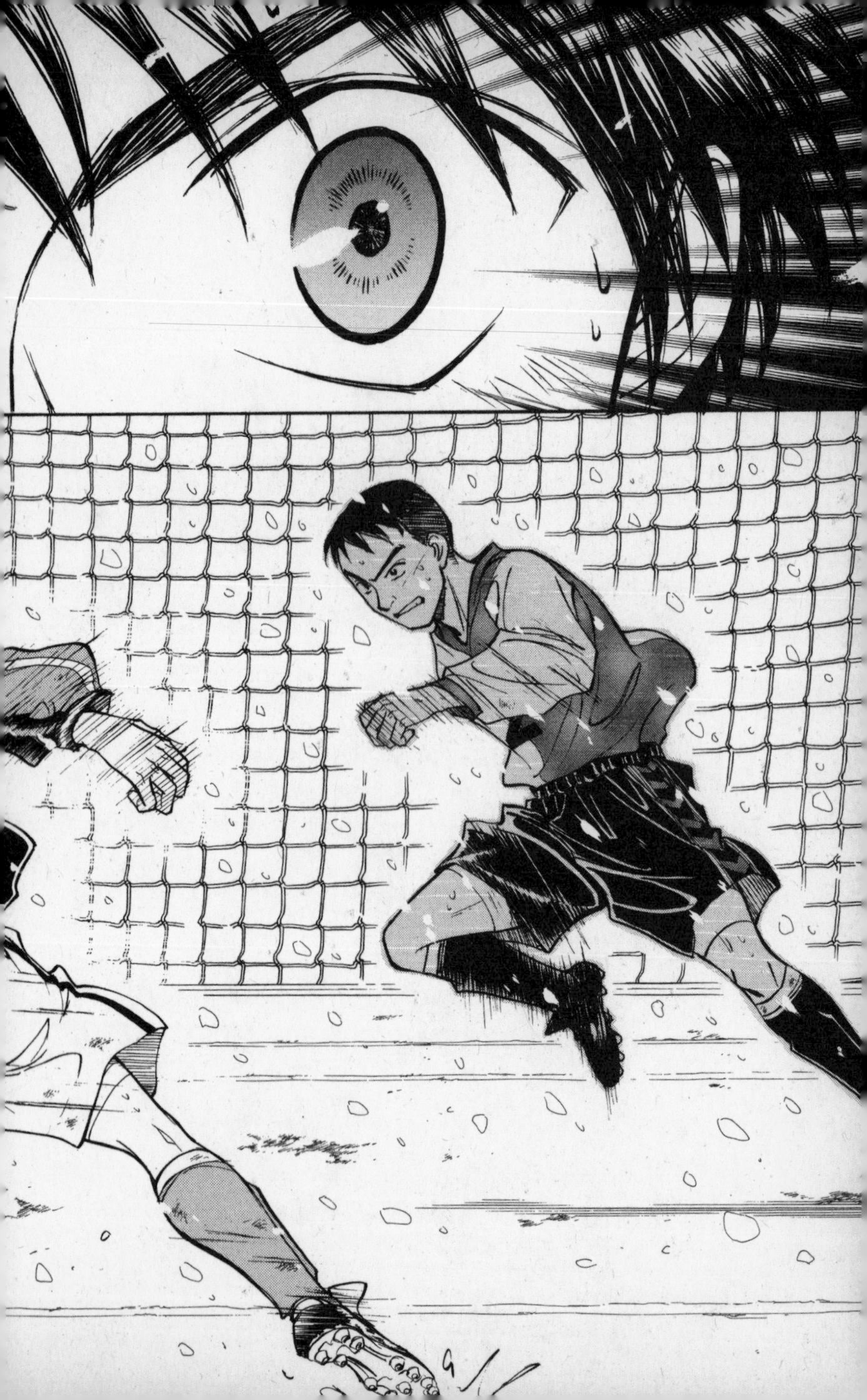

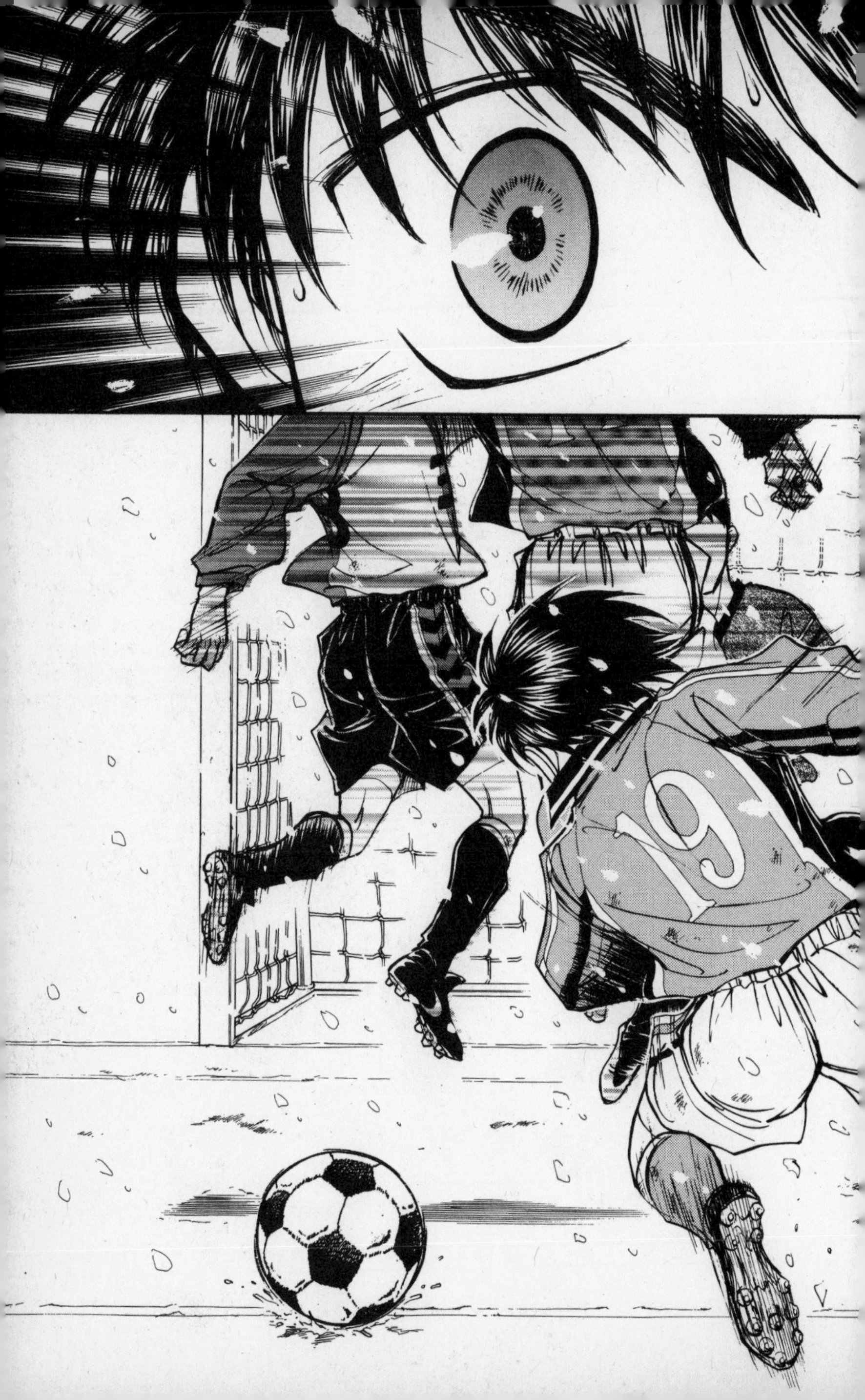

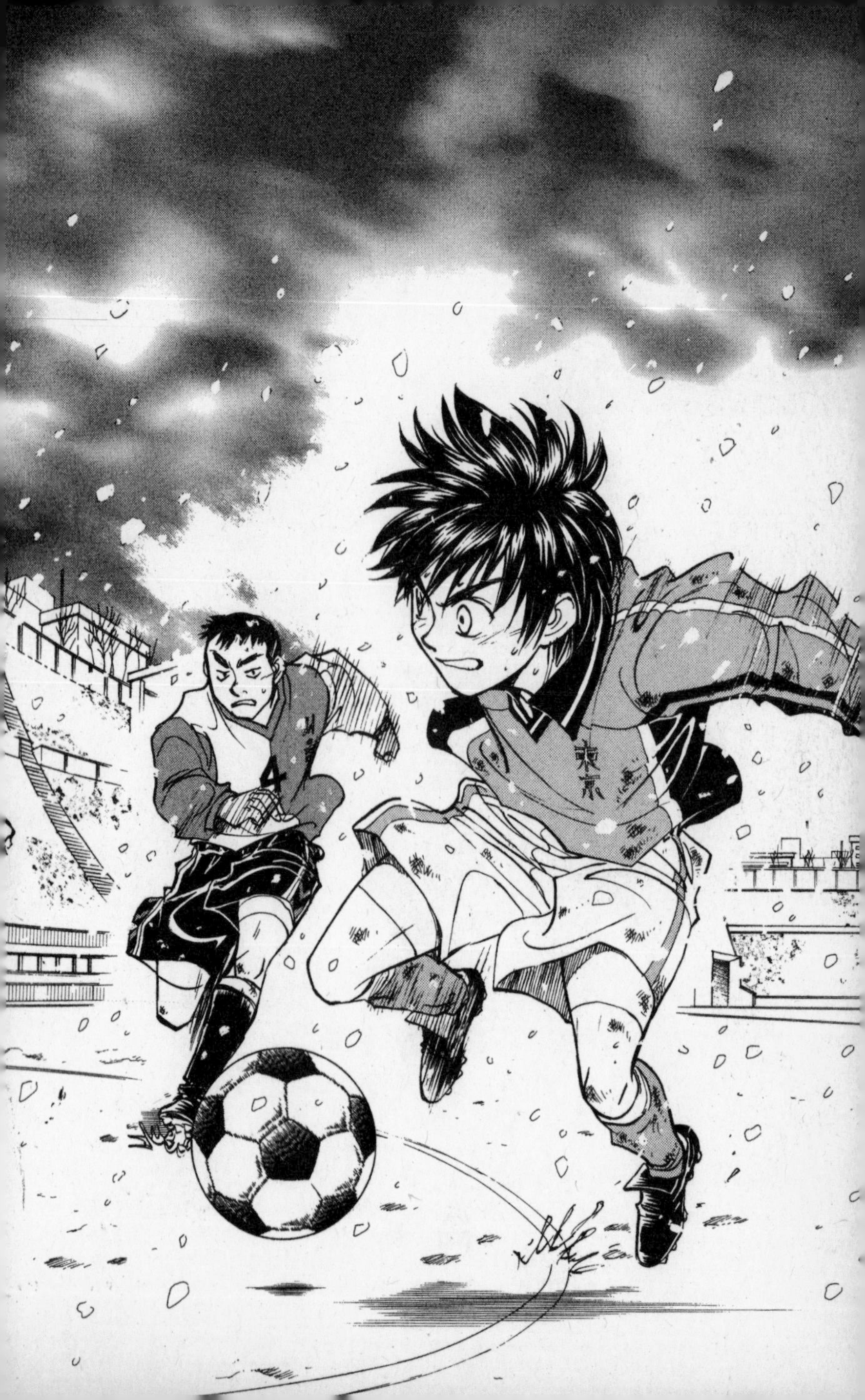

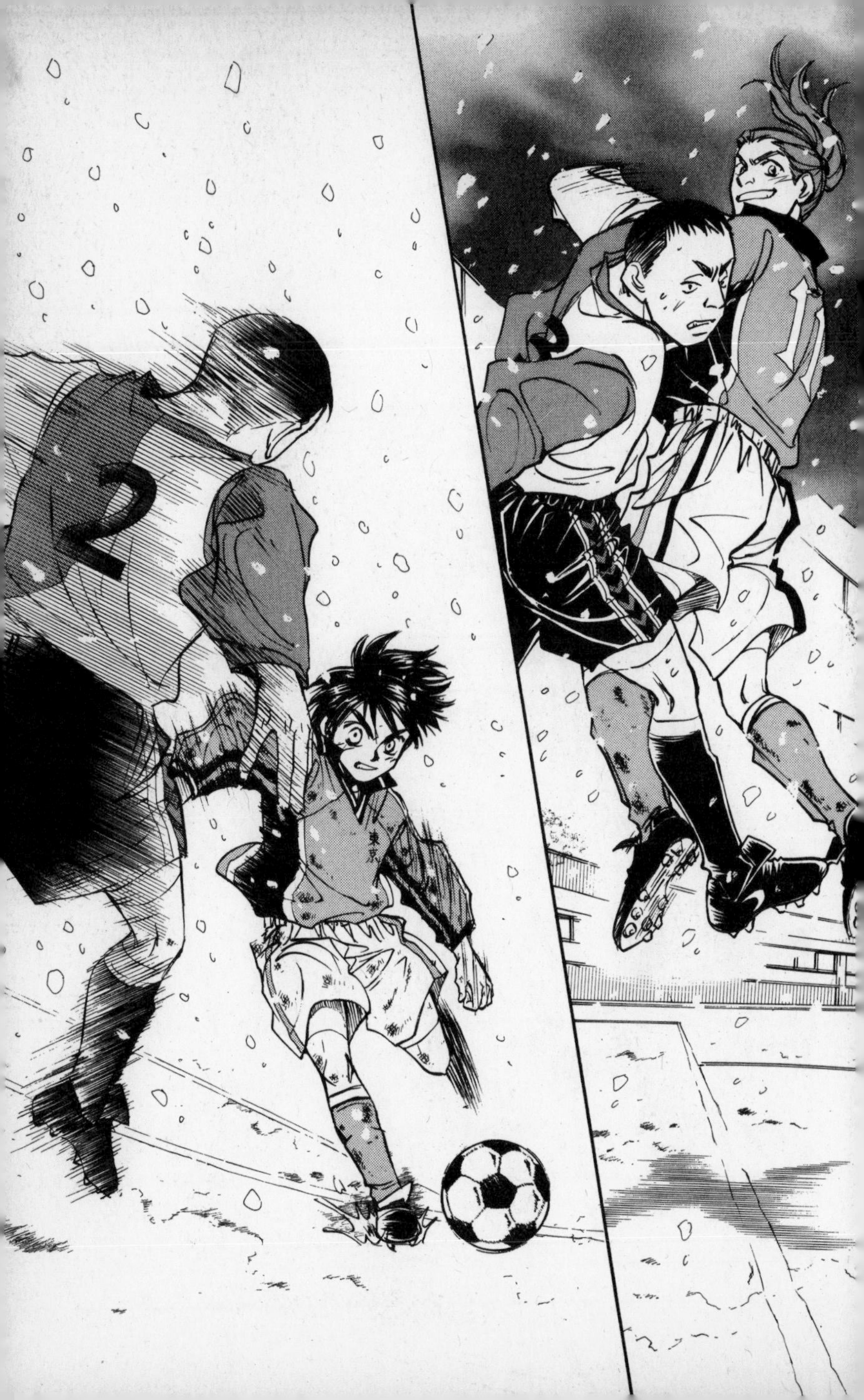

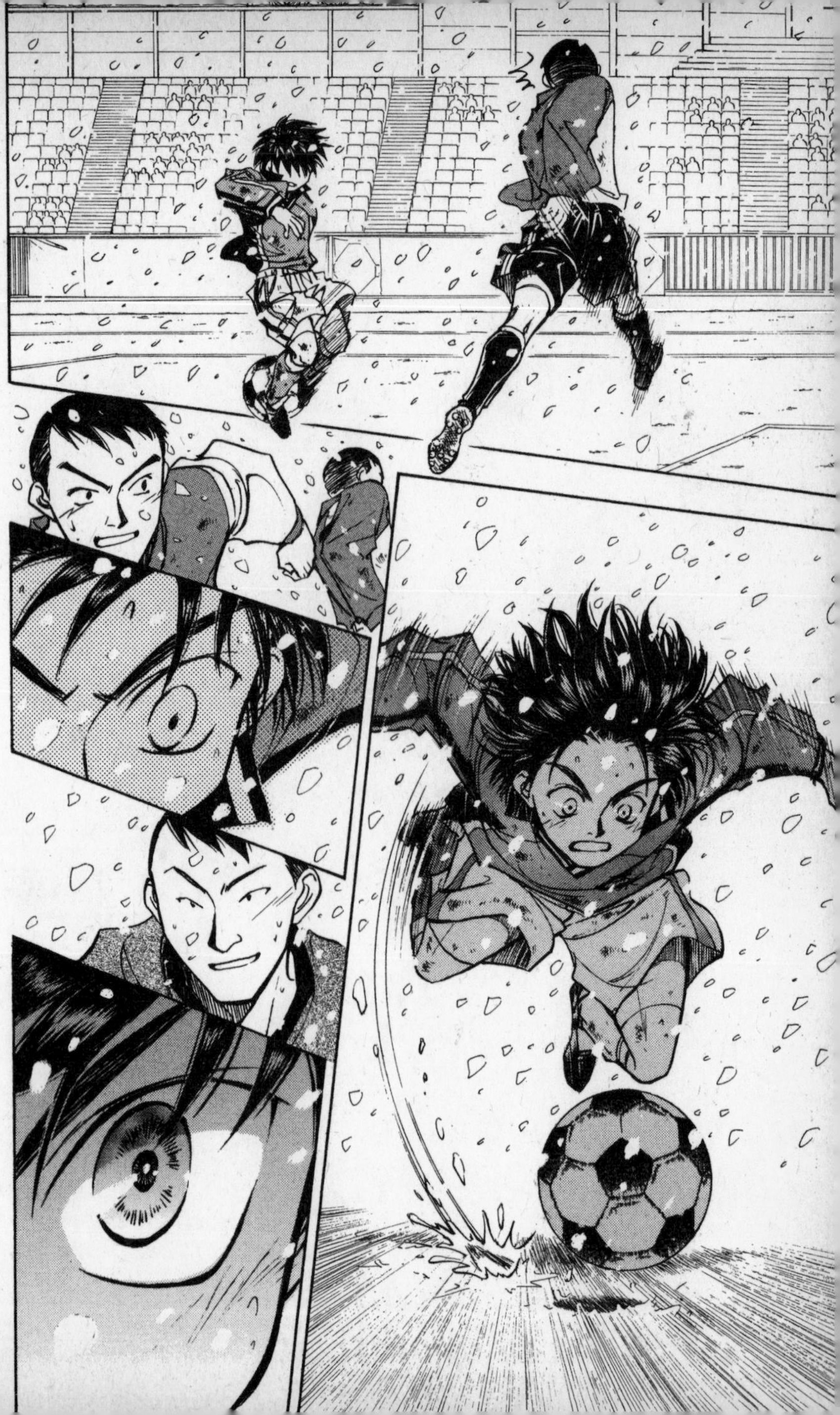

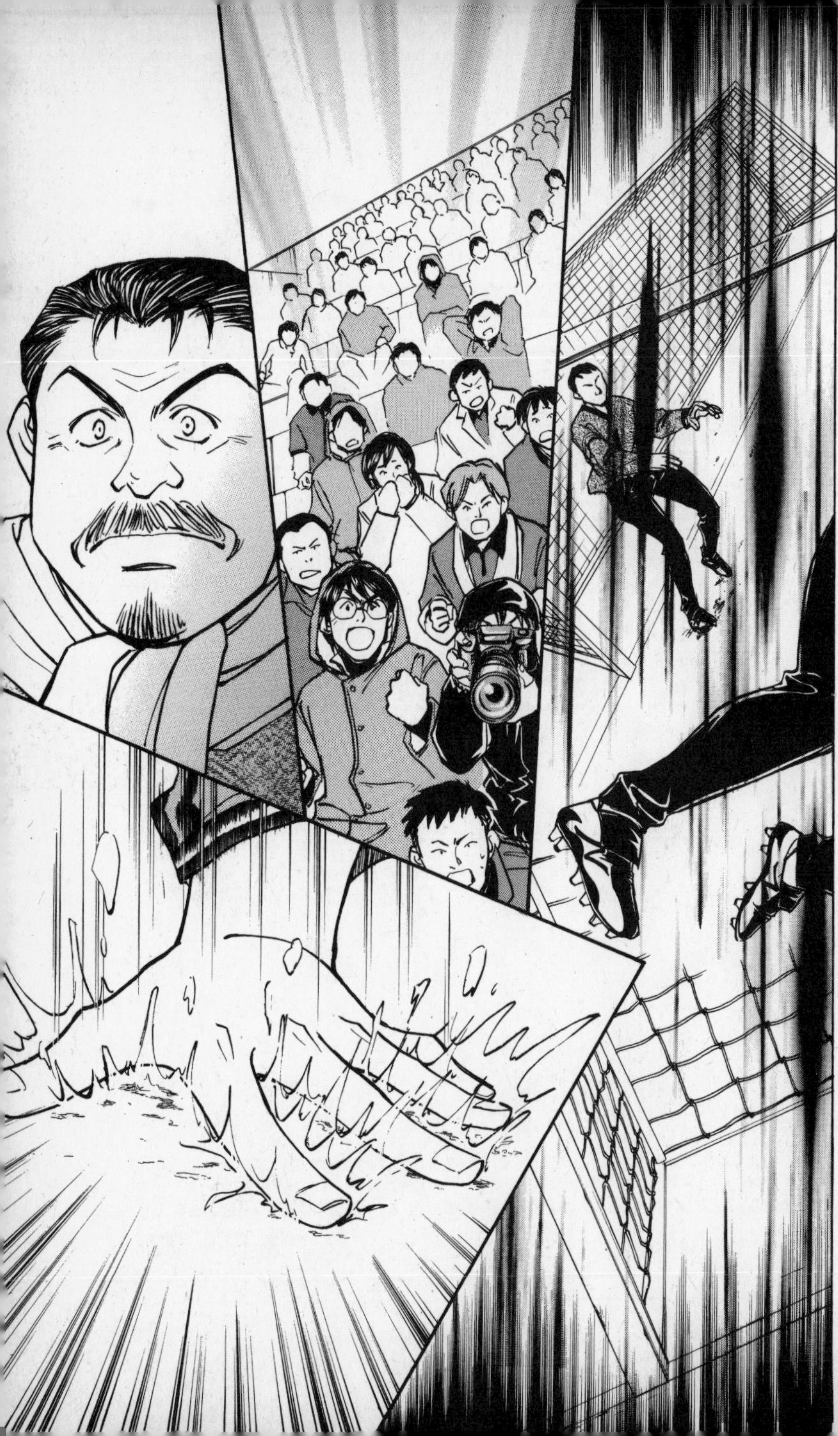

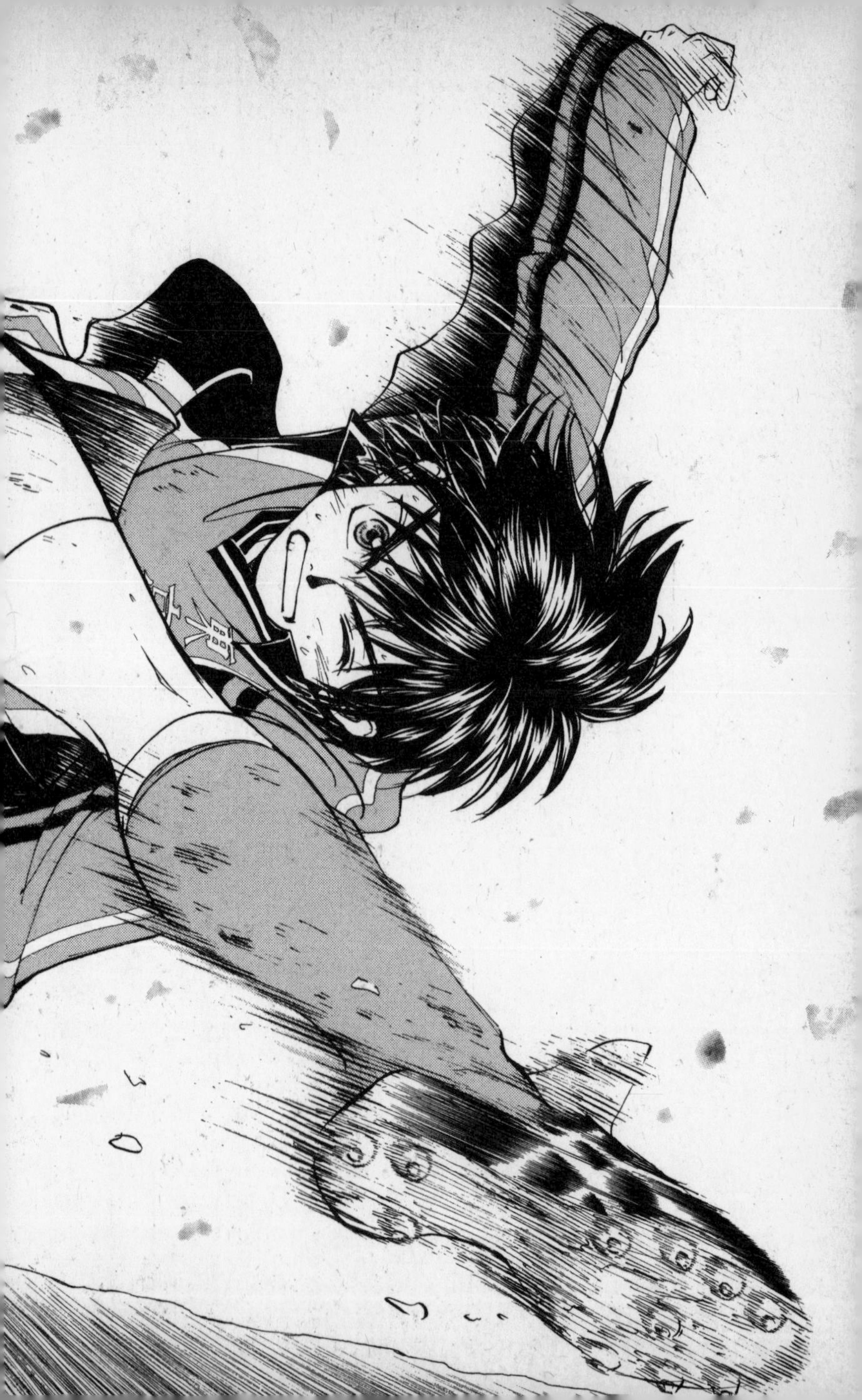

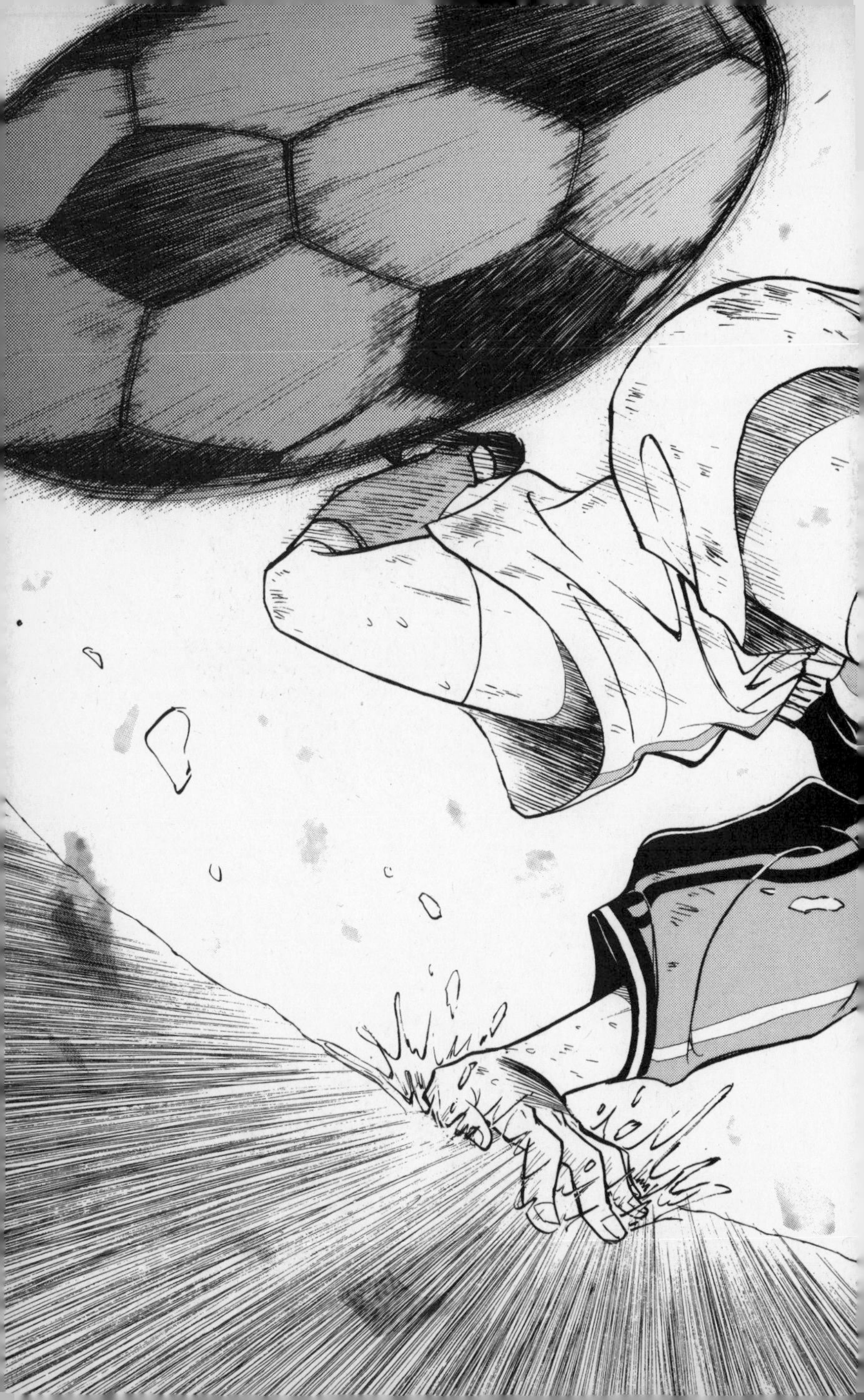

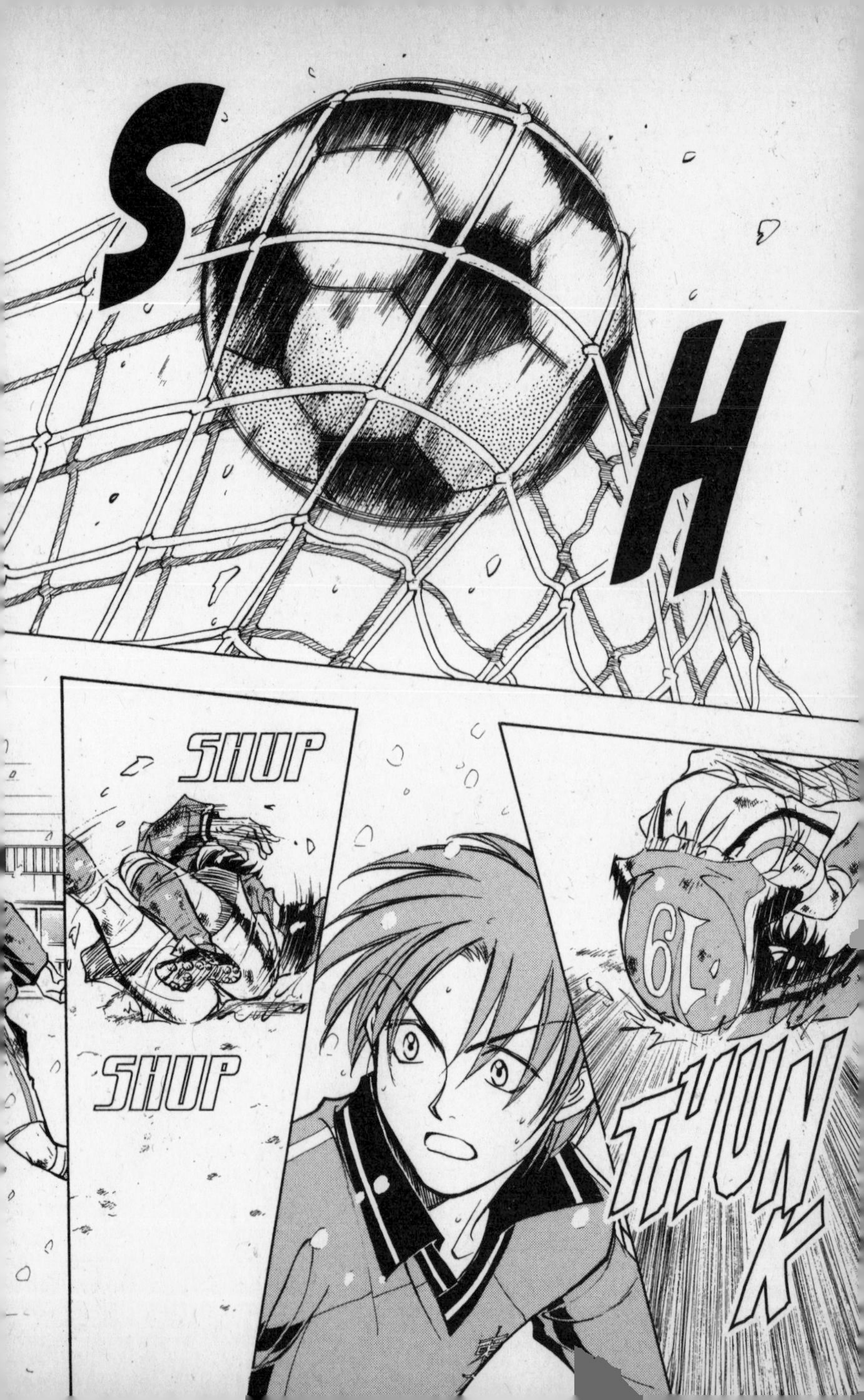
SH
THUNK
SHUP
SHUP

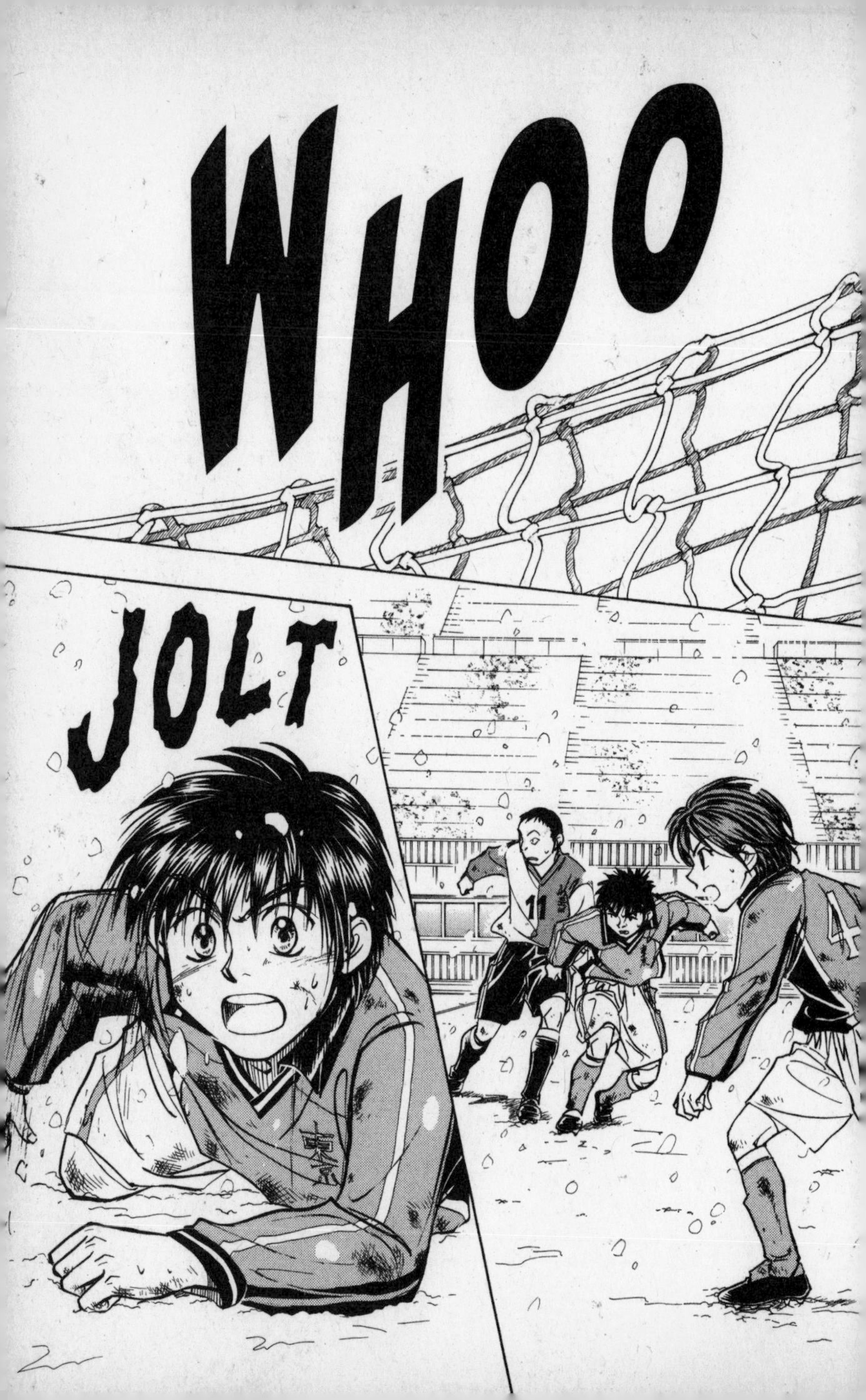
WHOO
JOLT

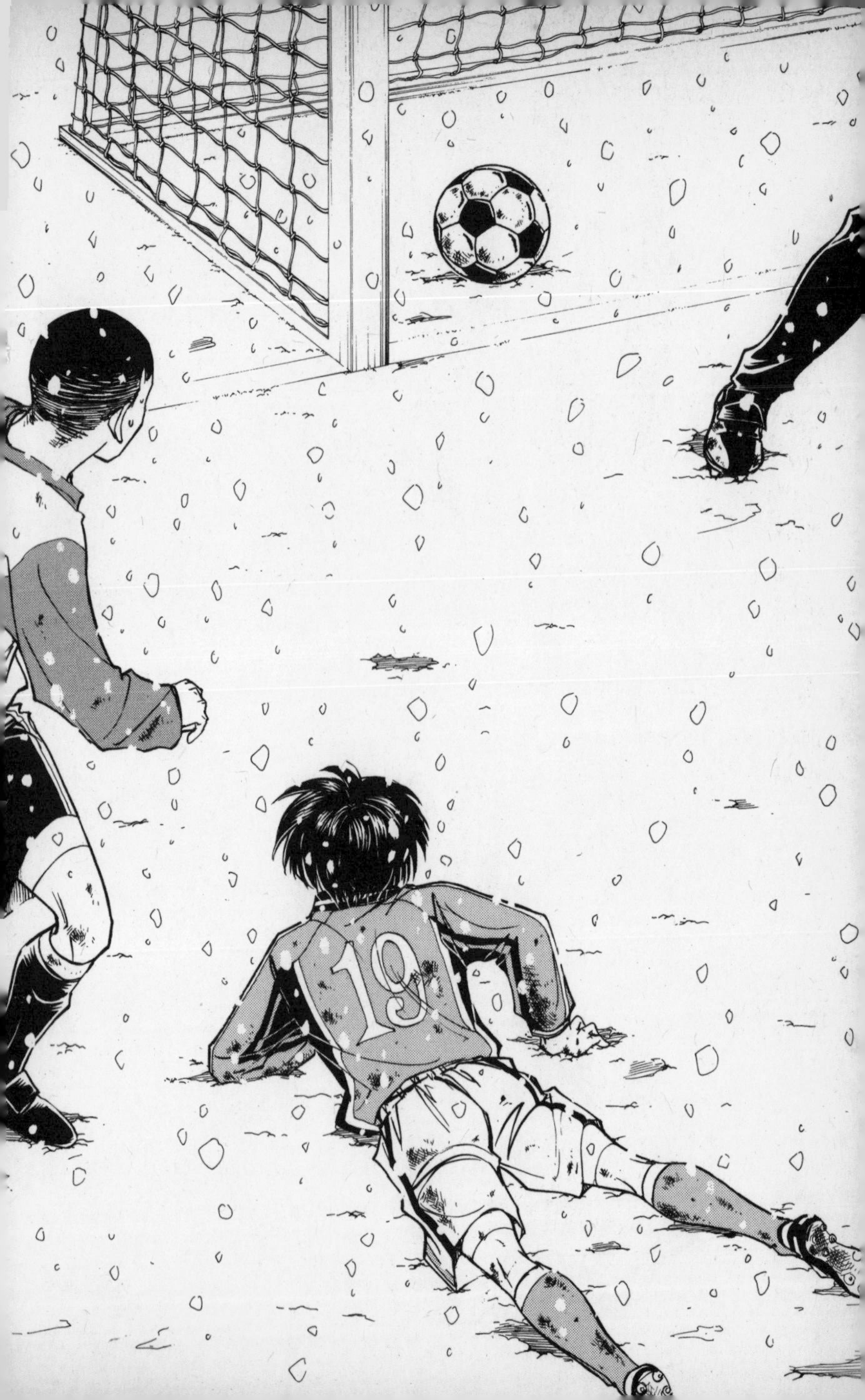

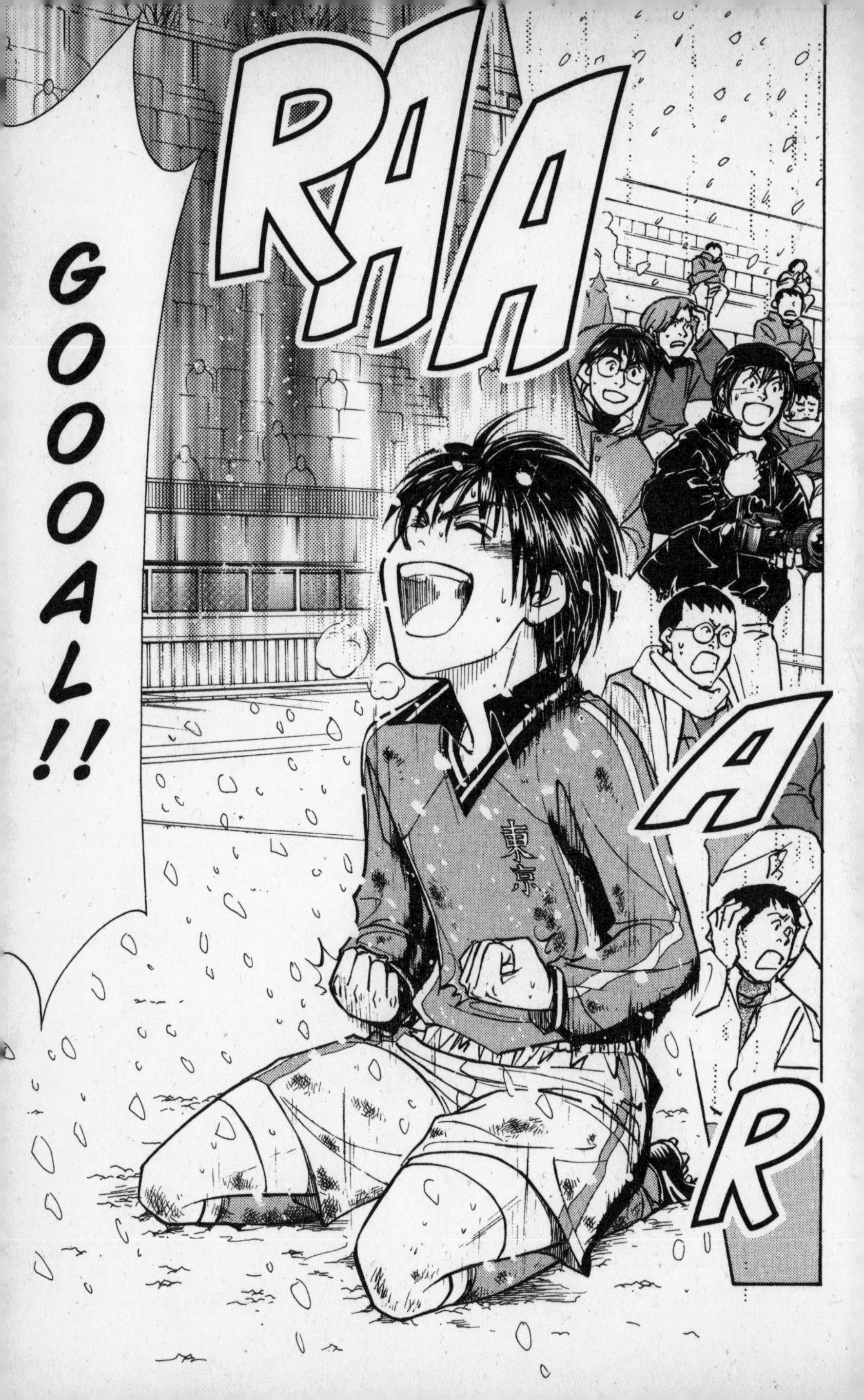
GOOOOAL!!
RAA
A
R
東京

HUSTLE!

PRODUCED BY: ASSISTANT F. JAGUAR

Was it a hand ball or not?

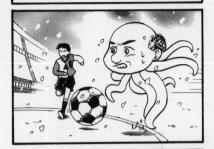

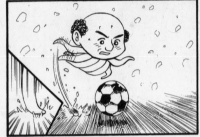

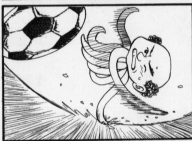

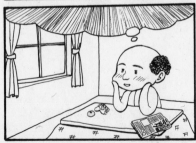

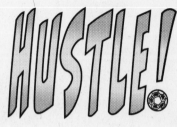

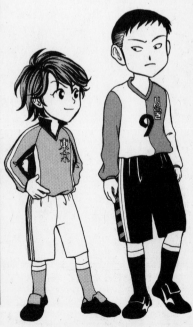

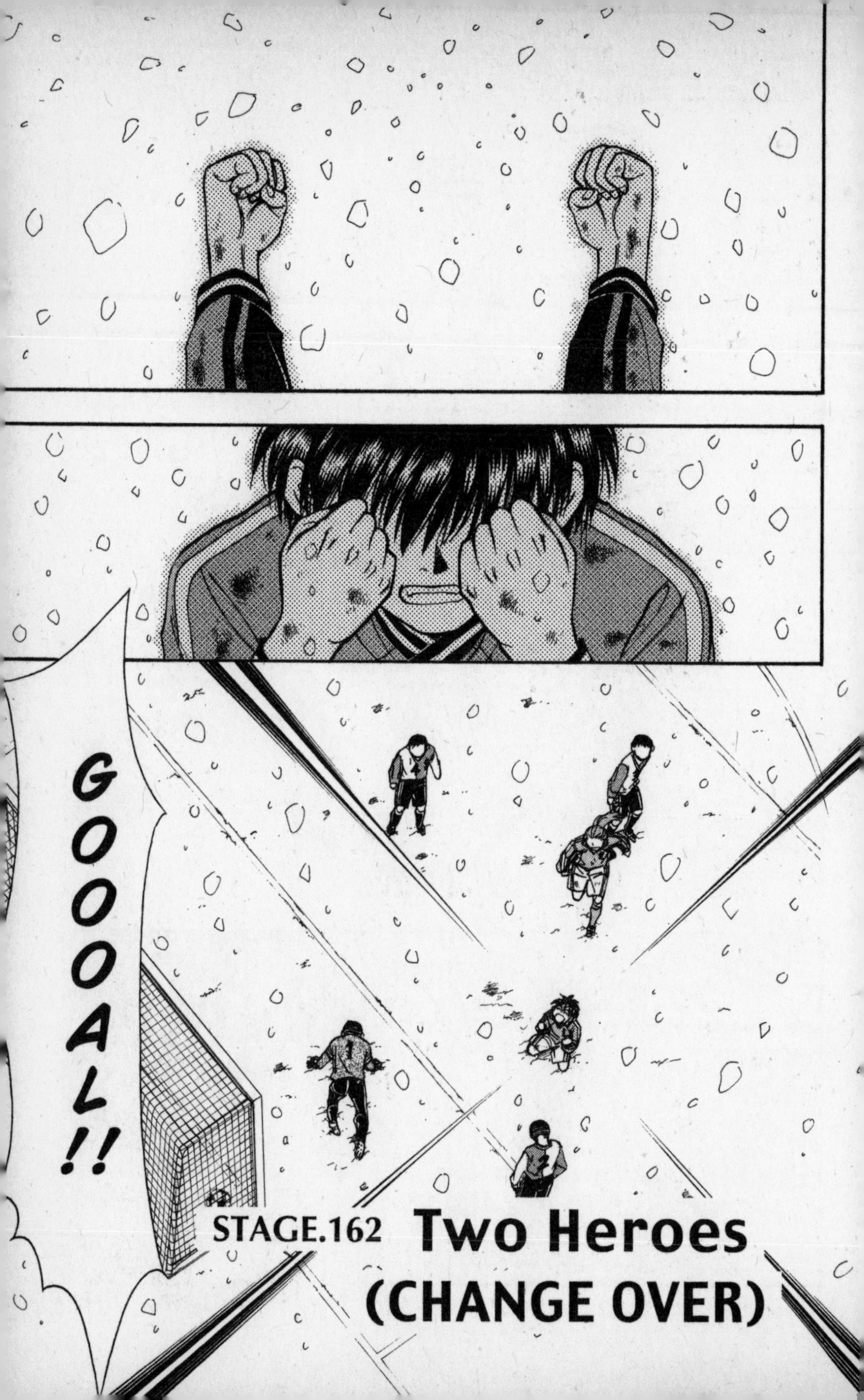
GOOOOAL!!

STAGE.162 Two Heroes (CHANGE OVER)

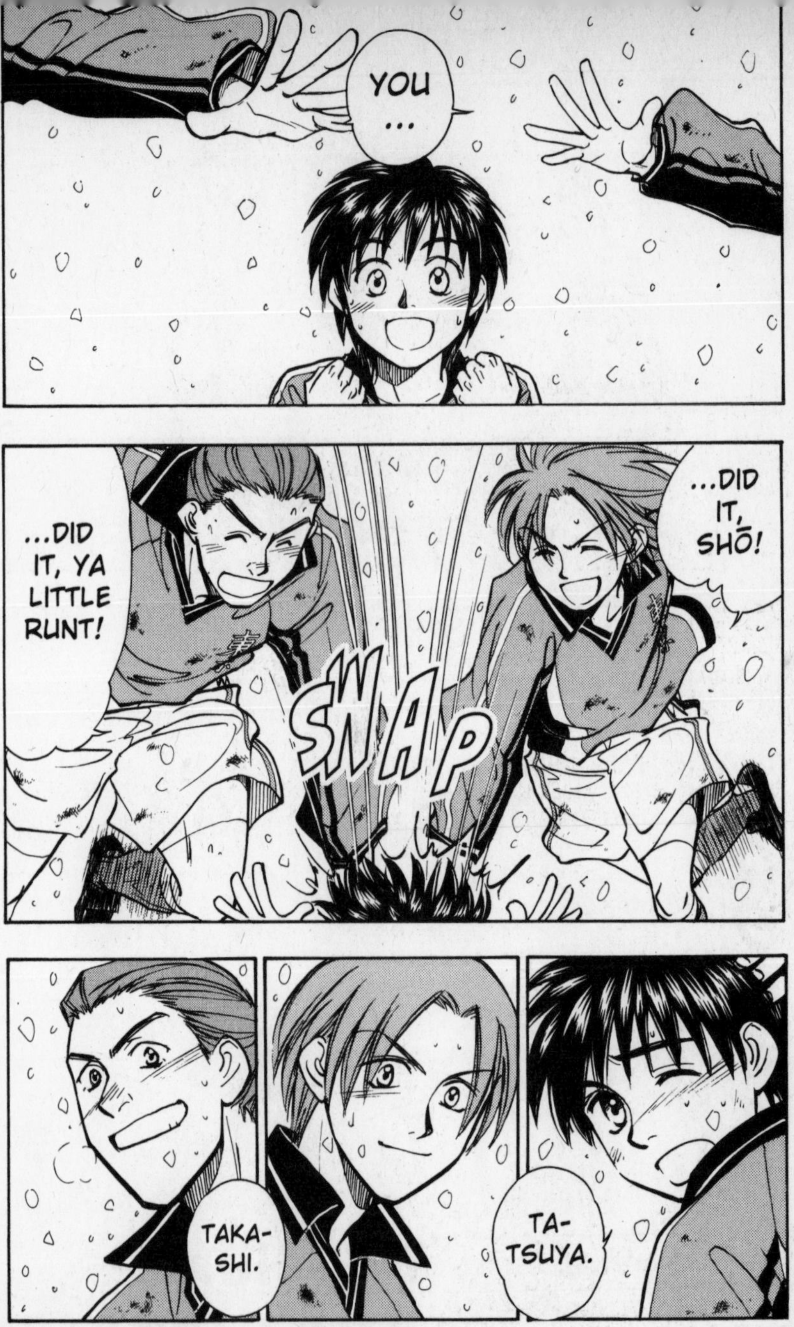
YOU ...
...DID IT, SHŌ!
...DID IT, YA LITTLE RUNT!
SNAP
TA-TSUYA.
TAKA-SHI.

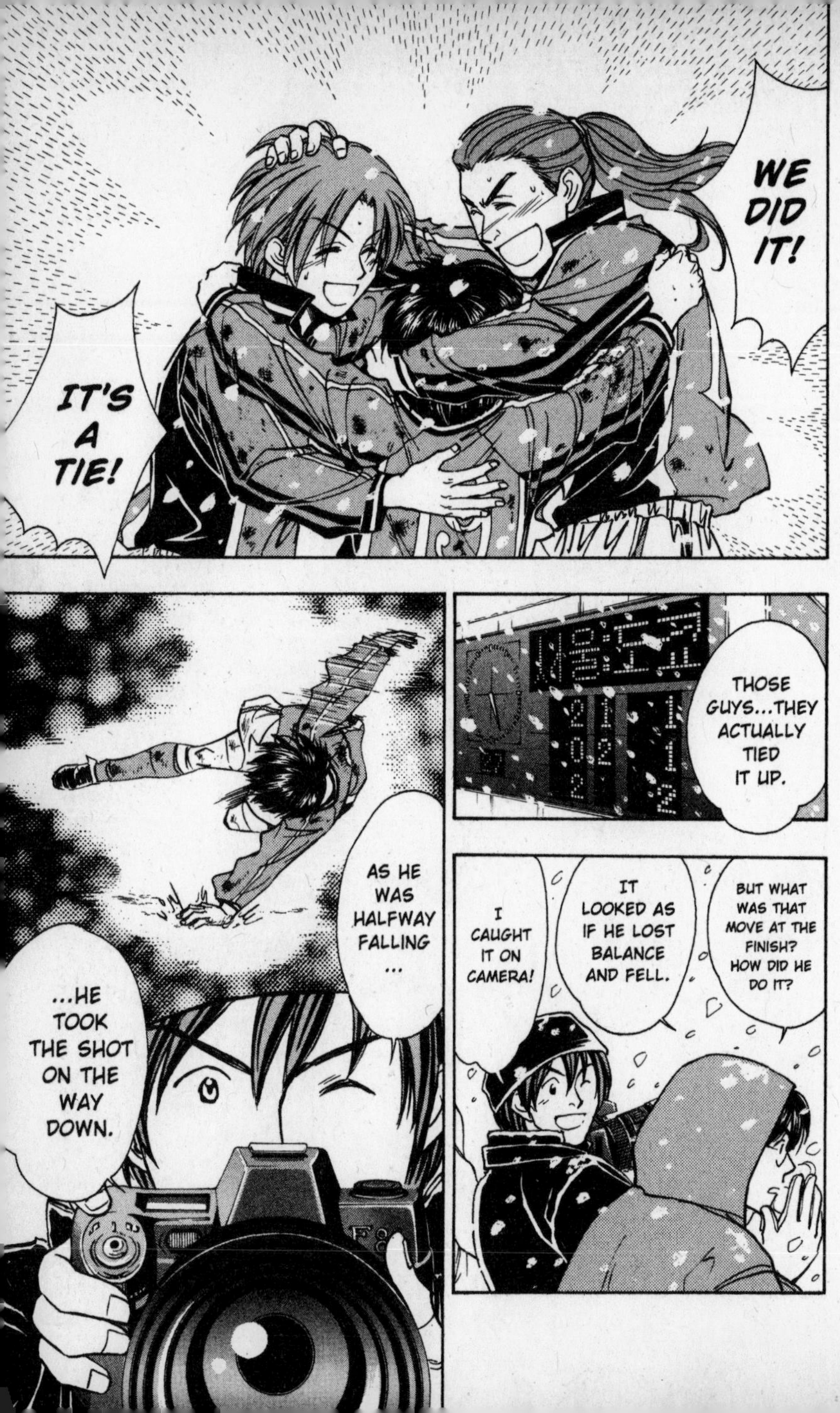
WE DID IT!
IT'S A TIE!
THOSE GUYS...THEY ACTUALLY TIED IT UP.
BUT WHAT WAS THAT MOVE AT THE FINISH? HOW DID HE DO IT?
IT LOOKED AS IF HE LOST BALANCE AND FELL.
I CAUGHT IT ON CAMERA!
AS HE WAS HALFWAY FALLING...
...HE TOOK THE SHOT ON THE WAY DOWN.

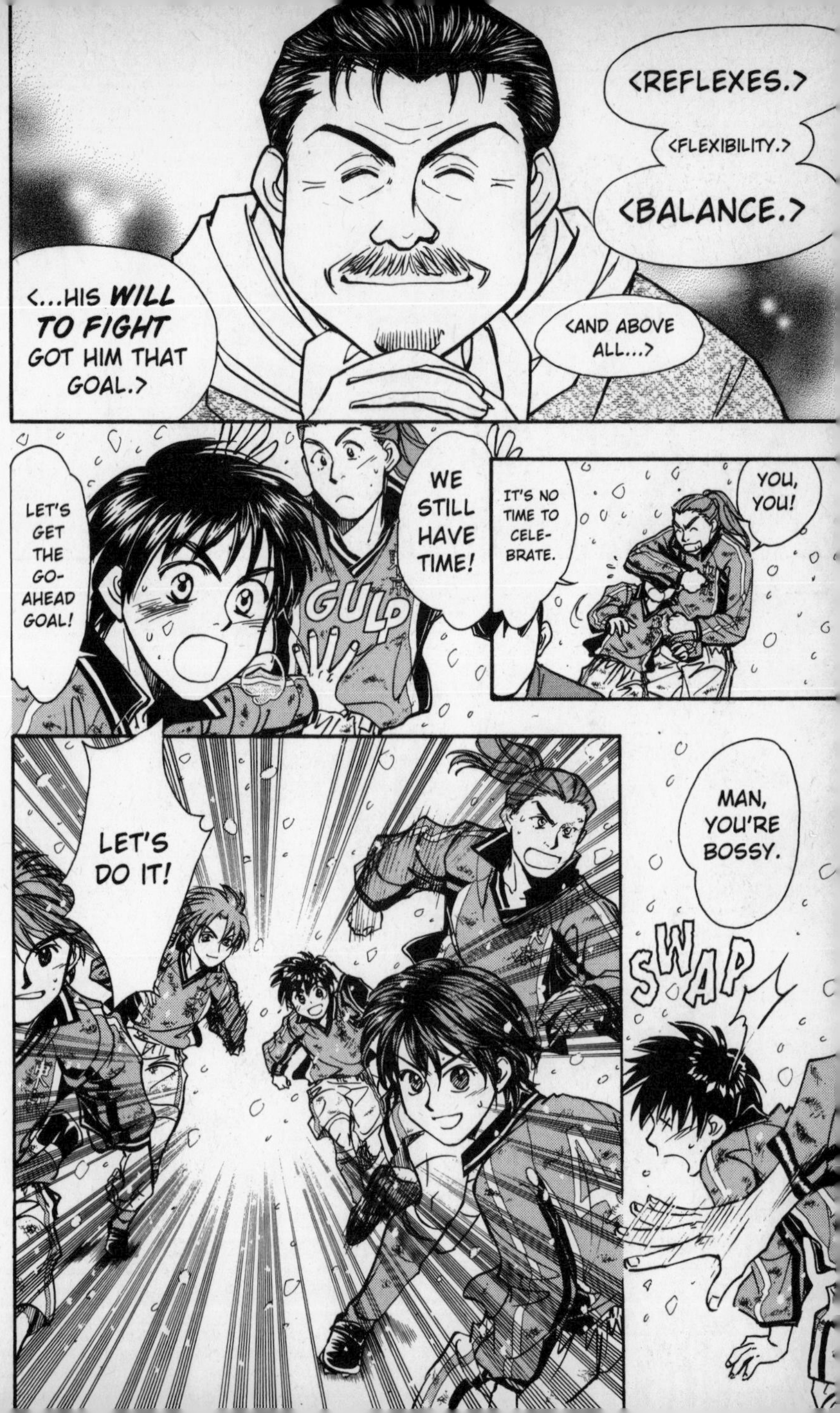
<REFLEXES.>
<FLEXIBILITY.>
<BALANCE.>
<AND ABOVE ALL...>
<...HIS **WILL TO FIGHT** GOT HIM THAT GOAL.>
YOU, YOU!
IT'S NO TIME TO CELE-BRATE.
WE STILL HAVE TIME!
GULP
LET'S GET THE GO-AHEAD GOAL!
MAN, YOU'RE BOSSY.
SWAP
LET'S DO IT!

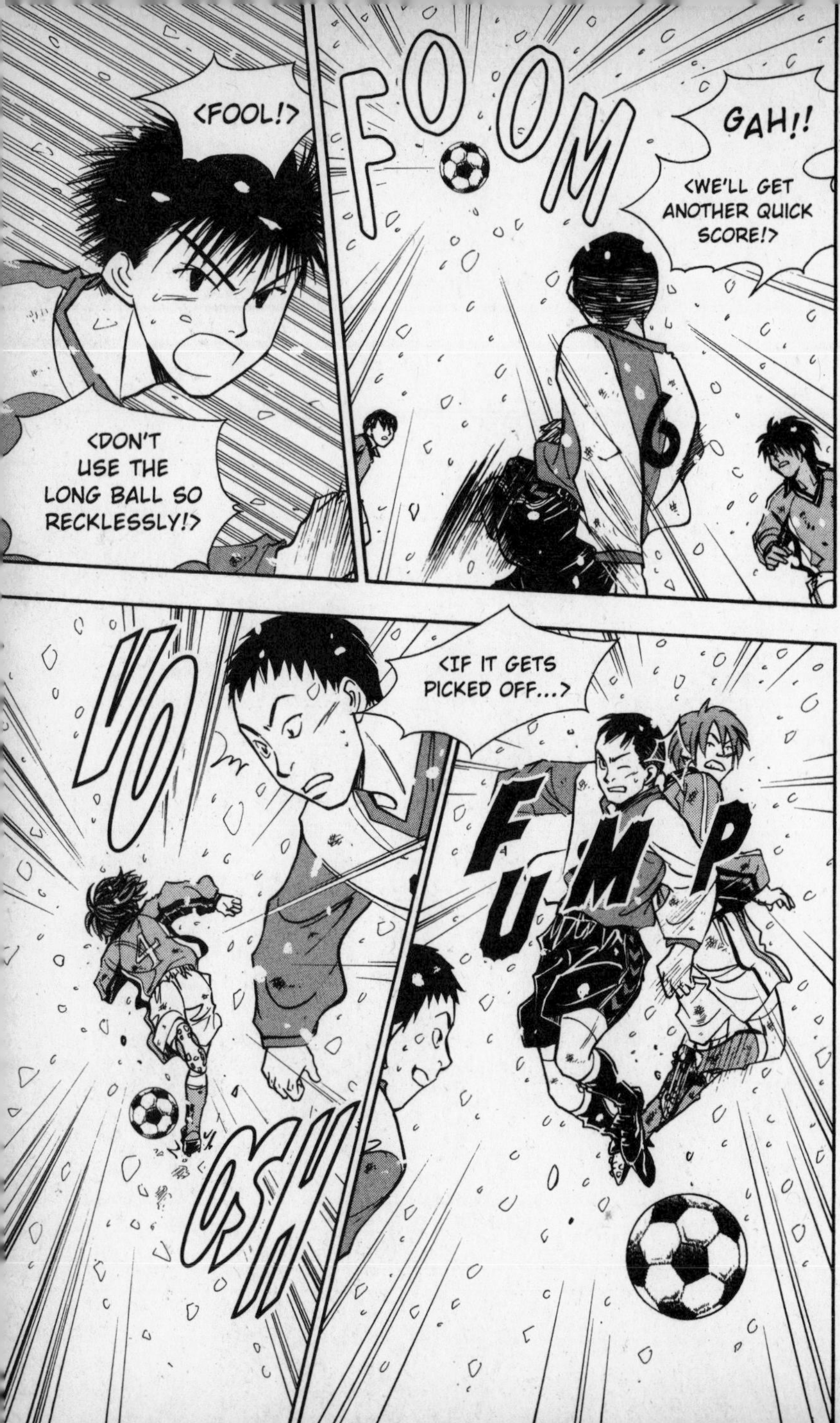
FOOM
GAH!!
<WE'LL GET ANOTHER QUICK SCORE!>
<FOOL!>
<DON'T USE THE LONG BALL SO RECKLESSLY!>
<IF IT GETS PICKED OFF...>
FUMP

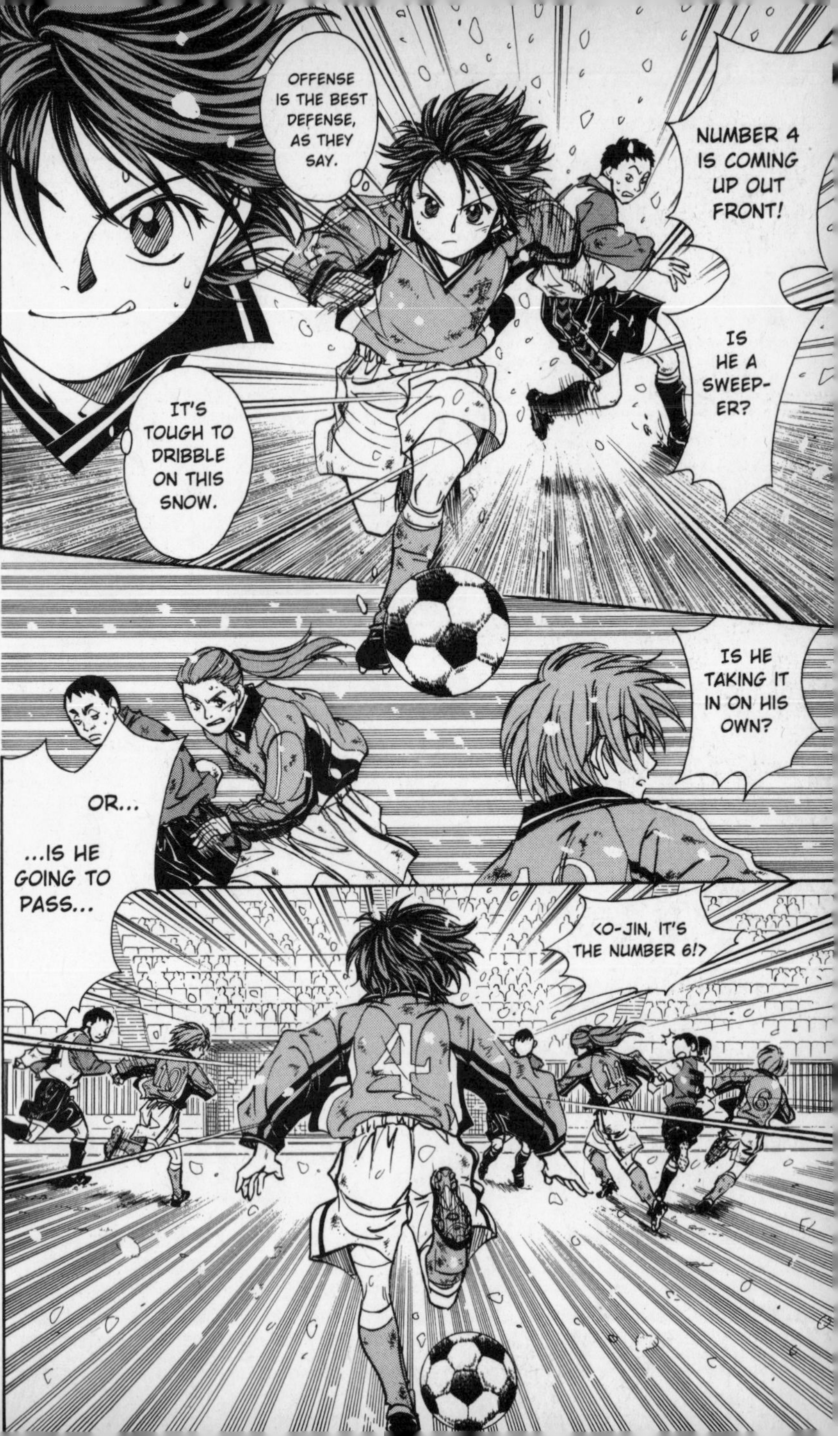
NUMBER 4 IS COMING UP OUT FRONT!
IS HE A SWEEPER?
OFFENSE IS THE BEST DEFENSE, AS THEY SAY.
IT'S TOUGH TO DRIBBLE ON THIS SNOW.
IS HE TAKING IT IN ON HIS OWN?
OR...
...IS HE GOING TO PASS...
<O-JIN, IT'S THE NUMBER 6!>

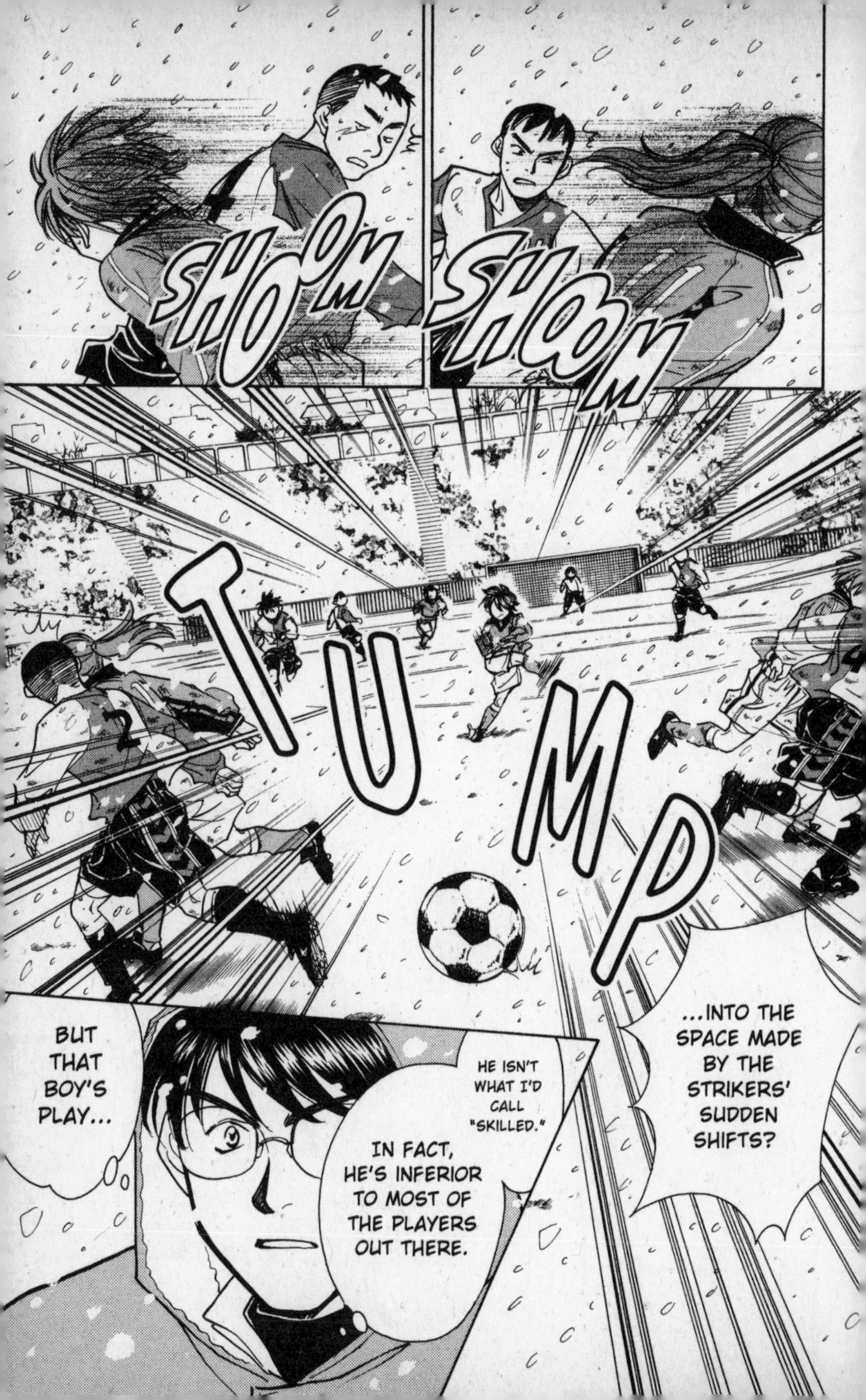
SHOOOM
SHOOM
TUMP
...INTO THE SPACE MADE BY THE STRIKERS' SUDDEN SHIFTS?
HE ISN'T WHAT I'D CALL "SKILLED."
IN FACT, HE'S INFERIOR TO MOST OF THE PLAYERS OUT THERE.
BUT THAT BOY'S PLAY...

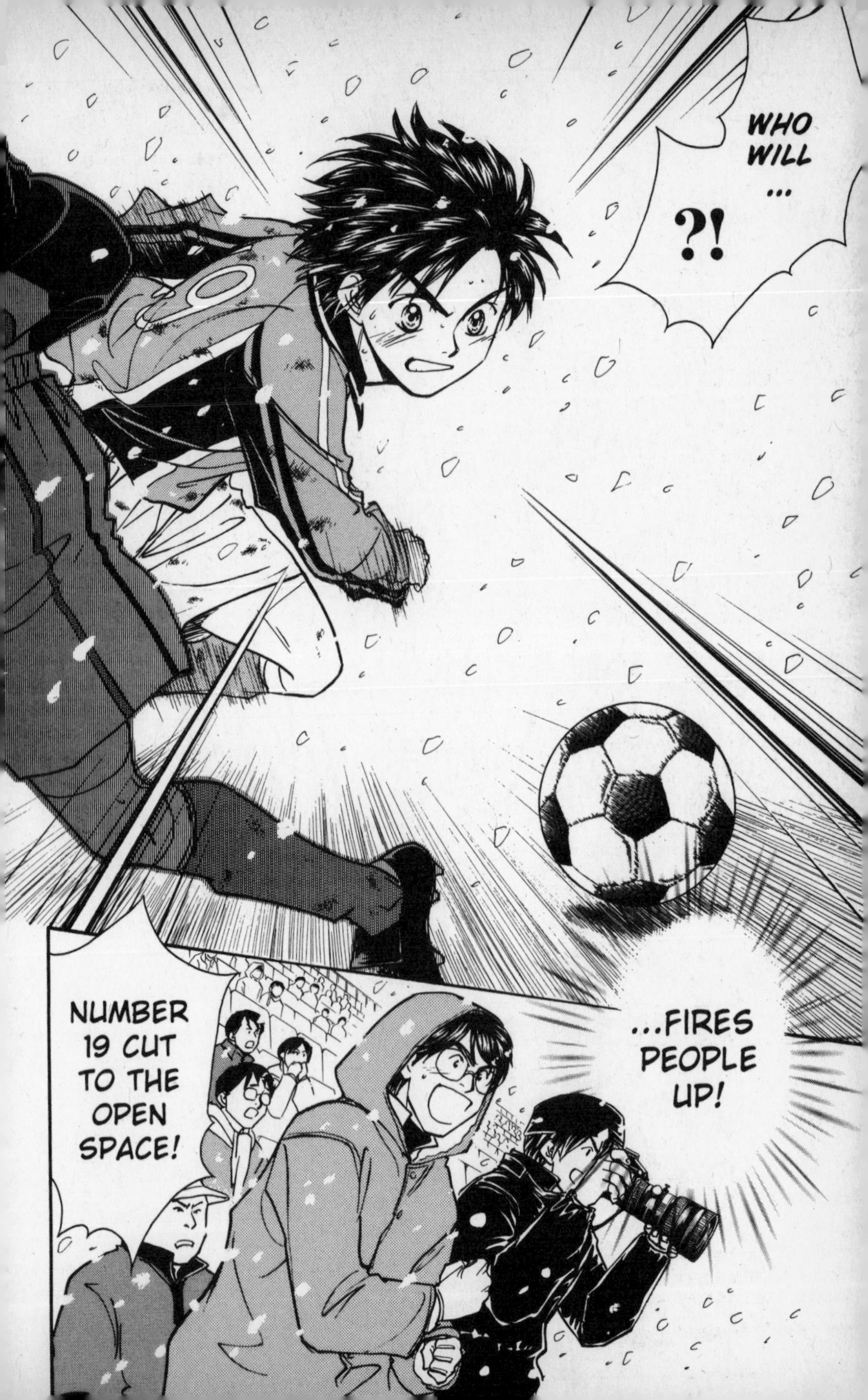
WHO WILL ...
?!
...FIRES PEOPLE UP!
NUMBER 19 CUT TO THE OPEN SPACE!

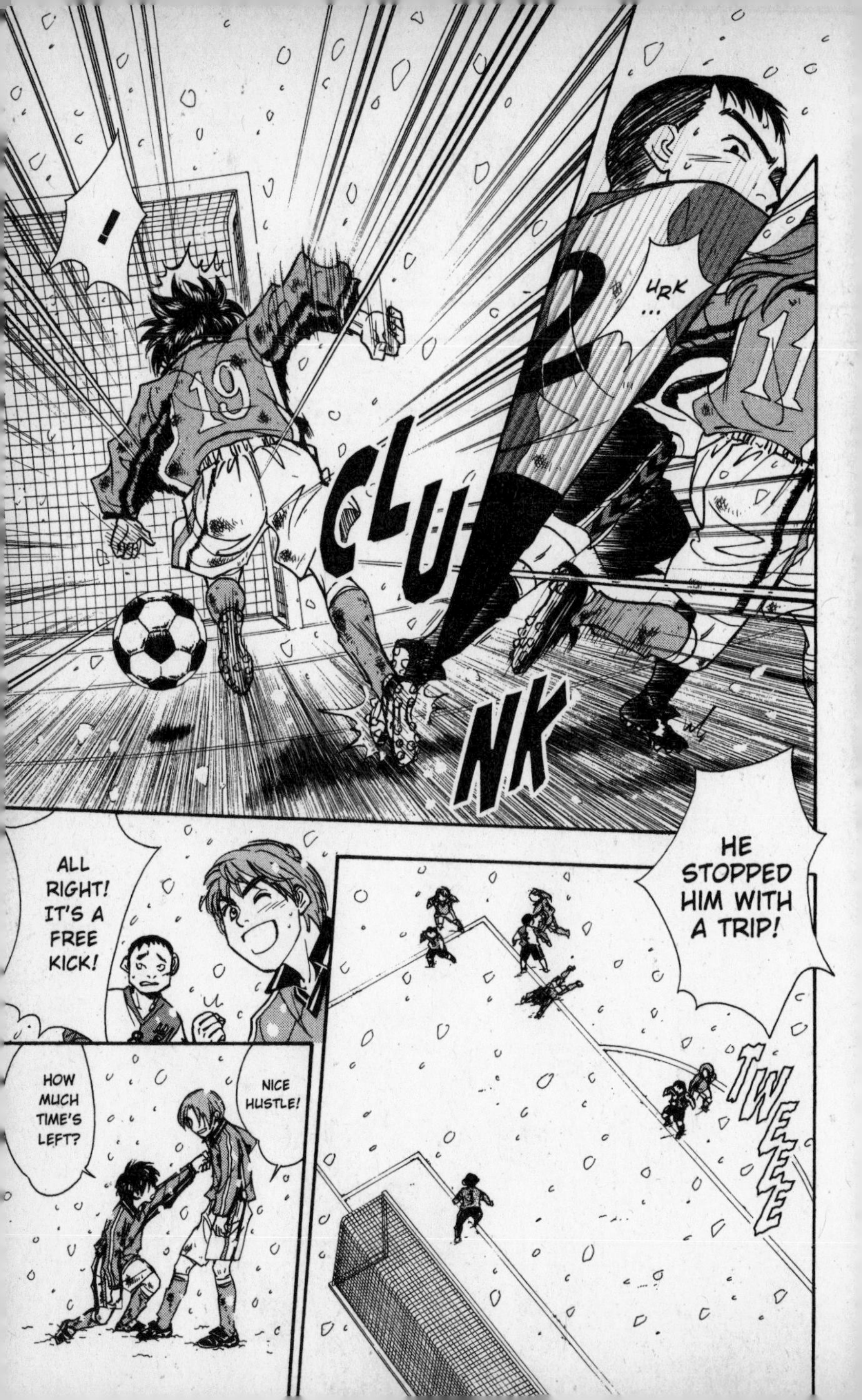
URK...
!
CLUNK
HE STOPPED HIM WITH A TRIP!
TWEEEE
ALL RIGHT! IT'S A FREE KICK!
NICE HUSTLE!
HOW MUCH TIME'S LEFT?

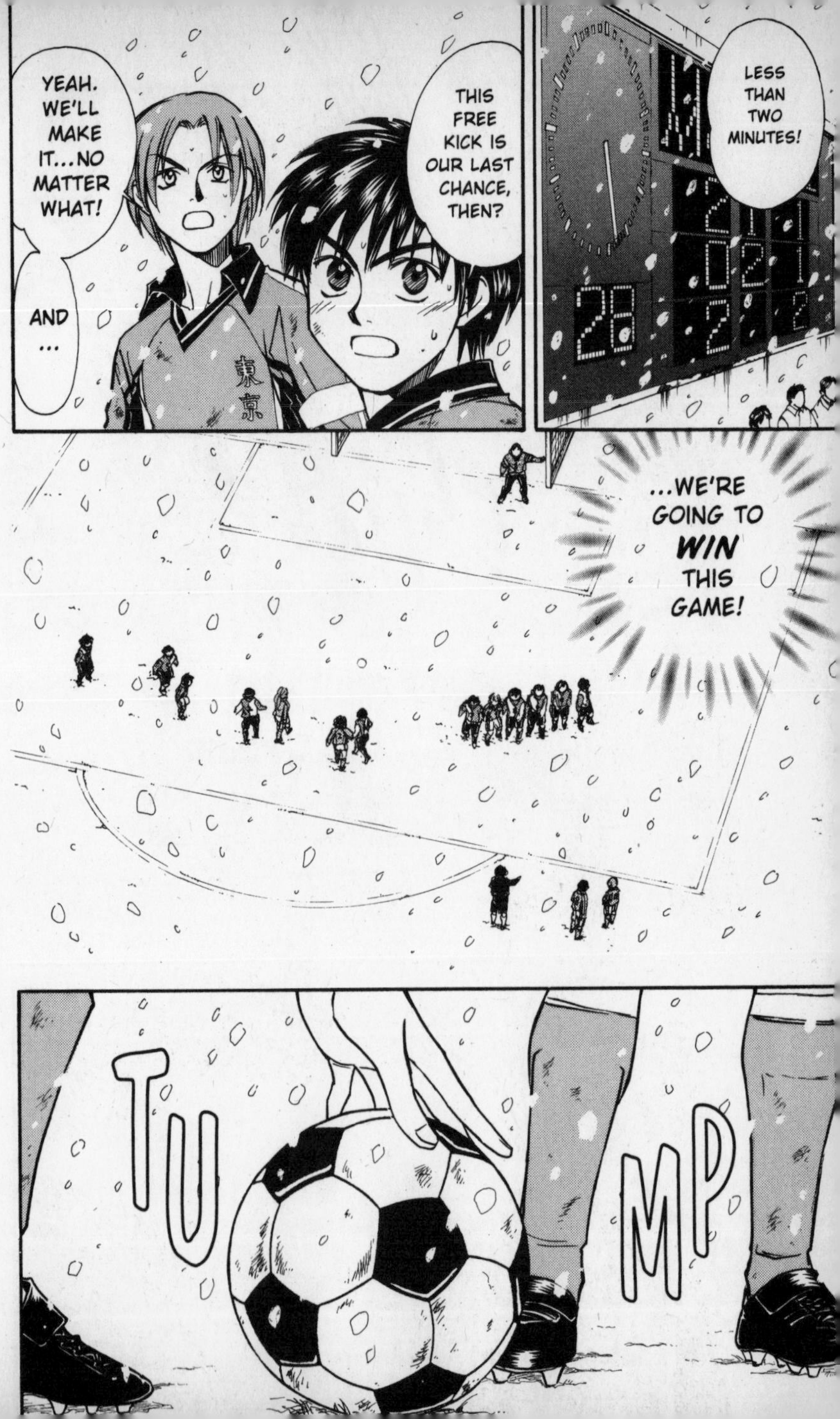
LESS THAN TWO MINUTES!
THIS FREE KICK IS OUR LAST CHANCE, THEN?
YEAH. WE'LL MAKE IT...NO MATTER WHAT!
AND ...
...WE'RE GOING TO WIN THIS GAME!
TUMP

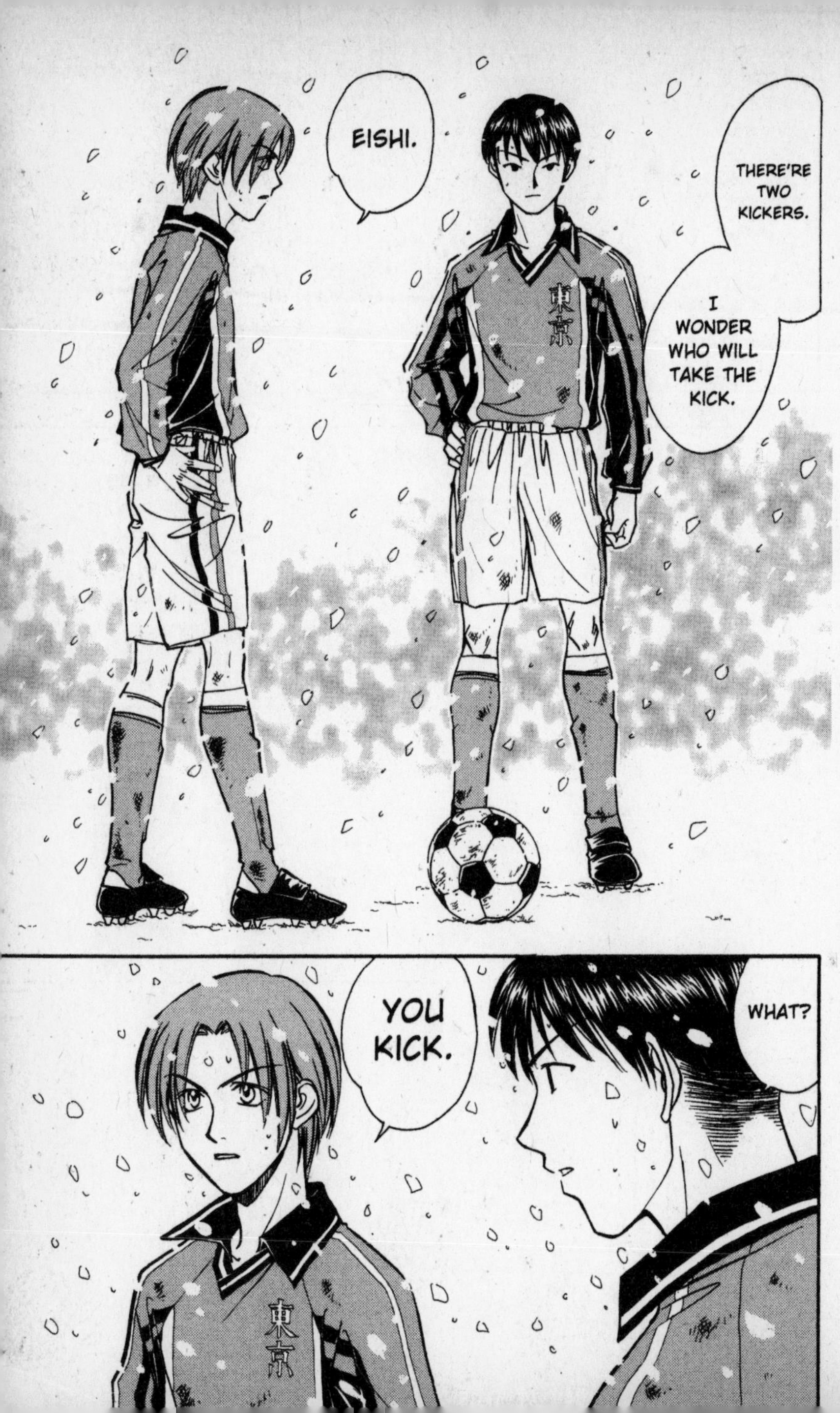
THERE'RE TWO KICKERS.
I WONDER WHO WILL TAKE THE KICK.
EISHI.
YOU KICK.
WHAT?

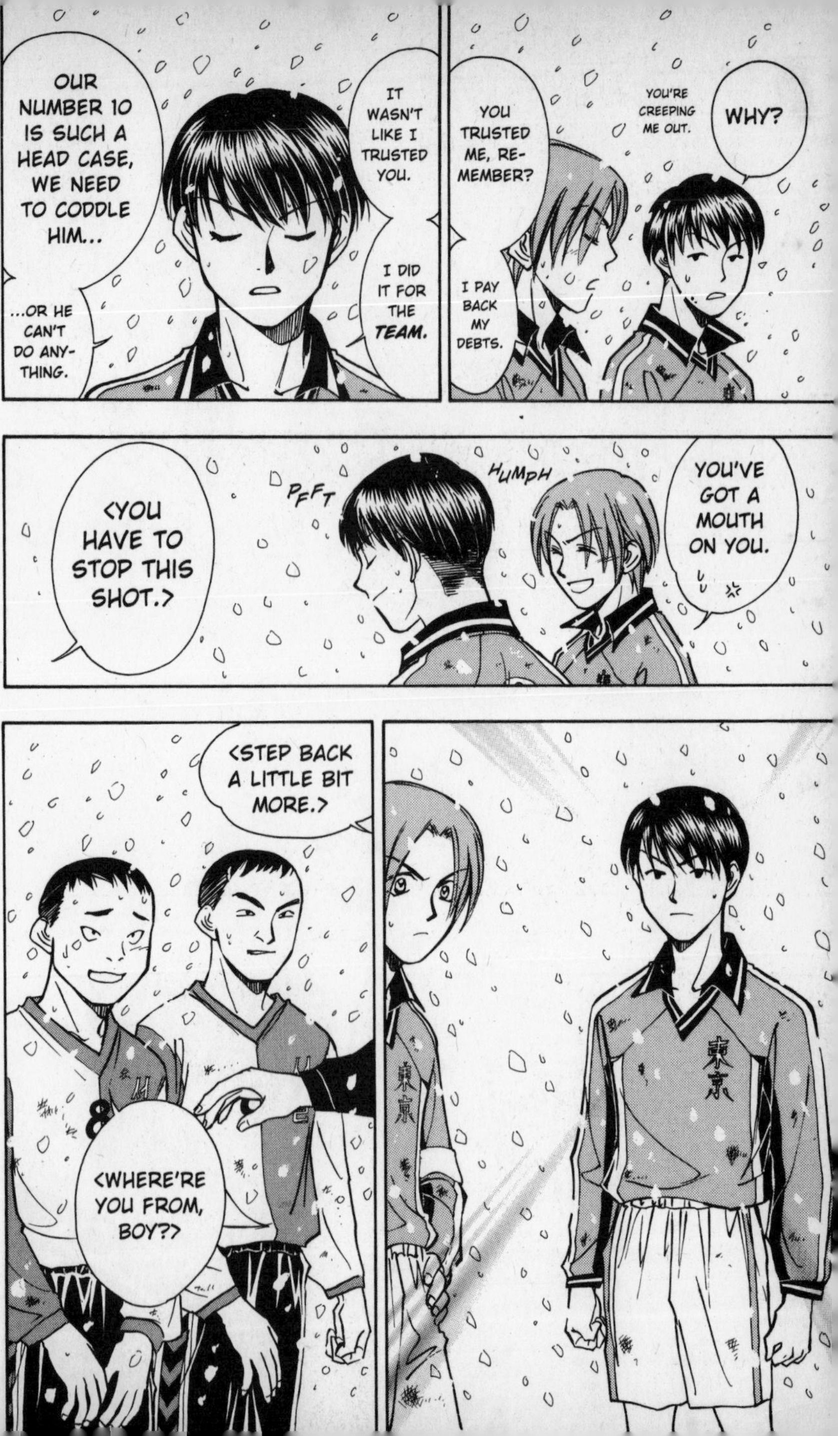
WHY?
YOU'RE CREEPING ME OUT.
YOU TRUSTED ME, REMEMBER?
I PAY BACK MY DEBTS.
IT WASN'T LIKE I TRUSTED YOU.
I DID IT FOR THE *TEAM.*
OUR NUMBER 10 IS SUCH A HEAD CASE, WE NEED TO CODDLE HIM...
...OR HE CAN'T DO ANYTHING.
YOU'VE GOT A MOUTH ON YOU.
HUMPH
PFFT
<YOU HAVE TO STOP THIS SHOT.>
<STEP BACK A LITTLE BIT MORE.>
<WHERE'RE YOU FROM, BOY?>

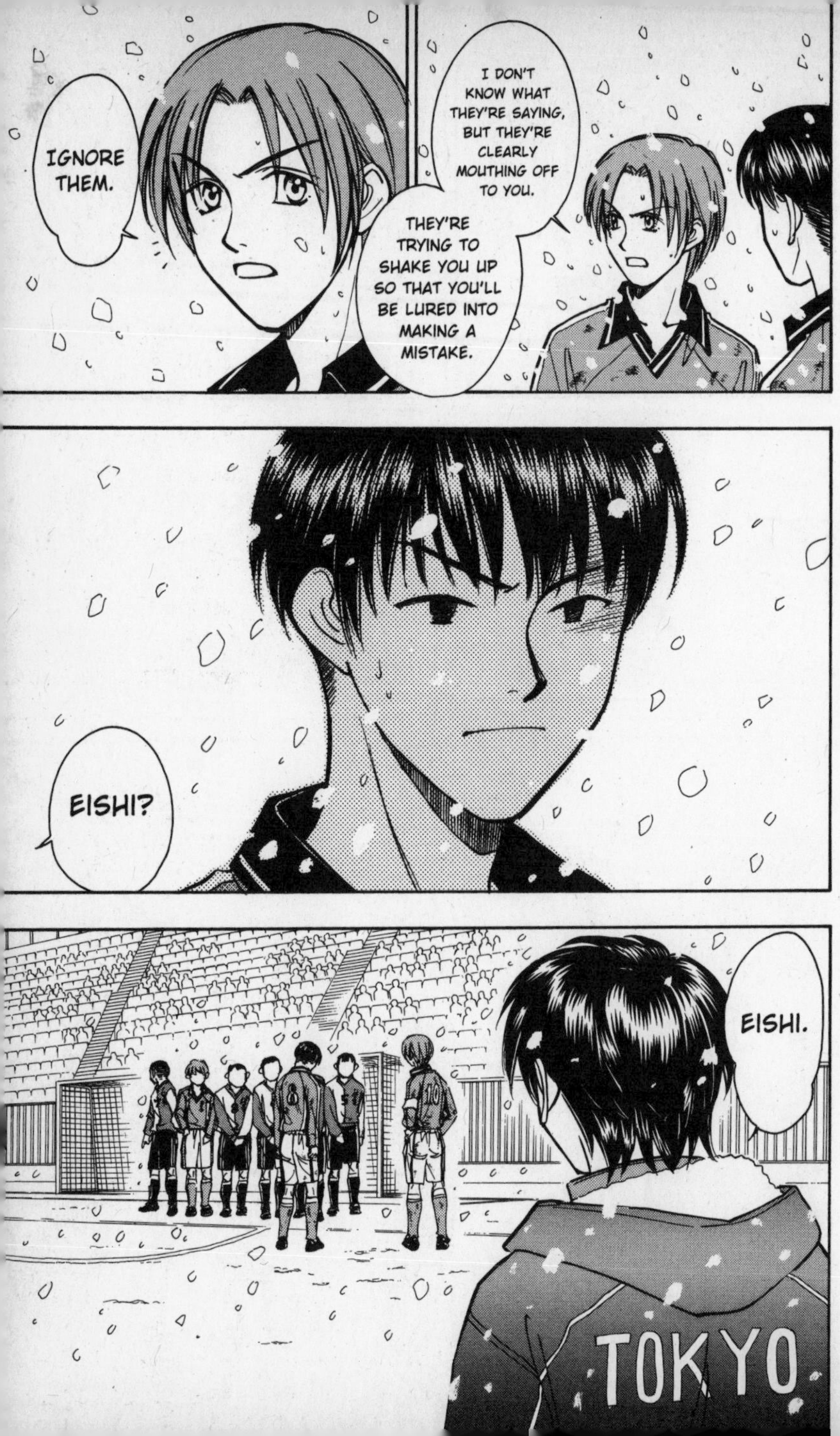
I DON'T KNOW WHAT THEY'RE SAYING, BUT THEY'RE CLEARLY MOUTHING OFF TO YOU.
THEY'RE TRYING TO SHAKE YOU UP SO THAT YOU'LL BE LURED INTO MAKING A MISTAKE.
IGNORE THEM.
EISHI?
EISHI.
TOKYO

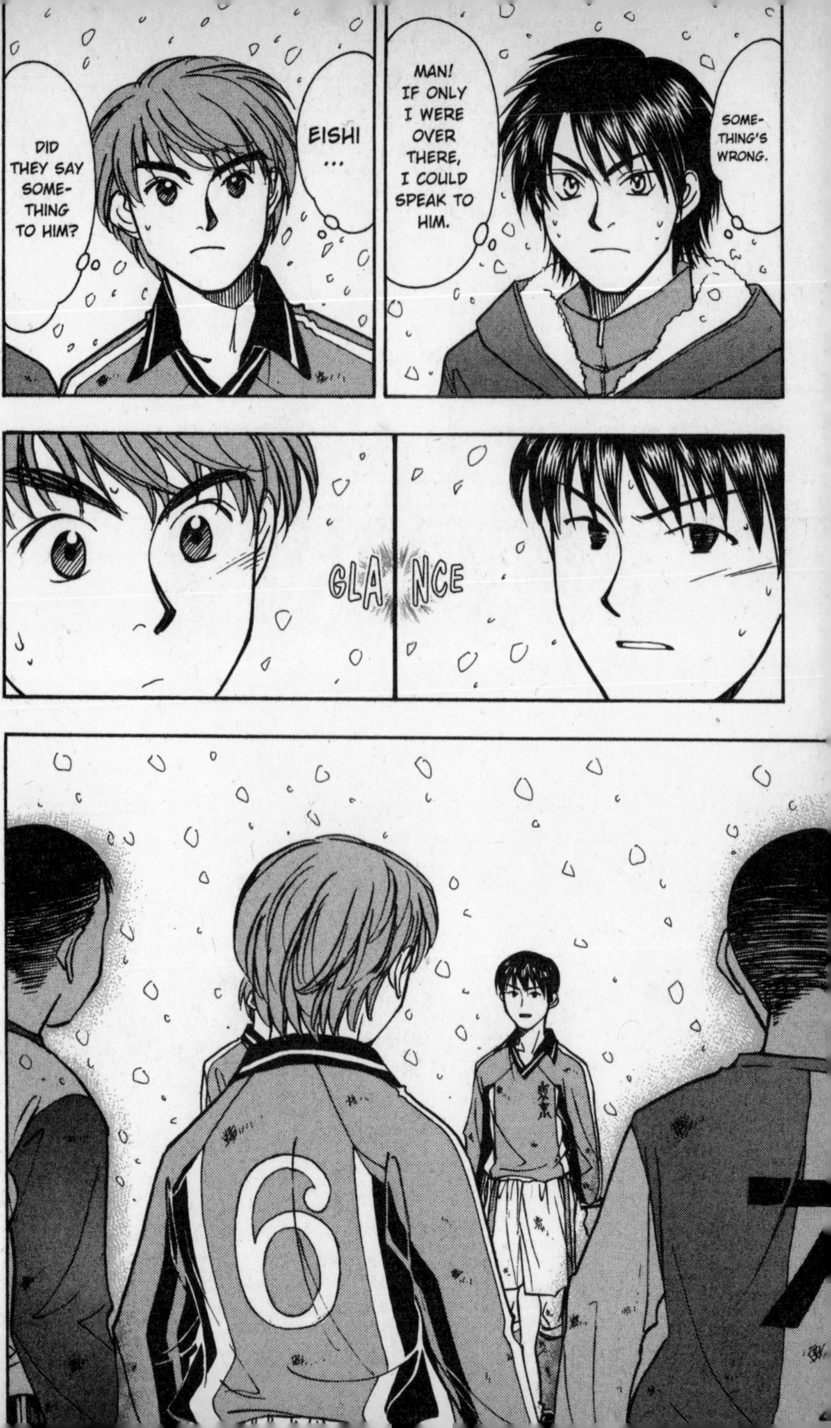
SOME-THING'S WRONG.
MAN! IF ONLY I WERE OVER THERE, I COULD SPEAK TO HIM.
EISHI...
DID THEY SAY SOME-THING TO HIM?
GLANCE

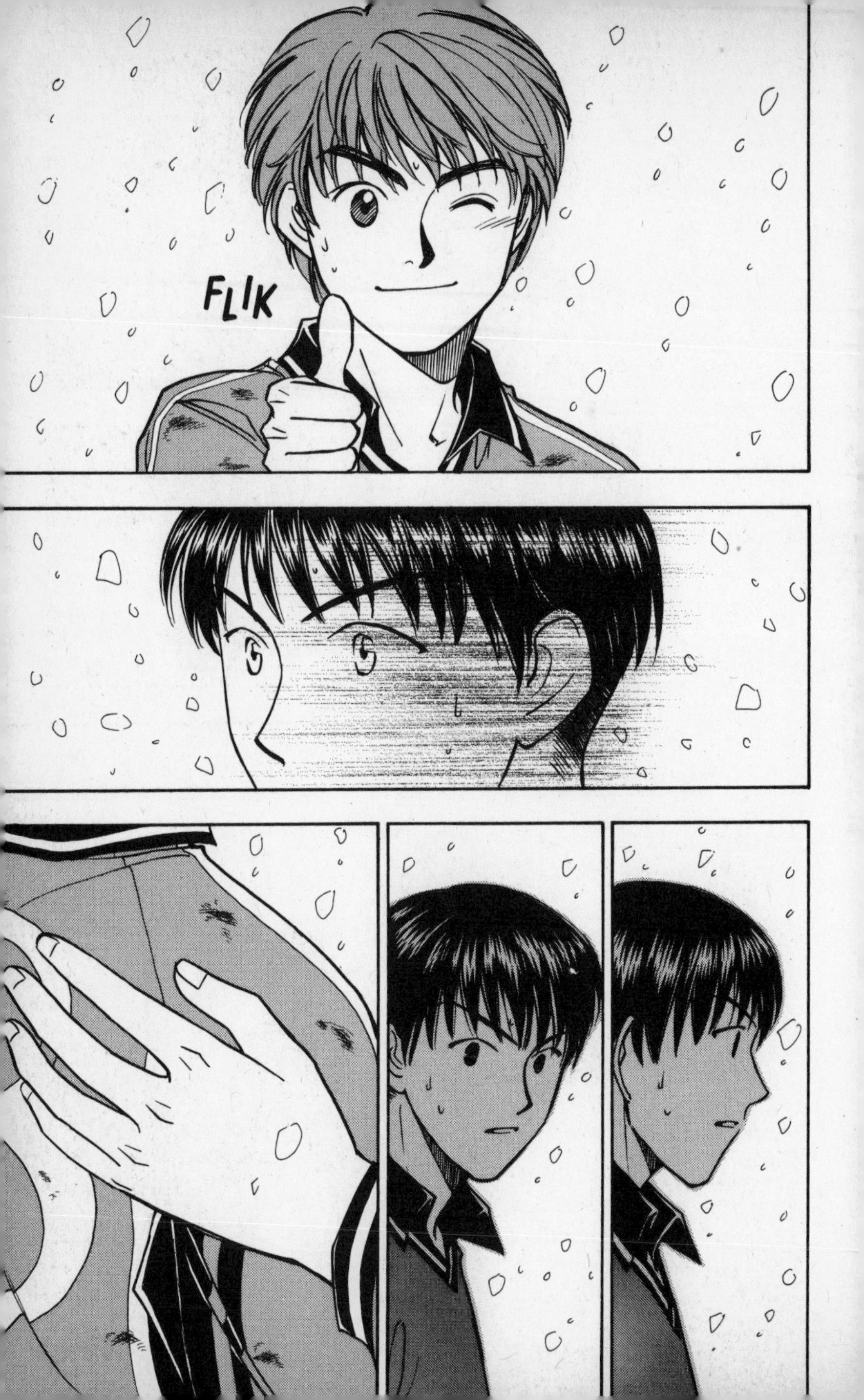
FLIK

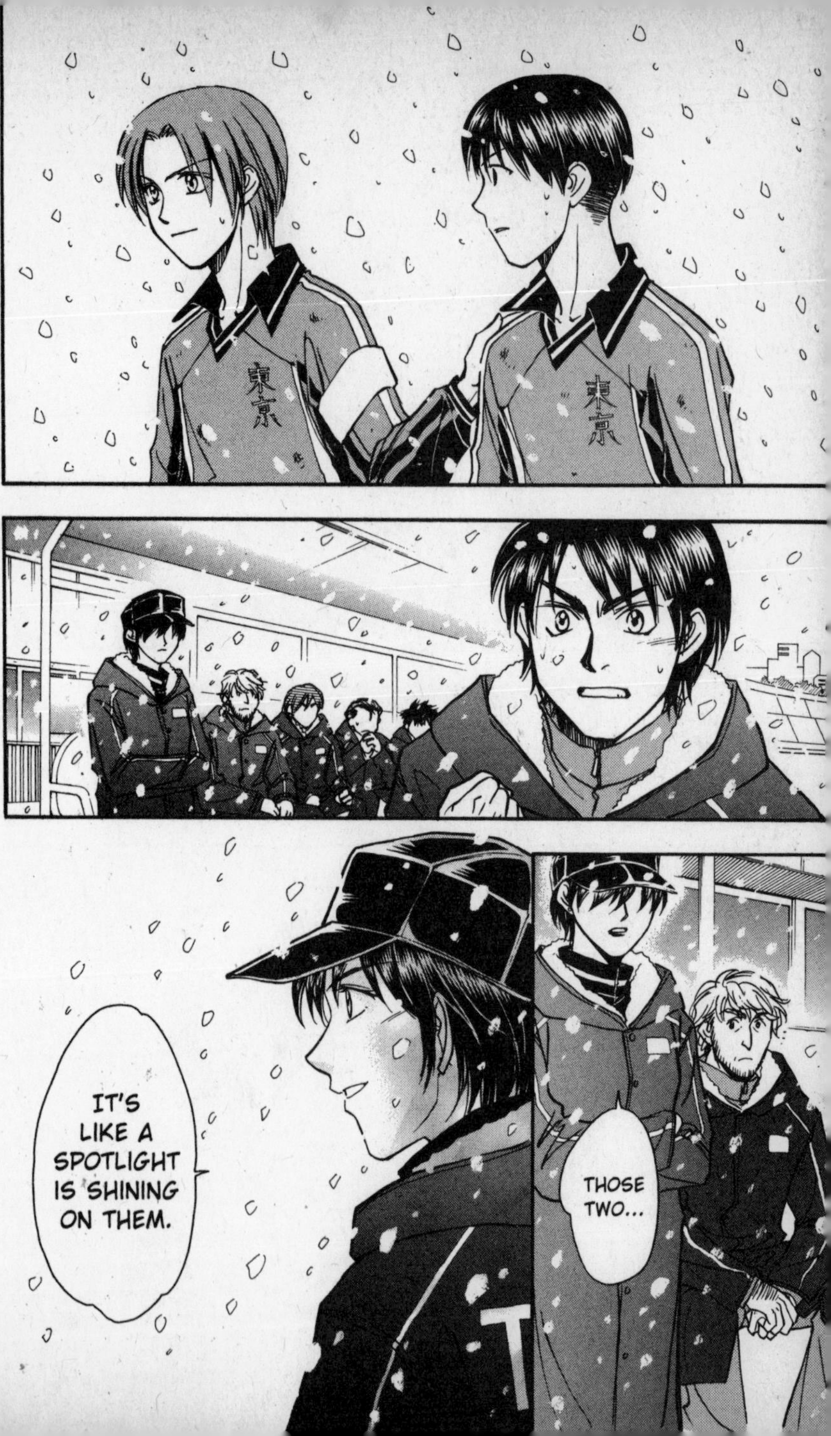
東京
東京
THOSE TWO...
IT'S LIKE A SPOTLIGHT IS SHINING ON THEM.

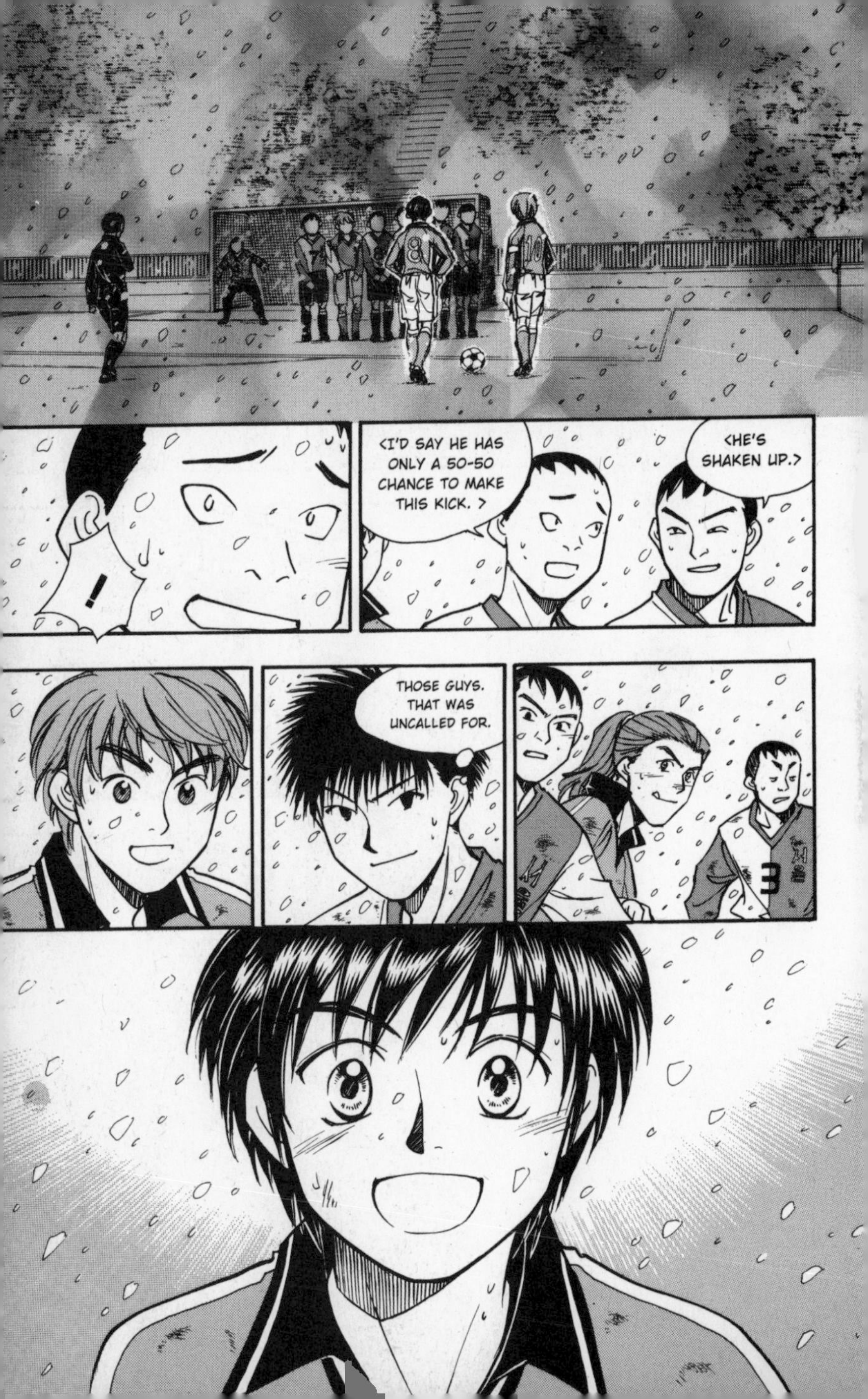
<HE'S SHAKEN UP.>
<I'D SAY HE HAS ONLY A 50-50 CHANCE TO MAKE THIS KICK. >
!
THOSE GUYS. THAT WAS UNCALLED FOR.

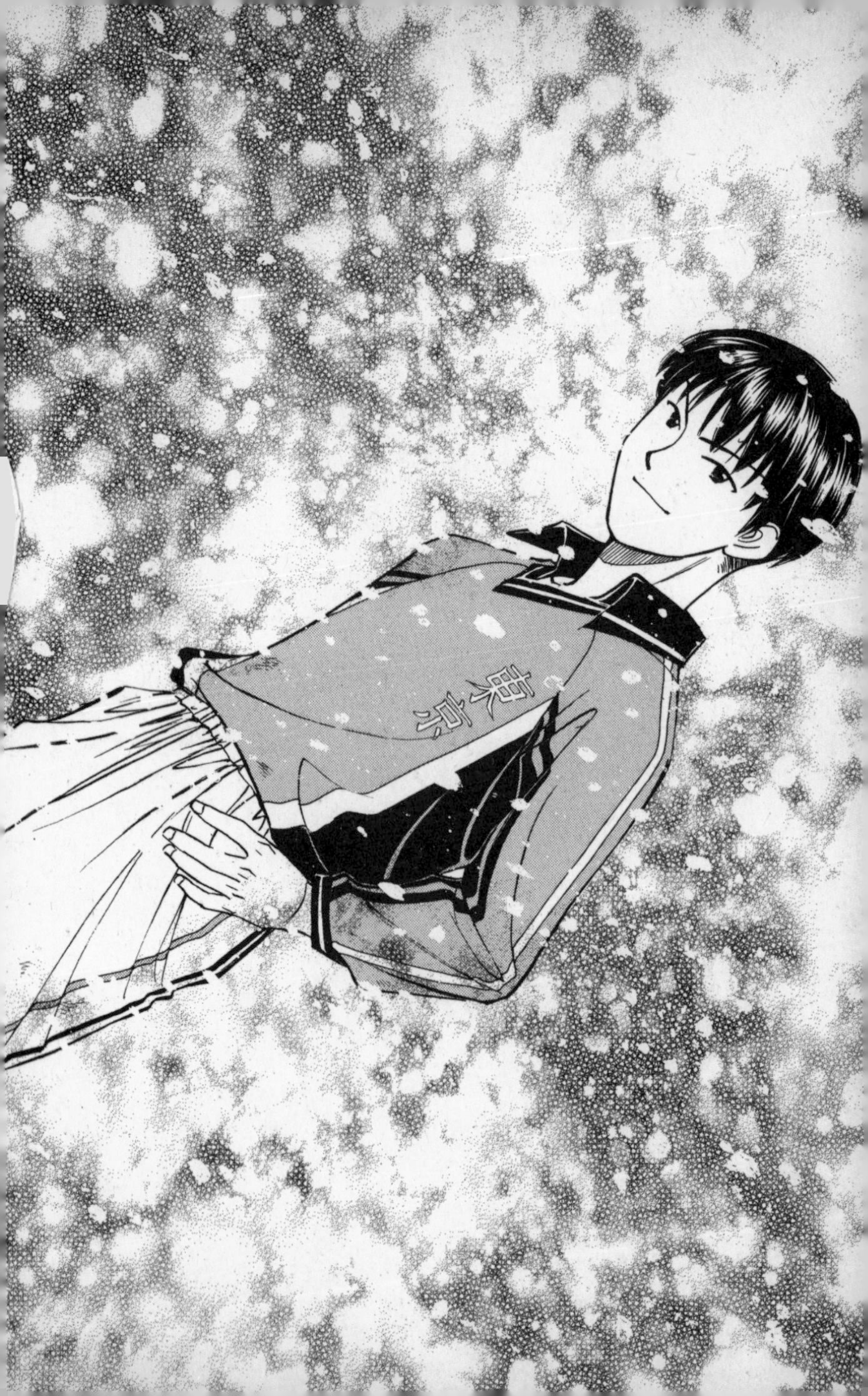
東京

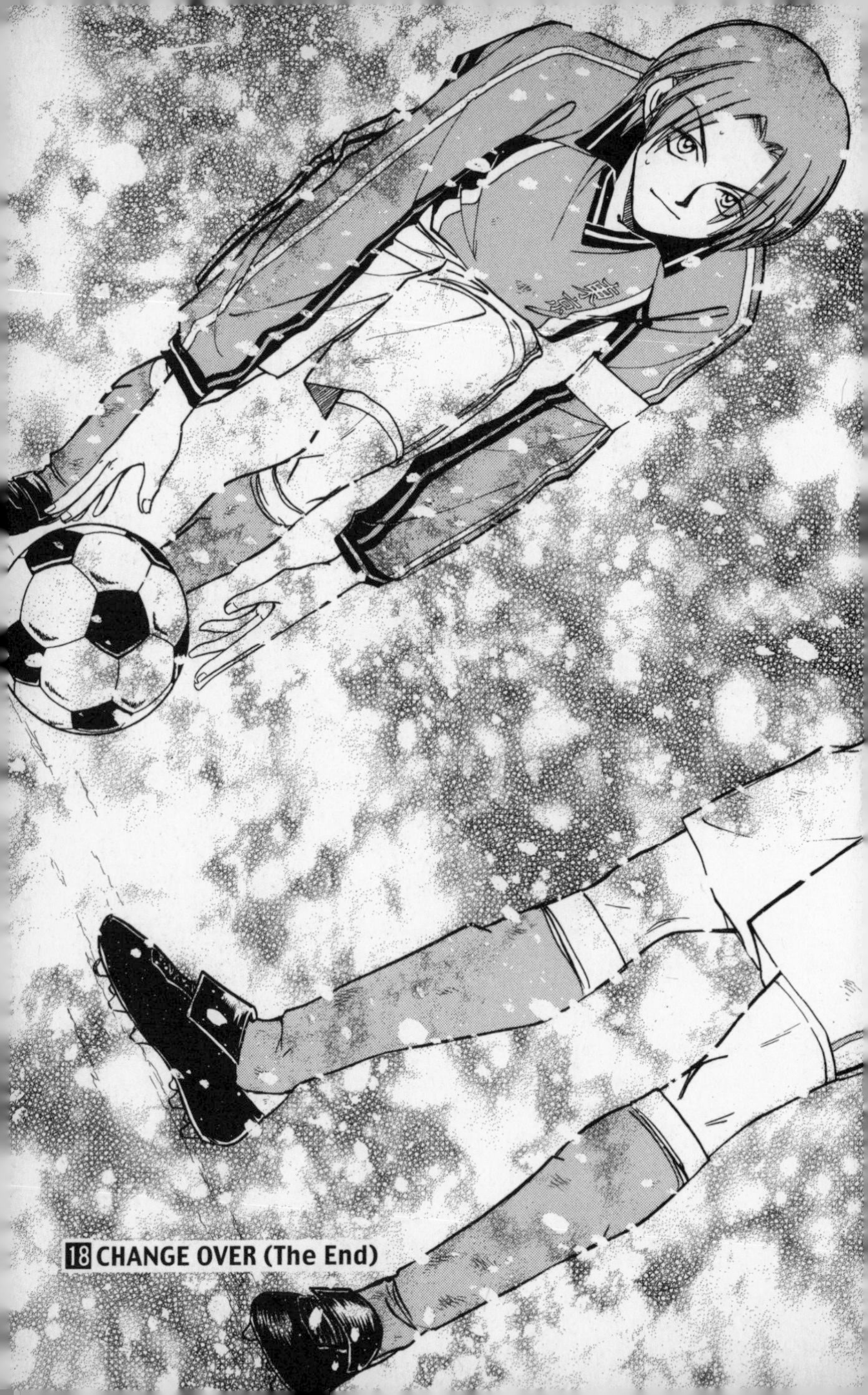

18 CHANGE OVER (The End)

Next in Whistle!

TURNING POINT

When the Tokyo Select Team returns from South Korea,
they have little time to reflect on the lessons learned before
they are thrown into a new maelstrom. They've been invited
to play in the Japan Toresen—a national tournament for the
best youth teams in the country! It's a major turning point,
both for the players and their coaches, as they are called on
to take the team to a new level.

Available May 2008!

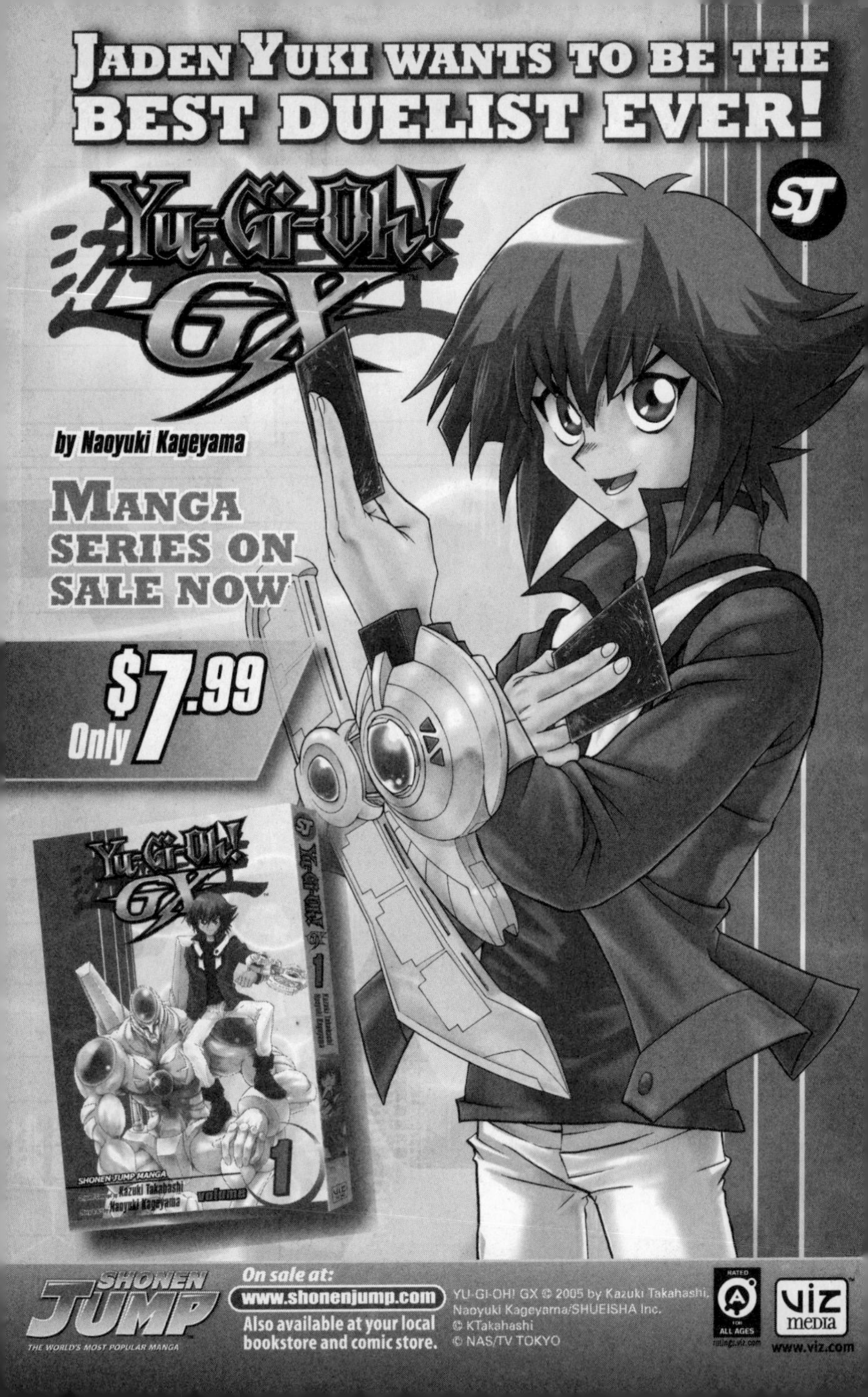
JADEN YUKI WANTS TO BE THE BEST DUELIST EVER!
SJ
YU-GI-OH! GX
by Naoyuki Kageyama
MANGA SERIES ON SALE NOW
Only $7.99
YU-GI-OH! GX
SHONEN JUMP MANGA
Kazuki Takahashi
Naoyuki Kageyama
1
SHONEN JUMP
THE WORLD'S MOST POPULAR MANGA
On sale at:
www.shonenjump.com
Also available at your local bookstore and comic store.
YU-GI-OH! GX © 2005 by Kazuki Takahashi, Naoyuki Kageyama/SHUEISHA Inc.
© KTakahashi
© NAS/TV TOKYO
RATED A FOR ALL AGES
VIZ MEDIA
www.viz.com

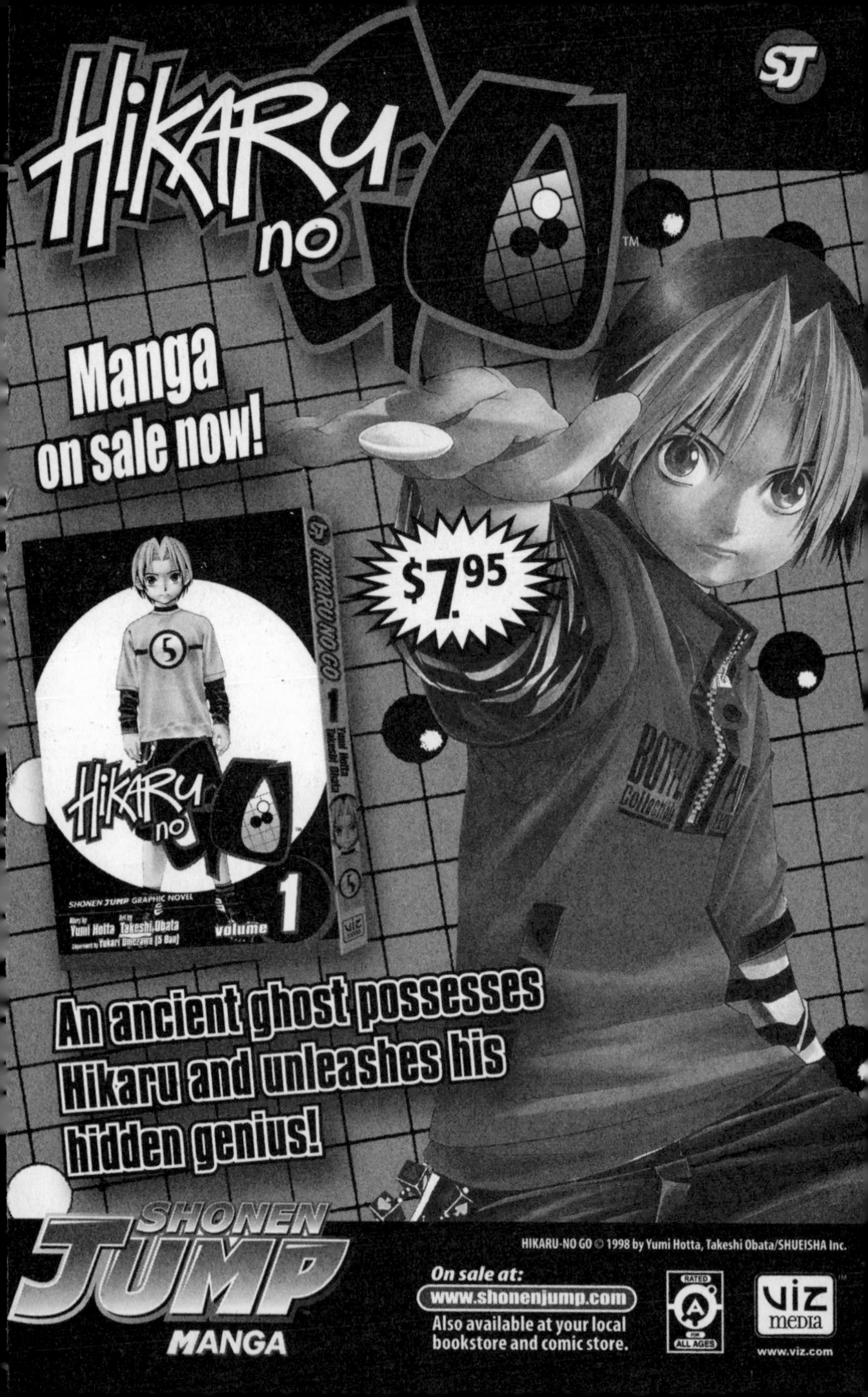
SJ
HIKARU no GO™
Manga on sale now!
$7.95
HIKARU NO GO 1
Yumi Hotta
Takeshi Obata
HIKARU no GO™
SHONEN JUMP GRAPHIC NOVEL
Story by Yumi Hotta Art by Takeshi Obata
Supervised by Yukari Umezawa (5 Dan)
volume 1
An ancient ghost possesses Hikaru and unleashes his hidden genius!
SHONEN JUMP MANGA
HIKARU-NO GO © 1998 by Yumi Hotta, Takeshi Obata/SHUEISHA Inc.
On sale at:
www.shonenjump.com
Also available at your local bookstore and comic store.
RATED A FOR ALL AGES
VIZ media
www.viz.com

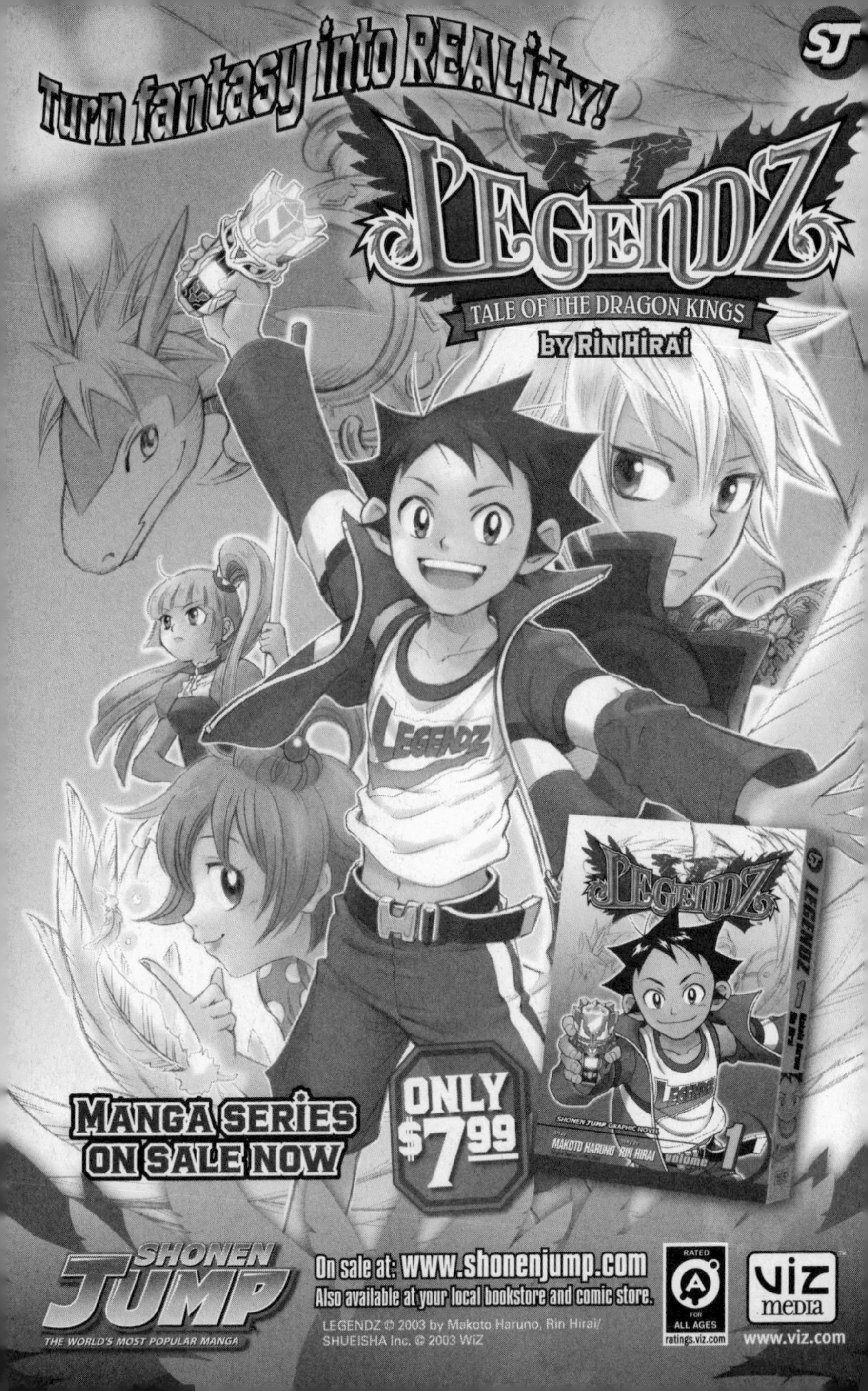
SJ
Turn fantasy into REALity!
LEGENDZ
TALE OF THE DRAGON KINGS
BY RIN HIRAI
LEGENDZ
MANGA SERIES
ON SALE NOW
ONLY
$7.99
SHONEN JUMP GRAPHIC NOVEL
MAKOTO HARUNO
RIN HIRAI
volume 1
SHONEN JUMP
THE WORLD'S MOST POPULAR MANGA
On sale at: www.shonenjump.com
Also available at your local bookstore and comic store.
RATED
A
FOR
ALL AGES
ratings.viz.com
VIZ media
www.viz.com
LEGENDZ © 2003 by Makoto Haruno, Rin Hirai/
SHUEISHA Inc. © 2003 VIZ

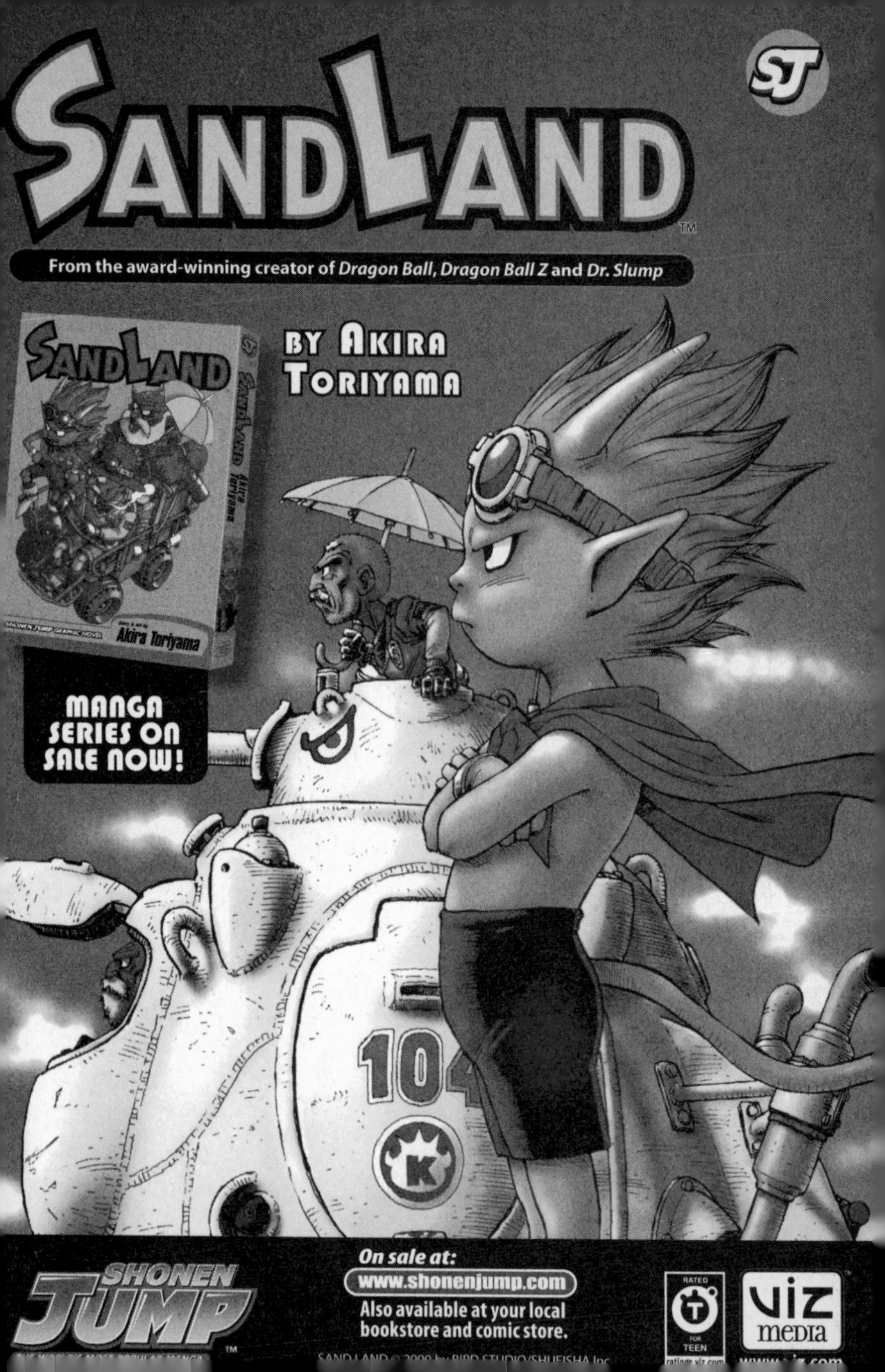

SANDLAND™
From the award-winning creator of *Dragon Ball, Dragon Ball Z* and *Dr. Slump*
BY AKIRA TORIYAMA
MANGA SERIES ON SALE NOW!
On sale at:
www.shonenjump.com
Also available at your local bookstore and comic store.

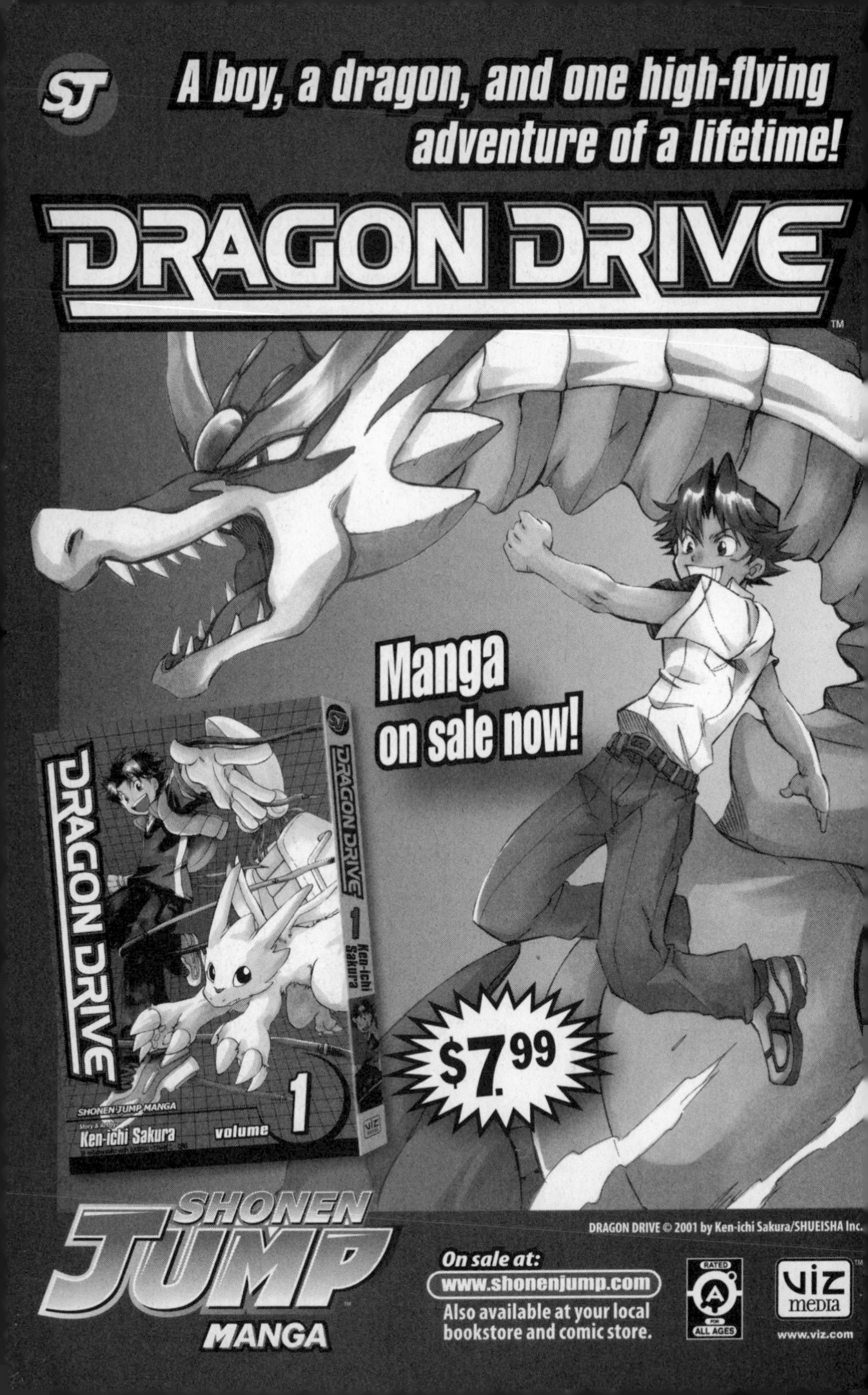
SJ
A boy, a dragon, and one high-flying adventure of a lifetime!
DRAGON DRIVE™
Manga on sale now!
DRAGON DRIVE
SHONEN JUMP MANGA
Story & Art by
Ken-ichi Sakura
volume 1
DRAGON DRIVE 1 Ken-ichi Sakura
$7.99
SHONEN JUMP MANGA
DRAGON DRIVE © 2001 by Ken-ichi Sakura/SHUEISHA Inc.
On sale at:
www.shonenjump.com
Also available at your local bookstore and comic store.
RATED A FOR ALL AGES
VIZ media
www.viz.com

Tell us what you think about SHONEN JUMP manga!

Our survey is now available online.
Go to: www.SHONENJUMP.com/mangasurvey

Help us make our product offering better!

THE REAL ACTION STARTS IN...

SHONEN JUMP
THE WORLD'S MOST POPULAR MANGA
www.shonenjump.com

ST ADVANCED

ST

VIZ MEDIA

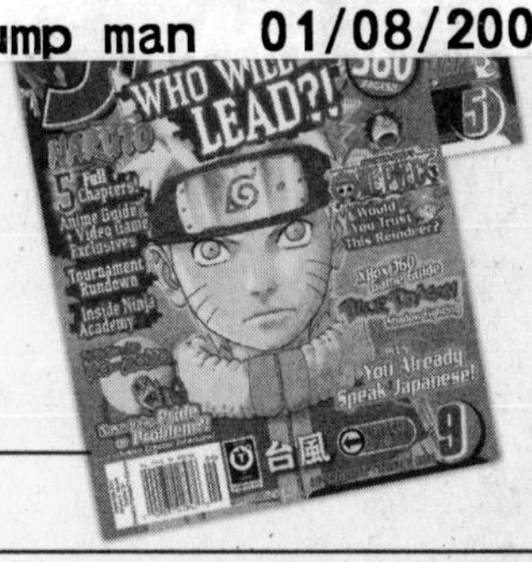
WHO WILL LEAD?!
NARUTO